Consistent Democracy

Consistent Democracy

The "Woman Question" and Self-Government
in Nineteenth-Century America

LESLIE BUTLER

OXFORD
UNIVERSITY PRESS

OXFORD
UNIVERSITY PRESS

Oxford University Press is a department of the University of Oxford. It furthers
the University's objective of excellence in research, scholarship, and education
by publishing worldwide. Oxford is a registered trade mark of Oxford University
Press in the UK and certain other countries.

Published in the United States of America by Oxford University Press
198 Madison Avenue, New York, NY 10016, United States of America.

Library of Congress Cataloging-in-Publication Data
Names: Butler, Leslie, 1969- author.
Title: Consistent democracy : the "woman question" and self-government in
nineteenth-century America / Leslie Butler.
Description: New York, NY : Oxford University Press, 2023. |
Identifiers: LCCN 2023032469 (print) | LCCN 2023032470 (ebook) |
ISBN 9780197685839 (hardback) | ISBN 9780197685846 (epub) |
ISBN 9780197685860
Subjects: LCSH: Women—Suffrage—United States—History—19th century. |
Women—Legal status, laws, etc.—United States—History—19th century. |
Democracy—United States. | United States—Politics and government—19th century.
Classification: LCC JK1896 .B88 2023 (print) | LCC JK1896 (ebook) |
DDC 324 .6/230973—dc23/eng/20230808
LC record available at https://lccn.loc.gov/2023032469
LC ebook record available at https://lccn.loc.gov/2023032470

DOI: 10.1093/oso/9780197685839.001.0001

Printed by Sheridan Books, Inc., United States of America

*For Bob, partner extraordinaire
(in tennis, marriage, and life)*

Contents

Acknowledgments

SO MUCH ABOUT writing a book is an exercise in isolation—alone with your sources, alone at your computer, alone in your head. This fact makes the moments of engagement and connection with others stand out in bright, wondrous relief. It is a pleasure to be able to thank the many institutions, agencies, and individuals who eased the isolation and provided critical support at every stage.

My interest in the questions this book examines began many decades ago. As a graduate student, I was trained in American intellectual and cultural history, Victorian intellectual history, and American women's history, and this project has delightfully fused all three fields. The scholarly works I first discussed in a small directed readings seminar with Nancy Cott introduced me to the imaginative research methods and the sophisticated analytical tools of women's history. I have been able to continue those discussions in my own teaching. I'm grateful to the many students in multiple iterations of two courses, "Gender and Power in US History" and "Debating Democracy in Nineteenth-Century America," for thinking through vital texts and topics with me. Beyond the classroom, I want to thank Evan Sternick, Emily Baxter, Lucy Pollard, Zoe Friedland, Natalie Vaughan, Louisa Auerbach, Andrew Joubert, Max Weintraub, Ashley Hess, Sarah Engelman, and Maud McCole for research assistance.

Even with such wonderful students, time off from teaching and service has been indispensable to (finally) completing this book. A Senior Faculty Fellowship from Dartmouth College gave me the time and freedom to recast a project in which I had begun to lose interest. A summer fellowship from the National Endowment for the Humanities (NEH) allowed me to spend a lively two weeks in Charlottesville, Virginia, discussing Alexis de Tocqueville. I thank the co-conveners Arthur Goldhammer and Olivier Zunz and all of my fellow seminar participants, especially Jean Pedersen. A year-long fellowship from the NEH enabled me to sketch out drafts of several chapters in the recast project. Finally, I was lucky enough to spend a wonderful year as the Billington Visiting Professor at Occidental College/Huntington Library in 2020–2021, which was critical to completing a draft of the whole manuscript. I thank Alex Puerto, Sharla Fett, Marla Stone, Steve Hindle, and my excellent Oxy students for making that year as productive as possible amidst the COVID-19 shutdowns. The terrifically engaging group of Long-Term Fellows at the Huntington Library provided a generous and encouraging community at a crucial stage in this book's completion, even though the pandemic frustratingly limited our face-to-face interactions.

I have presented portions of this work, in its various phases of existence, at many venues and have benefitted from collegial critique and thoughtful questions: in the United Kingdom, the Institute for Historical Research, University of Nottingham, University of Leicester, the British American Nineteenth Century Historians (BrANCH) conference, and History of Ideologies conference at Queen Mary University; in Germany, the Muhlenberg Center for American Studies (at Martin Luther University of Halle-Wittenberg); and in the United States, the American Antiquarian Society, Clark University, the Huntington Library, Occidental College, and multiple Organization of American History (OAH), American Historical Association (AHA), and United States Intellectual History (USIH) conferences.

Many colleagues have generously read or discussed parts of the manuscript at various stages. I thank Claire Rydell Arcenas, Carla Bittel, Molly Farrell, Lynn Festa, Sarah Igo, Amy Kittlestrom, Jim Kloppenberg, Jonathan Koch, Trent McNamara, Johann Neem, Susan Pearson, Jennifer Ratner-Rosenhagen, Erik Redling, Dan Rodgers, Kyle Volk, Caroline Winterer, and Rosemarie Zagarri. I also want to acknowledge five senior colleagues/mentors who are sadly no longer with us but whose writing and generous conversation have done so much to shape the way I think about the nineteenth century: Charlie Capper, David Brion Davis, Michael O'Brien, Cynthia Russett, and Frank M. Turner.

As the book began to take on something resembling its final shape, helpful conversations with Thomas LeBien, Priya Nelson, and Tim Mennell pushed me to clarify my thoughts and sharpen my arguments, as did four anonymous reviews. I am grateful to them all. At Oxford, Susan Ferber supported the project and provided an exceptionally close and careful reading of the penultimate draft. Lari Heathcote of Newgen steered the manuscript through the production process with patience and professionalism. Anne Sanow and Ken Hassman did the difficult but critical work of copyediting and indexing.

The Rockefeller Center at Dartmouth funded a manuscript review in 2021, where I benefited enormously from the feedback of many wise and wonderful colleagues. Thanks goes to Jason Barabas and Lynn Spencer for making that happen. I cannot thank Corinne Field and Caleb McDaniel enough for the care and thoughtfulness with which they engaged the project at a rough and raw stage. Boundless gratitude goes as well to my fabulous Dartmouth colleagues for their generosity of time and attention in reading the draft. Lisa Baldez, Bob Bonner, Udi Greenberg, Darrin McMahon, Jennifer Miller, Miriam Rich, and Luke Swain: your collegiality is a rare and wonderful gift. I also thank Cecilia Gaposchkin for her friendship and, in her capacity as department chair, for facilitating a change in my teaching schedule to accommodate the final push. Gail Patten, Bruch Lehmann, and Chelsea D'Aprile, though chronically understaffed and overworked, have made the History Department at Dartmouth a well-run and happy place.

Friends outside the seminar room kept my spirits high. The tennis community in the Upper Valley provided good sport and good fun, always reminding me of the therapeutic benefits of hitting a ball hard. Keri Craft and Susan Zak shared the ups and downs of my work on this book, offering commiseration and distraction in perfect measure. Over countless hikes and cross-country ski adventures, Viva Hardigg has been an unfailing source of support and solidarity, from discussing the finer points of nineteenth-century "woman question" novels to reading and commenting on this book's introduction.

If indeed "there is no school like the family school," as the advice author William Alcott put it, then I have been a most fortunate pupil at every stage of my life. I married into a family that has embodied love, support, and resilience. Pat and Wally Bigbee, who still tackle the hills of New Hampshire and Vermont when they come to visit, have also provided admirable models of grandparently energy. Jamie, Alison, Katie, and Jess always have my back. It's an amazing thing moving through the world with four sisters, like having a permanent and portable force field. Their partners John, Michael, Greg, and Tony (and my five nephews Conor, Liam, Ben, Charlie, and Quinn) introduced some fun gender diversity into our family. I could type "thank you thank you" for as many pages as this book is long and it would never come close to conveying how much I owe my incredible parents, Frank and Mary Butler. They seem always to know when and how to support, nudge, encourage, tease, console, or cheer me in the right proportions. At critical moments, they also sent Lou Malnattis pizza and Garrett's popcorn (if you know, you know). Everything I aspire to be in a parent, I have learned from them.

That brings me to my immediate family, the household of lovely men in which my thinking about the nineteenth-century woman question took shape. I have worked on this project so long that my three sons Will, Matt, and Cameron have somehow transformed from little boys into young men. From dance parties to card games, movie nights to family doubles, time with the boys is the best of times. They are the most delightful of companions.

Finally, there is Bob, best of husbands, best of men. It is hard to put into words my gratitude to him. He has entered into this project thoroughly, following me down rabbit holes, talking through ideas at every stage, and reading and editing draft after draft after draft. And yet once again, that is the least of it. The dedication of this book says everything but also so very little.

Introduction

WILL DEMOCRACY ENDURE as a form of government? Do Americans want it to? Whom do they trust to vote or hold office? These and other vital questions are regularly and volubly discussed across newspapers, cable news programs, and online comment sections. The same corners of the media landscape also reveal full-throated disagreements on a more specific set of questions concerning women. How much autonomy should they have over their own lives? Does equality extend into the marriage relationship, and are sex roles therein predetermined? What role should mothers play in the civic education of their families?

These are today's questions, but they were also the nineteenth century's. Founded as a republican exemplar of a government rejecting both monarchy and aristocracy, the United States by the third decade of the nineteenth century had become the proving ground for vibrant mass-based popular government. The spectacle of this young nation drew the attention of the world. A government that was by design all male embraced its maleness overtly, first in a partisan political system that functioned as a brotherhood and then through the mass mobilization of soldiers during the Civil War.

Even so, nineteenth-century observers asserted that the global fate of democracy depended on American women. Opinion was split over what exactly that widely broadcast assertion meant. Some insisted that America would cease to be a beacon of inspiration if its female citizens continued to be excluded as full democratic participants. Others argued with equal vigor that democracy's survival required women to forego the franchise and thus avoid altogether the corrupting world of grubby politics. This book explores how such arguments grew from a rich, nuanced, and prolonged dialogue about whether consistency in American self-government could or should be attained.

The exclusionary tendencies of nineteenth-century America's all-male citizenship and suffrage are well-known. Nearly all recent accounts acknowledge the paradox of what John Stuart Mill in 1835 memorably termed democratic America's "aristocracy of sex."[1] However familiar his critique might appear, it is still striking how residues of Old World hierarchies managed to "retain their privileges" in a nation incessantly proclaiming political equality and "universal" suffrage. A modern democracy seemed peculiar indeed if only a minority of its citizens enjoyed political power and social prerogatives. And yet the norm for the majority of nineteenth-century Americans was governance by others more than genuine self-government.[2]

The paradoxes of the United States as a self-conscious democracy did not end with its minority electorate. For here was a democracy that also denied every right of citizenship—and of basic personhood—to millions of enslaved people, female and male alike. Efforts to dismantle sex-based disabilities grew directly from the antislavery campaigns that had been launched to address this most profound American inconsistency. Almost all the main actors in the early quest to win political rights for women had first participated in campaigns to end Black enslavement. This is a story that grew more complicated and contentious as victories were scored and time passed. Scrutiny of women's disabilities escalated—but were not really remedied—by a civil war that uprooted slavery and remade democratic citizenship. Attempts to sever suffrage rights from manhood acquired momentum during Reconstruction's second founding, attaining institutional heft in the national women's suffrage organizations launched in the late 1860s. Those groups would wage a multidecade campaign to amend the US Constitution. But the power of racial exclusivity proved resilient, and some of the activists who made the greatest efforts to obtain the political enfranchisement of white women displayed an ugly acceptance of racism that surfaced, in stubborn new forms, over the long post–emancipation period.

Consistent Democracy establishes a new vantage on this arc of history fixed in Americans' collective memory. It does so by offering an intellectual history of the arguments, advocacy, and commentary concerning democracy and the so-called woman question that circulated as published opinion, a concept the book develops across time and space. Far-flung print networks allowed observers to acknowledge contradictions, analysts to set forth various solutions, activists to set social change in motion, and conservatives to defend the status quo. By the time the country faced its greatest crisis in an epic civil war, bold calls—elaborated in print for American and international audiences—demanded America become a consistent democracy. Building on the revolutionary-era claim that political legitimacy derived from the consent of the governed, a potent new proposition was forged. America's democratic experiment required consistency in applying its founding principle to its entire adult population.[3] Included in this powerful formula was an insistence that all who were governed must be granted the electoral tools to have their say. Activists, however, shared cultural space with a variety of other voices. Understanding the history of democracy and the woman question requires attending to the broader set of conversations that preceded, paralleled, or otherwise swirled around the organized campaign for women's rights. Doing so demonstrates what reformers were up against and reveals a rich vein of popular political thought.

Several critical features of nineteenth-century discussions of democracy have faded with the passage of time. Some of the richest commentary from this earlier era ventured beyond matters of inclusion or exclusion, of who possessed or did not possess the right to vote. As the first generation to grapple with democracy in actual practice and not just theory, observers asked more rudimentary questions. They took little for granted. This is evident in the incisive commentary of essayists like Mill, who was a canonical advocate of women's rights and believed that popular government represented the "inevitable result of the tendencies of a progressive civilization." Just how the world-historic shift to democratic rule would alter the future remained uncertain for Mill, as it did for countless others. Among his many contributions to the debate was his elaboration of that uncertainty in an apt metaphor. If democracy represented an inevitable tendency, one could not stop it. But "like other great powers of nature," this tendency "may be guided to good" or left to wreak havoc. "Man cannot turn back the rivers to their source," Mill noted, "but it rests with himself whether they shall fertilize or lay waste his fields."[4] Many US-based observers, discussed in the first part of this book, shared Mill's anxious optimism that a great democratic river would nurture national progress, at least if various reformers succeeded in guiding it so that it might overcome the most glaring shortcomings. Yet many commentators—even, as the second part of this book shows, within reform communities—expressed fears that the alternative outcome was more likely. The most alarmist warned that fields might be laid waste by what they considered to be a flood of new and ill-equipped voters.

When nineteenth-century writers imagined globalizing democracy as a natural and irresistible force, they directed readers' attention to the overall impact of an untried form of government. A different set of concerns emerged when observers considered the interplay between collective popular government and individual capacity. Here uncertainty also reigned. Did political participation require specific resources—economic, moral, intellectual— in the individual? Or did it provide an indispensable spur to the development of individual faculties? Answers to such questions abounded and changed over time and according to which individuals were being discussed.

Powerful understandings of self-government informed commentary about how women's inner-directed lives might be enhanced (or, as critics would have it, compromised) by active participation in America's boisterously democratic public life. The ubiquitous "self-governing" language of the nineteenth century owed much of its potency to how it evolved beyond an original, and limited, meaning. A moral concept that had first been applied to an individual's ability to exercise control over the self was widened by a revolutionary new order that rested, as James Madison put it, on the "capacity of mankind for self-government." By 1840 or so, this more political meaning of the concept had become common parlance, and the adjective "self-governing" was attached to any polity in which a broad collective of the "people" exercised control over how they were governed. Still, the individual and moral connotations lingered.[5]

Disagreements over the most suitable mode of self-governance for the female half of the American population were the pivot on which nineteenth-century "woman question" disputes turned. Was individual autonomy the overriding objective? Or did even that aspiration invite a level of social dislocation and discord that would spell the doom of the American family and, by extension, the country? Could the vital principle of self-government provide the impetus for breaking down the male monopoly on political rights, including the right to vote or to hold office? Why was it that so many who were proving themselves capable of self-governing as individuals were not allowed to play a role in the larger political endeavor of American self-government? Self-government in this sense, with its link both to individual autonomy and to the collective process of self-rule, helps restore some of the democratic connotations of nineteenth-century terms—connotations that have sometimes been obscured by their connection to more familiar, and still vital, theoretical traditions such as liberalism.[6]

The formulation of self-government brought together women's standing as individuals, as members of family-based households, and as constituents of the body politic. This triad can reveal the starkly different conditions experienced by actual women living in nineteenth-century America. Any project that attempts to discuss something like the female "half of the population," a period phrase that appears repeatedly in the pages that follow, must acknowledge, and avoid, a tendency to generalize outward from the experiences of free, white, middle-class women whose lives generated greater documentary records than did those of women in more challenging circumstances. The quest for generalizations about the entire female population obscures the distinctive experiences of those who, having left a fainter trail, can too easily be marginalized or left out altogether.[7] What is needed is a balanced recognition of two equally true propositions. All women living in the mid-nineteenth-century United States lacked the ballot, which had become the critical mode of access to collective self-government. But if meaningful self-governance entails the control and regulation of one's own personhood, radical disparities rather than commonalities emerge as obvious and essential to historical analysis.

The most desperate circumstances were endured by enslaved American women, deprived by law and by routinized violence of meaningful individual autonomy. The extreme vulnerability of that population, which numbered above two million people upon ratification of the Thirteenth Amendment in 1865, included the theft of their labor, the alienation of their progeny, and their inability to resist violations of their bodily integrity.[8] The denial of basic personhood to these women left them overtly other-governed. Two other groups were susceptible to control by others, though in neither case did conditions approach the deprivations experienced by women bound as slaves. The sizeable number of free women of color within the United States faced precarious circumstances. Being deprived of full civic standing before 1865 and suffering lingering disabilities in the post–emancipation period, this group lacked individual legal recourse if violated or defrauded. Their vulnerability existed both beyond and within their own households.[9]

Finally, all married women, regardless of skin color, race, or lineage, lived under the governance of household heads via common-law doctrines that operated robustly through the 1840s and were only gradually dismantled thereafter. A status termed "coverture" legally subsumed a married woman in the person of her husband, under whose "protection, wing, and cover" she remained. Married women were thus other-governed by husbands who, in theory, shielded them from menaces external to households.[10] It was only custom, rather than rights or legal protections, that prevented domestic spaces from becoming sites of demeaning exploitation by male patriarchs. As long as coverture persisted, only property-owning free, single, adult, white women enjoyed any semblance of meaningful autonomy. Yet even this rare group shared with others what the visiting Englishwoman Harriet Martineau in 1837 termed the "political non-existence" of American women.[11]

During the decades tracked in this book, Americans' large-scale version of a self-governing democracy rose to prominence, elicited international scrutiny, and sparked an important dialogue about its shortcomings. Government of, by, and for the people endured a great trial of civil war that ended human bondage and launched a second founding but left key questions unresolved. *Consistent Democracy* recovers the range, depth, and complexity of debate over the promise and peril of self-government. It shows that at every stage of this tumultuous and transformative century, the place of women—enslaved and free, Black and white—hovered around the uneasy questions observers and commentators asked of America's still uncertain democratic experiment.

Clarifying key concepts makes for good intellectual history. A cluster of the most important terms used in this book requires some detailed explanation. This will allow readers to appreciate how three key concepts relate to nineteenth-century usage, extend (and in some instances modify) a vast existing scholarship, and derive from specific methods of research.

The phenomenon of the "woman question" anchors the book as a whole. This phrase emerged in print in the late 1830s, experienced a major spike in usage in the 1860s and early 1870s, and continued to be a feature of commentary at the turn of the century. A sense of familiarity and weariness often greeted new additions to what was more than once dismissed as "the interminable woman question." The meaning appeared to readers as both obvious and imprecise, and the valence shifted over time. Though generally phrased as a singular, in fact the phrase contained multiple subquestions. These included considerations of women's education, labor, marriage and family dynamics, legal standing, and political rights. Many such issues had been pondered for decades, even centuries. The French came closest to the nineteenth-century terminology with what they termed the "*querelle des femmes*."[12]

The conceptualization of a singular woman question typified a distinctive feature of nineteenth-century intellectual life. As historian Holly Case has explored, this "age of questions" witnessed a proliferating tendency of "querists" to publish one or another perspective in an "x question" format: the temperance question, the labor question, the money question.[13] This formulation imposed a certain structure to debates, with varied consequences. It elevated the visibility of a problem and accorded legitimacy to the discussion of particular issues, while leaving others unaddressed. Querists often constrained the scope of the discussion and channeled it into well-worn grooves; the very abstraction of the x question formulation flattened categories that were always far more complex and nuanced. Nowhere was this more evident than in the case of the doubly singular phrasing in the "woman question," which both collapsed distinct questions under one rubric and erased meaningful differences—of race, class, religion, age, marital status, and region—among women. A default assumption about exactly which women were being considered when the woman question was broached tended to push aside Black women, whether they were enslaved or free. Discussions in the Black press mitigated this tendency, but as a mode of intellectual exchange, the querist approach generally aligned with larger nineteenth-century racial biases.[14]

The questions posed by journalists, intellectuals, and other querists were no less consequential for who and what they omitted. Their work collectively established a decades-long framework—with a common vocabulary and a conventional set of topics—that new contributors could join with a self-conscious awareness that a discussion had already reached an advanced stage of consideration.[15] The coherence was more apparent than real, and nineteenth-century querists regularly pursued their own lines of inquiry in ways that could more often muddy than clarify a topic. Agreement on basic terminology between authors addressing even the same question was the exception to a more general rule. Disputants in the "slavery question," for example, routinely talked past one another as to whether the key issue at stake concerned race, labor, rights, section, political economy, religion, or democratic consistency.

Varied meanings of the "woman question" ran a particularly wide gamut. Radical abolitionists meant something quite narrow and specific when they introduced the phrase into print in the late 1830s. Others picked and chose: exploring girls' access to education or married women's property rights could be the theme for some; for others it might be the physiological discussion of women's health and how it related to the tyranny of fashion. Even when it came to the question of women in politics, specific issues blurred into one another and sometimes confounded back-and-forth argumentation. The debate might center on the advisability of women speaking publicly, of gathering petitions for a reform effort, or of attending a rally for the party of one's husband. Or, alternatively, the key issue might involve whether American women had access to the ballot box, could sit on a jury, or hold formal political office.

Querists entered into conversation with one another by advancing ideas and convictions through a realm that I term "published opinion." The ideas of well-known activists, especially those in the antislavery movement, and canonical political thinkers such as Mill and Harriet Martineau, circulated in an expansive media landscape. A staggeringly large set of conversations about the woman question appeared, sprawling across the pages of all kinds of printed material and defying any clear-cut ideological categorization.[16] These discussions can be found in a range of genres and in texts of varying degrees of formality and sophistication, in political tracts as well as travel writing, domestic advice manuals, sermons, magazine articles, and illustrations. The nineteenth-century United States was not just awash in printed type but inundated by mass-circulated visual materials that reflected and shaped how Americans thought about men, women, slavery, race, and class, as well as their democratic government.[17]

Published opinion differs from the familiar concept of public opinion, which carries connotations of representativeness and coherence—of somehow capturing what a collective body of people thought at a given time. Published opinion carries no such baggage. It can encompass a raucous, genre-crossing, sometimes serious, sometimes superficial body of material that circulated to readers in word and image. Even seemingly frivolous contributions reveal assumptions and attitudes that convey much about vernacular political thought. A dragnet-approach to recovering the huge volume of opinion-making—an approach only made possible by the digitization of so much primary material in recent decades—shows how media formed historically specific systems of intellectual exchange.

Interpreting this multitude of individual sources and making sense of the collective whole requires the time-honored tools of intellectual and cultural history: reading texts carefully and critically, drawing out the connections among them, and delineating the multiple contexts in which they were engaged. Digitization too has facilitated this work, enabling me to follow textual breadcrumbs from source to source and recover forgotten conversations, an endeavor that until recently would have been impossibly laborious, if not thoroughly random.[18]

The robustness of published opinion was facilitated by two related nineteenth-century developments, one social and one technological. The first was a rise in literacy—already comparatively high in the North American colonies at the time of the Revolution and continuing to grow through the nineteenth century, especially among urban and northern populations, including male and female, white and Black Americans. The birth of the common-school movement in 1830s Massachusetts accelerated a process already underway. The second development centered on the expansion of print, which was fueled by successive technological innovations (associated first with the steam and rotary press and then with telegraphy) and a commercial infrastructure that allowed for increasingly rapid and efficient distribution of books, periodicals, and newspapers.[19]

Nineteenth-century print culture created an exuberant forum, with a relatively low barrier to entry, especially after the 1830s. There were obvious limitations to the print format. Urban centers along the northeastern seaboard dominated the market, though regional publishing hubs could also be found in the Ohio River Valley and across the urban South. White men produced far more material than any other group, though white women were highly significant commentators as well on the topic of democracy and the woman question. A vital Black press, which included newspapers and religious organs, emerged in the northern cities in the late 1820s and continued to grow in size and importance every decade thereafter. Though most of these papers were edited by Black men (with the important exception of Mary Shadd Cary at the *Provincial Freeman* in Ontario), a small but crucial group of Black women contributed to published opinion by offering poetry, fiction, and political and social commentary.[20]

Print regularly brought international voices before American readers, thus expanding frames of reference and terms of debate. Texts were able to travel freely and rampantly amidst a robust culture of reprinting and the absence of any international copyright mechanisms.[21] Further, print enabled ordinary (literate) people to express themselves—in articles, letters, and standalone pamphlets—placing canonical, noncanonical, and at times obscure or anonymous writers in meaningful conversation with one another.

Published opinion facilitated the political thought and attitudes of a wide sector of the American population. When it came to the woman question, that thought and those attitudes were far more vast and ideologically diverse than has previously been recognized. While activists contributed only a fraction of what was put forth, they proved critical in shaping discussion. Their distinctive contribution and effort can only be fully understood when considered as part of the larger print world to which they appealed. This larger context reveals the challenges activists faced as they made the case for what they would come to call a "consistent democracy." As a mass-circulation phenomenon, published opinion framed, structured, and shaped how the reading public encountered significant questions. Evidence of published opinion's power in this regard can be found in how closely movement activists, and their critics, tracked and monitored its output. The people whose voices and words fill the following pages entered into these discussions by asking new questions or reformulating old ones; making assumptions explicit or putting familiar viewpoints into pithy and memorable expression; arguing with and refuting earlier works; and giving voice to perspectives often marginalized from mainstream discussions. Across each of these facets, this lively debate was a vital embodiment of democratic practice, of how a democratic people understood itself and its polity.

The third and most intricate concept to be delineated is that of democracy itself. Published opinion from the period emphasized several key aspects of this phenomenon in both targeted exploration and the increasing regularity of treating apparently unrelated topics as part of a democratic ethos. The fact that querists never formulated a specific "democracy question" was hardly an indication of lack of interest. Indeed, the enormous pull and vast sweep of this topic—in practice, in political maneuvering, and in the world of ideas—made it an indispensable part of how nineteenth-century writers reflected upon a modern world then coming into being.[22] Democracy was a force that eluded containment in any one formulation and whose very definition provoked vigorous debate. To capture the essence and significance of popular government involved not a rote list of criteria but the crafting of metaphors that conjured up natural forces or, more simply, evoked the spirit of the times.

A few working assumptions about the attributes of this profound development in human history did emerge when democracy was taken up and self-consciously analyzed. The novelty and potency of mass democracy became a common theme, as did its supposedly preordained global reach and its tendency to recast both affairs of state and daily life. Even those who emphasized its shortcomings and potential to inflict harm approached popular government differently than had earlier generations, who considered its intrinsic fragility as axiomatic. By the early nineteenth century, democracy appeared to be a mode of government with prospects for endurance, though these prospects depended on adaptability and on the prudence of populations to constitute themselves and their societies in ways that might avoid grave dangers. The ability of popular rule to twin broad input with legitimate and effective state authority still carried with it a hint of doubt, a whiff of instability. Ultimate outcomes would depend on the nature of those people who, at large, were assuming the reins of sovereignty.

The enormous body of scholarly literature on democracy has echoed several of these earlier themes, while dispensing with others. Among the most lasting legacies of the nineteenth-century world was the establishment of popular government as "a yardstick of all politics," as historian Jürgen Osterhammel puts it. In the twentieth and twenty-first centuries, even authoritarian regimes have designated themselves as "people's republics."[23] The initial emphasis on the multiplicity of the term, and of its meaning as fundamentally contested, has emerged as among its most essential characteristics. James Kloppenberg's authoritative work has framed the matter with particular elegance: "Disagreements about democracy constitute its history."[24] Even if one limits the scope to work concerning democracy in the United States, scholarship is marked by eclecticism. Organized warfare of the Democrats and Whigs or Democrats and Republicans continues to attract attention, and the contours of these partisan contests still yield vital insights. Studies of a democratizing republic have grown to include other sorts of mobilizations, however, and have taken up everything from the Workingmen's Party to the collective efforts of evangelical reformers (as well as those who resisted them), to the Colored Convention Movement of the late antebellum period and the opinion-shaping efforts of the Garrisonian abolitionists. In the field of early American democracy studies, variety and multiplicity are the rule.[25]

The expectation in the nineteenth century that governments-of-the-people would expand globally was prescient in some ways, but proved to be a half-truth in others, especially in the short term. Britain attained economic and geopolitical hegemony while incrementally expanding access to the franchise. It also witnessed a broad-based movement for its implementation via the Chartist campaign of the 1830s and 1840s. France had briefly adopted mass voting during its revolution of the 1790s, and that example was revivified by a left that, after the country's 1830 Revolution, offered universal suffrage as the "sacred ark" of democracy. Expansion of the French electorate to include all adult men was achieved, however, not via the robust and open public deliberation imagined by reformers but under the auspices of an autocratic Second Empire. A more promising road to democratic forms was taken by South American republics created as the Spanish empire disintegrated and citizenship established popular rule as a critical component of modernity. But a far gloomier story prevailed elsewhere, most notably across colonies within the continents of Africa and Asia. For the majority of the world's population, the nineteenth century was not an age of democracy but of imperial subjugation. The distinction between self-governing polities and those remotely governed by others was mirrored in the racial logic employed by the United States (among other settler democracies) that distributed power internally between its white and nonwhite inhabitants.[26]

The variety of democratic projects heightened the nineteenth-century interest in the chain of actions that occurred before and after voting and made these as important as the particulars of election day itself. For many theorists and observers of democracy, voting appeared as much a responsibility as a right. That right was therefore accompanied by high expectations about following public affairs with care and deliberation in order to discharge one's democratic duty. At one end of a spectrum was an unthinking drive to the polls that seemed devoid of actual meaning; excessive American partisans here seemed little better than those French voters who had succumbed to direction from above. The polar opposite of such "false" democracy involved political engagement on a regular basis. At its best, this version of enfranchisement entailed a process that would stimulate—and thereby enhance—individuals' intellectual and moral capacities to exercise reason, judgment, and a commitment to collective advancement. Out of this formulation came both an emphasis on the internal capacities of the ideal voter and a set of reflections about beneficial and detrimental modes of political mobilization.[27]

To focus attention on democracy in a book about the woman question is to bring to light something that has always been there, like a piece of furniture or a patterned wallpaper that has become so familiar we cease to see it. Contested ideas about democracy lurk behind nearly every aspect of American history. To the extent histories of the women's movement self-consciously situate their narrative as a part of this story, they have largely made democracy a fixed threshold to be attained: women, or groups of women, are either included or excluded, via the suffrage.[28] The story changes when one treats, as this book does, democracy as a dynamic concept with diverse meanings that varied according to a set of contingent circumstances. What results, I hope, is an account that restores some of the unpredictability and unevenness to past developments experienced by actors themselves.

So what does the patterned wallpaper reveal? For starters, it makes clear that woman questions were intrinsically democracy questions. That is, in asking and answering questions about women's roles, responsibilities, and rights Americans were compelled continually to assess and reassess their political ideas and assumptions. Some Americans made arguments for women's full inclusion in the body politic and a consistent democracy involving all adults. Others gave reasons why this was unwise, dangerous, or unnecessary. In doing so, they probed the meaning of their democratic experiment—an experiment that was still contested the world over. Thinking and arguing about women and self-government was a major preoccupation of published opinion across the century, outside the women's movement as well as within it. It did not require a movement for a variety of commentators—foreign observers, legal scholars, political thinkers—to note the enormous exclusions that accompanied such general categories as "consent of the governed," "rule of the people," and "universal suffrage." That these exclusions did not elicit the same level of outrage as the contradictions of a slaveholding democracy spoke to the utter brutality and violence of slavery as well as to the enduring religious, legal, and ideological underpinnings of women's subordination in the household.

Varied answers to the democratic version of the woman question proliferated across the nineteenth century, in travel narratives and treatises, novels and newspapers, and short stories and sheet music. Collectively they reveal both Americans' democratic aspirations and their democratic anxieties. Consistent democracy was a compelling answer but one that proved difficult for even movement figures to uphold in the face of racial, ethnic, and class differences that increasingly marked the expanding nation. Many Americans expressed concern that the wrong kind of people were being empowered, that government by the people was too precarious a proposition to include *all* the people. In other words, resistance to women's full inclusion in the body politic had as much to do with ideas about democracy as ideas about women. This meant that even as advocates for women's full political participation made strides, they always faced two distinct, though overlapping, intellectual obstacles laid bare in published opinion—stubborn notions about the limits on women's self-governance and enduring anxieties about the full implications of a consistent democracy.

Even as nineteenth-century Americans expressed their anxieties and uncertainties, many observers, in their most optimistic moments, found exhilarating features of the democratic world they saw emerging. The first to express doubt were also the first to experience bracing visions of what self-government at its best might become. For them, to live in a democracy was to entrust public matters to a broad portion of a population where differences of social rank and economic status held less sway than in any previous social formation. It required embracing egalitarian values as a bedrock principle and organizing institutions and distributing power in ways that might achieve the most ambitious of a country's founding commitments. It involved validating social mobility and the essential wisdom of ordinary people. How precisely to locate women, Black and white, within an ethos that routinely fell well short of its highest aspirations, was then, and remains now, an open question.

Prelude

POSING THE WOMAN QUESTION IN 1838

THE FIRST ARTICLE to be titled "The Woman Question" appeared in print in 1838. Inquiries about "woman" had been posed for decades, even centuries, but the late 1830s represented a distinct moment. One of the "most vexed questions of the day" seemed poised, if only it received a thorough discussion, to end in "enlarging the privileges of woman." Then the "few relics of former oppression of the gentler sex by the stronger" would cease to exist. Or at least that was how matters were framed for readers of the *Western Messenger*, a reformist Unitarian journal managed by editors in the booming cities of Louisville and Cincinnati. Sixteen measured paragraphs from a young Harvard-trained minister named Samuel Osgood thereby put in motion a consideration of "what is technically called the woman question."[1]

This little-heralded essay was among the first in a cascade of American articles and orations to employ a title that would still be in use after Osgood's death in 1881. Over the course of the century and peaking in the post–Civil War years, a throng of contributors to magazines and journals, fiction writers, and public lecturers would provide extensive commentary and analysis of the legal, social, cultural, religious, vocational, economic, and political disparities American women faced. This collective charting of the contours of the woman question would furnish a critical mode through which many Americans would form opinions about a whole series of salient topics.

Osgood is hardly a recognized figure in the story of women's struggle for expanded rights in America. Far more familiar are the abolitionists who were in that same year experiencing the "woman question" viscerally as one of the roiling disputes within Anglo-American antislavery organizations. The phrase appeared in William Lloyd Garrison's *Liberator* just a couple of months prior to Osgood's *Western Messenger* article, which is likely where Osgood encountered it. What would eventually become a stock formula, isolated in quotation marks, initially referred to a conflict over a procedural question: Should antislavery organizations whose membership was heavily female allow women to exercise the same roles and responsibilities that their male counterparts did? Or should the sex-specific roles that pervaded nearly every aspect of American life also prevail in these groups? The Boston-based *Liberator* took a bold stand on these questions. Garrisonian abolitionism would become a critical incubator of women's activism over time, providing an ideological and organizational training ground for a generation of women's rights reformers.

Articles like Osgood's convey much about the larger culture in which reformers' ideas circulated and were discussed. Were those ideas treated respectfully or with ridicule? Did commentators frame the subject of women's equality as plausible or preposterous? The story of democracy and the woman question is incomplete if based solely on the movement activists who were intent on pushing change forward. Osgood's 1838 essay helps map woman question debates both chronologically and culturally, delineating the specificity of this moment in time and this corner of published opinion.

———

The *Western Messenger* addressed a specific segment of American readers, an audience of primarily white, self-identified liberal Christians who valued that journal's connection to New England Transcendentalism. These readers were eager to track what the future might hold, and the *Messenger's* predictions of continuing progress contributed to an upbeat sense of optimism. The editorial tone contrasted with the excited and excitable ferment of other arenas of published opinion in the lively American media landscape of the 1830s. The magazine's signature feature was its preference for what Samuel Osgood termed "calm and profound discussion" over a more pervasive spirit of "angry controversy and vicious abuse." Its comparatively staid contents were typical of a range of general interest magazines that offered tempered reflections on the prospects for human improvement just over the horizon.

This posture could be seen in a self-consciousness about posing questions in the first place. Osgood counted among the most remarkable features of the day the incessant habit of "inquiring into all manner of subjects" and "asking all sorts of questions." The barrage of interrogatories challenged "old opinions" and "established ideas" that had survived recent revolutionary upheaval. Even during this period of less violent change, all aspects of life seemed ready to be recast. This process depended on circulating discussion of unresolved questions to a periodical-reading middle class, whose collective opinion would help determine the fate of any given issue. American improvements rested on such mechanisms of debate, as did the fate of reform in England, and the shift toward constitutionalism and human betterment in France. An international set of authors and readers agreed on one basic point: to avoid grappling with pressing questions was to fall short of what the moment demanded. The nineteenth century was in the process of becoming nothing less than an "age of questions."[2]

The *Western Messenger* exemplified the eclectic range of issues suitable for inquiry. Dotting its contents were reflections on the "Catholic question" and "the question of Miracles." Cautious considerations of the "Slavery question" and the "Texas question" tackled subjects that particularly bedeviled progressives residing in the borderland between a free North and a slave South.[3] And so it was that through the routine asking of questions, a systematic, albeit brief, discussion of women came before the readership of this journal. The moderately reformist Unitarian readership was especially fertile ground for identifying topics that might take longer to appear in other venues. The journal had, after all, featured the early verse of the Transcendentalist intellectual Margaret Fuller. Its editors paid particular attention to subjects that had relevance beyond the United States, within an "international public sphere" similarly concerned with human progress.

The cosmopolitan questioning mode did not extend uniformly across the United States. It held greatest appeal in the improving areas of the free states where a common reformist outlook in political and cultural matters prevailed.[4] The most enthusiastic proponents of the style of free-form question-posing were Christians who subscribed to strands of Protestantism that had cast off inherited Calvinist austerity and dogmatism. To such communities of earnest, progressive moralists, what was "technically called the woman question" was simply the latest in a string of problems to be taken up and worked through.

Radical reformers were also highly attuned to the age of questions, though not in the same way that moderate reform-minded journalists like Osgood were. Activists aligned with Garrison devoted attention to the woman question not in the spirit of broad-based inquiry but to convey their depth of conviction. The emergence of Angela and Sarah Grimké as fiery antislavery lecturers had generated a flurry of responses, even though they were not the first to address what critics called "promiscuous" (or male and female) audiences. That distinction belonged to African American author Maria W. Stewart, who spoke at Boston's African Meeting House and other venues in 1832–1833. Yet if the Grimkés' lectures were not the first, they mattered in how they drew the attention of the press and the denunciation of the Massachusetts clergy. The prolonged press and pamphlet interchange that followed sought to delineate the proper scope for white womanhood. The sisters' incisive publications—especially Sarah's *Letters on the Equality of the Sexes* (1838)—made this a pivotal episode in the history of American women's rights advocacy.[5]

Antislavery disputes over the woman question advanced in spurts that laid bare increasingly consequential divisions within the movement. Quaker poet John Greenleaf Whittier had warned the Grimké sisters in private letters that attention to their own "trifling oppression" and "paltry grievances" undercut their work to remedy the lives of the enslaved. The burning of Pennsylvania Hall by an anti-abolitionist mob in the early summer of 1838 heightened Whittier's concerns, and he denounced continued agitation of the woman question in the pages of the paper he edited, the *Pennsylvania Freeman*. When a contributor objected to his constrained vision, he dug in: "We do not see what the 'woman question' or the 'peace question' or the 'moral reform question' or the 'temperance question' have to do with our cause." If Whittier believed the proliferating tendency of question-posing muddled the clarity of a single-issue movement, others like Garrison's close ally Maria Weston Chapman believed a true understanding of the cause of antislavery engaged reformers in "numerous unpopular questions."[6]

This rift only deepened over the next couple of years. Garrison's commitment to women's equal standing within the organization—their ability to vote within antislavery societies and to hold office if elected by others—prompted an effort to oust him from power. The Garrisonians' demand for equal voting rights internally was curious given their insistence that men abstain from voting in the larger American electorate (part of their "nonresistance" strategy). New York-based abolitionist Henry Stanton hoped that the meeting of the Massachusetts state organization early in 1839 would permit him to contest these twinned heresies—empowerment of women and withdrawal from politics—that in his view set the Garrisonians apart from American democratic norms.[7] A process begun by Whittier and fueled by Stanton reached a crescendo in dual ruptures of 1840. First, Garrison consolidated his influence within the American Anti-Slavery Society that May, when the organization embraced the equality of women and men within its ranks. The following month, the London World's Anti-Slavery Convention refused to seat women delegates and Garrison removed himself from the deliberations in solidarity. Whittier, saddened over the schism, nonetheless defended the

Londoners: they were, he remarked, interested in abolishing slavery and not in "subscribing to our Yankee doctrines of equality or sexless Democracy."[8]

Whether one displayed the calm of the querist or the passion of the activist, the place to ventilate emerging issues were the newspapers, periodicals, and tracts that made up a nascent system of mass communications.[9] Opinion-shaping work across the media was the path to considering or implementing social change. Abolitionist Wendell Phillips could have been addressing the "Slavery Question" or the "Temperance Question" when in 1851 he forecast how "the greatest question of the day" (that of extending political rights to women) would be resolved. All that was needed was the basic "opportunity to argue the question" and to "set it full before the people." Once that essential step was taken, reformers could leave it up to "the intellects and hearts of our country" to do their work through the "institutions under which we live."[10] In Phillips's concise account lay something bolder than the Enlightenment notion that truth would prevail through free and open discussion. Reformers in nineteenth-century America took for granted that once answers to questions achieved broad assent, democratic mechanisms would convert those solutions into functioning realities. Popular pressure applied to representative governments urging the enactment of new laws might fit the bill in some instances. As often as not, a shift in attitudes would serve as the lever of progressive reform. In a government by opinion, published opinion was the indispensable tool.

Did 1838 represent a new era? So proclaimed the Garrisonians, leaving Osgood to reflect in more measured terms. He vaguely nodded toward what had come before, noting how "words that seemed a wonder and abomination in the mouth of Mary Wolstoncraft [sic] have now become familiar sounds." The Englishwoman who earned renown in the 1790s became for him a stand-in for the whole range of debates over the preceding half-century, which had extended the *querelle des femmes* among literary figures in the sixteenth century. The age of enlightenment and revolution, with its fashioning of new selves and societies, still reverberated in its questioning of traditional sex roles. Two emergent strands of thought endured through nineteenth-century considerations of women. Philosophers and historians associated with the Scottish Enlightenment elaborated a stadial theory of history that understood women and families as central to the progression from savagery to civilization. An elevation of women's status was linked to the crucial role they played in families' progressively elevated morals and manners.[11] A more radical group of writers reworked classical republican and natural rights themes to ponder the social, structural, and psychological apparatus of sex differentiation and the unequal relations prevailing between men and women. A strand that emphasized women's rights deriving from the fact of their personhood, not their familial role, was developed by Mary Wollstonecraft in *The Vindication of the Rights of Women* (1792), French philosopher Condorcet in "On the Emancipation of Women" (1790), and Massachusetts-based writer Judith Sargent Murray in "On the Equality of the Sexes" (1790).[12]

Early Americans had drawn on both the stadial theory of history and the equal rights tradition as they worked out their republican experiment. The chief responsibility of the wife and mother in supporting this new republican order was to nurture civic virtue in their husbands and sons. Though early Americans did not specify free, white women when they discussed "republican motherhood," the category was effectively limited in this way. The discourse carved out new political space for some women, while also underscoring the importance of education for this segment of the population. An ignorant woman, early Americans could agree, seemed unlikely to be a good republican wife or mother. Though there were few legal alterations in women's status during the early national period, the opening of educational opportunities shaped new possibilities. Just how political and politicized republican women should be remained unclear. From the 1780s to the 1820s, some (white, educated) women participated in a broad range of public and political activities, and for a thirty-year span in New Jersey, women who could meet the property requirement even voted in elections.[13]

But by the time Osgood wrote his article on "The Woman Question," what the historian Rosemarie Zagarri has convincingly termed a "backlash" had pushed women out of politics and recast partisan activity in overtly male terms. American men and women who had grown uneasy about the intensely partisan politics that had pitted Jeffersonians against Federalists looked to women and the household as a domestic refuge from the unruly passions of the competitive electoral sphere. Women lost the vote in New Jersey in 1807, as did African American and immigrant men, harbingers of a trend that soon became unmistakable: the inclusion of nearly all white men in a system of "universal suffrage" that pulled down economic barriers and replaced them with those of sex and race. By the 1830s a new language and culture of domesticity had emerged that reworked the civilizational theory of the Scottish Enlightenment for a new democratic, market-oriented era. Middle-class white women in the home were lauded across published opinion as the shapers of morals and the selfless nurturers of the husbands and male children who made up a white American political nation.[14]

By the 1830s the backlash against earlier claims for female equality had rendered them increasingly obscure, even perverse. Wollstonecraft's posthumous reputation had been tarnished by her purported violation of sexual mores. Osgood's reference to "the wonder and abomination" that had greeted her words in the 1790s was packed with innuendo, a nod to the "fog of censure" that had enveloped her weighty intellectual legacy. Rather than recall her plea for the education of girls or her extension of John Locke's theory of knowledge, a clergy hostile to her argument for women's rights transformed her into a symbol of licentiousness. As such, she was used to discredit later female reformers and to make earlier pleas for sexual equality all but invisible. The varied transgressions of visiting British radical Fanny Wright in the 1820s, for example, could be more easily condemned once women's rights advocacy was tarnished as a sexually irregular, atheistical intrusion. A vigorous statement of equality between the sexes written by Irish Utilitarians William Thompson and Anna Wheeler, *Appeal of One Half the Human Race* (1825), was not even reprinted in the United States.[15]

In a pattern that would repeat throughout American history, efforts to turn back earlier advances encountered new challenges of their own. These challenges appeared in women's extra-electoral political activity—including abolition—and in the largely unrelated rebalancing of legal power within households. Patriarchal households that persisted across eighteenth-century upheavals seemed, in a self-consciously progressive age, to be out of sync with the times. Multiple aspects of the legal edifice of coverture were subjected to scrutiny, and would ultimately be reformed. Whether such alterations were the current that would lead to further change, or a countercurrent to the masculinization of politics, remained uncertain.

Osgood's short essay steered a moderate course through these conflicting developments, as he rejected both a status quo that had admittedly "tyrannical" vestiges and radical alternatives that seemed to go too far. He urged women's education, acknowledged their ability to speak in public (on certain subjects), and even encouraged their literary aspirations. He drew the line, however, at political participation and shuddered at the idea of women voting, serving on juries, and holding office. He enlisted Frenchman Louis Aimé-Martin to legitimate this distinction, applauding his *On the Education of Mothers, or the Civilization of the Human Race by Women* (1834). As a disciple of Jean Jacques Rousseau, Aimé-Martin pitted domesticity and the "religious mother" against the "orator" and the "politician," insisting that the former was woman's only appropriate path to influence or power.[16] With a flourish that was both cosmopolitan and vaguely spiritual, Osgood used Aimé-Martin's work to meet his own criteria for question-formation. Having applied principles of rationality and uplift to the social position of women, he proposed a twofold solution: to curtail the most egregious elements of male dominance, while justifying women's continued exclusion from politics.

Discussions of the woman question would evolve as activists and querists shaped and framed the subject for the broader readerships each aspired to reach. Garrisonians weathered the schism and made women's equality a recurrent feature of the *Liberator* over the next two decades. Women arose to positions of leadership in these reformist circles, which became a crucial training ground for future leaders of the women's right movement. For the reformers fired by Garrison's example, the woman question was not so much an invitation to debate, or even to persuade, as to pronounce a fierce and lasting commitment to topple what appeared to be the most persistent of all human categories of inequality. Frederick Douglass, the powerful African American abolitionist who had once been Garrison's protégé, captured an essential spirit of the reform program when his own newspaper in late 1847 placed on its masthead the rousing sentences "Right is of no sex. Truth is of no color." Twenty years into her marriage to Garrison's one-time nemesis Henry Stanton, Elizabeth Cady Stanton could rejoice how Garrison's organization had been the only one "on God's footstool where the humanity of woman is recognized" and contained the "only men who have ever echoed back her cries for justice and equality."[17]

Osgood meanwhile continued his querying and stuck to the distinctions he had drawn in 1838. Just as he had made no effort to give earlier revolutionary thinkers their due, he ignored proto-feminist works like Elisha Hurlbut's *Essays on Human Rights* (1845), which extended the natural rights tradition.[18] When he returned to the woman question in 1854, Osgood simply repeated his simultaneous denunciation of both patriarchal excess and female political activity from his *Western Messenger* essay. Over the fifteen years since "The Woman Question" piece had appeared the broader cultural contours had shifted dramatically, thanks in large part to a vibrant period of women's activism. This change could be registered in the way Osgood moved from open-ended questioning to outright alarm. Deploying a language of peril, he fretted over "the voice of Mary Wollstonecraft" (whose name he now spelled correctly), who had claimed "masculine freedom." The eighteenth-century

English radical seemed to generate "a thousand echoes" among a new generation of American women, and he urged the "mothers and sisters in our Israel" to push back against the threat. As he shifted from framing questions to exhortation, he adopted a sharp tone that was absent in 1838. For women to begin "crowding to the ballot-box, screaming in the caucus, or snatching at the staff of office" would be nothing short of a calamity, he insisted. His views proved quite popular. His book sold steadily across the middle-class North; the reissue in 1876 was at least the sixth edition.[19]

In the years between the initial publication of Osgood's book in 1854 and its last edition in the Reconstruction era, the woman question became ubiquitous. Beginning as a sporadic theme in only the most "advanced" journals, a movement and a civil war elevated it into an incessant and more complex discussion that migrated across genres. Later in the century, women's access to the ballot became the focal point of the dialogue, featured in song sheets and lithographs no less than in essays and orations. But the same basic conundrum emerged out of this intense period of discussion: What did it mean that the world's leading exponent of democracy barred the female half of its population, of all races, from becoming full-fledged and equal participants in the process of self-government?

PART I

American Democracy, American Women

I

Observing American Democracy

AT THE VERY same time that the woman question roiled Northeastern abolitionists and piqued interest among readers of the *Western Messenger*, a trio of commentators explored the topic in original, systematic, and enduring accounts of American democratic governance. Two young French aristocrats and an eminent English woman of letters composed their writings after extensive travels across the United States. They observed the young nation during Andrew Jackson's presidency and amidst turbulent events across the Atlantic world. Revolution was again in the air: the Bourbon monarch Charles X was driven from the throne in France; anti-absolutist fervor was evident in the Italian states and in Poland; and new republics continued to emerge from the wreckage of a centuries-old Catholic Spanish empire. In Britain, Parliament extended the franchise for the first time in centuries, an insurgent Chartist movement demanded universal suffrage, and a mighty experiment of Caribbean emancipation released hundreds of thousands from bondage.

There was no better site than the oldest New World republic for careful consideration of what problems might be solved in a new order of things and what difficulties would continue to fester. The bracing democratic moment inspired visiting writers who offered something more than the sensational travelogues that had become all the rage by the 1830s. In the six books they produced between 1835 and 1840, Alexis de Tocqueville, Gustave de Beaumont, and Harriet Martineau compiled pioneering analyses of a people who were ruling themselves. The world was put on notice for what the American example of self-government might mean for all humankind.[1]

The European attention flattered Americans' conviction that their enterprise had global importance. All three authors made the exceptions, exclusions, and apparent anomalies of American democracy important parts of the story they told. They pointed out shortcomings of democratic society and governance and were especially frank in condemning the most extreme inconsistencies between principle and practice. The institution of slavery and the pervasive system of racial inequality garnered the most scrutiny, but all three authors considered the place of free white women in democratic society as well. They surveyed American family life, considered the education of girls, and inquired into the way marriage conventions distributed authority within households. How, they wondered, did democracy shape these institutions that organized women's lives? Their answers varied and were not always pleasing to American readers, but a tone of cool detachment rather than sensational polemic made their works signal contributions to an age of questions. The dialogue in published opinion that followed ensured that key formulations of Tocqueville's *Democracy in America* and Martineau's *Society in America* would become touchstones about the merits and deficiencies of democracy as it related to women no less than to men. From this flurry of commentary and response, a novel set of problems was framed that had an enduring impact on how Americans understood their country's defining commitment to self-government.

To Show What in Our Days a Democratic People Really Was

By the 1830s, it was hardly original for European writers to opine about what America claimed to represent and how its citizens either lived up to or fell short of their country's high-minded professions. Nor was it unusual for American writers to respond loudly, whether by glorying in the stray compliment or, far more frequently, by striking back in irritation at European fault-finding. The rarefied Anglo-American "paper war" that began the nineteenth century was quite heated in outlets that circulated to a limited audience. As that cultural form waned, a new publishing phenomenon arose that operated on a broader scale. Beginning around 1825, travelogues became the first mass cultural exchange across the Atlantic about America's democratic experiment. What was distinctive about these robust-selling European accounts of the United States were the responses and counterresponses that stretched on for decades.[2] Multivolume books, supplemented by countless magazine articles, appeared so abundantly that one London periodical apologized in 1835 for being unable to even list the flood of new works by visitors to America.[3]

These travel accounts gave Americans the sense that they were like "persons surrounded by mirrors," as one New Englander put it. Finding themselves the object of constant scrutiny, they caught "their likeness from every quarter, and in every possible light, attitude, and movement." Self-righteous pride in the innate superiority of their republican institutions coexisted with a defensiveness about their "peculiar" institution of chattel slavery. The moral vulnerability of the United States on this issue continued a dynamic that dated from the 1770s, when Samuel Johnson famously chided American revolutionaries for yelping for liberty while holding others in bondage. The dehumanizing and corrupting institution of slavery became a central theme in nearly every travel book in the post-1825 boom. Among the most notorious was Frances Trollope's *Domestic Manners of the Americans* (1832), which invoked Irish poet Thomas Moore. In a sign of the times, Moore linked American's hypocrisy about slavery not simply to vaunted liberty but to aggrandizing democratic professions that masked the ugly reality of disastrous misrule.

> *Who can, with patience, for a moment see*
> *The medley mass of pride and misery,*
> *Of whips and charters, manacles and rights,*
> *Of slaving blacks, and democratic whites,*
> *Of all the piebald polity that reigns*
> *In free confusion o'er Columbia's plains?*[4]

Frances Trollope's acid tone built upon *Travels in North America* by Basil Hall from 1829, and their works became the two classic statements of Tory derision toward the American example.

As transatlantic transit was made easier and more rapid by steamship, the spate of travelogues only increased. Emulators of Trollope and Hall were joined by British radicals and by a growing number of non-British commentators. In time, this corpus would include figures such as the Swedish writer Frederika Bremer, who was among the few to center analysis of women and the household. US newspapers and journals routinely reviewed and commented on these publications, further publicizing them even as they excoriated "the ribaldry, the exaggerations, the falsehoods of the score of tourists in this country." Financial incentives favored drama over description, invective over investigation. Though the German American Francis Lieber had long lived in the United States, he contributed his own volume titled *The Stranger in America* (1833–1835), where he recalled a publisher advising him that "the severest books against the United States sell rapidly, and often run through several editions." This dynamic reached a crescendo in the 1842 *American Notes* of famed novelist Charles Dickens, whose damning portrait sparked waves of outrage, then counter-outrage, and even a mock reverse travel narrative by a "Quarles Quickens," whose real interest was simple self-aggrandizement.[5]

Gossip, national chauvinism, and frivolity fueled interest in the travelogue genre, but beginning in the 1830s some fashioned it into a tool for advancing social knowledge. British philosopher John Stuart Mill never traveled to the United States, but he became a lifelong student of American democracy largely as a result of his immersion in those travel accounts. The "intelligent study of foreign countries," Mill wrote, in one of three lengthy reviews on the subject, had begun "to be turned to some account" as a mode to better understand the world and to achieve insight into what the future held. Political institutions, slavery, commerce, manners, education, religion, family, local governance, transportation, prisons, hospitals: all were ripe for constructive scrutiny, by those with a capable eye for discerning what did and did not work. Harriet Martineau was so enthralled with the possibility of the genre that she began composing a guide to foreign observation as she crossed the Atlantic. *How to Observe Morals and Manners* (1838), an early treatise on sociological method, elaborated the appropriate stance of the traveler/observer, a strategy for what to observe, and a method for studying the dynamic and complex interaction between a people's stated ideals (or morals) and their practices (or manners).[6]

The transformation of travel accounts from the luridly sensational to knowledge-producing endeavors recast how American democracy was discussed both within and beyond US borders.[7] Hall, Trollope, and Dickens each caricatured democracy by drawing attention to mediocre politicians, uncouth public spaces, the over-familiarity of lower-class folks, and Americans' rampant money-grubbing ethos. The frontispiece to Trollope's book, featuring a drunken male citizen, captured this more effectively than a torrent of mere words. The more nuanced treatments that would soon appear and call attention to the woman question were crafted as self-conscious alternatives to such accounts. Trollope herself forecast this development when she closed her volume with the prediction that "abler pens" would presumably take up the "more ambitious task of commenting on the democratic form of the American government."[8]

As Trollope's book appeared in print, the young French aristocrat Alexis de Tocqueville sailed home ready to wield such an "abler pen." The literary talents he possessed made the most of a series of notebooks he had compiled while in the United States, which overflowed with observations and detailed records of his conversations with more than two hundred Americans. He had landed in Newport, Rhode Island in 1831 with Gustave de Beaumont, his close friend and traveling companion. The delicate political situation in France following

FIG. 1.1 Detail from Auguste Hervieu, "Ancient and Modern Republics." This frontispiece to Trollope's book set the tone for the ensuing volume, which examined "the great experiment, as it has been called, now making in government, on the other side of the Atlantic." In a public space, likely a stagecoach station, a drunken white man, empty "mint julap [*sic*]" cup in hand, leans back unsteadily in a chair, with his feet rudely propped on the table. The image emphasized the book's purpose, announced in the preface, "to show how greatly the advantage is on the side of those who are governed by the few, instead of the many." There is good reason to believe the preface was not written by Trollope herself but by the publisher, as an overt piece of anti-Reform Bill propaganda. From Frances Trollope, *Domestic Manners of the Americans* (1832). Courtesy of Rauner Library, Dartmouth College.

the ascension of Louis-Phillipe to the throne had spurred the pair's trip, which they justified as part of a commissioned study of American prisons. Although they dutifully prepared their joint survey of the penitentiary system, they devoted effort to ambitious, individual projects that appeared in French in 1835. While Beaumont's novel *Marie, Ou L'Esclavage aux Etats-Unis* would not be fully translated into English until the mid-twentieth century, Tocqueville's *Democracy in America* soon appeared in British and American editions that sold nearly as well as the original French. In writing it, he told a friend, he "wished to show what in our days a democratic people really was." The work became an immediate and enduring success.[9]

Tocqueville's book did more than any other nineteenth-century text to spark conversations about how American democracy worked. Its very title was significant, in that it severed the rhetorical connection that partisans had established in linking "Democrat" to the winning electoral coalition that had brought the Jacksonians to power throughout the 1830s. A Frenchman aloof from partisanship (though he consulted with far more Whigs than Democrats), Tocqueville offered neither a partisan screed nor the sort of brief for or against popular government that American travelogues often became. What set his account apart was its comprehensiveness and attempt at balance. Appearing in two volumes over five years, *Democracy in America* generated extensive discussion that effectively neutralized and normalized a contentious word. By 1839, anti-Jacksonian Whig Calvin Colton observed how no one attempting to gain power in the United States could "dispense with" the term. "Whatever their principles, radical or conservative, their best passport is democracy."[10] For the rest of the nineteenth century, "republic" and "democracy" would be used interchangeably as impartial terms to describe the American system. And from its publication to the present, *Democracy in America* would be read and quoted by figures across the spectrum of national politics.[11]

Tocqueville presented a sympathetic yet critical perspective on a phenomenon he believed to be both universal and "providential." That stance was truly remarkable given that his own relatives had perished by guillotine during the Reign of Terror, which had been justified as an expression of popular will. From the opening pages, the book announced that Tocqueville was not settling scores but establishing his own philosophical gravitas. "A great democratic revolution," he wrote, "is taking place among us" in Europe as well as the United States.[12] The Frenchman was thus not hoping merely to "satisfy a legitimate curiosity" but to establish the world-historic significance of this great shift and to "learn what we have to fear or to hope" from the inevitable expansion of popular rule.

His approach combined the social with the political, the empirical with the abstract, and the descriptive with the philosophical. Only such a multifaceted, broad-based approach would suffice, he explained: "A new science of politics is indispensable to a new world."[13]

Generations of scholars have delineated how *Democracy in America* laid out the compatibility of democracy and religion, how it fretted over potentially tyrannical majorities, and how it cast light on civil society's associations as the tool for the collective management of public affairs. A common thread tying those themes together was Tocqueville's view that, despite nineteenth-century anxieties, ordinary people were already elaborating self-governing norms and demonstrating that they possessed the independence and judgment that such responsibility required. Basil Hall's 1829 book had expressed skepticism on this front, a view the British *Quarterly Review* summarized by conceding that while there may be "many individuals of excellent moral principle and habits" in the United States, they exist "in spite of the prevailing system." Democracy, the Tory publication was certain, "administers no stimulus to produce such character" and was instead marked by the "fluctuating will, and coarse passions of an illiterate, conceited, encroaching, and sottish populace."[14]

Tocqueville inverted this familiar formulation by highlighting the energy and dynamism that he witnessed across the American citizenry. The active participation of ordinary people was more important than the design and workings of the federal constitution, the judiciary, or state legislatures that he also discussed. The most vivid sections of his work highlighted the do-it-yourself civic culture in which Americans solved problems like fixing roads, distributing Bibles, or combating drunkenness. Through these activities, which operated outside the electoral machinery, Americans learned the vital habits that fitted them for self-government. Engaging in local government, like the New England town meeting, further taught Americans the habits and "mores" necessary for self-rule. Such participatory governance benefited the collective, in its attainment of the common good; it also cultivated the individual and instilled in each person the sense that one's own moral and mental development would be advanced while joining with others.[15] Tocqueville conceded that democracy in America could often be clumsy, erratic, and mediocre and that aristocracies were "infinitely more clever" at legislation and produced superior statesmen than those elevated by "universal suffrage." But democracy awakened in the citizenry "an all-pervading and restless activity, a superabundant force, and an energy," which he considered to be its "greatest advantage." Participation, especially at the local level, provided a crucial "school" of liberty, giving citizens a taste for it and teaching them how to exercise it. The "humblest" individual could not help but be altered by engaging in political activity—one's established ways of thinking would be unsettled, and one's "circle of ideas" would be extended. Democracy was, in short, educative.[16]

Political participation seemed to Tocqueville particularly crucial in avoiding one of the most dangerous tendencies of democratic society—the retreat into private self-seeking at the expense of the common good (or "individualism," a word first used in English by his translator Henry Reeve). This tendency preoccupied Tocqueville, especially in the darker, more philosophically probing second volume that appeared in 1840. But the Frenchman ventured that Americans' associational activity and political participation could combat this potential drift into selfish apathy.[17] He reiterated this main point in one of the rhetorical inversions he prized: "Elected magistrates do not make the American democracy flourish; it flourishes because the magistrates are elective." A democratic political system gave rise to a democratic political culture that promoted an engaged citizenry. And that citizenry made all the difference.[18]

Of Tocqueville's many readers across the North Atlantic world, none was as discerning as John Stuart Mill. Mill's enthusiasm—for Tocqueville's methodological intervention, his philosophical stance, and his specific observations on the workings of American democracy—spilled out across fifty-odd pages of an important essay in the 1835 *London Review*. Tocqueville's book, Mill felt certain, represented a "new era in the scientific study of politics." Mill especially appreciated the Frenchman's reflections on associations and local government as "schools" of liberty—sites that provided "the means of training the people to the good use" of their political power. He lingered on that point. Actual school instruction was obviously indispensable, but "what really constitutes education is the formation of habits." One does not learn to read or write, let alone how to swim or ride a horse, merely by being told how to do these things, but by actually doing them. So only "by practising popular government on a limited scale" would a people "learn how to exercise it on a larger." For Mill, as for Tocqueville, democratic participation provided the crucial education for democratic citizens. A crucial question going forward would be to what extent this formula applied to those beyond the adult white men to whom this society had awarded the franchise.[19]

An Aristocracy of Skin and Sex

John Stuart Mill admired *Democracy in America* despite his own emphasis on the bundle of inequalities and hierarchies that the book's title obscured. In paired essays from 1835 and 1836 Mill elaborated a key point and questioned Tocqueville's decision to cordon off slavery into a separate chapter devoted to the country's "three races." Mill preferred a more direct method when he insisted that only "a mere perversion of terms" allowed one to "call the government a democracy" where the "entire white population" of some areas sought to "rule by force and are supported by the labour of others." He detected traces of the slave South's blatant racial aristocracy across the post–emancipation North. In that region, "all free persons having the slightest admixture of negro blood" were ruthlessly denied political rights, banned from social intercourse, and relegated to menial labor.[20]

Mill combined his comments on American racial slavery and caste with a more novel observation, which connected extreme racial prejudice to a lingering sexual hierarchy that also tarnished America's democratic example. In the United States, he wrote, "one entire half of the human race is wholly excluded from the political equality" of which Americans so loved to boast. Constricted social position and prospects made women there even "more dependent than in Europe." He then added a formulation that would echo across nineteenth-century women's rights activism. "In the American democracy," he maintained, "the aristocracy of skin, and the aristocracy of sex, retain their privileges."[21]

Tocqueville had addressed the anti-egalitarian trends of democratic America highlighted by Mill, but in doing so he sought to make sense of inconsistencies rather than to critique them. A concluding chapter to volume one tackled the subject of racial dominance while the second volume, published in 1840, offered rich reflections about white American women. The former topic included a sharp condemnation of slavery, a withering account of the forced removal of Native Americans, and an acknowledgment of the discrimination faced by free Black Americans. But Tocqueville explicitly set the status of these subordinated groups outside the framework of popular rule and seemed hesitant to fully apply his formula of "tyranny of the majority" to the hold that white Americans had on all the country's resources and opportunities. In his telling, subordinated racial groups had largely come to accept their inferior position within the status quo. The "servility" of the "Negro" was a foil to the "anarchy" of the Indian and neither really diminished his larger claims about the democratic equality that suffused a society governed by white American men. "Violence made him a slave," Tocqueville observed about "the negro," but "habituation to servitude has given him the thoughts and ambitions of one." That assessment unsurprisingly ignited denunciations from the nascent Black press; its writers perceived his words as another example of placing the onus for oppression upon the oppressed.[22]

Tocqueville promised readers that his friend Beaumont would feature the dynamics of America's "three races" prominently in his forthcoming book, the main goal of which was to reveal the warping effect of racial exclusivity in democratic America. The entire plot of *Marie*—a combination novel/social scientific study—revolved around a French immigrant gradually coming to the unpleasant realization that race considerations dominated the American republic and were likely to erupt in apocalyptic violence. A traveling Frenchman meets an older Frenchman named Ludovic who tells the story of how he fell in love with the beautiful Marie Nelson, who inherited the invisible "taint" of her mother's "negro" ancestor. The novel then flashes back to Ludovic traveling to survey first-hand the extent of the country's white racial tyranny. While Marie has resigned herself to her status as a racial outcast, her brother George resists American colorism at every turn. Ludovic's path repeatedly overlaps with that of his prospective brother-in-law, who defiantly acknowledges his "colored" status in a series of confrontations: his ejection from the white seating area of a New York theater, a violent election-day skirmish, and a foiled plot to unite Black and Indian forces and launch an armed rebellion in North Carolina. The book's bleak outlook on America is evident in the final paragraph, when the French narrator to whom Ludovic (now a recluse) has told his story flees the country he once admired and weeps "with joy" upon his return to Europe.[23]

The "aristocracies" of skin and sex elicited still more detailed attention from Harriet Martineau, who might well have read Mill's memorable formulation while she was in the United States. She was midway through her own two-year-long stay when Mill's review of Tocqueville's first volume appeared as a standalone pamphlet, and she would have been keen to learn the views of a leading intellectual who inhabited the same cultural milieu that she did in London. Martineau had launched her writing career in the radical Unitarian group clustered around the *Monthly Repository* and was even present at the 1830 London dinner where Mill first met Harriet Taylor, the woman who would eventually become his wife. Though never friends, Mill and Martineau shared an enthusiasm for political economy and utilitarian philosophy, and each supported the democratizing Reform Bill of 1832 and the abolition of West Indian slavery in 1833. Both also entertained an early skepticism toward the rationales provided for sex as a barrier to political rights within systems of representative government.[24] As each took up this topic in print during the mid-1830s, a connective thread could be found in the phrasing they borrowed from the 1825 tract by two Irish-born Utilitarian-Socialists. William Thompson and Anna Wheeler's *Appeal of One Half the Human Race* disputed the claim advanced by James Mill (John Stuart Mill's father), in his 1820 essay "On Government," that women did not need political rights because their interests were adequately represented by men.[25]

When Martineau arrived in New York in the fall of 1834, she was already known as the author of the immensely popular series *Illustrations of Political Economy.* The craze for these laissez-faire morality tales had made her a celebrity of sorts, just as her use of an ear trumpet, to compensate for partial deafness, made her a mild curiosity. One poet in Richmond, Virginia conveyed in verse his or her interest in the Englishwoman, rhyming "Was she grave as judge? Did she talk like a book? // [A sort of man-woman,] and how did she look?"[26] The wonder of Martineau lived up to some of that hype, and her fame grew as she traveled to a wider range of places and spoke to a larger group of interlocutors over two years than Tocqueville and Beaumont, neither with a preexisting reputation, had in their nine months. Transported by wagon, stagecoach, horseback, and steamboat, she journeyed from Canada to Georgia, Connecticut to Kentucky. She stopped at farmhouses, watering places, estates, and log cabins and conversed with former presidents (James Madison in Montpelier), senators (Henry Clay in Kentucky), and abolitionists (Maria Weston Chapman in Massachusetts), as well as countless men and women from all walks of life. In contrast to Tocqueville's relatively homogenous circle of informants, largely from New England and New York, Martineau proudly recorded the range of people with diverse opinions whom she encountered: Whigs and Democrats; worshippers from multiple religious denominations; slaveholders, colonizationists, abolitionists, and enslaved persons; farmers, merchants, and lawyers; Native Americans from different tribes; and free Black Americans. She placed particular emphasis on her access as a woman to domestic spaces from which male travelers were likely excluded. "The nursery, the boudoir, the kitchen," she explained, "are all excellent schools in which to learn the morals and manners of a people." These sites led her to topics that the Frenchmen had made little effort to explore.[27]

Martineau's stated goal made her more attentive to democracy's anomalies than to its achievements as she sought to assess how well the American experience matched its original principles. Martineau paired the pronouncements made in the Declaration of Independence about equal rights and the consent of the governed with the country's deep and abiding faith in what she termed, likely through a dialogue with Madison, "the capacity of mankind for self-government."[28] That approach of seeing if principles matched practice struck Martineau as eminently fair, as it allowed her to evaluate American "Institutions, Morals, and Manners" by an "indisputable, instead of an arbitrary, standard." Like Tocqueville, she considered herself a sympathetic and friendly observer, boasting that she began her travels "with a mind, I believe, as nearly as possible unprejudiced about America." Across her two volumes, she highlighted many admirable features of the country but pulled no punches in offering distinctly negative findings about the treatment of "people of colour" and what she termed, with lasting effect, the "political non-existence of women." Her interactions with Garrisonian abolitionists and with Black and white activists inspired in her a belief that Americans would soon reckon with slavery—the "one tremendous anomaly" that needed to be "cast out." She thus confidently, if naively, looked forward to the Americans' successful elimination of that "deadly sin against their own principles" in the form of slavery and racial exclusivity.[29]

Martineau was far less specific about how America's aristocracy of sex might be dismantled, but she was sure that its toppling was only a matter of time. She was especially chagrined that neither American women nor American men seemed particularly bothered by the former's exclusion from political life, a clear betrayal of the country's central "democratic principle." Instead, Americans loved to boast of the "chivalrous" treatment accorded to (white) women. Their intellect may be "confined" and their weaknesses "encouraged," but they were always given the "best place[s] in stage-coaches" and praised with "oratorical flourishes" on public occasions, thus given "indulgence" as a "substitute for justice." Americans could achieve consistency by expanding the "equal political representation of all rational beings," with the "fair exceptions" of "children, idiots, and criminals, during the season of sequestration." This would allow women who were adults, of sound mind, and not convicted of a crime to participate in a government that taxed them, regulated their marriages, imprisoned, and even enslaved them. The last of these comments showed that Martineau, like the Garrisonians, did not conflate a purportedly universal category of "woman" with the particular subset of free white women seen in most "woman question" discussions in this period.[30]

Supplementing Mill's language of aristocracy with that of despotism, Martineau marveled that "the most principled democratic writers on government" sank into "fallacies, as disgraceful as any advocate of despotism has adduced," when they attempted to justify a political system that was the exclusive preserve of men. Thomas Jefferson had warned that men and women could not safely gather "promiscuously" (i.e., men and women together), while James Mill had maintained that adult women were already represented by fathers or husbands. To rebut such obvious cant would be like trying to "dissect the morning mist," Martineau contended. She then predicted with a calm certainty that the denial of the "equal rights of both halves of the human race" could simply not be sustained. Readers might laugh at women's political equality in 1837, she wrote, but so too did the "kings of Europe" once laugh "at the idea of a commoner" leading a nation. The "true democratic principle," she argued, using a favorite phrase, could never be "seriously controverted, and only for a short time evaded."[31]

Martineau's critique of women's "political non-existence" was striking and novel. It borrowed from the language of those who objected to the legal obliteration of personhood via enslavement or, in the case of married women, their status as *femes covert* at common law. But Martineau's assessment went further by asserting that people denied formal political participation were reduced to nonentities. This claim rested on a prior commitment to universally applied interior or subjective modes of self-governance: the individual self-rule that she and many other nineteenth-century observers viewed as a necessary precursor to collective self-rule. Her fear was that the constricted circumstances of women's lives denied them the vital resources that a human being required to be autonomous. Such denial did even more elemental—certainly more existential—damage than their exclusion from political rights and responsibilities. Most of Martineau's criticism centered on married women's disabilities. But in general, she believed American norms violated the country's ideals so egregiously when it came to women that the violations could not be sustained indefinitely. "Sooner or later," she predicted, women who had long been compliant would rise up to "burst asunder the bonds, (silken to some, but cold iron to others) of feudal prejudices and usages."[32]

Martineau's imagery revealed her awareness of the multiple experiences contained within the category of "American woman." Her reflections—in *Society in America* and then in *Retrospect of Western Travel* (1838) and "The Martyr Age" (1839)—contrasted with Tocqueville's reference to the singular "Negresse" and to Frances Trollope's depiction, without much elaboration, of the experiences of free Black women in the North. Martineau offered up searing depictions of enslaved women whom she observed "ploughing in the field," in dingy dresses with "vacant countenance"—a disturbingly sharp contrast to the "bright" and "brisk" children she witnessed in slave quarters, before the institution of slavery rendered them "slow and stupid." Martineau insisted that the system of bondage that so brutalized the enslaved as they matured also took a toll on white women enslavers. She repeated the horrifying tale, told to her by a New Orleans acquaintance, of Delphine Lalaurie, whose serial abuse—torture and even murder—of the women she enslaved revealed "a cruelty so excessive as to compel the belief that she was mentally deranged." For Martineau the lesson was that the "exercise of irresponsible power" corrupted and distorted all who encountered it. Lalaurie may well have been insane, Martineau conceded, but "there remains the fact that the insanity could have taken such a direction, and perpetrated such deeds nowhere but in a slave country."[33]

Martineau understood that slavery and racial hierarchy set women against each other, even if most situations were less dramatic than in the Lalaurie anecdote. She mocked her Southern white female acquaintances for constantly asking her if she found the enslaved people to be "generally happy." Martineau wondered that these white women "never seemed to have been asked, or to ask themselves," if they would be happy in similar circumstances. While white slaveholding women benefitted economically from the system of coerced labor and were clearly complicit in the maintenance of human property, Martineau emphasized how white men reaped the greatest rewards from this system. The benefits to white men and the complicity of white women were the point of the devastating story she recounted about a white "southern lady" who claimed to be quite fond of the "very pretty mulatto girl" she owned. The girl appealed to the white woman "for protection" from the aggressive, unwanted attentions of a white man who had come to visit. The white woman attempted to protect the enslaved girl, but she eventually took "pity" on the white man who claimed he simply could not live without this object of his desire. Martineau reported, without elaboration, that the white woman ended up selling "the girl to him for 1,500 dollars."[34]

Free Black women also appear in Martineau's work, though the encounters she described were more distant than intimate. She recounted her relief at having arrived in Cincinnati, "intensely thankful to be once more out of sight of slavery." While dining in a hotel restaurant, she was thrilled to see a "better thing than I saw at any other table in the United States, a lady of color breakfasting in the midst of us!" Her rejoicing spoke to the exceptional nature of this occurrence, as patterns of segregation marked most of her encounters with people of color in the free states. Though she attended an abolitionist meeting in Boston with white and Black women, she was taken aback by a white woman abolitionist inquiring if it "revolted" her feelings to meet in a racially mixed assembly.[35]

In *Retrospect of Western Travel* (1838), Martineau told an extended version of the story of Elizabeth Freeman (Mum Bett), the enslaved woman who

BLACK AND WHITE BEAUX.

FIG. 1.2 Auguste Hervieu, "Black and White Beaux." Though few contained images, most early travel narratives commented (as did Martineau) on the multiracial nature of the "free" states. Frances Trollope's earlier discussion accompanying this image betrayed some of her usual condescension but, in the context of the larger text, was remarkably restrained. Here Trollope praised the "toilet" of the "sable goddess" and her "black beau" and contrasted their fashionable elegance and devotion with the less admirable picture in the window, where a "very pretty white girl" was accompanied by two men who both had "their hats on, and one was smoking!" From Frances Trollope, *Domestic Manners of the Americans* (1832). Courtesy of Rauner Library, Dartmouth College.

successfully sued for her freedom in Massachusetts and helped bring about the end of slavery in that state. Martineau learned Freeman's story from the children of Theodore Sedgwick, the young lawyer who had argued Freeman's case. But Freeman is the clear heroine of her own story in Martineau's telling. Amidst the revolutionary-era talk of freedom and equality, she called on Sedgwick to inquire if she "could not claim her liberty under the law." When a surprised Sedgwick asked her what "put such an idea in her head," Freeman demonstrated familiarity with the Massachusetts constitution and Declaration of Rights, quoting its "born free and equal" language. Given Martineau's emphasis in *Society in America* on judging the United States by its adherence to its founding ideals, the fact that she made a formerly enslaved Black woman the upholder of those ideals is striking. Freeman's "name ought to be preserved in all histories of the state as one of its honours," Martineau insisted. Offering the first discussion of Elizabeth Freeman to appear in a book (Catharine Maria Sedgwick would later publish her own version), Martineau gave her story national and international attention.[36]

The Marriage Compact in America

In the methodological work she wrote while sailing across the Atlantic, Martineau reasoned that "the marriage compact" presented the "most important feature of the domestic state on which the observer can fix his attention." Tocqueville and Beaumont shared her appreciation for the significance of the institution and how it related to self-government, broadly understood. The authority exercised by the husband and father over every American household drew their attention and raised questions for each about the connection to America's democratic principles.[37]

Martineau's intellectual interest in matrimony had been fueled by discussion of this topic within London reform circles of the 1830s. As she traveled across the United States, she treated the institution as a critical gauge of the country's "treatment of women." The fact that "one sex overbears the other" within households as well as in public life revealed another way the country had "fallen below" their "democratic principles."[38] She found a more receptive audience for this argument than for her plea for women's enfranchisement. In multiple encounters, "liberal-minded" Americans had expressed embarrassment and even outrage over the lingering remnants of the common-law doctrine of coverture, which held that a married woman (a *feme covert*) was legally merged into the person of her husband. Martineau's uneasy conversations about the injustice of this practice revealed the persistence of an early national discourse of republican conjugality, which, in its elevation of marital harmony over patriarchal authority, had furnished a critique of the wife's legal non-personhood. American public culture from the late eighteenth century had begun to consider mutually supportive marriages as a sort of republic in miniature, imagining both polity and spousal harmony as "chaste, disinterested and free from the exercise of arbitrary power," in the words of historian Jan Lewis. Such republican idealizations did not seek complete equality between husband and wife as much as a rejection of overweening patriarchal tyranny. The misrule of an overbearing husband threatened republican good-feeling and thus needed to be "totally banished," even if longstanding legal principles remained in place.[39]

The deficiencies of American marriage surfaced as a recurrent theme in *Society in America*. Martineau emphasized variety and variability. Unions in slave states were assessed in the worst light. Jealous—and ultimately powerless—enslaved couples directed violence against one another as those reduced to chattel status were denied that "holy and constant love, free preference, and all that makes marriage a blessing instead of a curse." Martineau condemned a system that thwarted the natural "chastity" she observed in conversations with formerly enslaved women. Free white spouses on plantations were unhappy in entirely different ways. Marital estrangement resulted from the all-too-common behavior of "licentious" masters toward the enslaved women under their control. A lengthy discussion of the sexual economy of New Orleans allowed Martineau to elaborate on the harms of a social order based on racial subjugation and (sexual) "treachery." She explained how purportedly free, mixed-race women were coerced into relations of concubinage, in which white men took up with mistresses they kept separate from the white family in their households. This system, with its assault on "domestic purity and peace," injured all but the white men. Every "quadroon woman," Martineau wrote, believes her white partner will prove an exception to the "rule of desertion," while every "white lady believes that her husband had been an exception to the rule of seduction."[40]

Martineau also detailed several aspects of wifely subordination practiced by "American women," here using a universalizing category that applied to white, middle-class women residing in the free states. She objected to the way society positioned marriage as "the only appointed object in life" for women whose limited educations presumed an eventual husband and children. Nondomestic occupations thus became an aberration, regardless of whether family life matched a particular woman's talents, interests, and desires. If Martineau judged American norms to be better than those of England, the stated approach of her work had made clear that this was not the appropriate standard of judgment. The question to be posed was: Did the institution of marriage adequately reflect America's democratic ideals? The answer, she thought, was no. Marriage in democratic America suffered from the "inequalities of the partners in mind and occupation" and would remain an "imperfect institution" so long as "women continue to be ill-educated, passive, and subservient; or well-educated, vigorous, and free only upon sufferance."[41]

A separate chapter explained married women's legal disabilities with such clarity and force that it garnered instant authority. Sarah Grimké almost immediately put Martineau's findings to use, citing them in her *Letters on the Equality of the Sexes* (1838). Through fine-grained distinctions between the states, Martineau contrasted the civil law regimes in Louisiana and Missouri with the more stringent application elsewhere of coverture. She happily reported that in some states, efforts had been made to eliminate the most objectionable aspects that limited a wife's property-holding, inheritance, and access to divorce. The incremental approach, she maintained, was promising but hardly sufficient. Even a partial restriction of women's due right to property was a violation: since they lacked a voice in selecting representatives, they never gave "consent of the governed" to states that unjustly disposed of their property. The tension between a wife's legal subordination and the need in a democracy to achieve the active consent of all adults, regardless of sex, was among Martineau's most original contributions.[42]

Beaumont and Tocqueville offered alternative perspectives on the relationship of husbandly authority to America's democratic principles. Both men noted and condemned the fragility of conjugality for the country's non-white inhabitants. *Marie*'s basic plot—detailing the vulnerability of free Black and mixed-race Americans in a culture hostile toward "amalgamation"—was stretched in one dialogue to focus on the South's enslaved population and the impossibility there of any semblance of "conjugal tenderness." One character remarks that the "loves of a slave leave no more trace on society than does the breeding of plants on our gardens." Tocqueville echoed this passage in "The Three Races" chapter of *Democracy in America*, where he linked marital fragility and familial disorder to a diminished capacity of nonwhite peoples for self-government. His two racialized categories—a singular "Negro" and an Indian "savage"—took the male subject to stand in for the whole group. In the case of the "negro," Tocqueville argued that slavery deprived its victims of "all the privileges of humanity," including the bonds of family. The rupture of family ties made "woman" little more than the "temporary companion of [the enslaved man's] pleasures."[43]

Tocqueville's second racialized group, the Indians, suffered from a different but similarly destructive familial disorder, which stemmed from what he deemed their collective penchant for excessive freedom. Europeans had initiated, through their greed, the scattering of native kin groups, but Tocqueville thought that the "savages" themselves exercised choice in stubbornly remaining "scarcely conscious of the authority of the family." What he saw as their refusal to bow to the will of another produced a debilitating inability to "distinguish between voluntary obedience and a shameful subjection." The end result was an aversion to all familial tutelage that would mold and transmit an enduring sense of domestic duties and rights. Tocqueville's lament that Indians understood freedom as the "escape from all shackles of society" found a counterpart in the chapter from Beaumont's *Marie* that culminated in the tragic suicide of a spurned Ottawa wife.[44]

The purported domestic disorder of the enslaved and the dispossessed indigenous population threw into relief the quite different experience of free white families. Democracy's impact on the family was manifold. It weakened the bonds of patriarchy; it altered the relations between fathers and sons and among male siblings; it granted girls a degree of independence and autonomy they enjoyed nowhere in Europe; and it shaped the relations between husband and wife. *Marie*'s opening chapter (titled "American Women") established the seeming paradox that the American girl enjoyed an unusual degree of freedom but was reduced to a "nonentity" when she became a wife. Tocqueville gave this transformation a more positive slant, which he developed at some length in the second volume of *Democracy in America* (1840). Across five chapters, he linked American marriage to democracy more explicitly than had ever before been attempted.

The confidence and poise of American girls struck Tocqueville and Beaumont, who saw them as evidence of democracy's impact on the daughters of white, middle-class households. Beaumont recalled hearing a twelve-year-old gravely debate the best form of government (her answer: a republic), while Tocqueville reported being "frequently surprised and almost frightened" by the boldness of girls' talk. He marveled how "they manage their thoughts" easily in conversations, in which even "a philosopher would have stumbled." The American girl "thinks for herself, speaks with freedom, and acts on her own impulse." Tocqueville believed this striking autonomy resulted from diminished patriarchal authority and the resulting need for girls to protect themselves and their chastity. Whereas girls in aristocratic France were educated to remain innocent and almost childlike in their ignorance of the ways of the world, American girls needed "precocious knowledge" on all manner of subjects. In short, a "democratic education" was needed to protect young women from "the dangers with which democratic institutions and manners surround them." This democratic education emphasized autonomy and self-control over religious strictures or seclusion from society. The Americans sought "to arm" a girl's "reason" and cultivate the independence that would give her "confidence in her own strength of character."[45]

Then came marriage. In that institution the autonomy and independence Tocqueville witnessed in the American girl completely disappeared, and in her place was a wife whose independence was "irrevocably lost in the bonds of matrimony." If a father's house had been an "abode of freedom and of pleasure," that of a husband resembled a "cloister."[46]

How to reconcile such an abrupt reversal of circumstance? Undoubtedly for readers today, as for some in 1840, no effort to reconcile this apparent inconsistency can satisfy. Tocqueville's comments only underscored the imperative, announced loudly by Martineau and others, to relegate coverture to the dustbin. And yet Tocqueville did attempt to resolve the apparent tension, in democratic terms, by claiming to discern what women actually preferred. The move from girlish freedom to wifely submission made sense only if one appreciated the continuities between the "early culture of the girl" and the person of the wife. "Her habits are different," Tocqueville explained, "but her character is the same."[47] The key to this explanation lay in the free choice that American women no less than men enjoyed in selecting partners and voluntarily entering into marriage when ready to do so. This voluntary consent struck an aristocratic European as a dramatic departure from approaching marriage as a union of property rather than of persons.

Tocqueville struggled to stretch the voluntary nature of marital choice to cover women's self-abnegation upon marriage. Women willingly accepted marital submission, he claimed. They were neither dupes nor victims of "simplicity and ignorance," but actually made it "their boast to bend themselves to the yoke." Each woman, he argued, prepared herself for this step and greeted her subordination with equanimity. In fact, it was the very democratic education that made American girls so independent and autonomous before marriage that allowed them to relinquish those traits upon marriage and to shift from being a self-governing person to an other-governed one whose individuality could be further developed through the key female roles of wife and mother. The American woman learned "by use of her independence" to surrender it "without a struggle" when the time came to make this sacrifice. Tocqueville's language emphasized the bold resolve he professed to observe: married women, in making this leap, demonstrated "independence," "strength of purpose," "calm and unquenchable energy," "courage," "inward strength," even "virile habits."[48]

American marriage was democratic not just because it was voluntary, however. Tocqueville shifted from the question of how individuals paired with one another to how their interaction, as authoritative male head and subordinate female partner, shaped and reinforced the crucial habits that made democracy possible. If the language remained the same from Tocqueville's discussion of mores and habits in volume one of *Democracy*, the points he made in the second volume's discussion of marriage were distinct and original. Native Americans in the earlier schema failed to differentiate between voluntary obedience and shameful subjection; (white) American women within families made no such mistake. In consenting to authority and continuing to submit to that rightful authority, wives modeled key democratic practices. By deferring to their wives' judgment and exhibiting "a profound respect for [their] freedom" (within their sphere), men modeled reciprocal democratic habits that made the American family serve as a site of political socialization. It modeled consent and limited authority within a well-regulated social order. And this was how Americans understand, Tocqueville explained, "the equality of the sexes."

At a time when the "woman question" had re-emerged, Tocqueville took pains to qualify the sort of equality that Americans nurtured within family life. They generally did not believe that "the subversion of marital power" was a necessary consequence of "democratic principles" and instead understood that in the family, as in the larger community, "the object of democracy is to regulate and legalize the powers that are necessary, and not to subvert all power."[49] Tocqueville found that men and women alike assented to this "opinion," and this assent was as crucial as the moment when a wife accepted the "yoke" of marriage. In his telling—based on limited interaction with actual women—he claimed to have heard no women complain of "conjugal authority" as a "usurpation of their rights." This was a curious definition of "equality between the sexes"—as his awkward attempt to pair "yoke" with consent suggested—but Tocqueville nonetheless insisted that American marriage represented some sort of democratic modification of the institution and granted dignity and reciprocity to men and women alike.

Dissenting voices made clear that marriage was not as voluntary as he imagined and that the story of self-abnegating American women who gladly "bend themselves to the yoke" of matrimony was a convenient fiction. The entire plot of Beaumont's novel had pivoted on the impossibility of interracial marriages in America. Other observers questioned how "voluntary" marriage could actually be when it was the only route to economic security for most women. Coercion seemed a better way to describe the situation forced on women who had to accept a marriage offer, as the reformer Lydia Maria Child noted, simply out of desperation or "dread" of "being dependent."[50] Where Tocqueville glimpsed democratic progress and a supposedly greater equality between the sexes, Martineau saw only a missed opportunity. In her eyes, marriage not only exacerbated the larger inequalities and injustices of American society but failed to serve as the appropriate means of democratic political socialization that it could ideally be. Not unlike Mary Wollstonecraft before her, she imagined marriage as a true partnership of equals who would mutually improve one another and thereby society as a whole. This was impossible as long as society tended to make women "weak, ignorant and subservient" and men "tyrannical." Only equality and a free range of moral action could make marriage an appropriately democratic institution, which Martineau argued was both crucial to the self-reliance of men and women and "essential to the virtue of society."[51]

On this subject, perhaps more than any other, Tocqueville's impressions from 1831 felt stale by the time he published them in 1840. His view that women were cloistered in the home missed the whole range of associational activity to which they had been active contributors, and which showed that the interplay of educative participation and collective purpose might apply to both sexes. The five years between the appearance of the first and second volumes witnessed the emergence of the woman question as a significant topic in published opinion, with new avenues opened by Martineau's *Society in America* (1837), the controversy over the Grimké sisters' public speaking, and the publication of Sarah Grimké's *Letters on the Equality of the Sexes* (1838). That Tocqueville was not aware of these developments seems clear by the relief he expressed that American women had not been infected with any of the dangerous sex radicalism he encountered in France. It was to the credit of the Americans that they did not confuse "the different characteristics of the sexes" and pursue a misguided and unnatural kind of equality that would produce "weak men and disorderly women." He likely had in mind here a range of figures, including novelist George Sand, utopian Saint Simonians, British freethinker Fanny Wright, and other figures who noisily "clamor[ed] for the rights of women" while "trampling" upon hallowed duties.

Having heard none of this talk during his tour, Tocqueville had only praise and admiration for American women who correctly understood "that species of democratic equality which may be established between the sexes." In fact, he concluded his discussion of women in just the sort of chivalrous terms

Martineau would have loathed. Were he to be asked, as he concluded his two-volume study, "to what the singular prosperity and growing strength" of the Americans "ought mainly to be attributed," he would reply: "To the superiority of their women."[52]

The Observed Respond

If Americans of the late 1830s and early 1840s were "like persons surrounded by mirrors," they had a hard time looking away. Tocqueville and Martineau's works generated broad domestic discussion. Weighty thirty-page essays, lighter magazine reviews, and countless newspapers squibs took on their own momentum, which transformed observation into conversation.

Tocqueville—hailed as a genius, a friend of popular government, and a flatterer of American women—drew especially lavish praise from US writers. Even when reviewers remarked on specific errors, they noted that the "seriousness, dignity, and good faith" of his work admirably distinguished it from the "flippancy and vulgarity" of so many other "foreign books on America." In one of a cluster of book-length engagements with the theme of democracy from the late 1830s, Whig writer Calvin Colton quibbled with Tocqueville on several key issues but still granted him his due. Colton marveled that the first volume of *Democracy in America* had begun "at the beginning, dove to the bottom, and pervaded all the known and unknown regions of American society." Its sheer comprehensiveness had drawn out from America's "profundities a vast amount of its hidden secrets" and had "fished up pearls and treasures of inestimable value."[53] The attention drawn to Tocqueville's "Three Races" chapter, in contrast, elicited more controversy than praise. More than one contributor to the *Colored American* took issue with it, including a rare female correspondent who complained that the "disgusting trickery" of the "slaveocracy" had stoked the Frenchman's prejudices. Some white reviewers denounced the chapter as typical European meddling, while others approved his endorsement of Black deportation to West Africa as a means of eliminating a "staining" racial presence.[54]

Extensive notice of *Democracy in America* contrasted sharply with the reception of Beaumont's novel *Marie*, which barely registered in US print culture. A novel that was acclaimed in France—where it went through multiple editions and won a prestigious prize from the Académie Française—was not fully translated into English or published in the United States until the mid-twentieth century. The easiest explanation for that absence was its affront to many American audiences, from its unsparing criticism to the implication that Europe was preferable to the New World to its focus on an "interracial" relationship. Even Beaumont's marriage to the granddaughter of Lafayette (which made him half-American, as he liked to say) did not ease the book's path to American publication. With no American or British editions in print, the book became known mainly from a handful of reviews in periodicals, including one by John Stuart Mill, who contended that no other book "represented American social life in such sombre colors." Abolitionist Maria Weston Chapman, who thought the novel revealed "the severity and truth" of "the vices of the American people," began a translation in the mid-1840s but completed only two chapters. It would thus be left to Harriet Beecher Stowe to achieve America's breakthrough antislavery novel, some fifteen years later, with *Uncle Tom's Cabin*.[55]

Somewhere between the two extremes of effusive praise and studied avoidance lay Americans' responses to Martineau's work. Her forceful opinions on slavery were embraced by abolitionists who featured excerpts in their periodicals and published a compilation of her antislavery commentary as a separate pamphlet that identified her as an "ardent admirer of democracy." But to most others, her "advanced" position on slavery was used to explain—and to discredit—the "ultra" comments she offered about women and self-government. Colton castigated the Englishwoman's "seditious labors" that blended the disorder of "amalgamation" with the "rights of women." Some of the antebellum South's earliest systematic defenders of slavery ventured further. South Carolina ideologues rejected the basic premise of *Society in America*: that nineteenth-century Americans actually believed the high-minded affirmations of their 1776 Declaration of Independence. A Charleston journal waved away Jefferson's two core concepts by dubbing both equality among humans and the consent of the governed to be "false in theory and impracticable in application." Another Charlestonian, bestselling novelist William Gilmore Simms, conveyed the same point, but only after deploying a withering attack on Martineau and her travels. His lengthy broadside denouncing *Society in America* went through multiple incarnations, as it moved from the pages of the *Southern Literary Messenger* to a stand-alone pamphlet (which he dedicated to South Carolina's Congressional delegation), and, finally, to a place in *The Proslavery Argument*, an influential collection of writings in 1852.[56]

Some Americans instead tried to break the cycle of ill-tempered defensiveness in response to outside criticism. These authors took the stance of querist in engaging reasonably with Martineau. Their efforts stood out for their very ordinariness. Their contributions to published opinion have not been remembered for their brilliance, but they reveal how foreign observations spurred Americans' introspection about their democracy. Indiscriminate abuse was not constructive, advised James T. Boyle, the author of a full pamphlet-length "impartial review" of *Society in America.* Americans would do better and "display much more wisdom" by carefully reading the work and "calmly deciding" its worth "on its merits." He cautioned readers that they were under a double scrutiny, "that both the work, and the manner we treat it, are before the world."[57]

The insistence that Americans would burnish their reputation by rising above indignant reaction to foreign observation was echoed by George Sidney Camp in the first American-authored comprehensive account of popular government. Much of Camp's *Democracy* (1841) defended the emerging notion of collective "self-government" against those who seized on the "tyranny of the majority" as the key Tocquevillian assessment of democracy. This concern had been foregrounded by early British reviews of Tocqueville, mostly in a conservative vein, and inspired Camp to offer a counterbalanced view of what he considered Tocqueville's more significant theme: the elevation of the citizen through political participation. "Let [the citizen] feel that he and his children are integral parts of the nation . . . parties to its laws, and equal partakers of its rights and privileges," he wrote, "and you increase, as much as human means can, the force of his moral motives and the energy of his active powers."[58]

This body of commentary demonstrated how scrutiny of American democracy led to questions about the place of women within it. Camp resisted being drawn too deeply into this issue, though he acknowledged the asymmetry of denying a voice in national affairs to "females, infants, idiots, and maniacs." He appreciated what Tocqueville did not—that women possessed "all the requisites of political freedom" and that as a consequence, their exclusion might not hold up under close inspection. The continuing disfranchisement of women, he wrote, involved "questions which I do not care to discuss," and then he abruptly and awkwardly set the topic aside. Remaining silent as to whether or not Americans consistently applied principles of self-government, he announced that he "would rather admit the invalidity of the exception than impair the force of the general rule." Truncated in this way, the work of reconciling democratic principles and the exclusions of sex would be left to others who picked up where Tocqueville and Camp left off.[59]

As James Boyle engaged with Martineau's *Society in America* point-by-point in his pamphlet, he granted the question of women's political rights a thorough hearing. By rejecting Martineau's views with reason instead of ridicule, he tacitly admitted being challenged by them. Her arguments in the chapter on "The Political Non-existence of Women" were, in his opinion, "so peculiar that no one has deemed them of sufficient consequence to demand a serious refutation." Refutation he would provide, though not before first identifying areas of consensus. Here he conceded that her lament about the constrained opportunities available to women ought to be distributed in full to "every family throughout the Union." The notion of ending men's monopoly on political power, however, struck him as too advanced. Boyle supported his position by laying out the travails of child-bearing and by raising what he thought was the absurdity of women bearing arms. Full citizenship, he believed, along with other Martineau reviewers, must be based on physical defense of the country from foreign enemies. He admitted that some aspects of coverture could be "ameliorated," but he asserted that women's welfare and liberty (along with that of "our children") were safely protected by men. Far from convinced, he nonetheless acknowledged that Martineau brought "more cogent arguments to support her mistakes than many can bring in defence of truth."[60]

Martineau's paragraphs on the "political non-existence of women" became perhaps the most frequently quoted section of *Society in America*. The ad hominem attacks on her "women's rights" posture in that chapter were mitigated by her established presence as a bestselling author and by a prim demeanor that shielded her from the attacks on her sexuality that had targeted Mary Wollstonecraft and Frances Wright. Her book and her subsequent journalism ensured she would feature regularly in the American press for decades. Attempts to depict her as a "female brawler" fell flat, as did efforts to associate her work with the "unsexing" of American society, "the prostration of all decency and order," and the "reign of wild anarchy and shameless vice." After all, even Boyle had admitted that Martineau might be "in error" but that "her errors are not ridiculous." An English novel, *Woman as She Should Be* (1843), turned the tables by having a reasonable woman spar with an "ultra Tory" acquaintance over "that chapter" of "Miss Martineau's" new book.[61] Across American published opinion, Martineau's case for women's political representation encountered less ridicule than one might expect, and even those reviews that expressed strong reservations featured extensive quotations that circulated her basic arguments to more and more readers. Her forward-looking affirmation of democratic progress fit the mood, and the "political non-existence" chapter was thus reprinted—in its complete form—in the more radical corners of the Jacksonian press. Unlikely journalistic figures such as Orestes Brownson and John L. O'Sullivan deemed her discussions worthy at least of airing fully for a forward-looking American public.[62]

Several distinctive features ensured that Martineau's work endured as a touchstone for further women's rights advocacy. Her evocative phrase "political non-existence" borrowed the language of coverture for married women and crafted, via the principle of consent of the governed, a critique of all women's exclusion from the ballot box. That pivot transfixed young women like Bostonian Caroline Dall, née Healey, and her friend Ednah Dow Cheney, née Littlehale, whose aspirations for full citizenship would be strengthened in part by the formula that appeared in Martineau's work. When future congressman George W. Julian of Indiana encountered her book a decade after its appearance, he realized that it "pithily states the substance of all" that had been ventured regarding women's full political participation. Unable to contest its points, he embraced them. For decades to come, he linked his

HARRIET MARTINEAU.

FIG. 1.3 "Harriet Martineau." By 1850, thirteen years after the appearance of *Society in America*, Martineau was enough of a household name that *Peterson's*, an illustrated magazine for ladies, could publish this engraving with no accompanying story. The "unusually good" image, according to the magazine, illustrated itself "without words." From *Peterson's Magazine* (January 1, 1850). Courtesy of the Henry E. Huntington Library.

commitment to political antislavery to the cause of women's enfranchisement. Perhaps the most striking rhetorical move of Martineau's work was its
concluding assertion, where she insisted that "the true democratic principle"
would cause Americans to implement equal political standing for "both halves
of the human race." She thus summed up her logic with a hint of a rallying cry.
"The principles once established, the methods will follow, easily, naturally,
and under a remarkable transmutation of the ridiculous into the sublime."[63]

2

Domesticating Democracy

IN 1841, CATHARINE BEECHER turned to Alexis de Tocqueville not to explain her country, but to save it. As the successful educator transitioned to a new phase as a popular domestic advice guru, she enlisted the Frenchman's reflections on American women, marriage, and the family to make her case that the efforts of white, middle-class women were indispensable to the fate of democracy. An excerpt from Tocqueville's chapter on "How Americans Understand the Equality of the Sexes" extended across five of the book's opening ten pages and set the tone for Beecher's *Treatise on Domestic Economy* (1841). Other Tocqueville passages—his thoughts on the inevitability of popular government and his commentary on Americans' manners—were peppered across subsequent pages. This commentary from the newly published second volume of *Democracy in America* (1840) revealed the stakes of Beecher's reform efforts: the fact that "startled kings and sages, philosophers, and statesmen" had been "studying our institutions, scrutinizing our experience, and watching for our mistakes."[1]

The *Treatise on Domestic Economy* forged a curious connection between a paragon of middle-class Yankee values and an observant European aristocrat. Drawing so prominently on the views of "M. De Tocqueville, a writer, who, for intelligence, fidelity, and ability, ranks second to none," Beecher sought to bolster the credibility and timeliness of her own contribution to her national culture. The extensive circulation and longevity of the *Treatise* shifted the dynamic. In time, Beecher contributed as much to Tocqueville's popularity as she originally benefitted from his prestige. Twenty reprintings of her book appeared before 1869. It was then functionally replaced by a new volume she coauthored with her sister, Harriet Beecher Stowe. When readers who purchased the antebellum *Treatise* are added to those who borrowed it (from lending libraries or from acquaintances) and those who accessed its frequent excerpts in the press, it is safe to say that more Americans encountered Tocqueville's words via Beecher's extensive quotation than through any other single channel. How a guide to household management became a conduit for democratic political philosophy is a puzzle worth trying to solve.[2]

The links between domesticity and democracy were multiple, though they are not perhaps immediately evoked by phrases like the "Age of Jackson" or the "rise of American democracy." Scholars have shown how middle-class reformers sought to remake the family during this period in response to intense social and economic change—a growing market economy, continued geographical expansion into western territories, and the sense of dislocation and anxiety these forces produced.[3] Because these developments occurred simultaneously with the expansion of democracy, the latter's significance to the elaboration of domesticity can be difficult to see. But attending to the pervasive cultural program exemplified by Beecher's *Treatise* illuminates how Americans confronted the knotty problems of popular government in the decades before the Civil War. Alongside election parades, barbecues, and white workingmen's political mobilization, Americans appreciated the democratic elements of fireside discussions, gatherings around dinner tables, and white middle-class women's far-flung reform activity. At each of these disparate sites, Americans were working out what it meant to achieve a broad culture of "self-government."

The household became a space for fostering new governing modes, drawing scrutiny of the deep domestic roots that shaped popular government for either good or for ill. Fundamental questions surfaced, as they had in other eras and under other systems of government, about the relations between household and polity. How far, for example, should democratic equality extend? Should it remake relations within the household, traditionally a site of paternal male authority over dependent wives, children, servants, and slaves? What role did, or should, the family play in shaping democratic selves—in teaching individuals how to become self-governing and in preparing citizens for self-government? These questions connected ideas of equality and popular government with shifting gender norms and household prerogatives.

Beecher emerged as the foremost innovator of what might be termed "domesticated democracy," which refashioned ideas about republican motherhood for a new era. By the time she drafted her 1841 *Treatise*, she had resolved to claim the language of democracy—a terminology far too important to be left to radical or merely partisan voices. The first sentence of her book staked this claim: "American women" must "feel an interest in the support of the democratic institutions of their Country." She then identified "the principles of democracy" with the "principles of Christianity." That pivot depended on a reading of the Golden Rule that converted "do unto others as you would have them do unto you" into guidance about making hierarchical interactions across social rank more consistent with a democratic ethos then achieving cultural dominance. But the most striking position Beecher laid out in her introduction involved a syllogism whose power lay in its simplicity: the worldwide embrace of democracy depended on the success of American democracy; the success of American democracy depended on the intellectual and moral character of its people; the moral and intellectual character of its people depended on the efforts of American women. Ergo, American women were responsible for democracy across the nineteenth-century world.

For all her effort to align herself with the broader democratic ethos, Beecher's domesticated democracy was limited in ways that went well beyond her amply documented opposition to women's antislavery activism and, in later years, her hostility to women's political enfranchisement (a stance that set her apart from three famous siblings). Just as Tocqueville had linked a purported inability or unwillingness to form nurturing families among the enslaved and Native Americans to an unfitness for self-government, Beecher's vision was marked by a race and class specificity that was always implied but only sometimes stated explicitly. She repeatedly presented people outside her white, native, and Protestant middle-class readership as a corrupting and menacing force, capable of dooming the American democratic experiment.

Domesticity represented the most prolific and visible effort to reform families in these years, but its very dominance stirred countercurrents. The most thoroughgoing critiques came from utopian socialist reformers who imagined alternative family configurations. Their communitarian ideas received a full airing in Horace Greeley's *New York Tribune*, a paper that quickly became a significant force in reformist northeastern circles. Yet, as was the case with Beaumont's *Marie*, utopian socialists bumped up against limits on what was permissible to venture within published opinion of the 1840s. The hint of sexual irregularity proved a powerful weapon in ruling certain views out of order, as Greeley and his contributors learned. Greeley played a role in furthering the career of Transcendentalist intellectual Margaret Fuller, who arguably penned the era's most enduring critique of domesticity and the gender relations it affirmed. Her work in the early 1840s posed probing questions about the possibilities and limitations of American culture for women who longed to be fully self-governing.

Domus and Demos

Even a casual glance at early nineteenth-century published opinion reveals domesticity as a central preoccupation. So pervasive was the focus on home and family life in these decades that historians long ago dubbed it a "cult of domesticity," a phrase that has been routinely paired with the "Cult of True Womanhood" and the notion of "separate spheres." Such language evokes the era's accelerating social and economic change, with an expanding market economy that shifted the primary site of productive work away from home to the factory, shop, or office; entangled men in a ruthless world of buying, selling, winning, and losing; and uprooted individuals and families from traditional communities in the process. Social mobility coincided with geographic mobility. As Americans sought opportunity in expanding cities, booming canal towns, and the newly admitted states of the Old Northwest, they left behind the social worlds that had provided order and instruction.[4] Tocqueville had identified the psychic stress that democratic mobility (as opposed to aristocratic fixity) inflicted on individuals, who were free to improve their lot in life but then bore individual responsibility for any failure to do so. The "voluntary" nature of marriage also imposed some psychic burden: individuals could marry for love but the onus of that choice rested squarely on them. The simultaneously liberating and terrifying reality of such mobility explained why Americans, in Tocqueville's words, could seem "restless" and even melancholic amidst their abundance. Anxiety and ambition alike fueled a demand for the explosion of advice literature that instructed Americans on how to succeed, or at least how to hedge against the vagaries of the market. Domestic advice was part of this larger corpus of self-improving literature. Anxious ministers and white middle-class women responded to the dislocations of the era by turning cultural conventions into an easily understood code of behavior.[5]

Less obvious but no less significant was the democratic context in which domestic themes gained cultural heft. Nearly all American travel writing made some mention of home life, and the bulk of these works assumed familial and household structures had an intimate relation to Americans' distinctive form of popular government. What was at stake was the nation's democratic destiny, which all observers agreed depended on what took place within the intimate confines of shared living spaces. The incessant public commentary of traditionalists, domestic reformers, and still more radical critics of the family developed an American variation of a truism accepted across much of human history—that the entire scheme of a polity's governance depended on the proper ordering of its families. "The elements of the nation, nay, of the world itself," one volume asserted in 1838, "are prepared, to a very great extent, in our nurseries, and around the domestic fireside."[6]

Self-government provided the most important conceptual link between domesticity and democracy. The term in this period evoked both its older connotations and a more explicitly political sense ventured during the early years of American nationhood by James Madison, George Washington, and others. Originally referring to the habits of self-control that restrained passions and kept one on the path of righteousness, the term "self-government" became a staple of sermons and moral exhortation about the acquisition of a self-regulating regimen. Such a regimen was seen as a prerequisite for the kind of moral freedom that was untainted by license. Self-governance was thought to distinguish humans from animals—men and women alone among God's creatures were able to undertake the necessary practice and training in attaining it. A supposed disparity in the capacity of certain groups to develop internal self-governance allowed theorists and moralists to justify all manner of governance by others, including slavery. These were specious arguments, the *Colored American* told its readers in 1837, that simply repeated "what the despots of all ages and nations have said" to justify the permanent and arbitrary rule of some over others.[7]

By 1840, the term "self-government" had became a synonym for democracy or popular government. Tocqueville's English translator had used it in the first volume of 1835 to identify a core philosophical principle of the Americans ("that every man is born in possession of the right of self-government"). This potent association became commonplace across both England and the United States, with one essayist even insisting the term was of "American origin" and "very little known in Europe or Asia."[8] George Sidney Camp in another typical usage—from *Democracy* (1841)—explained that the Americans had for sixty-some years been "governed by a government" of their own establishment, laws of their own making, and representatives of their own selection. This, he wrote, "is self-government. It is free government." By the end of the decade, the term in its collective, political meaning was ubiquitous, with phrases like the "great question of self-government" and the "right to self-government," appearing regularly, including in President James K. Polk's message to Congress in 1847.[9]

The term's original moral connotations persisted, and for most of the nineteenth century suspicions remained about whether humans who demonstrated an inability to regulate individual desires and drives were fit to participate in politics. This moral emphasis did not simply coexist with the more novel emphasis on political forms; the dual meanings overlapped in ways that were taken for granted. Commentators insisted that collective self-government, no less than personal self-government, depended on the self-control and self-rule that held appetites in check. The quest for internal sources of restraint became a major preoccupation of American reformers and evangelicals who fretted as much about an age of "universal" suffrage and mass partisan mobilization as they did about the dissolution of authority that occurred in the expansion of market relations.[10] The temperance movement, which attracted adherents across the social spectrum, made palpable the connections among self-regulation, autonomy, and democratic citizenship. Similarly, diverse programs of diet and bodily reform flourished, including the gospel of "bran bread" inspired by Sylvester Graham whose strenuous regimen of food preparation and consumption promised to offer "the best manner of living in civic life." As the work of self-governance required self-knowledge, new modes and techniques of understanding the self were linked as much to democratic stability as individual fulfillment. From illustrations in anatomy and physiology to the brain "maps" of the phrenological movement (whose adopted slogan was "Know thyself!"), the stakes of self-cultivation were related to the viability of popular government.[11]

Family assumed utmost significance as the primary institution in which a person learned to be self-governing, both as a functioning individual and as a member of the polity. Amherst College president Heman Humphrey, a defender of a fading patriarchal authority, captured an assumption that went well beyond family traditionalists like himself. "Without family government," he proclaimed, there would "be very little *self-government* in any community." A vast set of publications emerged to aid the development of this process, produced by an American-based middle-class chorus of essayists, ministers, reformers, novelists, and editors, who collectively commented on the domestic bedrock of an expansive democracy. Americans of both sexes and all ages were inundated with guidance on how to be a wife, a husband, a parent, or a child, and how to create and sustain appropriately nurturing familial relations. This output sprawled in form and genre; it included courtship guides, etiquette books, family periodicals, dedicated lady's magazines, domestic manuals, child-rearing handbooks, and self-improvement guides, as well as fiction, poetry, and song. Book publishers witnessed a boom in sales and maintained the trade's momentum by segmenting targeted audiences, sometimes in terms of class or region but more often through age-specific materials.[12]

Guides appeared to tackle each and every life stage of a readership keen for basic instruction. Etiquette and courtship manuals were offered to the unmarried of both sexes, to be supplemented, after marriage, by books detailing the responsibilities of the "young husband" or the "young bride," and then the American mother and father. One savvy bookseller included space for a "beautifully engraved marriage certificate" to be added as a frontispiece, marketing the volume as a bridal gift. Nationally oriented magazines such as *Godey's Lady's Book* and *Graham's* appealed to newly formed families, whetting appetites for a steady diet of domestic material comprised of American-produced poetry, fiction, didactic instruction, humor, and increasingly lavish illustrations. Parenting handbooks, self-improvement guides, and novel-length depictions of family life filled bookcases of parlors, especially in the free states, as a realm where the American wife and mother presided. An explosion of juvenile literature capped off the flood of materials that equipped the family to pursue a version of socialization and self-making that set it apart from the inherited patriarchal household.[13]

If a new world, according to Tocqueville, required a new science of politics, so too did a new citizenry require a new guide to domestic life. As Americans pioneered untested forms of democratic government, they similarly worked to recast how individuals developed themselves within the context of private families. "This work is intended for American youth," announced William Andrus Alcott, one of the most prolific practitioners of conduct literature. "*American*! did I say? This word, alone, ought to call forth all your energies, and if there be a slumbering faculty within you, arouse it to action." Celebrated Massachusetts novelist Catharine Maria Sedgwick similarly rallied young women to glory in the original world they faced. For the first time in human history, she claimed, an individual's fate would be determined not by inherited rank but by her own character and effort.[14]

The central work of this "school of domesticity" was to educate all household members to become self-governing individuals and to prepare them to be citizens in a self-governing republic. If, according to liberal theory, the rights-bearing individual was born not made, in democratic practice the self-governing citizen was made not born. William Alcott confirmed this message in volume after volume, emphasizing not just that the difficult "work of self-government" was required of every "rational being" but that it demanded training and practice. Families provided the first school of self-government for children but also functioned as a continuing one for adults. Children would be taught to internalize norms, control impulses, and understand duties and responsibilities, as well as rights. Parents would serve as both instructors and models. Marriage would thus, according to Alcott, "complete the education of the parties themselves" and be the "means of human progress and improvement through another generation." The frontispiece to one of his volumes illustrated the point. A husband/father reads aloud to his wife and child in their well-appointed middle-class parlor, where the accessories of refinement (sumptuous textiles, elaborate mantelpiece, ornamental clock, and vase) share visual space with trappings of the classroom (volumes of books, a globe). As the caption informed the reader: "There is no school like the Family School."[15]

And yet the emphasis on self-governance surfaced a latent tension within domesticity concerning the legal obliteration, via coverture, of the personhood of American wives. Especially in those areas of the United States where slavery no longer existed, a collective commitment to democratic equality in public sat awkwardly alongside vestiges of household relationships marked by subordination and government by others. The problem of a married woman's civic personhood would begin to be rectified by specific reform legislation of the 1840s and 1850s enacted at the state level. The defining features of these

"There is no School like the Family School."

FIG. 2.1 "There is no School like the Family School." This frontispiece, from one of the nearly dozen advice manuals William Alcott wrote, captured the view of domestic writers that living together as a family provided a crucial education in the habits required for self-governing citizens. Family life was "the school of schools," with all other "places of instruction merely its subsidiaries." From William A. Alcott, *The Young Husband, or Duties of Man in the Marriage Relation* (1838). Courtesy of Rauner Library, Dartmouth College.

legislative efforts centered on property rights for married women and an easing of access to the ultimate remedy of divorce. Historian Carole Shammas has placed these piecemeal reforms alongside the more aggressive but simultaneous assault on southern slaveholding as different battle fronts in what she has termed Americans' "household civil war." Taking this panoramic view reveals how, over the course of the nineteenth century, a political society that had been comprised of households was remade legally as a citizenry of autonomous individuals, freed from dependencies that had survived America's revolutionary founding. Hard-won political and legal victories in this period were anticipated by shifts of public opinion, however, and the questioning of prevailing conventions had already brought change to everyday life and practice.[16]

The quest for more egalitarian, if not exactly democratic, marriages was evident in the domestic writing of the period. In 1838 publisher and political economist Matthew Carey excoriated newspapers writers who circulated "maxims and rules" that continued to counsel "a highly improper degree of subordination or subservience on the part of the wife" and a "correlative superiority or authority on the part of the husband." His own instructions, which relaxed authority while leaving marital hierarchy intact, was delivered first to husbands, then to wives, and finally to a couple together, whom he counseled to direct all their energies toward a harmonious union. Baltimore-based Unitarian minister George W. Burnap chastised men who viewed woman as "a mere doll" to be dressed up and installed in a home like a piece of furniture as well as those who treated her as a "domestic drudge" charged with feeding and clothing the family. Neither doll nor drudge was a "worthy conception of one half the human species." Burnap instead preached women's fuller humanity and the need to enliven and train all their faculties. There were of course familial, other-directed reasons for his view, but he insisted primarily on the benefits to woman herself—on the importance of adding to her inner "resources" and enlarging "her means of happiness."[17]

More than simply outmoded, patriarchal behavior neglected the crucial opportunity to mold and improve the character of all family members: husbands, wives, children, and servants alike. Lydia Maria Child, who authored two highly successful domestic advice manuals, urged mothers of girls to inculcate a correct understanding of matrimony as crucial to their continued individual development. If "formed with proper views," marriage could operate as a "powerful means of improving our better nature." Child's concise view captured a larger cultural ethos that intensified scrutiny of marriage, a phenomenon most dramatically evident in a fascinating "science of matrimony" that proliferated in the 1840s. This innovative body of material, growing out of an upsurge in phrenology, spoke to partners seeking compatibility rather than economic advancement, or even love.[18] The relentless focus on marital and familial relations was inhospitable to adults who never wed, as well as to childless couples. Alcott expressed a common suspicion of bachelors when he warned young men that an individual's "mind and feelings contract" in proportion to his disregard of matrimony.[19]

The quest for revamped marital norms and shifts in parenting advice held broad implications for the household. Earlier emphases on male patriarchy and the nurturing republican motherhood of the female spouse gave way to calls to make "fireside education" (as one advice manual dubbed it) the responsibility of fathers and mothers alike. Harriet Martineau, who remained single herself, nonetheless applied such perspectives to British society in her own 1849 domestic guide, which prescribed that "all members of a household" engage in the "process of education together."[20] Highly differentiated roles in the family persisted. Sons were told how cheerful submission to the rightful authority of their elders would aid in wielding authority later in life. For "he only is fit to command who has first learned to obey," Alcott informed young men. Girls received no such instructions. But even though "woman" would not be called upon to "preside in halls of justice or command armies," Alcott wrote, "it is required of her, no less than of the other sex, to do what is more difficult—to govern herself." Further, only by becoming self-governing herself could the wife help to nurture her husband and children in their similar journey toward self-government.[21]

White, middle-class female readers who became accustomed to the lessons that democracy depended on the home-based moralizing of mothers, daughters, and sisters found it easy to take a next step and devote themselves to inculcating the right values across members of society beyond their immediate family. Some even found an outlet in political engagement and campaigning, such as Whig women during the 1840 election.[22] More typical was the impulse toward social reform, which tended to make the always-implicit class and racial specificity of much of the domesticity literature manifest. So, for example, author Lydia Sigourney looked to "the zeal of mothers" to aid the "vital interests of our country" at a moment when it was exposed to "the influx of untutored foreigners" whom she considered "unfit" for American institutions. Native-born, self-governing citizens became for her the critical means to "neutralize this mass," to "rule its fermentations," and to "prevent it from becoming a lava stream in the garden of liberty."[23] Sigourney's logic was evident in middle-class women's embrace of temperance and other "benevolent reform" programs. The exercise of female moral authority in the public sphere was predicated on some (white, middle-class, Protestant) women's willingness to regulate others with apparent deficiencies in modes of family socialization. The tangled relationship between reforming middle-class women's moral crusades and their expanding role beyond the American home represented a critical nineteenth-century development.[24]

Reformers' attention to the supposedly insufficient training in self-government that non-native (and non-Protestant) white children received at times overlapped with even sharper racialized anxieties. The commercially successful *Fireside Education* (1838) opened with a startling contrast between the "civilized" members of the governing white middle class and the "savagery" of "red warriors." The difference, author Samuel Griswold Goodrich maintained, lay in the education that only a specific familial environment could provide, an echo of Tocqueville's comments on Native Americans' supposed inability to distinguish between "voluntary obedience and a shameful subjection" in rejecting family life altogether. Black Americans found themselves subjected to similarly disparaging remarks at a time when whiteness was becoming the chief badge of civic inclusion.[25]

Two patterns emerge in assessing how domestic published opinion circulated among Black Americans themselves. To state the obvious, neither exhortations on self-governance nor guides to family life held out much promise for the two and a half million Black Americans living in slavery in 1840. Where one's very ability to form and maintain a family depended on the will of one's enslavers, the "school of domesticity" had little purchase. Marriages were not only legally unsanctioned, but they could also be disrupted by forced separation through sale. Even for those enslaved men and women who managed against staggering obstacles to form partnerships and families, low literacy rates and the policing of print among the enslaved population would have made print-based guides to family life irrelevant. Instead, catechisms intended for slaves' oral instruction were master-centered, including consideration of the fifth Mosaic commandment to "honor thy father and mother." Proslavery evangelists turned this into a platform for seeing God's will behind the obedience owed to the true "masters" of the household: the white men who wielded absolute power over human chattel. The circumstances faced by people reduced to the legal status of property and subjected to routine acts of violent degradation made southern households the very antithesis of evolving free-state norms. As such, they remained the most significant battlefront in the larger "household civil war."[26]

The multiple ways slavery shattered the family and the household became a major theme of the antislavery argument, which Lydia Maria Child highlighted in her *Brief History of the Condition of Women* (1835) and Martineau echoed in *Society in America*. Virginia Cary's *Letters on Female Character* (1828) offered a rare example of southern domestic advice that lingered on the conditions of enslaved families. Her critique of masters in a chapter titled "Domestic Management" was surprisingly sustained even while Cary, herself part of a white slaveholding family, signaled an understanding of enslavers' prerogatives and their chafing at outside interference. After observing the corruptions of white women who inflicted physical punishment on Black dependents, Cary expressed regret at how enslaved young people were not guided more surely to observe "the holy law of obedience to parents." At least some fault was thus attached to the white Americans who disregarded nurturing "relative duties" among Virginia's "wretched people." Ultimately, a deeper and more obvious cause was at work, as Cary acknowledged in commenting on white Virginians' "indifference in maintaining the conjugal union among our servants." Left out of her observation was the ugly business of slave-trading that worked to split an untold number of unions.[27]

African Americans living in the free states created and circulated their own version of domestic literature through the Black periodical press. In doing so, they strove to demonstrate their own "capacity for self-government," both within their own communities and as part of the collective democratic exercise. Important African American newspapers such as *Freedom's Journal* (1827–1829) and the *Colored American* (1837–1842) combined antislavery politics and protest with articles and short stories dedicated to domesticity and self-improvement. "A good wife," a sermon reprinted in 1841 insisted, sat at the "head of a little society" that needed her example of "self-command." A brief admonition had earlier reminded readers that "every member of a family" played a role in increasing or decreasing the "amount of domestic enjoyment" and making the "home sweet and attractive."[28] Domestic ideals were echoed in the network of associational life constructed by Black churches, schools, and abolitionist organizations. When fugitive slave and abolitionist orator Frederick Douglass reproduced the certificate of his marriage to Anna Murray in his *Narrative of the Life of Frederick Douglass* (1845), he attested to the linkages between marriage and membership in a self-governing polity.[29]

WOMEN IN SLAVE-HOLDING COUNTRIES.

FIG. 2.2 This untitled image from the chapter on "Women in Slave-Holding Countries," in Lydia Maria Child's *Brief History of the Condition of Women* (1835) captures some of the ways the institution of slavery assaulted domesticity. The white woman does not fulfil her maternal duties, instead sitting barefoot enjoying a drink while taking a break from the leisurely activity of violin-playing. The enslaved woman is unable to care for her own child, whose outstretched arms she must ignore because she is busy cleaning the white woman's parlor. Meanwhile, outside the window, a white man brutally beats an enslaved woman tied to a post. Though this particular book was not a domestic manual, Child authored two of the earliest and most successful of the genre: *The Frugal Housewife* (1829) and *The American Mother* (1831). Courtesy of Dartmouth College Library.

Beecher's Domesticated Democracy

Catharine Beecher's *Treatise on Domestic Economy* linked democracy and domesticity explicitly in 1841 during a transformational moment in the author's life. Born in 1800, Beecher was the first of minister Lyman Beecher's thirteen children. She was a devoted daughter to her formidable father, whom she later remembered calling her "the *best boy* he had." Had she been a son, her path in life might have been clearer. Even as she worked to establish Hartford's Female Seminary, Beecher was aware of the comparatively easier time her brothers had in developing a coherent sense of self. Prescriptions made and expectations set during boyhoods and girlhoods framed what adult life would mean for the rest of this uniquely accomplished American family. All but one of Rev. Lyman Beecher's eight sons entered the ministry, and Henry Ward Beecher surpassed his father's renown as an evangelical pulpit orator. Catharine's three sisters traveled the accustomed route to respectable marriages and mothered multiple children to adulthood. Harriet Beecher Stowe and Isabella Beecher Hooker balanced their considerable spousal and maternal duties with public careers.[30]

Catharine, the oldest and initially by far the best known of her siblings, followed a different and less conventional path after her fiancé, a young professor at Yale College, died at sea in 1822. Resolving to remain single, she became her generation's pioneering female institution-builder and one of its leading published-opinion makers. She methodically extended her reach, from founding local schools (in Hartford, Connecticut and Cincinnati, Ohio) to becoming a national oracle of domesticated democracy, and masked her fierce tenacity and ambition by wearing her hair in girlish ringlets throughout her whole life.[31] While Beecher's growing certainty about her life's purpose was never an explicit theme of the *Treatise*, her firm sense of what might be accomplished by professing domesticity emerged repeatedly.

In affirming women as essential partners in their country's democratic venture, Beecher extended advice literature and ranged over a staggering array of topics. For her, self-government began with basic self-knowledge and self-care, which led her to include nearly a dozen graphic illustrations in her *Treatise* showing how the body worked. She complemented these anatomical and physiological lessons with an innovative exercise regime she called "Calisthenics" (a linguistic combination of the Greek words for "beauty" and "strength"). Her thorough hints about scheduling, avoidance of stimulation (with the exception of laughter, which she deemed to be healthy), architecture, cooking, and floral design came with flashes of spirit and imagination. In Beecher's hands, the "'science' of Domestic Economy" opened on to thousands of "important concerns," all of which she handled, according to the *United State Magazine and Democratic Review*, with "uncommon commonsense." Hers was a gospel of personal and collective self-regulation. Although she rarely relied on authoritative scriptural injunctions, she made domesticity central to the larger moral project associated with her father Lyman Beecher.[32]

The prominent invocation of Tocqueville in the opening chapter of a book that contained detailed instruction on everything from ventilating bedrooms to repotting houseplants was far from obvious. But with this framing, Beecher prepared the reader for a series of suggestions on how democratic values might

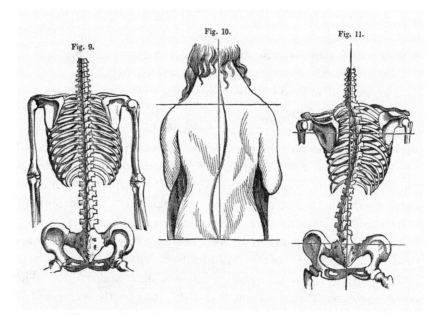

FIG. 2.3 These three images ("Fig. 9, Fig. 10, and Fig. 11") were among the "sumptuous additions and illustrative engravings" that appeared in Beecher's chapter "On the Care of Health." Beecher's emphasis on exercise (and loose clothing) attempted to combat the curvature of the spine that was both "common" and "the cause of so many diseases among American women." To be full partners in the project of American self-government, Beecher insisted, women had first to take care of their own embodied selves. From Catharine Beecher, in *A Treatise of Domestic Economy* (1841). Courtesy of Rauner Library, Dartmouth College.

shape a woman's daily interactions within her household. The hour when one arose from sleep became an aspect of Americans' commitment to equality, with early rising women shunning Europeans' aristocratic indulgence of remaining in bed while laborers toiled at sunrise. Another means for pushing aristocratic values aside came in reflections about how American women should interact with hired housekeepers—or whether they should employ such workers at all (a favored subject for William Alcott as well). Beecher's middle-class bias appeared in her lament about the "pride" and "insubordination" she found all too evident in those employees who displayed "a spirit not conformed to their condition." An equally dismissive account conveyed how relocation to the country's interior (e.g., Ohio and Kentucky) caused women to suffer from the deficiencies of the "ignorant foreigners, or shiftless slaves," whose work did not meet the standards of "better service" back East. Yet Beecher deployed the same softening imagery that prevailed in conduct literature and urged female employers to "exercise a parental care" over those they hired to keep the household running. And she contrasted the "leisure" of aristocratic societies with the dignity of work that structured the days of all members of a middle-class household, not simply the "help."[33]

It became one of Beecher's core convictions, developed over many years as an educator of girls, that women best fulfilled their own democratic mission by nurturing their capacity for individual self-governance while steering clear of direct involvement in the work of collective or political self-government. Like the authors of conduct manuals and self-help guides, she considered women's quintessential calling toward education, broadly understood, as work that would harmonize a household made up of self-governing individuals. The *Treatise*, unlike most of its counterparts, served as a resource for each of the varied stages of the female life cycle.[34] Beecher devoted the first third of the book to care of the physical self—to habits of diet, work, dress, and grooming. The several anatomical diagrams she included furthered her earlier admonition for girls to understand "the structure, the nature, and the laws of the body which you inhabit." Female readers had their own bodies in mind, then, as they read her instructions about freely circulated air, avoidance of overly stimulating food and drink, and exercise. The consistent message remained that such habits would both bring individual happiness and create the capacity to model bodily self-government in husbands, children, and domestic help. As the needs of infants were distinct, a separate chapter of physiologically inspired counsel laid out specific principles, while another addressed rearing older children (including the delicate issue of how to handle the impure thoughts of sons). An exploration of charity and social engagements delved into topics that were rightly women's responsibilities even after children had been sent out into the world.[35]

The framing of the *Treatise* around the country's future political prospects bore the imprint of Beecher's move from New England to Cincinnati the decade before she wrote it. A six-year residency, spurred by her father becoming president of Lane Seminary, enhanced the national perspective that she had already made a minor theme of her Hartford Seminary leadership.[36] Living in this river boom town fueled her mounting anxieties about America's democratic future. Lyman Beecher's initial concern for vindicating Protestant Christianity against aggressive Catholic proselytizing was soon eclipsed by divisions over immediate abolition. After a white mob launched a relentless assault against the city's Black population, his seminary witnessed ongoing debates over slavery in the winter of 1834, promoted, despite Lyman Beecher's objections, by some of his star students, including the future spouses of

Angelina Grimké (Theodore Dwight Weld) and Elizabeth Cady (Henry Stanton).

Catharine's participation in these debates took the form of a polemical exchange with Sarah Grimké, including her *An Essay on Slavery and Abolitionism: With Reference to the Duty of American Females* (1837). One of the most striking themes of Beecher's pamphlet was the damage inflicted on American life by the passions of hyper-politicized men. Using imagery that would have clashed with the uplift of the *Treatise*, she fretted how the "storms of democratic liberty" threatened destruction. She blamed the "spirit of the age," exacerbated by the "tendency of our peculiar form of government" to follow fickle public sentiment and a simple majority of votes. In this view, instability was the key obstacle to national success. Men in America's democratic political culture, whether native born or newcomers, introduced volatility with their "sensitive and pertinacious inflexibility" and their adherence to a "party spirit that rules by an iron rod and shakes its scorpion whip."[37]

The democratic anxiety found in Beecher's 1837 diagnosis of men's dangerous egotism and lack of restraint informed two related aspects of the *Treatise*, each establishing how the book's opening embrace of popular government was more conditional than absolute. First, as she completed the book upon her return to the East, Beecher proclaimed that "women have an equal interest in all social and civil concerns." She boasted that the "tendencies of democratic institutions" concerning "the rights and interests of the female sex" had been "fully developed in the United States." Second, and in a curious reliance on the passive voice, Beecher explained that to secure women's place in these democratic privileges, "it is decided" that they take a subordinate station in marriage and that they entrust their interests in political and civil concerns "to the other sex," without taking any part in "voting, or in making and administering laws." On the question of American marriage, Beecher and Tocqueville were of one mind, and it was on this subject in particular that she so extensively leaned on the Frenchman's words.[38]

Like Tocqueville, Beecher worked to reconcile the seeming contradiction between an adamant statement about equality and an affirmation of existing exclusions. If not exactly reconciled, this contradiction might at least be explained by her polarized views about democracy's prospects. Beecher observed that if the "mass of the people" were "intelligent and virtuous" then their innovative form of government would prove a success. Conversely, an "ignorant and unprincipled democracy" would be "more dreadful than any form of civil governance," since "a thousand tyrants are more to be dreaded than one." The key actors in determining which of these futures would materialize were the "army of teachers" that only women could supply, and female relatives. That mother who "writes the character of the future man," that sister who "bends the fibres that hereafter are the forest tree," and that wife who "sways the heart, whose energies may turn for good or for evil the destinies of a nation," were each vital to the shared American enterprise. Having turned to this sweeping manifestation of female influence, Beecher then summed up her key point: "Let the women of a country be made virtuous and intelligent, and the men will certainly be the same."[39]

Neither her anxiety about democratic politics nor her view of women as a restraining presence were unique to Beecher. Congregational minister Horace Bushnell, a Hartford neighbor, expressed a similar view of the passions and turbulence unleashed by democracy in a sermon on "American Politics," published shortly after the election of 1840. Bushnell voiced concern not just about the selfishness of politics but about the part women played "in these political strifes." He detected a "revolution" brewing in the "manners of the female sex," which when combined with the efforts of some men to "unite the ladies in their political demonstrations" created a potentially destabilizing world. If women no longer graced "the fireside by their retiring softness" and whispered calming words in the ears of their excitable husbands, what would be left outside the corrupting amorality of democratic politics? "Do save us," he implored, "one half of society free of the broils and bruises and arts of demagogy!"[40]

Beecher's faith in the power of female nurture to counterbalance the male "agitation" over slavery led her to avoid escalating disputes between advocates of colonization (initially a position embraced by most of her family) and abolitionists (whose ranks gradually drew more and more of the Beecher siblings). She persisted in her 1837 stance that Black people were Christian brethren to be pitied for wearing, in their dark complexions, the "badge of degradation of station." But she would leave it to her younger sister to draw out the logic of how female virtue might explore Black suffering more thoroughly, in a work that helped to shift perceptions across the North. Unlike with Beaumont's *Marie*, an agitated readership for Stowe's *Uncle Tom's Cabin* (1852) was primed by the Fugitive Slave Act (1850) to hear its message. That context made it perhaps the most consequential work of fiction in all of American history. Catharine played a role in the making of the novel. In the first place, it was to Catharine that Harriet Beecher Stowe first wrote about housing a "charismatic" fugitive named John Andrew Jackson, whose 1850 escape provided Harriet a compelling firsthand account of the slavery's brutality. More in keeping with Catharine's domestic mission was the fact that she helped make her sister's literary labors possible by moving in with her as she wrote, minding the many Stowe children, and keeping the household running.[41]

Radical Critiques of the Family

Domesticity prevailed across published opinion, but its vision of the American family did not go uncontested. These decades of economic dislocation and experimental reform also witnessed new efforts to reassess this most fundamental of social institutions. Communitarian utopias figured as yet another theater in the roiling "household civil war" of the era. Their appearance coincided with the rise of Mormonism, the Shakers, and the Oneida community, three other responses to this culture's recasting of household dependent relationships and gradual elevation of individuals via incremental legal reforms. The most prominent of the communitarian efforts were based on the principles of French philosopher Charles Fourier, whose ideas found a receptive American audience in Albert Brisbane. Fourier's "utopian socialism" criticized present-day civilization for wasting effort in competition and repressing men and women's natural passions. Instead, he imagined society reorganized into cooperative, associational communities, called "phalanxes," where men and women would together engage in productive work. As Brisbane and his allies promoted their Americanized version of Fourierism, they promised "a perfect system of Democracy"—one that would "extend Liberty and Equality, now restricted to the narrow field of Politics, to every department of Society and human life, and render them Social and Universal."[42]

Fourierite and similar programs would receive a major boost from a crucial ally, the entrepreneurial newspaperman Horace Greeley. Having established the *New York Tribune* in the spring of 1841, the savvy Greeley within months added an oversized weekly version. For just two dollars a year, subscribers in towns, farms, and villages across the free states could receive by mail the metropolitan and Whig-friendly perspectives of a paper "calculated to promote Morality, maintain Social Order, extend the blessings of Education, or in any way subserve the great cause of Human Progress to ultimate Virtue, Liberty, and Happiness." Across the 1840s and 1850s Greeley turned the *Tribune* into one of the most influential reformist organs in America. Soon he would add a European edition, giving his paper a global reach. Through the *Tribune's* pages, readers encountered a wide range of voices and a bracingly cosmopolitan set of conversations about the democratic possibilities of the moment.

In a regular column—one widely reprinted in other newspapers—Brisbane informed readers of the possibilities of thoroughgoing reform.[43]

Economic and political discontent drove the enthusiasm for what came to be called "Associationism." The ongoing depression that followed the Panic of 1837 made many Associationists receptive to its vision of cooperative and harmonious living. For others, such as radical journalist Parke Godwin, the dire economic situation also revealed the failings of both democratic politics and the Democratic party, with which he broke over its insistence on laissez-faire policies. The version of popular government being "spouted in ward meetings" and "slavered through the columns of newspapers," he wrote in his 1844 pamphlet *Democracy: Constructive and Pacific*, needed to be transformed into the "God-ordained principle of social government" that could only be achieved via cooperative, harmonious cohabitation. Godwin thought both parties had badly misdirected their energies into superficial and carnivalesque partisan antics. The Whigs' "Log Cabin Campaign" for "Tippecanoe" William Henry Harrison epitomized the superficiality of an electoral system geared to entertainment and mobilization rather than elevation and the amelioration of suffering.[44]

Efforts to replace outdated—and ostensibly failing—social formations accelerated in the early 1840s. Among the most famous of these were the Massachusetts-based Brook Farm (founded by Transcendentalist George Ripley and his wife Sophia in 1841); the New Jersey-based "North American Phalanx" (established by Brisbane and others in 1843); and the Northampton Association of Education and Industry (1842), whose explicit abolitionist and interracial commitment attracted Black activists including Sojourner Truth and David Ruggles. The following year, Amos Bronson Alcott (cousin of William Alcott) began a smaller and even more short-lived experiment in communal living at Fruitlands (1843). In keeping with the notion of an overlapping "sisterhood of reforms," utopian socialists often combined their unconventional mode of living with such other efforts to remake the self, including abolition, diet reform, temperance, and education, as well as experimental alternatives to the nuclear family.[45]

Thus, investigation into gender norms generally accompanied utopian socialist efforts, as it did in the overt patriarchy of Mormonism or in the complicated regimen of (male) sexuality at John Humphrey Noyes's Oneida community. Brisbane and his fellow Associationists revisited the family as a key hindrance to progress, presenting it not as the ballast of self-government but as the epitome of modern selfishness and egotism. Such explorations followed Tocqueville, Martineau, and Beecher in questioning whether and how democracy related to household norms. But the way Associationists imagined the emancipation of women from "traditional" roles offered a near inversion of the cult of domesticity. By implementing democratic principles within their own perfectionist communities rather than at the ballot box, American Associationists promised to release women from the drudgery of daily labors. "WOMAN HAS NOT BEEN FREE," George Ripley exclaimed in the pages of *The Harbinger* (the organ of Brook Farm), but forced into an economic dependence upon men. Fourierites vowed to liberate women along with men by eradicating separate and isolated family units and cooperatively redistributing daily household labor and childcare. This formula promised the same efficiencies in "private life" that cooperative production would yield as an alternative to the wasteful competitiveness of market capitalism.[46]

Central to this innovation was an awareness that women performed the monotonous, boring, and "fatiguing beyond all conception" labor that kept families functioning. To those who explained that women's character had larger reserves of patience and selflessness that suited them to such toil, Brisbane thundered: "It is not so." Women's "destiny" in his conception involved something higher than wasting "her life in a kitchen" and in the petty and routine cares of a household. "Nature made her the equal of man," he proclaimed, declaring her to be capable of industry and of cultivating the arts and sciences no less than the items of "domestic economy" discussed in Beecher's *Treatise*. Women's destiny was "not to be [man's] inferior, to cook and sew for him, and live dependently at his board" but to achieve genuine equality and a fully flourishing individuality.

But experimenting with heterodox gender and sexual norms could run afoul of published opinion. Critics soon found in the Fourierist writings plenty of ammunition to attack the program and to slander Greeley's reputation as a reformer. In the winter of 1846–1847, a nasty public dispute with Henry J. Raymond, a former employee of the *Tribune*, peaked with accusations that Greeley's paper sought to destroy the Christian family. Raymond sketched the dystopian results of a scheme that would alienate parents from children and upend the position of "wife," if that term would even "be then retained." A woman shorn of matrimonial and maternal duties, Raymond feared, "will keep her own time, retain her liberty of heart and action, and be in short entirely independent of her husband in all respects." This would reduce the institution of marriage, so central to God's design, to a mere "co-partnership." In his coded language about the loosening of "passions" and the removal of "restraints" on men, Raymond also hinted at his awareness that Fourierism did not accept the permanence of existing sexual mores. Part of

Fourier's social regeneration involved a "new amorous world" created by the unfettering of sexual attraction.[47]

Salacious details quickly emerged after the *Tribune* contributor Henry James Sr. translated and introduced *Love in the Phalanstery* (1849) by Fourierist acolyte Victor Henniquin. Controversy ensued across the press, demonstrating how charges of supposedly libertine sexuality posed the same challenge to reformers in the 1840s as they had earlier for Wollstonecraft and Fanny Wright. A spate of nineteenth-century sexual reforms lent new relevance to the polemical assaults. These efforts varied a good deal, including Mary Gove's "reform physiology," which dared teach women about sexual matters; attempts to institute truly voluntary (and therefore dissolvable) unions; and direct assaults on monogamy. Controversy and scandalous insinuation did not bother with distinctions, collapsing all these reforms in a vague but effective charge of "free love." This slur was attached to any arrangement that seemed to challenge the boundaries of male-female interaction.[48] Stung by the uproar, James and Greeley alike modulated their positions. The newspaper editor became scrupulous in clarifying that he did not approve of the most sweeping forms of familial or household reform. Such aversion to controversy would make Greeley an unreliable partner for women's rights advocates over the quarter-century that followed, a fact that would become especially apparent when the *Tribune* opposed women's voting rights during Reconstruction. The influential paper would, however, continue to cover important developments in the emergence of America's organized women's movement and serve as a conduit for international discussion of it.

Greeley also played a role in the publication of one of the most provocative and original works on the "woman question"—one of only a handful of crucial book-length texts to appear between Mary Wollstonecraft's *Vindication of the Rights of Woman* (1792) and Simone de Beauvoir's *The Second Sex* (1949).[49] In drawing Margaret Fuller away from New England to the bustling and cosmopolitan New York scene, Greeley helped provide the independence and horizon-expanding perspective crucial to her development as the author of *Woman in the Nineteenth Century* (1845), a book he published. Greeley had been intrigued by her essays for the Transcendentalist organ *The Dial*, as well as by her many translations and frequent interactions with utopian socialists. So, partly at the suggestion of his wife Mary Greeley, the newspaperman convinced Fuller to join the otherwise all-male *Tribune* staff as literary critic. Both the newspaper and the city proved hospitable new homes for her intellect.[50]

Margaret Fuller.

FIG. 2.4 W. J. Linton, "Margaret Fuller." Horace Greeley included
this portrait of Fuller, the only image of someone besides himself,
in his 1868 autobiography. Perhaps seeking to remind readers of his
early women's rights credentials, at a very different stage in the movement, he devoted a whole chapter to Fuller. He called *Woman in
the Nineteenth Century* the "loftiest and most commanding" (if not
necessarily "the clearest and most logical") assertion of the "right of
Woman to be regarded and treated as an independent, intelligent, rational being, entitled to an equal voice in framing and modifying the
laws she is required to obey." From Greeley, *Recollections of a Busy Life*
(1868). Courtesy of Dartmouth College Library.

Woman in the Nineteenth Century is a challenging text, steeped in myth-
ology and Romantic philosophy and written in an allusive style. The range
and richness of the book surely accounts for its resonance with so many different readers, including those interested in the possibilities and limits of self-
government for women. In both her initial *Dial* essay—"The Great Lawsuit.
Man *versus* Men. Woman *versus* Women" (1843)—and the expanded book,
Fuller deplored the whole domestic advice industrial complex that formed
conventional opinion. She complained of endless lectures on "some model-
woman" and "little treatises" that sought "to mark out with due precision the

limits of woman's sphere." Fuller had minimal patience with any notion of sex-based spheres. Believing men and women shared masculine and feminine traits, she insisted it must be left to individuals to chart their own paths. She thus urged "every arbitrary barrier thrown down" and "every path laid open to woman as freely as to man." In this context came the pithy and memorable expression about what employments and activities women might pursue. "Any!" she insisted. "Let them be sea-captains, if you will."[51]

The elliptical title of the *Dial* article ("Man *versus* Men. Woman *versus* Women") had implied that the "woman question" formed one part of a larger human question, that of achieving individuality in opposition to conventional roles. Womanhood and Manhood had never yet been realized, she wrote, predicting a "new manifestation is at hand, a new hour in the day of man."[52] In ways that Catharine Beecher had resisted, Fuller channeled her own life experiences in framing what inequality meant at the individual level. There were intriguing parallels in the backgrounds of the two women. Both were accomplished daughters of demanding fathers who encouraged their intellectuality. Both had been entrusted, as the oldest sibling, with the care and formal schooling of younger sisters and brothers. Both lived a single life (Fuller's marriage having come just on the eve of her death). Fuller added German Romanticism and New England Transcendentalism to her native skill, ambition, and familiarity with unmarried women's various roles and forged a striking vision of female autonomy. While Beecher founded schools, Fuller created new opportunities for women in intellectual terms through a series of exhilarating Boston-based Conversations. Over the course of several years, she fostered an extraordinary group of women including Sophia Ripley, Lydia Maria Child, Elizabeth Cady Stanton, Caroline Healey Dall, Julia Ward Howe, and Ednah Dow Cheney. It was through the Conversations that Fuller had first come to know Mary Greeley.

As she expanded "The Great Lawsuit" into a book three times its length, she wrestled (as had Harriet Martineau) with the gap between American ideals and American realities. Fuller was no naive believer in America. To the contrary, she thought the country had done all it could to undermine its promise and hinder its achievement. Here Fuller mentioned the treatment of both African Americans and Native Americans, a topic she had handled unsparingly in *Summer on the Lakes* (1843). Dispossession, slavery, racial discrimination: these "deeds are the scoff of the world," Fuller acknowledged. And yet she still found liberatory potential in the United States and in its indispensable idea that "all men are born free and equal"—a statement of "golden certainty" intended "to encourage the good, to shame the bad." Surveying the hypocrisy all around her, she could not help but believe that so much talk of freedom and equality "must be mingled with some desire for" the things themselves. Though she had remained aloof from the Garrisonian abolitionists for years, by 1845 she saw that it was these "champions of the enslaved African" who led the way forward. They recognized that the struggles against slavery and for women's emancipation followed from the same principles; both insisted on the right of all individuals to self-governing autonomy.[53]

Fuller recognized that some institutional and legal change would be necessary to enable women to achieve meaningful autonomy, but, unsurprisingly as a Transcendentalist, her focus remained always on the internal obstacles. So, while overhauling the disabilities associated with coverture, especially property rights and custody of children, was important, changing the mindset of men and women alike was crucial. What woman, no less than man, needed, Fuller wrote, was "as a nature to grow, as an intellect to discern, as a soul to live freely and unimpeded, to unfold such powers as were given her." But such unfolding was impossible amidst existing domestic practices. Women were at once infantilized (as evident in the phrase that lumped together "women and children") and rendered subject-less or self-less by being told repeatedly that they were "made *for man*."

Fuller looked forward to a new era in human relations that would allow both men and women to achieve equality and a fully flourishing individuality. Marriage, family, and the household would have to be reimagined, for a household could be "no home unless it contain food and fire for the mind as well as for the body." Too many wives languished in non-nurturing conventional marriages, which bore all the ill effects of women's subordinate and dependent position in society. This was surely bad for women. But Fuller urged that women's "excessive devotion" to man harmed both sexes—at least spiritually—as it "degraded" marriage and "prevented either sex from being what it should be to itself or for the other." In short, marriage was a flawed institution because it made the woman "belong to the man, instead of forming a whole with him." What was needed then was what Fuller labeled "self-subsistence" and "self-dependence." These were not masculine but human traits. Fuller also carved out a social and cultural space for "bachelors" and "old maids," whose decision not to marry, she insisted, represented a wholly suitable life path.[54]

For the next five years, living among New York journalists and then European revolutionaries, Fuller discovered a novel enthusiasm for the possibilities of democratic change. Her increased discussion of political issues aligned with the cluster of intellectuals around Greeley's *Tribune*, a group whose seriousness set their work apart from what fellow Transcendentalist Ralph Waldo Emerson belittled as the "foaming foolishness of newspapers." Her book reviews mixed the erudition of her *Dial* writings with a self-conscious adoption of the *Tribune's* signature pose of reformist critique and forecast of new worlds soon to be born. Commentary about slavery and racism dotted her contributions, notably in an important review of Frederick Douglass's *Narrative* and an allegorical dialogue "What Fits a Man to Be a Voter," written as Black men struggled—unsuccessfully—for equal suffrage during the 1846 New York State Constitutional Convention. Fuller discussed poverty and prison reform in these years and condemned the US war against Mexico. An especially memorable New Year's Day column for 1846 had her looking around the world and noting that "it looks as if a great time was coming, and that time one of Democracy. Our country will play a ruling part." How the United States waged the iniquitous war in Mexico would reveal whether the American eagle would "soar upward to the sun" or "stoop for helpless prey" like a marauding vulture. Fuller dared to hope for an American Phoenix to herald a rebirth, but she acknowledged this bird had "first to be purified by fire."[55]

Fuller's earlier ambivalence about American democracy was even more strongly revised as she witnessed the European political upheavals of the late 1840s. Her stubborn faith in a more equal and free future seemed to be shared by figures such as Italian revolutionary Giuseppe Mazzini, whom she met in London early in a three-year European sojourn. Dispatched as a foreign correspondent for the *Tribune,* she witnessed firsthand the revolutionary struggle in France that led to the establishment of the Second Republic and universal (manhood) suffrage. When Fuller set sail to return from Italy to America in the spring of 1850, she was primed to shape discussion for an American public accustomed to her overseas reporting for the *Tribune.* Having just turned forty, Fuller seemed uniquely well-placed to pair her gusto for the global march of popular government with reflections on the widening possibilities for American women, an issue notably underdeveloped in her writing for the *Tribune.* The wreck of her ship off Fire Island, New York took her life and that of her new husband and infant son. How family life might have shaped Fuller's discussion of the woman question had she returned is uncertain.

More apparent is that by 1850 *Tribune* readers were alive to a subject that organized women's rights activists had just begun elevating to prominence. Travel writers had subjected American democracy to thorough scrutiny, raising questions about the place of women within it. Domestic writers worked to provide answers to these questions. By insisting on the need for all members of the household to become self-governing and to foster the self-governing capacities of each other, they helped build a consensus around ending the legal obliteration of wives' personhood via coverture. That consensus yielded legislative results, as states across the country began passing married women's property laws.[56] But these domestic writers drew a bright line between the process of individual self-governance and participation in collective self-government. Beecher followed Tocqueville in claiming that American wives enjoyed greater equality in marriage than anywhere else. If they benefited from democratic norms, they in turn were responsible for ensuring that popular government succeeded by modeling self-governance while also restraining the overly zealous passions of their husbands. Fuller's volume, which one newspaper recognized was the first book to argue for "'Woman's Rights' since the days of Mary Wollstonecraft," doubted any women could be fully self-governing under existing familial practices.[57]

Wanting to stay abreast of reform and deprived of Fuller's pen, Horace Greeley solicited New York writer Elizabeth Oakes Smith to reflect on "Woman and Her Needs" late in 1850. For Smith, this newly urgent issue, which included pleas to enfranchise women, emerged seamlessly from the national founders who had dared to articulate the "inalienable rights of life, liberty, and the pursuit of happiness." These men "might have foreseen that at some day their daughters would sift thoroughly their opinions" and apply the lessons to their own claims.[58] The call, by American women, for a consistent application of these high-minded democratic principles was at hand.

3

To Make Democracy Consistent

BY THE 1850S, a movement for women's rights had emerged as an international sensation. Out of the fierce struggle against slavery and racial caste, a group of women and men organized and worked to make women full partners in American democracy. This new effort sought to topple what John Stuart Mill had called in 1835 America's "aristocracy of sex." The rhetoric of this first national women's rights movement alternated between the grand scope of human history and the particularities of America's distinctive creed. Each framework was effective in its own way. Sex inequality was without question the "hoary-headed error of all times," as *New York Tribune* contributor Elizabeth Oakes Smith put it, one that had been "intermingled in every aspect of civilization." To dismantle hierarchies with such deep roots had world-historical implications. But it was no less true that what Harriet Martineau had termed the "political non-existence of women" also violated the self-evident truths of America's founding. Barring women from political participation was out of sync with rights-derived political truths that demanded governments base their "just powers" on the all-important consent of the governed.[1]

An organized movement for women's rights is often dated to 1848, a pivotal year that saw revolutionary change spread across the world and roil the United States. An exemplary founding text, written by Elizabeth Cady Stanton, was among that year's most lasting achievements. Similar to French writer and political activist Olympe de Gouges's 1791 reworking of the Declaration of the Rights of Man, the Declaration of Sentiments deployed revolutionary language to create a document that was, in the words of historian Lori Ginzberg, simultaneously "familiar and breathtaking, mainstream and radical."[2] Calls for women's political inclusion preceded this moment: what set the Seneca Falls convention apart was less its message than its means. The one hundred

people who signed the convention's resolutions vowed to use "every instrumentality within our power" in a coordinated effort to "employ agents, circulate tracts, petition the State and national Legislatures, and endeavor to enlist
the pulpit and the press in our behalf." Published opinion would be as important for future activism as appeals to the halls of government. The first two
national conventions—both held in Worcester, Massachusetts—reveal the ef-
fectiveness of a strategy that could draw attention beyond the United States.

Seneca Falls is often understood as the first step toward a long-awaited
women's suffrage amendment that would only be achieved many decades
later, in 1920. Shorter-term consequences of the 1850s conventions have
generated less scholarly discussion than might be expected. Scores of women
as well as men entered the public arena in the 1850s, through speeches and
sermons and in convention halls and lecture platforms. They met in regional
and national conventions nearly every year between 1848 and the outbreak of
the Civil War and established the first "woman's rights" periodicals. The reach
of their ideas extended well beyond their own meetings. Women in general
were newly visible—as bestselling authors, as lecturers and performers, and
in political circles—and women's rights garnered the attention, even when
hostile, of the wider culture. Through such efforts, the theme of female self-
government already circulating in domestic literature acquired a radical and
politicized tinge.

By the late 1850s, activists had arrived at a formulation stunning in its
economy: that the United States could never be a "consistent democracy"
without women's full inclusion in the polity. *Consistent Democracy: The
Elective Franchise for Women. Twenty-Five Testimonies of Prominent Men*
(1858) gathered quotations from a series of writers, ministers, educators,
politicians, activists, and jurists. The fact that all these testimonies came
from white men is both ironic and a reflection of a key dynamic at work in
producing and circulating such a document. Frederick Douglass, one of the
most prominent male activists not included, understood what was involved.
There was a good deal women could do—and must do—to advance their
own interests, Douglass explained, but "not so in the matter of voting." That
work required the effort of actual voters who must "like true men and true
[d]emocrats, batter down the thick walls erected against woman at the ballot
box." Excluded from political power, women had no choice but to depend on
the enfranchised to change the rules. But they (along with their male allies)
could at least ensure that the question of women's political participation
became inescapable in published opinion by the time the country faced its
greatest crisis of all.[3]

That Women's Rights Were Human Rights;
and ... That Women Were Persons

A survey of published opinion reveals how attention to women's political enfranchisement intensified across the 1840s. Though the woman question began to be discussed anew in the late 1830s, Harriet Martineau's analysis of the "political non-existence of women" in the United States provided a rare commentary on voting rights specifically. The Garrisonians had thoroughly debated women's rights and responsibilities, but in their rejection of electoral politics, their insistence on women's balloting did not apply outside antislavery organizations. Margaret Fuller's focus on inner freedom led her to largely ignore women's potential political engagement. But an explicit call for women's enfranchisement emerged from several quarters across the 1840s, as various thinkers, activists, and ordinary Americans considered how female voting might make the practice of American democracy more consistent with its theory.

One of the most spectacular of these calls came from writer John Neal, who brought a provocateur's pizzazz to the topic. Though not a well-known figure today, the native Mainer generated considerable attention with his speeches and essays urging women's equal rights, including the right to vote. Perhaps it was his legal training that allowed Neal to cut through what he dismissed in 1824 as the "blarney" and "sentimentality" that muddled discussions about women's restricted sphere. He published essays on the subject while living in London and interacting with Jeremy Bentham and his young teenaged protégé John Stuart Mill (Neal later claimed to have influenced both men on women's rights). He brought these decades of prior theorizing to the New York stage in a blockbuster 1843 lecture on "the Rights of Women." The venue and billing ensured high visibility for the event, and prior publicity drew over two thousand into Manhattan's cavernous Broadway Tabernacle.[4] The evening was such a sensation (as remembered by observers even years later) that it led to a follow-up event in the same auditorium, this time a public debate between Neal and two other male writers on the question "Do Women Enjoy All the Political Rights to Which They Are Entitled?" The extensive press coverage these events aroused, stretching from Maryland to Missouri, generally mocked Neal's answer in the negative. One reviewer captured the prevailing tone of press coverage by grumbling that Neal's "absurd stuff" about women and politics amounted to little more than "prattle" by a fool who should be reduced to wearing a child's "pantalets and flannels for the remainder of his existence."[5]

Neal's lecture, which he reprinted in the popular weekly *Brother Jonathan*, focused on the inconsistency between America's political ideals and its treatment of women. He refuted the claim of Tocqueville and Beecher that American women enjoyed greater equality than women elsewhere, maintaining instead that a greater gap existed between "the rights of the Men, and the rights of the Women" in America than "among any other people upon the face of the earth." He nonetheless relied on a variant of American exceptionalism, as he placed gender norms in the United States alongside various "barbarian" and "savage" cultures to whom Americans fancied themselves superior. Only in democratic America with its claims to "universal" suffrage, he asserted, did the exclusion of women provide such a clear contrast. Here women were reduced to "nobodies": no "vote can she give, no office can she hold." Barred from all "powers of self-government" regardless of status, marriage imposed the "additional disqualifications" of coverture.[6] Neal reiterated these claims as he sparred with Park Benjamin on the debate stage, and conducted a lengthy debate in the pages of the *Brother Jonathan* with a twenty-seven-year-old woman, Eliza W. Farnham, a reformer soon to be appointed a warden of the women's prison at Sing Sing.

Across several months and some 30,000 words, Neal and Farnham discussed everything from the application of American democratic principles to women to the significance of biology, social class, economic opportunity, and marital relations. While Neal maintained that participation in the polity was essential, a marker of full selfhood and citizenship alike, Farnham dissented both from the political argument and the broader case for women's equality. She stressed instead women's spiritual superiority and claimed that women's freedom centered on their domestic and social roles, which were founded in nature. A woman's true "declaration of Right is, 'I am a wife and mother, To be these is my freedom,'" she wrote, "'to be other would be slavery.'" But Neal insisted that self-government was a human, not male, imperative. If "free men must be allowed to govern themselves," he asked, then "why not Women?"[7]

The law was another important venue for thinking through the inconsistencies of American democracy. This was unsurprising given how prominently early critiques (including Martineau's) presented the common-law disabilities of wives as contrary to Americans' commitment to self-government. Two judges—Timothy Walker of Ohio and Elisha P. Hurlbut of New York—directly addressed the political dimension of common-law disparities as each systematized American law. Their treatises moved from an initial critique of the American wife's lack of legal personhood to an indictment of barring women, regardless of marital status, from the franchise. Observing that the common law of "the husband and wife" is a "disgrace to any civilized nation," Walker argued that women's exclusion from voting, if applied to men, would represent "the exact definition of political slavery." That assertion came in his *Introduction to American Law* (1837), his intended replacement of Blackstone in US legal instruction. Hurlbut's commentary, by contrast, was part of a sweeping contribution to a new theory of human rights in a treatise that would become a key reference point for later women's rights activists. *Essays on Human Rights* (1845) bore less resemblance to Walker's work than to the efforts of Montesquieu, Condorcet, Jeremy Bentham, and James Mill in attempting to lay out internally consistent schemes of governance that acknowledged and tried to rectify apparent discrepancies or anomalies.[8]

The two jurists, significantly, arrived at this similar conclusion even though they differed profoundly in their political sensibilities. Hurlbut eagerly embraced his radical status and displayed a penchant for "advanced" thinking in his early and zealous advocacy of the "new science" of phrenology. The establishment-minded Walker was more circumspect. Over time, as a women's rights movement began to gather momentum, Walker's moderation led him to repudiate the most radical implications of his critique. For example, while in 1849 he repeated his belief that making sex the basis of a citizen's exclusion from politics was an anomaly, he conceded that it might be better for all involved to keep women removed from the raucous electoral process. His anxiety about "the noise, the glare, the turmoil, [and] the corruption" of American elections only deepened in the face of recurrent election-day riots across the following decade. By 1850, he had begun to draw a careful distinction between justice and expediency. Before a Harvard audience, he echoed Horace Bushnell on the "broils and bruises" of politics as he worried that "rude encounters of the bar-room, the hustings, the stump, the caucus, or even the senate" would cause females to suffer the indignity of being "unsexed" if they ever were to join the American political nation. The political nonexistence of women might be inconsistent, he concluded, but it might be advisable nonetheless.[9]

Religion, no less than the law, represented a critical site for questioning women's subordinate status in America, a project begun in earnest with Judith Sargent Murray in the 1790s and continued by the Grimké sisters in the 1830s. Unitarian minister Samuel J. May, a close associate of William Lloyd Garrison, extended this theological project in his 1845 sermon *The Rights and Condition of Women*, which took Galatians 3:28 for its text: "There

FIG. 3.1 David Claypoole Johnston, detail from "Women's Rights." This 1849 image, one vignette in a series of illustrations for *Scraps*, imagines the coarsening influence that political participation might have on women, along the lines that Timothy Walker and Horace Bushnell feared. Women punch other women, engage in glaring stand-offs, and harangue passing men to support their cause. Violence at polling places and election-day riots in the 1850s exacerbated longstanding anxieties that these spaces were unsuitable for women and would "unsex" them. Courtesy of American Antiquarian Society.

is neither male nor female, for ye are all one in Christ." Insisting that the fate of women's rights and democracy were linked, May denounced "the utter annihilation, politically considered, of more than one-half of the whole community."[10] How could a democracy sustain such an annihilation? He surveyed the significant matters confronting his Syracuse parishioners in the current election, including the new constitution for the state of New York, a measure to ban intoxicating liquors, and the outbreak of hostilities with Mexico. These were all topics of concern to women and their perspectives were as important as those of their male fellow citizens. To bar them from political participation was both an injustice to women and a loss to the polity. The sermon made May the first minister in the United States to call for the enfranchisement of women. Through a curious fluke of transatlantic print networks, May's words circulated overseas and caught the attention of British abolitionist Anne Knight, who soon began sending a leaflet quoting the minister (without attribution) to women in her reform circle.[11]

A lengthier contribution came from the pen of Elizabeth Wilson, a theologically rigorous Presbyterian living in Cadiz, Ohio. In 1843, she had been refused access to the pages of the Philadelphia-based *Evangelical Repository*, which had featured an anonymous writer who argued that "the devil" was the force driving the "disorganizing, revolutionary tendencies" of women's rights. Her rebuttal began a multiyear process of research and writing that would combine her existing mastery of scripture with material culled from the Grimké sisters, Lucretia Mott, Lydia Maria Child, Harriet Martineau, and Elisha Hurlbut. Cumulatively, these secular voices imbued her work—*A Scriptural View of Woman's Rights and Duties* (1849)—with a critical language of democracy and "human rights." As she worked on this synthesis, Wilson came to appreciate the significance of what became a 376-page tour de force. Once her book found a publisher, she offered a forthright assessment of the "chaotic state" of women's rights theory, claiming that it was a shame that such a vital topic had "not been systematized by any person." She presented her own volume as "the first that ever has attempted to give a scriptural view of woman's rights and duties." This formulation might have been too modest. Her division of this mammoth work into sections devoted to the position of women in the family, church, and state had no real equivalent across the range of nineteenth-century writing, scriptural or otherwise.[12]

The tone of Wilson's work alternated between the defensive and the assertive. She expressed trepidation that her book would be taken up "for the purpose of sneering at the contemptible 'Woman's Rights Question.'" But she resolved that since "women's rights were human rights," the whole question was essential to the well-being of the human family. Wilson's interpretation primarily concerned Christian revelation, but she rooted her analysis in the context of American democracy. Like Catharine Beecher before her, Wilson saw an affinity between (Protestant) Christianity and democracy. "A scriptural form of government *is* democratic, a government from the people," she contended, "and we are so ultra as to believe that *women are people*!" She thus urged that the words "'white male' be stricken out" of state constitutions as a qualification for the right of suffrage and "*person* substituted in its place." Her argument gathered force through the rhetorical contrast she continually drew between American democratic ideals and their less-than-democratic realities, which she labeled "tyrannical," "despotic," and "aristocratic." She understood the "aristocracy of sex" as only the most pervasive—because it existed in every household—of a whole series of undemocratic American transgressions that included slavery and Indian removal. Anchoring her insight that America was a "great hereditary aristocracy" was her novel conception of what she termed "husbandly authority," which she rooted in Blackstone's coverture and in the eighteenth-century work of British clergyman William Paley—two products of monarchical patriarchy that inexplicably continued to hold enormous influence within supposedly democratic American culture.[13]

The privileges and authority vested in every husband had become so pervasive in American culture, Wilson lamented, that women were subsumed in its logic even if they had not taken marriage vows. The "spurious authority" of all men over all women was akin to the degrading despotisms of "popery" and chattel slavery. Under such conditions, Christian women were denied the chance to seek "inspiration" and "active agency" as the Bible demanded. Wilson built an alternative case from the words of the prophet Isaiah: "And kings shall be thy nursing fathers, and their queens thy nursing mothers." In her exegesis of this passage, she discerned a divine decree to distribute rights, duties, and the power to rule to male and female believers in equal measures. She "earnestly importun[ed]" all women to investigate and discuss this most pressing question, even in the face of "sneers, and sarcasm, and menaces of men." There was "no excuse for woman's not understanding her rights in this enlightened age." The book concluded on a note of optimism. In the six years she had labored on it, much had changed. A "star had recently appeared in the east," she wrote, which promised to usher in a "better day." What Wilson had in mind was a convention in Seneca Falls, New York. In the summer of 1848, some three hundred men and women met in the Wesleyan Chapel there to discuss the "social, civil, and religious condition and rights of woman" and to launch a movement.[14]

The First Collective Protest against the Aristocracy of Sex

Seneca Falls was a fairly modest affair—hastily planned and attended by men and women mostly living in upstate New York—but it was crucial in self-consciously calling a sustained campaign into being. The "Declaration of Sentiments" produced by the participants explicitly conceived of the gathering as only the first of "a series of Conventions, embracing every part of the country." A follow-up convention in Rochester occurred just a month later. And the subject of women's rights traveled, with Frederick Douglass, to the Colored National Convention in Cleveland that September. Regional and national gatherings in various cities in Ohio, Massachusetts, Pennsylvania, and New York soon followed. The "convention era" in women's rights thus inaugurated, these meetings became a regular feature of the 1850s.[15]

The Declaration of Sentiments anticipated more than conventions as they contemplated the "great work before us." Though the signers expected "no small amount of misconception, misrepresentation, and ridicule," they determined to use "every instrumentality within our power" to accomplish the work of achieving women's rights, vowing to "circulate tracts" and "enlist the pulpit and the press in our behalf." This aspect of the mission was quickly understood by others. One newspaper in Albany complained about these women making an "agitatory movement" with the goal of "revolutionizing public opinion."[16] Intervening in and trying to sway published opinion would form a significant part of the women's movement strategy going forward, as convention proceedings were joined by *The Lily*, founded by dress-reformer Amelia Bloomer as a temperance organ originally in 1849 but soon dedicated to women's rights, and *The Una*, started by abolitionist Paulina Wright Davis in 1853.

The impact on published opinion became especially evident with the first national convention, held in Worcester, Massachusetts in the fall of 1850. Unlike Seneca Falls, the convention in Worcester was planned months in advance, brought together over a thousand people from multiple states, and garnered wide attention. Hosted in a booming manufacturing town, conveniently situated on multiple railroad lines, the convention gathered some of the most prominent New England and northeastern reformers of the day, including Lucretia Mott, William Lloyd Garrison, Wendell Phillips, Frederick Douglass, Lucy Stone, Paulina Wright Davis, William Alcott, and Stephen and Abby Kelly Foster, as well as Sojourner Truth. Truth, who would be a vital presence in the movement for decades, had been born in slavery in New York State and had lived for a time in a utopian community, the Northampton Association of Education and Industry, founded by abolitionists who were also dedicated to women's equality. She thus brought a reservoir of experience and knowledge about the contradictions of democratic America. It was no accident that abolitionists comprised the bulk of attendees at Worcester: the call for the convention placed the event squarely within "the upward tending spiriting of the age," of which the "great question of Woman's Rights, Duties, and Relations" formed a signal part.[17]

Horace Greeley's *New York Tribune* became a crucial conduit for making the Worcester convention an internationally acclaimed event. A *Tribune* correspondent treated the occasion with the utmost seriousness and cautioned readers not to believe caricatures they might read in the "corrupt and venal press." Though the ambivalent Greeley himself doubted that the franchise offered a magic cure-all for women's grievances, he claimed to be perfectly "willing to give the [d]emocratic theory a full and fair trial."[18] The *Tribune's* coverage reached London, via its recently launched European edition, and caught the attention of John Stuart Mill. "I have been put in spirits," he swiftly wrote his fiancée Harriet Taylor, "by what I think will put you in spirits too."

What had elevated his mood was the *Tribune's* "long report" about Worcester, a meeting "chiefly of women" but with "a great number of men." Mill was especially impressed with the quality of the addresses and could not recall "any public meetings of agitation comparable to it in the proportion which good sense bears to nonsense." Delegates, he marveled, sounded "almost like ourselves speaking." Certain that the Worcester Convention was not an isolated New England event, Mill optimistically predicted that there was a chance of "something decisive" actually being "accomplished on that of all practical subjects the most important." He urged his fiancée to complete the important essay on the subject that had been occupying her for more than a year.[19]

The essay, "The Enfranchisement of Women," was published anonymously in the London quarterly *Westminster Review* the following summer. Harriet Taylor Mill (now married) had already drafted key parts of it and was just waiting for the right time to present it publicly.[20] While American events prompted its publication in 1851, the essay considered the significance of women's political equality in broader, more philosophical terms. Taylor Mill refuted a series of well-known objections, dispensing with the argument from custom, the tautological definition of women's sphere, and the vague but strongly felt prevailing belief that women were ill-suited for politics. The "real question," she maintained, boiled down to whether it was "right and expedient that one-half of the human race" should live in a "state of forced subordination to the other half." The only reason to answer the question in the affirmative was the simple one that "men like it." That is, she observed, it was "agreeable" to men that they "should live for their own sake" and "women for the sake of men."[21]

Both John Stuart Mill and Harriet Taylor Mill saw women's enfranchisement as a logical, even necessary, extension of America's democratic ideals. Taylor Mill revealed no familiarity with Seneca Falls or the Declaration of Sentiments, but she quoted the full preamble of the Declaration of Independence and insisted that no "American democrat" could "evade the force of these expressions" unless by "dishonest or ignorant subterfuge." Mill himself appreciated the directness of Worcester activists' demands. They were "outspoken like America, not frightened & servile like England," with the resolutions "asserting the whole of the principle." Neither was surprised that this effort was being led by abolitionists. It was "fitting," Taylor Mill observed, that those reformers working to remove "the aristocracy of color" from the "democratic soil of America" should also be the "originators, for America and for the rest of the world, of the first collective protest against the aristocracy of sex."[22]

The *Westminster* essay engaged but reconceived a whole cluster of ideas developed earlier by Tocqueville, Martineau, Fuller, and Beecher. Taylor Mill detailed the way social norms stunted the mental and moral faculties of women, concentrating their attention only on "petty subjects and interests," and thereby made them dangerous companions to men. Claims that marriage was an educative or "improving" institution rang hollow as long as most such unions were partnerships of unequals. Women's education, she complained, remained largely passive and focused on turning women into agreeable companions to men rather than fully developed and autonomous selves for whom the "dignity of thought itself" was stimulated by "a field for its practical application." The truly beneficial "mental companionship" in an ideal marriage could only occur when it involved "active minds, not mere contact between an active mind and a passive" one. Such an imbalance rendered marriage no "school" for either husband or wife.

The negative consequences of unequal marriages extended far beyond the household, Taylor Mill argued, in a bold remixing of Tocqueville and Beecher's emphasis on domesticity. Women who were debarred from the elevating impact of political participation threatened rather than protected democracy. She acknowledged the novelty of her formulation and its rejection of the conventional wisdom that maintained women's influence was "the great counteractive of selfishness." This spectacular misreading of reality failed to appreciate that constricting a woman's interests to the household only replaced "individual selfishness" with a "family selfishness" and further eroded the already-limited resource that was "public spirit." Inequality within the household amplified the negative qualities of women's political disfranchisement and threatened to make democracy unsustainable. The "emancipation of women"—something "the modern world" loved to boast it had accomplished but which it had actually barely begun—was thus crucial on two fronts: it would allow women to finally become self-governing individuals and it would help ensure that a self-governing polity would flourish.[23]

In an impressive transatlantic feedback loop, Taylor Mill's essay—inspired by her reading about the Worcester convention in the *New York Tribune*—rapidly traveled from its London publication back to both the *Tribune* and to Worcester. Greeley reprinted the entire text, devoting seven full columns to it. A few months later, Harriet Taylor Mill's oldest son Herbert Taylor personally delivered "a few copies" of the essay, in pamphlet form, to Lucretia Mott, when he traveled to Philadelphia on business. Mott then sent a copy to Garrison and urged him to reprint the "very fine" essay in the *Liberator* and to send it to their women's rights colleague Lucy Stone.[24] Then in October of 1851, the essay was featured prominently and repeatedly at the Second National Woman's Rights Convention, also held at Worcester. There, speaker after speaker quoted approvingly a foreign source that had quoted approvingly their own words from a previous convention.

Convention president Paulina Wright Davis hailed Taylor Mill's essay in her opening remarks to the gathered. Cady Stanton, unable to attend, sent in a letter proposing a resolution to extend "the right hand of fellowship" to "Mrs. Mill" in thanks for her "able exposition of our rights, and that complimentary review of our last Convention." And a letter from England sent by Harriet Martineau stressed how the piece (which she, like many, mistakenly attributed to "one of our very first men John S. Mill") demonstrated the "interest excited" across the ocean by this latest American reform effort. Wendell Phillips was so taken by this "thoughtful and profound article" with its "singular clearness and force" laying out "the leading arguments for our reform" that he worked quotations from it verbatim into five of the ten resolutions he presented to the convention. The essay instantly became a core tract of the women's movement: quoted, excerpted, and reprinted for the next half-century. Mill's initial sense that the Worcester convention was "almost like ourselves speaking" had acquired new meaning.[25]

Both advocates and opponents of women's rights grappled with Taylor Mill's essay more than any of the handful of other international circuits produced by the Worcester meeting.[26] Unable to ignore such a high-profile intervention, proslavery ideologue and avowed conservative Louisa Susannah Cheves McCord used a review of "Enfranchisement" to offer the lengthiest and most acrid response to the new movement. Her article, which repeated Taylor Mill's title with a slight modification (turning the intentional "women" into the more abstract "woman") appeared in a journal edited by William Gilmore Simms, the proslavery critic of Harriet Martineau. Martineau's reputation for taking a radical interest in America had clearly persisted, as McCord assumed it was the *Society in America* author who had also written the *Westminster* essay. McCord too was eager to link democracy, abolition, and women's rights but drew a contrary set of meanings than had Martineau, the Worcester activists, and Taylor Mill.[27]

McCord thanked the author of "Enfranchisement" for "saving us the trouble" of connecting reforms as an interlinked whole. Taylor Mill's claim that "sex and colour are accidental and irrelevant to all questions of government" struck McCord as both laughable and frightful, offering a forceful reminder that slavery and patriarchy were simultaneously under assault. Any disruption to the tightly nested set of hierarchies on which slave societies, in particular, rested posed a grave danger. Her emphasis on the racial dimension of mastery over slaves, and the sexual grounds for the authority of husbands over wives, led her to insist that notions of equality or individual rights must be carefully contained within the world of electoral governance where white men's dominance was foundational. Echoing Simms and others from the 1830s, McCord ridiculed those "mouthing over Mr. Jefferson's 'free and equal' sentence" and dismissed the "mischievous fallacy" contained in "the six unlucky words" of that "blundering" phrase from the 1776 Declaration of Independence.[28]

McCord took umbrage less at a convention of wild-eyed fanatics in New England than at the attention it received from a London quarterly. When a "grave periodical allows such sentiments to soil its pages," she warned, "it is time for us to cease to laugh" and to recognize the "mischievous effects of a progressive system of reform."[29] Here she adopted the acerbic style perfected by Scotsman Thomas Carlyle, who had recently published his infamously ven-omous "Discourse on the Negro Question" (1849). Taking a cue from Carlyle, McCord denounced the conventioneers, with equal parts disgust and conde-scension, as "petticoated despisers of their sex," "would-be men," and "moral monsters." She found it unfortunate that "this move for woman's (so-called) enfranchisement" was "entirely . . . of American growth," even if she thanked "Heaven" that "our modest Southern sisters have held aloof from the defiling pitch." The problem with "progressive" systems of reform was their tendency to be contagious. The *Westminster* essay ominously suggested how "the poison is spreading" across the Atlantic and might not be easily contained.[30]

Along with rejecting egalitarian democracy, McCord dismissed any con-cept of democratic individuality elaborated by Margaret Fuller. Poignantly, an unmistakable note of resignation accompanied her brittle conservatism. Life was not a picnic, she recognized, but suffering was an inescapable part of humanity. The strong oppressed the weak; men oppressed women; the master class oppressed the enslaved. And so one must muddle through, learning to accept one's place. Many women of "dominant intellect," she wrote, were forced to "submit to the rule of an animal in pantaloons," in every way their "inferior." Again, not a picnic, but such was God's will. Though her empathy did not extend to enslaved people, it did encompass, in a remarkable passage, what today might be called gender-nonconforming individuals. Using the examples of "Thomas" and "Betty," she acknowledged that some men were clearly more womanly and some women more manly than others. Thomas might make "a capital child's nurse," for example, and Betty could probably

"beat Thomas hollow in a stump oration." Similarly, McCord's own "dominant intellect" towered over the inferior mind of her "animal in pantaloons"
husband David James McCord. But Thomas, Betty, and Louisa were merely
"individual exceptions to a general rule" and accordingly had to acquiesce.
Individuals counted for little against the force of the social order. The injustice may be real, but so too was the need for conformity and forbearance.
And, for woman at least, there might even be something higher and noble;
Christlike, she could become "life's devoted martyr."[31]

So blunt was the anti-egalitarianism of McCord's rebuke that it provoked
a multipart response in *The Lily*. "Senex," the pseudonym of New York lawyer
Anson Bingham, devoted three separate articles to denouncing the "rant and
howling" tone and profoundly anti-democratic "ruffianism" of the *Southern
Quarterly* article (which he assumed had been written by a man). While the
"ferocious appetite" for might over right, in matters of slavery as well as patriarchy, offended Bingham's own political sensibility, he seemed (like McCord
herself) particularly disconcerted that such views would gain a receptive
hearing outside of the fanatical region in which they originated. He singled
out the New York–based *Democratic Review*, which, in spite of its pretensions
to being the "leading light of radical democracy," Bingham dismissed as the
venal "organ of the Slave interest." The "alacrity" with which that and other
"mercenary papers" in the North echoed McCord's extreme views did not
bode well for democratic progress. Against "common sense, common intelligence and common justice," these papers had "hired themselves out" to the
slaveholding South in its effort to "adopt as American and Christian customs,
Pagan brutalities exercised toward the women by their heathen husbands,
more than two thousand years ago."[32]

The First of Woman's Rights . . . Is the Right to a Fair Hearing

Most Americans plotted themselves somewhere on the spectrum between
the "ultraism" of Worcester and the reactionary proslavery conservatism of
McCord. Such was the case for Catharine Beecher, who used the appearance
of an organized women's movement to publicize her plan of higher education and teacher training for women. Expanded opportunity, not the ballot,
would offer, as her book title suggested, the *True Remedy for the Wrongs of
Women* (1851). If Beecher was leery of the movement, she still believed that
women had legitimate grievances. Practical reforms, therefore, rather than
the tart "vituperation and ridicule" of McCord, was the appropriate response.

Beecher's was a viewpoint shared by many Americans. Certain elements of coverture had come to appear archaic by the middle decades of the nineteenth century, and the democratic process showed itself able to guide gradual change. Reformers petitioned, made their case from the lecture platform and in print, and met at conventions. Over the course of the 1850s, state after state recognized property rights for married women and passed laws easing access to divorce. Black and white women alike worked for—and in several cases won—expanded roles in churches, earning the right to hold leadership positions and even to be ordained. In short, to many observers, establishing and protecting the personhood of women did not necessitate extending full political rights, a measure at which even some attendees of the early women's rights conventions had balked.[33]

Activists remained a small, radical minority, but the emergence of the movement assured that commentary on the "woman question" saturated published opinion in the 1850s, spreading out across intellectual life, popular culture, and party politics alike. Elizabeth Oakes Smith's columns for the *New York Tribune* exposed the many readers of that popular newspaper—with a circulation of two hundred thousand by the late 1850s—to women's rights issues. Following the plan set forth in the Seneca Falls Declaration of Sentiments, women's rights activists organized regular conventions and blanketed the press with their message. The frequent local and national conventions were crucial both for recruiting new adherents to the movement and for shaping the wider public conversation. Occurring nearly every year until the outbreak of war in 1861, these gatherings simultaneously advocated and modeled a vision of participatory democratic citizenship. As events, they brought men and women together to submit reports, give and listen to addresses, record minutes, structure debates, and draft and vote on resolutions.[34]

The conventions generated extensive press coverage, sparking discussions in "ladies' departments" and "family circle" sections of periodicals and attracting some respectful commentary even from skeptics. The *New York Evangelist* found the 1856 convention held at Broadway Tabernacle "a model for our democratic assemblies." The moderate weekly acknowledged that the phrase "woman's rights" was a "bug-bear that frightened many sober people," but it declared that the "first of woman's rights . . . is the right to a fair hearing." Proceedings from conventions were then published separately, reprinted in friendly periodicals, and reviewed in newspapers, thus extending the reach of the arguments they articulated and the citizenship practices they performed. Reformers in the women's movement, like those in the Colored Convention movement, were highly attuned to the workings of published opinion, as internal debates over establishing "national organs" in these years reveal.[35]

Lecture tours also brought visibility to women's rights in the 1850s, especially as a burgeoning celebrity culture transformed orators into regional and national figures. Sojourner Truth and Lucy Stone, who had both been present at the first national convention in Worcester, made names for themselves through their public speaking across the decade. Truth's life story as well her charismatic oratory was a draw. She had not only been born into slavery but had escaped, successfully sued a white man to recover her son, and dictated her autobiography before going on tour with British abolitionist George Thompson in 1851. Her speech at the 1851 Akron women's rights convention electrified the crowd, and she became a regular presence at conventions over the following decades. Lucy Stone, an early female graduate of Oberlin College, also achieved a measure of celebrity and an income as a popular lecturer on behalf of antislavery and women's rights, touring the Northeast and Midwest in the "Bloomer dress" of pantaloons and short skirts.[36]

The biracial dimension of the movement, as well as the wearing of bloomers, came in for ridicule, as a lithograph from 1851 demonstrates. Displaying an awareness of the second national convention at Worcester, a lithograph titled *Bloomerism in Practice* envisioned dire social consequences of women's rights agitation (figure 3.2). Women decline to do their domestic work; men are forced to pick up the slack; and servants and slaves refuse to accept their subordinate positions. In its depiction of a social order where all hierarchies of race, gender, and class have been overturned, the lithograph embodied McCord's nightmare vision. In reality, the place of Black women in the movement was more complicated, the celebrity presence of Sojourner Truth notwithstanding. Black women participated throughout the convention era. Indeed, the Fifth National Convention, held in Philadelphia in 1854, relied heavily on the organizational efforts of two Black women from that city's vibrant free Black community: Harriet Forten Purvis and Margaretta Forten, daughters of businessman James Forten, who had been instrumental in the founding of the Philadelphia Female Anti-Slavery Society. And yet even if the presence of Black women was likely underreported by the white chroniclers of the movement, the particular concerns of Black women—enslaved and free—were only occasionally acknowledged in resolutions, speeches, and articles. Black women largely charted their own course in these years—a course that encompassed the freedom struggle in all its intersectional dimensions.[37]

By the mid-1850s a reader would have had to have made an effort not to encounter discussion of the woman question in print. When Fuller's *Woman*

FIG. 3.2 Adam Weingärtner, "Bloomerism in Practice." This lithograph both mocks the "Bloomer" style and conjures up McCord's fear of the unraveling of tightly nested hierarchies of class, race, and gender. As "Mrs. Turkey" smokes from an exotic pipe and "Mr. Turkey" does the sewing, two women, a white servant and a Black slave, return home from an electoral rally. The white servant's placard announces "No More Basement & Kitchen!," while the enslaved woman's sign reads "No More Massus & Missus." Weingärtner directly connected his image to the Second National Woman's Rights Convention at Worcester in 1851, as a framed sign from the convention hangs on the wall to the left (the words "Woman's Rights," "[conve]ntion," and "October 1851" are legible). From *Humbug's Museum Series* (1851). Courtesy of Social and Political Cartoons, Boston Public Library.

in Nineteenth Century was reissued in 1855, it sold three times as many copies in just a few weeks as it had in the preceding decade. Intellectuals who had remained aloof from the movement or chose not to consider the issue increasingly had difficulty avoiding it. Under some pressure from friends, famed minister and abolitionist Theodore Parker finally made his thoughts known, delivering his sermon *Of the Public Function of Woman* in 1853. He doubted women would "ever, as a general thing, take the same interest as men in political affairs," and he affirmed a fairly conventional view of the sexes—that man, with the "bigger brain," would always lead in matters of reason and intellect, while women would always lead in emotion. But his stature as an intellectual and reformer rendered highly valuable his (otherwise vague) assertion that "to make one-half the human race consume all their energies in the functions of housekeeper, wife, and mother, is a waste of the most precious material God ever made." His sermon was included as part of small bundle of Woman's Rights Tracts published in 1853. Ralph Waldo Emerson, Margaret Fuller's first and most significant interlocutor, also offered his thoughts, in an address before the 1855 Woman's Rights Convention in Boston. Titled simply "Woman," Emerson's comments were even more tepid than Parker's and, as the title suggests, dealt mostly in vague abstractions of the "Man is Will, Woman is Sentiment" variety. He rehearsed the conventional, Enlightenment-era view that women were "the civilizers of mankind," but he expressed discomfort with women exerting actual political power. Nonetheless, like Parker, his name was too valuable to ignore, and women's rights activists would count him for "their" side throughout the nineteenth century.[38]

The ubiquity of the woman question in the 1850s can be seen in the curious essay drafted—but not published—by Frederick Grimke, brother of Angelina and Sarah. He framed his piece, titled "The Rights of Women in a Democratic Republic," by asserting, first, that the topic was a "question of infinitely more importance than is generally supposed" and, second, that placing men and women on the same political footing "will be one of the greatest revolutions in human affairs since the beginning of society." Grimke was born in Charleston, South Carolina, but like his more famous sisters he moved North, becoming a judge in Ohio. His real passion was not the law but philosophical study, and when he retired from the court in the early 1840s, he began working on his magnum opus: *Considerations Upon the Nature and Tendency of Free Institutions* (1848).[39]

When precisely Grimke turned to the woman question is unclear but at some point in the 1850s, he had come to believe that "no question . . . which has ever been agitated, demands more thought, and a more unclouded judgment." Like a lawyer, he weighed the evidence carefully, drawing on history, biology, custom, and political theory. His meticulously reasoned essay considered the advantages as well as the possible difficulties that might result from women's political equality. He thought reform was inevitable but was likely to be incremental rather than sudden. Even so, it would represent a revolutionary break with centuries of history, akin to the struggle against absolutism that had dominated the recent past. The women's rights revolution would be "the most searching of all revolutions," and one which "no arm will have power to arrest."[40] Grimke's thorough attention to the subject reveals how inescapable it had become, even if he expressed ambivalence about publishing his reflections. His trepidation signaled that the ubiquity of a topic was not the same as acceptance of it.[41]

Indeed, derision and mockery accompanied increased attention. Even after a decade of women and men speaking on the subject from convention platforms, ridicule and jeers from some corners of the press persisted. The minstrel entertainment industry incorporated mockeries of women's rights into its programming starting around 1853. Men would appear in women's dress (and usually blackface) and perform parody songs, faux lectures, and mock sermons.[42] Blackface stage actor Julius Caesar Hannibal (William Levison), for example, used racist dialect to lampoon Black and white women meeting in "con-wenchon" and talking about Woman's Rights but never about "Woman's Leffs." Why, he wondered, did "dese woman's all want to be Captains, when old Human Nature formed em spressly for mates!" These stage caricatures of women's rights lecturers were familiar enough that a young Louisa May Alcott could by mid-decade entertain her friends and neighbors with her own "burlesque lecture" on "Woman, and Her Position," in the guise of authoress "Oronthy Bluggage."[43] Popular songs extended the amusement into the private sphere, as Americans purchased sheet music to play and sing along with at home. *Woman's Rights: A Right Good Ballad Rightly Illustrating Woman's Rights*, written by Kate Horn—"*Not* one of the woman's wrights [*sic*] convention"—spelled out, over several verses, what *were* and *were not* women's rights. It was, for example, "woman's right to rule the house and petty troubles brave." But it was *not* her "right to rule the head and treat him as her slave."[44]

Fiction, which had long provided a vital space to think through questions relating to women, the family, and the relations between the sexes, also reflected the visibility of the 1850s women's rights movement. One peculiar example promised to illustrate "the follies and delusions" of the nineteenth century, with the tagline: "This is the age of oddities let loose." Likely playing on the celebrity of Lucy Stone, who had just that year insisted on keeping her own name when she married Henry Browne Blackwell, *Lucy Boston, or Woman's Rights and Spiritualism* (1855) depicted a role-reversed dystopian future in which women have taken over the government of the state of New York. Chaos ensues. The author claimed to have written the novel for "all sensible people" who were "both disgusted with the follies and pained by the evils" of such bizarre fads as women's rights and spiritualism. Regretting that the author's wit was not quite equal to his zeal, one reviewer nonetheless hoped the book "would provoke a smile and serve to sharpen the public contempt of the very shallow theories that are afloat." This was but one example of anti-women's rights fiction that looked to the home as a source of patriarchal stability amidst a world in flux.[45]

The woman question became ensnared in and helped give shape to sectional polarization and party realignment, as clashes over the return of fugitive slaves and the territorial expansion of slavery escalated through the 1850s. The two main parties—the Democrats and the Republicans—employed ideas about women and the family as a convenient cultural shorthand for opposing world views. The Democrats, increasingly devoted to the protection of Southern slavery, unabashedly declared the United States a "white man's government" that was, as Senator Stephen Douglas put it, "made by white men for the benefit of white men" and "never should be administered by any except white men." Patriarchal fiction, which regularly appeared in Democratic newspapers, presented happy images of "male rule, submissive wives, and rigid gender roles," in the words of one historian. This view of the "white man's republic," comprised of formally equal white patriarchs governing their unequal dependents, united Democrats across regional and religious lines, and Democratic newspapers in the North no less than the South made clear there could be no relaxation of white male authority in the household or the polity.[46]

The newly formed Republican Party, organized almost exclusively in the free states, offered a clear alternative in connecting its central goal—the restriction of slavery's expansion—to a broader reform vision. The early Whig party's commitment to domesticity and the moral influence of women persisted within a political coalition whose base was in the Protestant nonurban heartland. Drawing together antislavery activists as well as evangelical reformers like Catharine Beecher, the Republican party represented a new force eager to remake the world in the image of Yankee righteousness and rectitude. With the encouragement of party leaders, Republican women thronged to rallies just as Whig women had. Their presence bolstered the partisan self-image of a relatively egalitarian pro-family political force destined to set the country aright.[47]

The election of 1856 set these two competing gender cultures in sharp relief. Nominating John C. Frémont as their first presidential candidate, Republican Party leaders turned his charismatic wife, Jessie Benton Frémont (daughter of the eminent Democratic politician Thomas Hart Benton), into a celebrity and quasi-running mate. "John and Jessie" essentially overshadowed "Frémont and Dayton" as campaign slogan, and women's support was organized through "Jessie Clubs." Republicans drew a distinct contrast between their candidate's robust, healthy companionate marriage—free hearts and free homes—and the suspect bachelorhood of James Buchanan, who lacked the "courage to take a wife."[48] Frémont campaign songs depicted Buchanan as decrepit and deficient, an "old fossil bachelor," as one song put it. The candidate's failure to commit to a marital union called his larger commitments into question. As another song observed:

> A bachelor, who, like his species, you know,
> Is afraid of the girls, and to union a foe;
> Then up and be doing, for danger is rife, —
> A man is but moonshine who has n't a wife.[49]

Democrats fought back, defending themselves as the party of manly rights and female subordination and tarring Frémont and the antislavery Republicans as the party of a variety of "fanatical" commitments that included women's rights, abolition, free love, and racial amalgamation. They pointed to Jessie Frémont's high profile and the passionate support of Republican women as proof of their claims about the party's unreliable adherence to male authority. Though Frémont lost, the 1856 campaign had drawn clear lines between the Democrats' embrace of a white man's democracy and the Republican alternative of an antislavery domesticated democracy.[50]

The Republican Party never actually committed to women's political rights, but it drew hopeful activists into its ranks as it consolidated support for a national reformist agenda. The Seventh National Woman's Rights Convention (New York, 1856), which took place shortly after Frémont's loss, made multiple references to Jessie Benton Frémont and included resolutions applauding the Republican Party and condemning the Democrats. Lucy Stone took the opportunity to survey the accomplishments of the decade. Back when the movement started, she reminded the convention audience, "the laws were against us, custom was against us, prejudice was against us." Though there was still much work ahead, much had been achieved. In nearly all the northern states, at least some version of married women's property rights had been acknowledged in law, and this had been accomplished through democratic processes. State legislatures elected by all-male voters had nonetheless recognized the need to remove the worst features of coverture and recognize the legal personhood of wives. "Never before," Stone asserted, "has any reformatory movement gained so much in so short a time."[51]

Consistent Democracy

By the end of the decade, movement figures had distilled their cause into an elegantly simple call for "consistent democracy." This was the title Lucy Stone and her friend and fellow activist, Worcester-based minister and abolitionist Thomas Wentworth Higginson, gave to the four-page leaflet they assembled and published in 1858: *Consistent Democracy: The Elective Franchise for Women. Twenty-Five Testimonies of Prominent Men.* Among those "prominent men" were John Neal, Elisha Hurlburt, Timothy Walker, Samuel J. May, and Theodore Parker, as well as Wendell Phillips, William Lloyd Garrison, and Higginson himself. The selection ranged backward over the previous twenty years, but the bulk of endorsements came from the more recent convention era of women's rights, which was a testament to how much the movement had done to shape opinion in the 1850s.[52]

Most of the selections made some version of one essential point—that a government claiming to be "of the people" could be no such thing if women were not included. "Our whole plan of government is a hypocritical farce," William Henry Channing declared in one example, "if one-half the people can be governed by the other half, without their consent being asked or granted." Another "testimony," an 1857 Ohio senate report supporting a petition for "female suffrage" in that state, asserted that to "declare that a voice in the government is the right of all, and then give it only to a part, is to renounce even the appearance of principle." (Technically, since the Ohio report here directly quoted, without attribution, Harriet Taylor Mill, at least one woman's words made it into the leaflet.) This demand for a "consistent democracy," which captured a core idea articulated in lectures, tracts, and convention proceedings, would remain the most powerful and enduring weapon in the movement's rhetorical arsenal.[53]

"Consistent" evoked the matter of inclusion and exclusion, but what of "democracy"? The vision of popular government that animated the contributors and the movement activists collectively was hard to pin down.

Fault lines and tensions were evident, even if they would not fully emerge until the next decade. As early as the Declaration of Sentiments, some movement figures drew contrasts between "women" and "ignorant foreign men," suggesting the ethno-racial and class specificity that often lurked behind their use of a purportedly universal category of womanhood. Such language highlighted contested assumptions about education and enfranchisement that remained latent in the 1850s. At this point, disagreements were generally muted, as prominent proponents of "consistent democracy" underscored the emphasis on engaged and active citizenship that Tocqueville had made such a central part of his analysis in *Democracy in America* and that Taylor Mill had reconsidered in light of women's disenfranchisement. Democratic participation was elevating, as important to the flourishing of women's citizenship as it was to the success of the polity.

Higginson elaborated these themes in two essays that would be reprinted and quoted for decades. *Woman and Her Wishes*, termed a "spicy pamphlet" by the *New York Tribune*, was written for the Massachusetts Constitutional Convention in 1853 while the 1859 "Ought Women to Learn the Alphabet" appeared in the new literary magazine, the *Atlantic Monthly*. In both essays, Higginson drew explicitly on Tocqueville, Margaret Fuller, and both Mills as he enveloped critical ideas in memorable and catchy formulations. He wondered, for example, if the great anxiety lurking behind resistance to women's equality simply came down to the question of dinner and who would make it.[54] For Higginson, as for Wendell Phillips, enfranchising women was crucial for women, but it would also be good for American democracy. After all, the "great educator of American men is the ballot-box, with its accompaniments," by which he meant "the whole world of public life—public measures, public interest, and public office." Why would Americans want to "rigidly exclude" women from this crucial "school of instruction"?[55]

The idea of "consistent democracy," at least as it applied to women, received philosophical ballast from across the Atlantic, courtesy of John Stuart Mill, who in the late 1850s produced his most elaborate analysis of self-government. His prodigious output in these years included two of the books for which he would become best-known: *On Liberty* (1859) and *Considerations on Representative Government* (1861). With these and other works, Mill endeavored to create an intellectual monument to his late wife and collaborator, who had died from consumption in 1858. They also reflected the maturation of his thinking about democracy, as he entered a new phase of his career as a "public moralist."[56] That the status and rights of women became a salient concern in Mill's writing was both a function of the commitment he and Taylor Mill had long shared as well as the changed context. In the years since Taylor Mill's 1851 essay had been published, British women had begun mobilizing to expand their rights with activism focused on reforming married women's property laws, making divorce more accessible, and expanding employment opportunities. Pioneering associations and organs (such as *The English Woman's Journal*, established in 1858 by Barbara Bodichon and others) represented just the beginning of an organized women's rights movement that would flourish in the 1860s. Helen Taylor, Mill's stepdaughter and loyal companion until his death, served as a liaison to this emerging movement over the next decade and a half.[57]

Mill might seem an unlikely proponent of consistent democracy to twenty-first-century readers. He is best known as a theorist of liberalism or liberal individualism. He shared with most nineteenth-century liberals a distrust of mass democracy and an uncertainty about the "capacity" of all people to be self-governing. His decades of reading and observation had made him wary of the United States both for its continuing embrace of slavery and because he had internalized Tocqueville's warning about the threat of apathy and potentially tyrannical majorities.[58] At home, his anxieties about "unintelligent" voters led him to flirt with various voting schemes meant to enhance the electoral weight of the "intelligent."[59] Finally, he excepted colonial peoples from his discussion of self-government, justifying Britain's imperial rule as a necessary if temporary civilizing measure. In short, Mill's views on democracy seem riddled with inconsistencies, or at least tensions.[60]

But to nineteenth-century Americans, Mill's reputation as a defender of popular government was established in the 1850s and would continue to grow until his death in 1873. That reputation was very much bound up with his commitment to women's enfranchisement, which provides a helpful index to important aspects of his democratic thought. In fact, his insistence on women's political participation fused his democratic aspirations and anxieties. He argued on the grounds of consistency. "All human beings," he maintained, "have the same interest in good government, are affected by it, and should have a voice in it." The "difference of sex" was as irrelevant to political rights as the difference of height or hair color. But women's enfranchisement was also important in ensuring that democratic government achieve its best quality, which was the educative impact on the citizenry. Influenced by his reading of Tocqueville, Mill considered representative government to be "the ideally best form of government" precisely because of the improving stimulus it provided to the faculties and perspectives of the people. Participation furnished the "education" of a "free people," by "taking them out of the narrow circle of personal and family selfishness, and accustoming them to the comprehension of joint interests, the management of joint concerns." Not simply voting but all self-governing practices—from service on juries and involvement in local government to engagement in voluntary associations and even worker-owned collectives—comprised the very curriculum of the democratic "school of public spirit."[61]

This view of democracy encouraged as broad an electorate as possible, which for Mill included women. No political system could be satisfactory, he asserted, from which "any person or class is peremptorily excluded" and in which "the electoral privilege is not open to all persons of full age who desire to obtain it." Writing from a country where a majority of adult men were not able to vote, Mill compared the political knowledge and savvy of a disenfranchised manual laborer to that of an "average woman of the middle class," who knew vastly less about politics and public matters than her "husbands or brothers." Enfranchising both groups would bring them within the frame of educative participation. *Considerations on Representative Government*, however, complicated matters by speaking about enfranchisement in these bold strokes while taking it for granted that certain requirements must attach to the franchise. What in a British context might have been a radical departure from the status quo could nonetheless justify a contradictory set of readings in the United States.[62]

Mill's theory of representative government advanced a principled, philosophical case for women's political participation. Any former excuses for their exclusion, he claimed, were entirely out of keeping with "the whole mode of thought of the modern world," which tended toward the expansion of individual autonomy and self-determination. One by one, Mill explained, reformers had pulled down the "remains of the mouldering fabric" of tyranny and injustice. He hoped the "inveterate prejudice" against women would soon disappear and that before another generation had lapsed, "the accident of sex" along with the "accident of skin" would no longer be deemed "a sufficient justification for depriving its possessor of the equal protection and privileges of a citizen."[63]

As he published these words, American activists were involved in precisely this struggle—a struggle Mill would come to consider a turning point in human history. An emerging figure in the antislavery women's rights wing of the Republican Party, George William Curtis, gave voice to this sense of national crisis when he addressed the Ninth National Woman's Rights

Convention held in New York in 1858. Democratic principle was the very "corner-stone of our political existence," he asserted, but at this moment the "most democratic country in the world" was bringing that form of government "into the foulest discredit." The quest to redeem democracy—and to make it consistent—would soon find new opportunities and face new challenges.[64]

Interlude

SELF-GOVERNMENT ON TRIAL IN 1863

"BECAUSE THERE IS a war, shall we no more argue the old questions?" So asked journalist Charles Nordhoff of the many thousands who read *Harper's New Monthly Magazine* in the midst of a transformative conflict. His choice of title implied there was something quixotic about returning to an abstract discussion of womanhood while all-too-concrete battles raged on. As Nordhoff assumed the mantle of Cervantes's knight-errant, he offered his "Tilt at the Woman Question" as proof of Northern resilience and devotion to progress. "I am determined to stir up old grievances to show our Southern brethren that there are still Yankees in the land." To maintain the United States was also to salvage that distinctive crusade for human betterment.[1]

Nordhoff's 1863 effort combined a six-page whirlwind tour of sex roles across history with a pointed inquiry: "In this hour of our national trial, who has sent our million of men to the field but the women?" Lack of space prevented him from detailing women's patriotism or exploring whether those who encouraged their male relatives to volunteer would also support the policy of forced conscription that Congress was then debating. Yet the draft of free adult men was one of two issues, both wholly unprecedented in American history, then roiling Northern politics. The other was the Republicans' embrace of a federally led program of emancipation. Revolutionary innovations stirred a fierce backlash from war critics, which manifested in partisan elections that year. Were opponents of the war to take power, an ignoble peace with the Confederates, and new guarantees to slaveholders, seemed likely.

The author Mary Abigail Dodge, known to her many readers by her pseudonym Gail Hamilton, urged her own mass audience to stay the course. In doing so, she appealed to deeper understandings and an intensification of existing commitments to American self-government. Writing for the *Atlantic Monthly* a month after Nordoff turned to *Harper's*, Hamilton noted how Americans had long "rolled our Democracy as a sweet morsel under our tongue" without considering fully its varied implications. Pro-Union women, no less than men, had an obligation to educate themselves and others more fully about the political ideas they were now defending with their lives. A "self-governing people should be a self-understanding people," she wrote, adding that only self-understanding could clarify the stakes of the war. As a stalwart Republican, Hamilton urged the North's loyal women to internalize democratic convictions, to broadcast these as widely as they could, and to redouble their efforts to sustain a war that was transforming the American republic.[2]

Loyalty—a concept that had been largely absent from the previous quarter-century of questions, observations, advice, and advocacy—was becoming a fixation of Northern published opinion by 1863, especially among those backing the Lincoln administration.[3] As a third season of military campaigning approached, and with Northern voters wavering about a negotiated peace, Gail Hamilton's "A Call to my Countrywomen" echoed the assertion made by Rev. Henry Bellows that same winter—that the country's fate depended not simply on "the fealty of her sons but of her daughters too." A February meeting called by Bellows in New York contrasted Northern women's comparatively tepid response to war with the ferocious, if ill-considered, devotion of Confederate women to their bad cause. Hamilton, who had taught for a while at Beecher's Hartford Female Seminary, agreed. She lamented how loyal Northern women "have not come up to the level of to-day" and did "not stand abreast with its issues." Their insufficient understanding prevented them from rising to "the height of the great argument." The solution was for female patriots to fix their "ardent gaze" upon the war's highest purposes and to attach themselves to a government, unique across the globe, that the sitting president would soon hail for being "of the people, by the people, and for the people."[4]

If Gail Hamilton fell short of Abraham Lincoln's rhetorical flourish, her reflections included women explicitly in ways the Gettysburg Address of November 1863 did not. In a string of wartime essays, she sought to valorize American democracy by venturing beyond simple flag-waving patriotism. Her own understanding of popular government came via a careful reading of Alexis de Tocqueville and John Stuart Mill. She marveled how *Democracy in America* had anticipated the core issues of suppressing the slaveholders' rebellion: how "to unite liberty with equality" and to "prevent democracy from

This may seem very bold, and all that sort of thing, on Julia's part ; but he cannot put his
arm round HER waist—and something has to be done, you know.

FIG. I.I. "This May Seem Very Bold . . ." Northern women's devotion and their loyalty to democratic principles under internal and external assault emerged as a critical theme in 1863. An ever-more costly war inflicted bodily damage on men like the amputee shown in this image, who received the gentle support of a fellow patriot. Her forward gesture of an embrace, the caption explained, resulted from his inability to put his arm around her waist and something "had to be done, you know." This "bold" gesture was a tiny indication of the transformative powers of a "people's" war. From *Frank Leslie's Budget of Fun* (June 1, 1863). Courtesy of American Antiquarian Society.

one day throwing itself into the arms of despotism, as a last refuge against anarchy." Tocqueville had, in the wake of his 1859 death, become newly relevant for her, and she supplemented the Frenchman's guidance with Mill's *On Liberty*, which she consumed "with great delight" in April of 1863. She warned that the very pride that Americans took in their emphasis on self-government and equality could become a "shame and curse" if the country failed to live up to its high ideals.[5]

In the months that followed Gail Hamilton's rallying cry, the crisis of political obligation and democratic citizenship inspired female loyalists to launch two contrasting organizational efforts. A variety of groups dubbing themselves Ladies' Loyal Leagues placed a variant of Catharine Beecher's domesticated democracy on a wartime footing. A more radical tinge was evident in the efforts of Elizabeth Cady Stanton and Susan B. Anthony, who had suspended women's rights conventions when the war began. Gathering in May of 1863 as "Loyal Women of the Republic," they established the Women's Loyal National League, a centralized effort that soon enlisted 20,000 members. The goal of the league was to collect signatures for a "mammoth petition" demanding nationwide emancipation. The group aligned this call for social transformation with an explicitly democratic vision of how the war would end those aristocracies that had corrupted what was still the world's leading republic.[6]

These female publicists looked back to history for models of female solidarity with male-led national causes. One contributor to the *Continental Monthly* focused on the social aspect of that inheritance in her assertion that "the colonial matrons of the country lived democracy before our forefathers instituted it." The political dimensions of the effort proved more divisive and ignited sparks at that initial May gathering in New York. A Wisconsin delegate hewed to a more moderate course when she objected to a resolution calling for women's enfranchisement, contrasting that "theoretical or clamorous" pursuit with the self-sacrifice of the revolutionary matrons who had brought the republic into being. Susan B. Anthony's response, which carried the day, explained how the new organization remained true to the founding by boldly enunciating "the fundamental principles of democracy and republicanism which underlie the structure of a free government" and then working to bring practice in line with those principles.[7]

Elizabeth Cady Stanton did something similar by echoing the key themes of Gail Hamilton's *Atlantic* article but deftly directing them to more sweeping ends. She replayed Hamilton's contrast between the enthusiasm of Confederate women for "the blessings of slavery" and the more tepid response of Northern women on behalf of the "blessings of liberty." She issued the same urgent call for a "universal, clearly defined idea of the end proposed" and insisted the aim lay in the eradication of slavery and the principled embrace of democracy for all. But she also asserted that "woman is equally interested and responsible with man in the final settlement of this problem of self-government." Given the scope of the crisis, the country could not afford to have half its population as "idle spectators" as democracy faced its existential trial.[8]

The Women's National Loyal League unambiguously defined the war in the first of eight resolutions its members passed. This was not simply a clash between South and North, or slavery and freedom, but an "irrepressible conflict between the aristocratic doctrine" and the "democratic principle that self-government is the inalienable right of the people." Rev. Antoinette Brown Blackwell, Oberlin friend and sister-in-law of Lucy Stone, gave this resolution more sustained explication when she argued that proponents of Southern slavery and European monarchism opposed the "one great idea" on which the United States was based. These internal and external enemies alike chafed at the democratic principle of the "consent of the governed." In soaring oratory, she sketched out a "life and death conflict between all those grand, universal, man-respecting principles, which we call by the comprehensive term democracy" and "all those partial . . . class-favoring elements which we group together under that silver-slippered word, aristocracy." If the war did not vindicate the principles of self-government against those of entrenched privilege, "it means nothing."[9]

Understanding the war as a conflict between democracy and aristocracy raised questions and expectations. Would all existing relics of aristocracy be overthrown, or just some of them? From the perspective of 1863, the answer was far from clear. Most likely to fall was the aristocratic privilege of trea-sonous slaveholders, whose claim to property rights in fellow human beings had provoked the conflict in the first place. Lincoln urged loyal citizens to "disenthrall ourselves" to "save the country," since "in giving freedom to the slave" Americans would "assure freedom to the free." A national commitment to emancipation accelerated across 1863 and seemed all but inevitable by the year's close.[10]

The toppling of America's aristocracies of race and sex, both distinct and entangled, seemed less certain. The experiences of differing groups of non-white women suggested both the limits and possibilities of a wartime dem-ocratic vision. More than a thousand miles away from the North's chief eastern cities, hundreds of Dakota women began 1863 in a crushed and cap-tive state. Published opinion provided a few glimpses of this suffering, in-cluding the illustrated weeklies and *Harper's Monthly*. The press had widely discussed the Mankato gallows erected months before, which on the day after Christmas 1862 became the site of the largest mass execution in American history. The hanging of thirty-eight men, whose death sentences President Lincoln had upheld from the more than 300 convictions, produced a lull in the struggles between the United States military and Sioux warriors. The hundreds of men who had gained a reprieve from execution were taken in captivity to Davenport, Iowa. In May of 1863, some 1,300 of these men's wives

and children boarded two packed steamers, undertook a round-about itin-
erary of two thousand miles, and were resettled at the isolated Crow Creek
reservation in present-day South Dakota. Their group's exile from Minnesota
proved to be permanent, even though some rejoined husbands and fathers in
territorial Nebraska in 1866.[11]

Dakota women had been given no opportunity to profess allegiance, as insurgent Confederate women had that very same year, when occupying Union
armies offered loyalty oaths. Racial assumptions drove this discrepancy, as
did a discourse of civilization that had victimized indigenous peoples long
before Tocqueville, Beaumont, and Martineau offered their commentaries in
the 1830s. Many white Americans assumed self-government was antithetical
to the supposed familial norms of Indians, a perception that continued to
exclude native wives and mothers from the category of "American woman."

Whether whiteness would operate as a totalizing force was in 1863 still to
be determined for the North's loyal free women of color and the South's newly
liberated freedwomen. Representatives from both groups of Black Americans
spent that pivotal year considering how wartime loyalty might create new
possibilities. Rapidly developing events inspired these women with a sense
of cautious optimism and a vision of a democratic future in which lingering
aristocracies of skin and sex might be toppled.[12] Black women authors used
their pens to nudge the Union effort in the direction of emancipation, away
from white supremacy and toward a new set of rights for all female patriots.

The poet and orator Francis Ellen Watkins Harper, whose literary persona
had been established before the war, found new ways to fuse her antislavery
Christian commitments with her burning anger at America's inconsistencies.
Born free in the slave state of Maryland and raised by her abolitionist uncle,
Harper was exhilarated by developments in 1863. She had chastised President
Lincoln for his "dabbling with colonization" the previous fall, but her assessment shifted after New Year's Day, when the president "reached out his
hand through the darkness to break the chains on which the rust of centuries
had gathered." His move to enlist Black soldiers represented another breakthrough.[13] Harper responded with poetry such as "The New Liberty Bell,"
which imagined a mother freed from a tyrant master who could no longer
"tear my loved ones from my clasp." The verse concluded with a bedtime
parenting scene: "In peace I lull my boy to sleep, / And watch his slumbers
calm and deep: / Oh Freedom give us rest!" Harper's twinning of family
and freedom would be a hallmark of her writing. She championed Black
soldiers fighting for their freedom, musing how the slave who had long been a
"despised and trampled on pariah" had become a "useful ally to the American

HARRIET TUBMAN.

FIG. I.2 John G. Darby, "Harriet Tubman." This woodcut illustration, used as the frontispiece in Tubman's postwar biography,
suggests the changes underway during the Civil War era. Tubman,
a "Moses of her people," demonstrated not merely loyalty but "heroism . . . rarely possessed by those in any station of life." From Sarah
Hopkins Bradford, *Scenes in the Life of Harriet Tubman* (1869).
Courtesy of the Henry E. Huntington Library.

government." How could that not lead to radical postwar transformation, a
"higher form of republicanism and a purer type of democracy"?[14]

Harper was joined by other Black women working to align racial advancement with the wartime rhetoric of an emancipated democracy. Mary
Shadd Cary, a pioneer Black editor who had moved to Canada, repatriated
to the United States and undertook the patriotic recruitment of Black men

to Union armies, an effort that also attracted Sojourner Truth. Abolitionist orator Sarah Parker Remond, who had embarked with Samuel J. May on a lecture tour in Britain in 1858, remained abroad but tracked American progress with a new intensity, as she explained the stakes of the conflict to British audiences eager for instruction. As women of color remained engaged with the democratic remodeling of nation and family across the next several decades, new images and ideas reverberated across published opinion. Truth continued to take special care curating her public image in photography, and Harper also soon appeared in image as well as word. In one of the earliest such depictions of a Black female author, she faced out from the page, as discussion turned from dismantling the aristocracy of skin to the lingering aristocracies of male privilege.[15]

And then there was Harriet Tubman, whose daring exploits as a military scout catapulted her to national fame in 1863. The scope of change in these years was immediately evident in the "spirited wood-cut likeness" that became a long-time favorite of hers. Gazing resolutely in the distance wearing a dress and a kerchief, Tubman stood gripping a resting rifle with both hands and military tents behind her. As one of the most arresting images of the period, it raised questions about what role a woman like Tubman might play in what had the potential to be a wholly new postwar order.[16]

If Tubman could wield a gun, might she also cast a ballot? The portrait, which circulated during Reconstruction, recalled the wartime displays of loyalty and heroism that made 1863 one of the most consequential years in US history. Interrelated events served to catalyze new questions about the categories of person, citizen, voter, and spouse. Through the transformative power of war, any chance of considering the woman question as a tilting at windmills, as Charles Nordhoff had, was gone. Grappling with self-government in general and women's self-governance in particular would be crucial aspects of the democratic republic's second founding.

PART II

Woman Questions, Democracy Questions

4

Amending Democracy

WITH VICTORY IN war, Americans saved democracy and began a longer
effort to reshape it. A second founding radically altered how the Constitution
situated each individual in a republic that had mobilized to suppress a rebellion and establish universal freedom. By the end of 1865, slavery's affront
to self-government ended when a Thirteenth Amendment was ratified.
A Fourteenth Amendment in 1868 conveyed the rights of equal citizenship
to all persons born within the limits of the country, regardless of race, sex,
or condition. A series of ambiguities about what citizenship did and did not
entail would be worked out over decades of struggle. In the shorter term, political enfranchisement, the subject of the Fifteenth Amendment enacted in
1870, would prove the thorniest Reconstruction question to work through.
The precise relationship between citizenship and voting had rarely been
addressed at the national level prior to 1865. For the next decade it loomed
as one of the largest questions the country faced. Whether to invest women
with the ballot and make them partners in the collective project of American
self-government became an all-important consideration.

The sweep of democratic change after the war was a predominant concern
of commentators across a wide range of venues and of activists who had pushed
for women's enfranchisement in the 1850s. The work of actually implementing
a new order fell to Republican officeholders, whose governing Congressional
majority equipped them with enormous power. Pressing challenges drove their
actions, and their key achievements were devised as part of the effort to bring
the defeated Confederate states back into the Union. To the dismay of those
movement figures urging a consistent application of principle, expansion of
the franchise was uneven, driven by the imperatives of disloyalty and emancipation. The perilous situation of the freedmen, as they faced rebellious white
Southerners, led to Black men's inclusion in the electorate. No comparable

gains were won by women, whose enfranchisement seemed to lawmakers to further no pressing objective. Democratic participation remained a male preserve across a period when possibilities seemed endless. In making expediency rather than consistency the basis of policy, Reconstruction leaders fell short of establishing a nationally protected right to vote. That limitation, the period's gravest constitutional flaw, has had implications that persist to our own day.

The roiling and cacophonous public discussion of postwar voting rights ranged across genre and revealed a wide array of viewpoints. The most dramatic and novel feature was the sustained engagement of nonwhite women in pursuing what Frances Ellen Watkins Harper termed "a higher form of republicanism and a purer type of democracy."[1] Harper's vision of the interlocked challenges of self-governance emerged as the major theme of the postwar flood of poetry, fiction, and oratory that established her as a vital cultural voice. Speaking to the particular circumstances of those who had suffered from antebellum bondage or caste, she warned that the overthrow of "slavery, as an institution" needed to be accompanied by an assault on "slavery, as an idea." Ratification of the Fifteenth Amendment was undisputedly necessary, Harper asserted, but it alone would be insufficient to establish a nation committed to the self-government of all its people. In staking out that ground, Harper occasionally criticized white women and Black men alike. Her vision embraced progress and principle and conveyed how America's democratic destiny would be achieved only if all lived up to a heightened set of expectations about educative self-rule.[2]

Radical constitutional innovation was accompanied by unusually self-conscious efforts to define and explain key provisions of American democracy. The late 1860s witnessed an explosion of what scholars identify as "popular constitutionalism," a phenomenon particularly notable in periods when shifts in organic law come up for broad discussion and debate. The phrase, meant to reveal the spread of constitutional interpretation beyond legislative halls and court houses to direct engagement by "the people," had its counterpart in the "popular political theory" of the second founding. A desire to influence change, or to contain it, fostered a noisy and wide-ranging dialogue among intellectuals and ordinary citizens alike. In the exuberant realm of published opinion, the woman question offered a way to gauge the extent and velocity of democratic change. Two competing conceptual models emerged as Americans debated the disabilities of race and sex. One presumed an "educated suffrage," in which a voter would require some sort of tutelage prior to going to the polls. The alternative, echoing the observations of Tocqueville and others, contemplated an "educative suffrage" that emphasized the stimulative effect of democratic political participation.

The intensity and stakes of Reconstruction-era debates recast the woman question as a collective exercise in democratic self-understanding. The prospect of enfranchising women loomed as Congress wrangled over the basis of the vote in Washington, DC and over competing versions of the Fourteenth and Fifteenth Amendments. The question mobilized proponents for and opponents against various state suffrage referenda. As activist women petitioned Congress for the right to vote, a broad swath of Americans had already begun a consideration of how such demands related to the requirements, purpose, and significance of the vote.[3] Fundamental questions of democratic theory surfaced. Should suffrage automatically accompany citizenship? If not, what should the criteria for enfranchisement be? Was voting a right, a privilege, or a duty? Should it secure self-protection or promote the greater good? Hovering above all was the matter of whether a second founding in the wake of emancipation demanded democratic consistency.

Society Is Once More Resolved into Its Original Elements

Defining citizenship, and sorting out its relationship to the vote, was no small task. It involved all three branches of the federal government as well as the ratification, by three-quarters of the states, of multiple amendments to the Constitution. The US Supreme Court played a crucial role. In fact, the whole era was bookended by two critical cases, both involving plaintiffs from St. Louis. Citizenship and voting were first coupled in the Court's judgment against Dred Scott in 1857. They were then decisively decoupled in 1875 when the same court ruled against Virginia Minor, whose legal strategy attempted to establish that every adult citizen, regardless of sex, was a legitimate voter. Harriet Robinson Scott and at least one of her two daughters were still living in St. Louis when Minor's defeat during the waning years of Reconstruction affirmed that nationally protected suffrage was limited to American men. Even when the Nineteenth Amendment was finally enacted, nearly fifty years later, the access to the franchise of Harriet's female descendants would remain precariously incomplete. Like other Black women across the Jim Crow South, they would be effectively barred from the polls, and from shaping American democracy, for almost another fifty years.[4]

FIG. 4.1 "Eliza and Lizzie, Children of Dred Scott," "Dred Scott," and "His Wife, Harriet." The Scott family story found its way into popular published opinion outlets in the aftermath of the controversial *Dred Scott v. Sandford* (1857) decision. *Frank Leslie's* published an interview, along with woodcut engravings of photographs by John H. Fitzgibbon, of the couple and their two daughters, on the cover. Harriet Robinson Scott had also brought a freedom suit against her owner, but for strategic reasons her case was submerged in that of her husband's. The citizenship and suffrage claims of Black women remained distinct from both those of Black men and white women in these years. From *Frank Leslie's Illustrated Newspaper* (June 27, 1857). Courtesy of Library of Congress, LC-DIG-ds-12470.

A century of partial gains and profound disappointments dramatized the expansiveness and force, as well as the limitations, that marked the late nineteenth-century intertwining of democratic suffrage with the woman question. One can begin that story with the intricacies of the Scotts' own case, which US Chief Justice Roger Taney used to resolve the most profound tensions of American constitutional democracy. His 1857 opinion, justly remembered as among the most notorious in all of US history, asserted that all persons of African descent were excluded from national citizenship. This sweeping assertion applied to the enslaved as well as to the half-million people of color who were nominally free. The logic behind his arranging the distinct categories of unfreedom, race, and citizenship depended on a toxic combination of subtlety and fraud. Taney pointed to Black people's blanket exclusion from voting (in a deeply flawed historical overview) as a way to establish that they had not been, nor could they ever hope to be, citizens. This opinion ignored the glaring implication for the millions of free women, white and Black. The largest class of the country's nonvoters would, by Taney's logic, be stripped of all privileges of American citizenship. Were such an understanding to be widely accepted, all those legal gains of the women's rights movement—especially those that had chipped away at common-law doctrines on a state-by-state basis—would in political terms add up to absolutely nothing.[5]

As it mobilized for war, the Lincoln administration revisited Taney's dubious formula. A specific question about the status of a Black ship captain required Attorney General Edward Bates to consider the basis of citizenship. His opinion, which was widely reprinted in the press, observed the oddity that Americans had never framed "the exact meaning" of the word nor elaborated "the constituent elements of the thing we prize so highly." Replacing historical analysis with an emphasis on wartime fidelity, he set forth an understanding of citizenship that involved a pact between loyal individuals and a government that furnished personal security. An individual's support for the government provided the main criterion, regardless of categorization by race or sex. In a direct rebuke to Taney, Bates's opinion used the example of women as a key part of separating citizenship from voting rights. Privately, he fretted about the dire consequences of stripping nonvoting women of their rights as citizens. Such a move "would be frightful" and "would overturn society—cut off more than half the people from family & inheritance, and destroy the government, by dissolving the reciprocal bond of allegiance & protection."[6]

The wartime recasting of the relationship among freedom, civic standing, and access to the ballot arose in less technical ways across published opinion, where its connection to nonvoting women was generally muted. Much of this public discussion reversed Bates's logic and instead affirmatively coupled the rights of the citizen and the possession of the franchise. Rhetorical power was more important than fine-grained categorical distinctions for a reform community stirred by Frederick Douglass's insistence that the "abolition war" must produce an "abolition peace." Douglass prominently issued that rousing call before Elizabeth Cady Stanton's National Loyal League, a group that at its inception found it intolerable that "all slaves, all citizens of African descent, and all women" lacked a voice in self-government.[7]

Douglass's wartime commitment to a vision of self-government for both sexes as well as all races was initially uncertain. What exactly did he mean when he insisted that a future American republic could become "incomparably better than the old Union" by "making every slave free, and every freeman a voter?" The mounting enrollment of Black male soldiers, whose allegiance furnished an unusually strong rationale for the ballot, led Douglass to discuss extending the franchise in ways that included all loyal men but not any women. His contention that war veterans were especially deserving of enfranchisement reflected a much broader tendency. The *Christian Recorder* was typical in its insistence that the "colored people of the South" deserved to vote "because hundreds and thousands of colored men have spilled their blood for the sake of the Union and universal freedom." The simplicity and force of this argument lent it persuasive power, and it garnered qualified support from Abraham Lincoln after he was reelected in 1864. When Andrew Johnson replaced the assassinated leader, presidential powers passed to a figure who stubbornly clung to limiting democratic rights to white men.[8]

Douglass situated his vision of soldiers becoming voters within a broadly theorized understanding of the significance of democratic participation. His most sustained discussion of the franchise, offered the same month as Lincoln's murder, presented the vote first as an essential tool of self-protection. The ballot was a uniquely effective instrument for freedmen to use in confrontations with Southern whites, who were likely to nurse grievances of battlefield defeat that might manifest in unrelenting oppression and violence. The protective elements of the vote overlapped with an equally crucial view of the franchise as a fundamental badge of citizenship and mode of collective self-assertion. No class of people, Douglass insisted, "without insulting their own nature could be content with any deprivation of their rights." The civic standing that accompanied enfranchisement was particularly important for Black Southern men striving to overcome slavery's degradation.

A third aspect mentioned by Douglass elaborated a social and quasi-psychological understanding of the ballot, one that echoed Tocqueville and Mill. To be denied the elective franchise in a democratic country imposed a "stigma of inferiority" that threatened to become internalized and self-fulfilling, he explained. As social creatures, humans cultivated self-understanding, at least in part, through the views of others. By depriving the freedmen of suffrage, he warned his largely white audience, "you affirm our incapacity to form an intelligent judgment respecting public men and public measures; you declare before the world that we are unfit to exercise the elective franchise, and by this means lead us to undervalue ourselves, to put a low estimate upon ourselves, and to feel that we have no possibilities like other men." All these arguments for enfranchisement might be applied to women as well, and across the 1850s, Douglass had often made that case explicitly. In the altered postwar context, he merely reiterated his longstanding support for women's voting rights while minimizing their relevance to the pressing situation of the freedmen. Setting aside the plight of the freedwomen, he cut off further discussion with the observation that the woman question "rests upon another basis than which our right rests."[9]

Many activists in the early postwar years shared Douglass's understanding of the multiple imperatives of enfranchising Black men. A growing number also extended the logic to argue for women's right to the ballot. "Voting with us is like breathing," Henry Ward Beecher claimed, as he insisted that democratic citizenship for any person was lifeless if not accompanied by participation in electoral politics. The AME's *Christian Recorder* quoted Beecher approvingly and predicted that "however far off we may be from universal suffrage, the civilized world is traveling thenceforward." "Universal suffrage"—stripped of its "male" qualifier—was a providential and "universal tendency." *Harper's Weekly* editor George William Curtis agreed, maintaining that the civil rights of Black men and women of all races would be "a mere mocking name until political power gave them substance."[10] Faith in the universalizing tendency of political participation to elevate and uplift regardless of color or sex produced a new organizational initiative, aimed at enfranchising freed people of both sexes alongside all adult free-born women. The vehicle for this integrated campaign was the American Equal Rights Association (AERA), launched in May 1866. Its founders sought to end the organizational segmentation of antislavery and women's rights activists and to pursue an ambitious agenda, framed in terms of the soaring hopes expressed by women's rights conventions of the 1850s. The new association announced its formation by proclaiming:

By the war, society is once more resolved into its original elements, and in the reconstruction of our government we again stand face to face with the broad question of natural rights, all associations based on special claims for special classes are too narrow and partial for the hour; therefore from the baptism of this second revolution—purified and exalted through suffering—seeing with a holier vision that the peace, prosperity and perpetuity of the Republic rests on EQUAL RIGHTS FOR ALL, we . . . bury the woman in the citizen, and our organization in that of the American Equal Rights Association.[11]

As the self-conscious inheritor of the antebellum convention movement, the association made the right of suffrage the first of eight constituting articles, clarifying the centrality of the vote for all the group's subsequent actions. This initiative built on a recently launched petition campaign demanding a suffrage that would universalize democratic rights and which represented the first appeal in US history for Congress to invest women with political power. Lamenting how the "partial application" of core aspects of self-government would result in "a discontented people," this petition appealed to the Constitution's guarantee that all states possess a "Republican form of Government." On behalf of "one half the entire population of the country," the petitioners urged Congress to "legislate hereafter for persons, citizens, taxpayers, and not for class or caste."[12]

It would fall to Republicans in Congress, not activists, to determine if voting rights followed citizenship in the newly reunited nation. Until 1867, the case for suffrage expansion of any kind was stymied by a combination of presidential opposition, the wavering of some Republicans, and a focus on establishing impartial birthright citizenship by passing the Fourteenth Amendment. It would be up to the 40th Congress, with its comfortable veto-proof majorities, to pursue a sweeping program of Radical Reconstruction over the objections of Andrew Johnson. Republicans united despite the mounting anxiety of moderates as they watched white male voters reject Black suffrage in all but two of the eleven state referenda on the issue. Skittishness about Black suffrage's unpopularity in the North was overcome by the urgency of a parallel initiative—one that imagined how the votes of the freedmen in the unreconstructed states could be a counterweight to white Southern political power.

A complicated constitutional feature of the first founding (the three-fifths compromise) had produced an anomaly and then helped to achieve a breakthrough during Reconstruction, in a high-stakes maneuver to create a loyal bloc of enfranchised Black Southern men. States whose treason had prompted emancipation stood to increase their national power, since the freed but still disfranchised African Americans in their states would count fully rather than at the constitutionally compromised rate of three-fifths of free inhabitants. This calculus inspired Congress to undertake two measures that neutralized the recalcitrance of former Confederates by opening the polls to Black men, while at the same time requiring loyalty oaths from Southern whites. The first and more convoluted initiative, inserted into Section 2 of the Fourteenth Amendment, introduced a new formula that would reduce a state's representation proportionally for all "male inhabitants" (over the age of twenty-one and citizens) who were denied the right to vote. States faced no penalty for restricting the suffrage of other categories of inhabitants. Those who were under twenty-one, lacked US citizenship, participated in the rebellion, or were not male could be denied the vote in ways that would not diminish a state's allotment of power.[13]

The second Congressional initiative undertaken ironically made the relevance of Section 2 obsolete by the time of its ratification. Congress undertook a more direct route to Black (male) voting in the Reconstruction Acts of early 1867. These acts established territorial governments across the former Confederacy and required new state constitutions to be framed through the participation of all men, regardless of race. The prevalence of the army, and the paramilitary nature of Southern political contests for several years thereafter, amplified the wartime connections between male voting and male capacity to provide military defense to the government. Simply put, the intertwining of ballots and bullets would continue to be a feature of Southern politics long after the disbanding of the Confederate military.[14]

Educated or Educative?

The convoluted voting measures of the Fourteenth Amendment stirred a furious response from women's rights activists, who had warned from the outset against solidifying an "aristocracy of sex" through partial measures. Having already assailed sex-specific language in state constitutions, they were understandably horrified to see the word "male" introduced for the first time into the federal Constitution. Stanton feared such an introduction would "take a century at least" to overcome. Outrage rippled through the reform community immediately. Bostonian Caroline Dall fired off exasperated missives to Senator Charles Sumner, complaining that Republicans had not simply fallen short of pushing for truly universal suffrage but had raised new hurdles to the achievement of this goal. She vowed to petition "here in Massachusetts against the erection of any new barrier of color, race, or sex."[15] But where principle and political calculation had combined to nudge enough Congressional Republicans toward the enfranchisement of Black men, no such clear imperative existed for women. Pleas for that version of a "consistent democracy" made little political headway in the late 1860s.

The Republican Party's growing emphasis on a race-neutral manhood suffrage notoriously split the activist community in ways that recalled the 1840 abolitionist schism over the "woman question."[16] A surface unity initially prevailed as a result of shared disappointment over the Fourteenth Amendment's voting provision. Some criticized the absence of any affirmative voting rights for citizens, while others denounced the amendment's reliance on the "male" terminology. The failure of state suffrage referenda campaigns in New York and Kansas in 1867 exposed a rift, however, and soon a dynamic emerged that pitted the interests of (white) women against those of the (male) "Negro." Heated rhetoric escalated with the 1868 launching of the *Revolution*, a weekly journal based in New York City and edited by Susan B. Anthony, Elizabeth Cady Stanton, and Parker Pillsbury. In derogatory asides that became increasingly ugly, this editorial trio dwelt upon the supposed "ignorance" and "barbarism" of nonwhite male voters compared to "Saxon" women. Uttering scornful comments about "Sambo" within reform meetings was bad enough, but such remarks aligned with the main themes of a racist presidential campaign by the Democratic Party in 1868. Anti-Black opinions eclipsed Stanton's earlier attacks that had included dismissive reference to "Patrick, Hans, and Yung Tung" (her personification of "unqualified" Irish, German, and Chinese men) who had no right to rule over her and other women.[17]

Movement activists were particularly outraged because the moment seemed so fortuitous, abroad as well as at home. The British Parliament seriously debated enfranchising women in 1866–1867, as it hammered out the Second Reform Bill. None other than John Stuart Mill, who had been elected to Parliament in 1865, presented a petition (signed by nearly 1,500 women) and then introduced an amendment that would strike the word "male" from the proposed bill and replace it with "person," thus enfranchising women who otherwise met the criteria (i.e., propertied single or widowed women). To American observers, this was a noteworthy development. Mill's stature had soared during the war, when two important articles and a steady stream of public letters established him as the most prominent Briton to back the Union cause. He was lauded across newspapers and magazines, and his authority working in a querist mode caught the attention of journalists, political figures, and reformers alike.[18] His election had enhanced his reputation. Mill's "amendment speech" delivered on May 20, 1867, reprinted as a pamphlet, became a canonical tract among women's rights activists. George William Curtis quoted heavily from Mill in framing his own argument for women's suffrage at the 1867 New York State constitutional convention as part of an Anglo-American effort. Defeat in both London and Albany did not dampen the optimism of reformers. For his part, Mill confided to an American correspondent that the Parliamentary vote had provoked "thought and discussion . . . in quarters where the subject had never been thought of before." The simple fact of raising the measure lent "an immense impulse to the question."[19]

Expectations were high as Congress set its sights on passage of a "suffrage amendment," after Ulysses S. Grant won an overheated presidential contest. Representative George W. Julian emerged as one of the most important voices for a consistent democracy where all adult citizens were voters. Having been persuaded by women's political claims from his reading of Harriet Martineau decades earlier, the Indiana Republican became an official member of the AERA and regularly pressed to include women as voters in a reconstituted democracy. The expansion of Black voting in Washington, DC, in the territories, and in the new state of Nebraska provided him opportunities to promote universal suffrage, but his boldest and most direct advocacy came when he proposed an amendment that declared "the right of suffrage in the United States shall be based on citizenship," without "any distinction or discrimination whatever founded on race, color, or sex."[20] When that sweeping formulation foundered, discussion turned instead on whether educational tests should be prohibited or allowed as long as applied "impartially," or without racial distinction.

The debate over prioritizing either Black men's or white women's political rights revealed a disagreement—partly opportunistic, partly philosophical—about the relationship between education and democracy. The *Revolution* had already made the case for "*educated* suffrage, irrespective of sex or color." Anthony summed up this view by insisting that "if you will not give the whole loaf of justice and suffrage to an entire people, give it to the most intelligent first." Other activists denounced "educated suffrage"—which they saw as a ready excuse for delaying the enfranchisement of former slaves—as divisive sloganeering. Fiery orator Stephen Foster declared himself "an enemy of educated suffrage, as an enemy of white suffrage, as an enemy of man suffrage, as an enemy of every kind of suffrage except universal suffrage." Foster's comments

stressed the educative uplift of the vote rather than the educated restrictive-
ness that used disqualifying tests to shrink the size of the electorate.[21]

Educat*ed* or educat*ive* suffrage? This seemingly small adjectival shift
hinted at two different visions of democratic citizenship, revealing longstanding ambiguities of how self-government should work in practice. Most
nineteenth-century advocates of popular government took the notion of
an "informed citizenry" for granted (even if what precisely constituted "informed" remained murky). The alternative—an ignorant or uninformed
citizenry—represented one of the most persistent fears about popular rule.
But emancipation had exacerbated older anxieties over race, ethnicity,
and class. In this new context, many Americans seized on "education" as
a proxy for "white" and "middle class." Advocates of "educated," "equal,"
or "impartial" suffrage in the 1860s explicitly offered these formulations as
alternatives to "universal suffrage." They accepted restrictions on voting,
such as tax-paying or literacy or education, so long as these were applied to
all adult male citizens. Anthony and others sought to extend this logic to
make the inclusion of educated women in the electorate the country's top
priority.[22]

What for analytical purposes we might term "educat*ive* suffrage" instead
emphasized the elevating and improving impact the franchise had on individual citizens. For readers of Tocqueville and Mill, it was an inescapable contention that one of the "greatest advantages of democracy" over other forms
of government was its broadening of citizens' perspectives when they were active and engaged. This proposition rested on the belief that self-government
provided its own education, and that no other special preparation was therefore required. It was the same reasoning that set antislavery immediatism
apart from schemes of gradualist emancipation. The editor of the staid *North
American Review* captured the key assumptions of this stance at war's end,
even if he did not spell out how they related to questions of women voters.
"Our war has been carried on for the principles of democracy, and a cardinal
point of those principles is, that the only way in which to fit men for freedom
is to make them free, the only way to teach them how to use political power
is to give it [to] them."[23]

Reformers had drawn powerfully on this understanding of educative suffrage as an argument for women's enfranchisement. As an especially careful
student of Tocqueville and Mill, Wendell Phillips had argued even before the
war that "if woman has a direct share in the government, that very responsibility will educate her. Responsibilities educate, not books, nor schools,
nor academies." Henry Ward Beecher insisted at the 1866 National Woman's

Rights Convention that "voting teaches," and "the vote is a schoolmaster." Phillips and Beecher retained a bias against immigrants, especially Irish ones, but their theory of educative suffrage nonetheless pushed them to imagine how universal suffrage might include even "ignorant foreigners" and the "wild rabble" coming to American shores. Through political participation— and not some abstract course of study—such newcomers would adopt the habits and practices of democracy and do so "ten times quicker when the responsibility of knowing these things is laid upon them." Surely, Phillips and others argued, the same was true for women.[24]

Even though "educative suffrage" functioned as an argument for democratic inclusion, the emphasis on education could at times risk confusion. This risk became apparent on the floor of Congress when Julian invoked Mill in support of his universal suffrage amendment. A brief exchange with future president James Garfield ensued, as the Ohio Republican tried to pin down whether Mill had made "ordinary wisdom" or the demonstration of literacy and numeracy the basis for enfranchisement. Garfield's call for clarification was understandable. Mill's writings on representative government had maintained both that the vote in and of itself was educative and that it must rest on some baseline educational achievement. Uncertainty about the precise significance of education would become a staple of suffrage debates for decades.[25]

In the end, the narrow version of the Fifteenth Amendment that was enacted only barred states from using "race, color, or previous condition of servitude" to determine qualifications for the ballot. A range of other restrictive measures—literacy, poll taxes, pauperism—would continue to pass constitutional muster, and the default assumption was that incapacity (however defined) would result in disfranchisement. Any lingering possibility of aligning the voting rights of women with those of African American men was dashed by the state-by-state ratification of process, a prolonged campaign completed in March of 1870. Stanton further damaged her already tarnished reputation when she opposed a measure she warned would "culminate in fearful outrages on womanhood, especially in the southern states." That incendiary appeal was only the loudest of her coded echoes of Democrats' ongoing fixation on the supposed threat of Black men. This language unfortunately overshadowed Stanton's powerful deployment of the charge that American democracy, now more than ever, was an "aristocracy of sex." An organizational split that surprised no one came when the AERA disbanded in 1869. At that juncture, two suffrage organizations emerged as fierce rivals that would only be reconciled, with lingering tensions, in 1890.[26]

Observing developments an ocean away from the political turmoil, Mill called for women to take their case directly to the people in broad-based appeals to principle. He felt certain that "the late glorious struggle" had convinced Americans that "the principles of your democratic institutions are not mere phrases but are meant to be believed and acted upon towards all persons." All that was needed now was "a sufficiently large number" of women to unite and demand the democratic political equality "which is now refused to no one else." He evaded Stanton's overtures as the rival organizations became embittered toward one another. But he was especially impressed by the efforts of Stanton-aligned Isabella Beecher Hooker, who had only recently read and become an admirer of Taylor Mill's 1851 "Enfranchisement of Women," and expressed approval of *The Woman's Journal*, started by those opposed to Stanton and Anthony. That organ had scored a coup by enlisting the renowned Julia Ward Howe, who early in 1869 was hailed by one New York periodical as "the most cultured woman who has yet taken ground publicly in American in favor of suffrage for women."[27]

Is It Not the Negro Woman's Hour Also?

In May 1866, as the new American Equal Rights Association hammered out its constitution, seventy-three-year-old Lucretia Mott called for a generational passing of the torch. "It is no loss, but the proper order of things, that the mothers should depart and give place to the children," she explained, and she then singled out two up-and-coming reformers by name. One was a thirty-year-old editor named Theodore Tilton. The other was African American poet and orator Frances Ellen Watkins Harper. It was not simply Harper's age that suggested she was the future of women's rights activism. She had after all only been born a decade after Elizabeth Cady Stanton and had already been a teacher, a lecturer, a wife, a stepmother, a mother, and a widow. Her novelty in 1866 resulted from a rousing speech she had delivered just before Mott hailed her prospects for the future. This performance, the most famous of Harper's long career, laid out the disabilities of both race and sex with a thoroughness and style that captured listeners' attention. As the first major convention address by a Black woman since the early 1850s, the speech appeared to be the sign of things to come.[28]

Harper's expansive view of democratic citizenship drew from her lived experience but also from her reading, as her nineteenth-century biographer conveys, of the "elaborate works" of "De Tocqueville, Mill," and others. The speech that so impressed Mott never directly invoked either author, but

Harper's underlying political assumptions at times echoed both. The stories she told about her own personal struggles gave visceral force to her ideas. Her inability to protect property in Ohio as a widowed woman in 1864 had been just as infuriating as her difficulty riding streetcars in Philadelphia as a "colored" person. The first showed that "as long as woman is unequal before the law," justice was partial. The second led her to warn her fellow citizens that a society could not "trample on the weakest and feeblest of its members without receiving the curse in its own soul." Pressing Black people down for two centuries had "crippled the moral strength" of the entire country. She hoped Americans would heed this warning and work to achieve "the loftiest manhood and womanhood that humanity can attain" via democratic equality in both local law and in a new constitutional basis for citizenship and suffrage. If Americans were to apply their noble principles on a consistent basis, they had to acknowledge what united them, even in the wake of a bitter civil war. "We are all bound up together," she reminded her listeners, "in one great bundle of humanity."[29]

Harper used this 1866 speech to establish a position distinct from the majority in her audience. "You white women speak here of rights," she said, while "I speak of wrongs." Her advocacy of universal suffrage departed from that of white women in what she saw as their fixation on a supposed panacea. Enfranchising white women would not "cure all the ills of life" for the simple reason that women were not angels but, like men, were divided into the good, the bad, and the indifferent. Harper did not consider the vote a cure-all. She considered it as merely an initial step toward progress that might allow some white women to overcome their indifference to the plight of Black women. "Talk of giving women the ballot box?" she asked. "Go on. It is a normal school, and the white women of this country need it." In this curious phrasing (the ballot box as "normal school," or teacher-training college), Harper embraced a notion of "educative suffrage" and expressed the hope that white women might benefit from its perspective-expanding impact. To become voters might help to lift them out of their "airy nothing and selfishness."[30]

A year after Harper differentiated the plight of Black and white women to the AERA, Sojourner Truth appeared before the same group to explain the divergent interests of Black women and Black men. With Harper on a tour among the freed people in South Carolina and Georgia, Truth imagined herself as "about the only colored woman that goes about to speak for the rights of the colored woman." She conjured up the spectacle of formerly enslaved men becoming "masters over the women," and she expressed grave

reservations about Black women's unequal treatment in courts, in the disparate wages they earned, and in their vulnerability to those men who sought
to take their money and then expected them to cook all their meals. "I want
to keep the thing stirring, now that the ice is cracked," Truth commented,
as she championed the freedwomen's cause. Her association of the freedmen
with patriarchal tyranny within their households was given a racist slant by
Frances Gage, who depicted men "not yet a hundred years removed from the
barbarism of Africa" having learned the arts of oppression from their former
masters. Gage recounted first-hand observation of marriages forced on
freedwomen by military officials in the Sea Islands. These instances revealed
vulnerabilities that would only grow more dire if Black husbands were given
political power and Black wives left without the vote.[31]

As Black women, Harper and Truth could dissect and interrogate the
terms of Reconstruction-era debate more easily than they could change them.
Even the activists moved by their dual performances seemed resistant to their
essential point: that Black women occupied a distinctive place and had strong
grounds for the self-protection—from Black men as well as white men and
women—that possession of the ballot could help provide. A core group continued to insist that Reconstruction was "the Negro's hour," and by that phrase
gave priority to the enfranchisement of Black men through a program of "impartially applied" manhood suffrage. Those who spoke for "women" had a
countervailing tendency to speak about "educated" mothers and wives who
were better equipped to use the ballot than those long degraded by slavery.
If the first group saw all Black persons as men, the latter saw all women as
white. In the case of Stanton and Anthony, the elevation of "woman" over
"the negro" all too often degenerated into race-baiting imagery. The stubborn
persistence of categories that erased them frustrated Black women, especially
as it forced them, at least in the narrow context of activist strategies, to choose
sides.[32]

Though she never wavered in her commitment to women's rights,
Harper's willingness to choose "race over sex" determined how she allotted
her time and whom she hoped to influence. While some reformers worked
to sway the votes of white men in the New York and Kansas referenda, she
instead reached out to newly freed Black communities in the South, which
she considered to be the "great theater for the colored man's development
and progress." She had been a print presence in those communities early on,
with five of her poems being included in Lydia Maria Child's *The Freedmen's
Book* (1865), a volume that sought to offer "strength and courage" to recently
emancipated people and to provide a "true record of what colored men have

accomplished, under great difficulties." Her poems celebrated emancipation, Christianity, and family. Her verse lauding how "the humblest home, with children/ is rich with precious gems" conveyed the centrality of domesticity to her vision of a fully reconstructed, democratic America.[33]

Harper became a Southern presence not just on the page but in corporeal form, as she undertook arduous and dangerous travels to nearly every Southern state during the early years of peace. Speaking to white and Black audiences in churches and schools, and in legislative halls and lowly cabins, she preached a message that embraced both national healing and racial equality. A reconciliation that increased "the privileges of one class" and curtailed "the rights of the other," she warned, would be no reconciliation at all.[34] The poetry she composed in this period offered didactic instructions about "clean" voting, with the character of "Aunt Chloe" haranguing Black men not to sell their votes as if these were individual possessions. Political power gained by men was a resource to be used for the good of communities, an understanding that made the ballot a collective as much as an individual right. Harper's emphasis worked to rebut a national racist discourse about freed people's excessive investment in politics and their susceptibility to fraud and manipulation. Former Confederate Eliza Francis Andrews rehearsed this charge in her reports about the "demoralizing influences" of Georgia elections held in 1867. She closed her account, written for the *New York World*, by derisively imagining the consequences of enfranchising both sexes of the formerly enslaved. The Radicals erred, she wrote, in not bestowing "the right of suffrage on negro women for they will always be cheap instruments, even after the men become too wise to be managed with cocks and bulls." By offering up nothing more than the gift of "a red silk parasol," Andrews claimed, votes could be purchased "from the most respectable old 'mammy' down to the rawest Dinah in the cornfield."[35]

Harper's understanding of postwar self-governance ventured beyond the electoral process, and broader themes mark both her Southern outreach and the fiction that resulted from her experiences among the newly liberated. The full development and flourishing of every "soul" made an enriching domestic environment and schooling as critical to emerging democratic norms as involvement in Reconstruction politics. Her analysis did not absolve Black men when they fell short of what they could be, but she placed greater confidence in their ability to improve than had Sojourner Truth. Insisting that the freedman needed "something more than a vote in his hand," she emphasized the value of "a home life" and "the marriage relation." Harper's aims differed from domestic writers she may seem to have superficially echoed. Like

Harriet Martineau, she viewed marriage as a force for the improvement of selves and society only when properly constituted. Hence, as she toured the South, she wrote a correspondent from Georgia in 1870 about the time she spent meeting privately with the freedwomen to "talk with them about their daughters" and to urge them to realize that "now is the time for our women to begin to try to lift up their heads and plant the roots of progress under the hearthstone." Some of her time, she added, was spent "preaching against men ill-treating their wives."[36]

A proper understanding of marriage had shaped Harper's fiction even before the war. Her very first effort—the short story "The Two Offers" (1859), which she published in the *Anglo-African*—depicted the contrasting choices of two cousins. Laura represents the shallow young woman who marries for the wrong reasons, dreading the "risk of being an old maid" more than a loveless marriage, while her cousin Janette embodies a more thoughtful approach to both love and vocation. The "offer" Laura accepts turns out badly; her husband viewed marriage not as a site "for the soul's development and human progression" but only as a "title-deed that gave him possession of the woman he thought he loved." This marriage represented "no affinity of minds, no intercommunion of souls," a fact that leaves Laura devastated. Janette, by contrast, from an early age learned the importance of autonomy and that the "true aim of female education," like male education, was the development of "all the faculties of the human soul." Watching her suffering cousin bolstered her conviction that "life was not given her to be frittered away in nonsense or wasted in trifling pursuits." She became "an old maid" but she found fulfillment in her writing and reform work, committing to antislavery and other "unpopular" but not "unrighteous" causes.[37]

A Harper novel serialized by the *Christian Recorder* across 1869 intertwined another depiction of marriage with a critique of the inadequacies of Reconstruction, then nearing its culmination. *Minnie's Sacrifice* generated considerable publicity in a paper that sought to add the formerly enslaved to its original audience of Northern free Blacks. The story followed two young, mixed-race people born in the South but raised and educated as white people in the North. As war breaks out, Louis and Minnie each discover their mixed-race origins; they are both the progeny of enslaved mothers and slaveholding fathers. They return home and dedicate themselves to aiding the newly freed people in creating a better civilization in the South.

Harper's characters rehearse crucial public debates from the era, and their dialogue often repeats lines drawn from the author's actual speeches. Thus, Minnie works with the freedwomen, teaching them more than "mere knowledge of books" and urging them to "plant the roots of progress under the hearthstone." Louis attends political meetings and encourages the freedmen to use their votes "not to express the old hates and animosities of the plantation but the new community of interests arising from freedom." He brings Minnie a newspaper reporting how Northern whites in "state after state" had voted down Black suffrage, because freedmen were supposedly "too ignorant to vote," thereby emboldening the Rebels in their own intransigence. Minnie concedes that the freedmen may lack schooling, but "they knew more than their masters" during the war, "for they knew how to be true to their country, when their masters were false to it." Louis agrees, imagining a future when "the Anglo Saxon race will blush to remember that when they were trailing the banner of freedom in the dust, black men were grasping it with earnest hands, bearing it aloft amid persecution, pain, and death."[38]

Through the fictional Minnie, Harper rendered Black women visible and held Black men accountable. As the couple discuss Southern politics, Minnie expresses her qualms that the nation was making "one great mistake" in approaching democratic reform in too limited and "partial" a manner by not enfranchising women as well as men. When Louis responds with the by-then familiar refrain "this hour belongs to the negro," Minnie asks him, "Is it not the negro woman's hour also? Has she not as many rights and claims as the negro man?" Louis expresses some ambivalence about having a wife exposed to the "rough and brawling" mobs at the polls and also some surprise that Minnie was "such an advocate for women's voting." To his admission that he did not realize she was "a strong-minded woman," Minnie states, "Surely, you would not have me a weak-minded woman in these hours of trial?"

Though she affirms her unwavering support for Black manhood suffrage, Minnie doubts the Black man had any meaningful reciprocal commitment to women's suffrage. "I know that he would vote against me as soon as he gets his vote," she confides. Adamant that a woman should have "power to defend herself from oppression, and equal laws as if she were a man," Harper has Minnie declare how broadly inclusive political participation was the safest and most just embodiment of democratic values. "Basing our rights on the ground of our common humanity is the only true foundation for national peace and durability. If you would have the government strong and enduring, you should entrench it in the hearts of both the men and women of the land." Louis voices his agreement, and they move on. In narrating these long conversations between husband and wife, Harper provides scenes from an appropriate and mutually improving marriage. Each partner supports but also challenges the other to clarify and live up to their ideals through "evenings . . . enlivened by pleasant and interesting conversations upon the topics of the day."[39]

Harper's view of Black women and men together contributing to a new era of democracy was echoed in one of several prints commemorating the Fifteenth Amendment in 1870. But only one. These lavishly colored items, ready for display in the parlor, memorialized the achievement of national Black suffrage and joined the mass-marketed illustrated scenes sold by the thousands to an audience of veterans and their families. A central collective image of the Black community marching in celebration was surrounded in these lithographs by vignettes depicting "the rise and progress of the African race in America." Men predominated in prints laden with scenes of military service, schools, and voting, all depicted as male.[40] *The Fifteenth Amendment*, illustrated by James C. Beard, differed in its series of surrounding vignettes that portrayed Black women as both contributors to and beneficiaries of ongoing Black progress. The schoolroom image features a Black woman instructing a classroom of boys and girls, with the caption "Education Will Prove the Equality of the Races." Another scene highlights the importance of marriage to notions of freedom in a wedding ceremony with the caption "Liberty Protects the Marriage Altar." A third vignette captioned "Freedom Unites the Family Circle" echoes domestic literature on the nurturing home embraced as a middle-class ideal.

This was far from an image of equal political participation. The women are confined to the traditional roles of education, marriage, and motherhood, while the two vignettes dedicated to politics—one of voting and one of holding office—show only men. But reading this image through the lens of Harper's work, as well as recent historical scholarship, suggests more expansive possibilities. While women are absent from formal political participation in the reconstructing Southern states, they were partners in African American communal representation and advancement. The captions under the political vignettes read "The Ballot Box Is Open to Us" and "Our Representative Sits in the National Legislature." Those pronouns can be read narrowly as referring to men or expansively as referring to the whole community of newly freedmen and freedwomen.[41]

FIG. 4.2 James Beard, "Education Will Prove the Equality of the Races," detail from *The Fifteenth Amendment*. Like many lithographs celebrating the ratification of the Fifteenth Amendment, this one centered Black soldiers and white and Black political leaders. Unlike the others, however, it did not erase the contributions of Black women from the story of Black freedom. Women were featured in three of the surrounding vignettes as teachers, wives, and mothers. Courtesy of the Henry E. Huntington Library.

To Prevent . . . the Country From Running into Foolish and Fanatical Extremes

As Harper struggled to keep Black women visible, discussions of citizenship and suffrage continued to flood published opinion in the late 1860s. The war had made the country's fundamental principles a matter of prolonged debate, and as Elizabeth Cady Stanton recalled later, those debates occurred not just in "Congress and state legislatures," but "in the pulpits and public journals, and at every fireside." So all-consuming was this "momentous question," George Julian claimed later, that even "our little boys and girls caught the contagion" of interest and seemed poised to surpass their fathers and mothers in their "knowledge of the fundamental principles of free government and the rights and duties of the citizen."[42] Popular children's magazine *The Youth's Companion* agreed. It published nearly a dozen articles on the subject, all intended "to place political facts before our youthful readers" so that they "begin the acquisition of knowledge early." Surveying British and

American developments in 1870, the Boston-based magazine marveled at the tremendous progress achieved in recent years. Not only had the freedmen been enfranchised—something that would have been unthinkable even a few years earlier—but a "strong effort" was being made to give women "the power to vote." Clearly, "public sentiment" had changed dramatically, and the magazine boldly predicted "still greater changes" in the coming year.[43]

The prospect of continuing change did not thrill all observers. Democratic skepticism appeared across published opinion alongside democratic enthusiasm, a contrast captured in song, image, and word. The spectrum of opinion can be charted in two illustrations, both published in popular illustrated weeklies in 1869, as ratification of the Fifteenth Amendment was before the states. The first image, by Thomas Nast for *Harper's Weekly* and titled "Uncle Sam's Thanksgiving," showed a multi-racial, multicultural group of men, women, and children sitting around a lavish feast with "self-government" and "universal Suffrage" as the table's centerpiece. At this table all were welcome—not just Black Americans but Native Americans and immigrants from across the globe—and, under the approving gazes of Presidents Lincoln, Washington, and Grant, they engaged in cross-generational, multiracial festivities. Nast drew on recognizable stereotypes of various racial and ethnic minorities that would have been familiar to readers of illustrated papers in these years. These could be reductively crude, even if the intent was inclusivity. But what is noteworthy is how centrally self-government and suffrage figured into the national self-conception Nast rendered.[44]

A cartoon that appeared in *Frank Leslie's Illustrated* only a few months earlier presented a starkly contrasting view (figure 4.4). Drawn by the artist "W. D.," this illustration invoked the model Roman matron Cornelia, mother of the Gracchi brothers Tiberius and Gaius, who according to legend had offered a sharp, maternal response to a rich lady displaying her fine jewels. When asked to display her own gems, the modestly adorned Cornelia pointed to her two sons and replied, "these are my jewels." *Frank Leslie's* 1869 version depicted Cornelia as a drunken woman (a "Rum'un") labeled "Universal Suffrage," sitting outside a storefront advertising "gin, rum, brandy." As a caricatured Irish American man looks on, she gestures toward her children/jewels, which are identified as "Female Suffrage" (an angry, spectacles-wearing Susan B. Anthony look-alike, wielding a cudgel labeled with the recently founded women's club Sorosis) and "Negro Suffrage" (a highly caricatured and racialized freedman). The threat of universal suffrage the image conjured relied on the interplay of ethnic, racial, class, and gender stereotypes. An

FIG. 4.3 Thomas Nast, "Uncle Sam's Thanksgiving Dinner." This image captures the height of democratic idealism after the war. Though Nast drew on recognizable racial and ethnic stereotypes, he depicted a multiracial, multicultural collection of people sitting around Uncle Sam's table, where "Self-Government" and "Universal Suffrage" feature prominently. Portraits of presidents Lincoln, Washington, and Grant watch over the proceedings, draped in a banner celebrating the Fifteenth Amendment. An image of Castle Garden (precursor to Ellis Island) is titled "Welcome." That inclusive message is highlighted by slogans in the bottom two corners: "Come One, Come All" and "Free and Equal." From *Harper's Weekly* (November 20, 1869). Courtesy of the Henry E. Huntington Library.

already overly broad and degraded electorate, the illustration suggested, could only produce undesirable progeny.[45]

Sheet music from the era reveals a similarly divided opinion. John W. Hutchinson, a member of the famous Hutchinson Family Singers, sang as enthusiastically for the cause of voting rights during the 1867 referenda campaign in Kansas as he had earlier for abolition. Finding the "national hymnology" on the topic of suffrage to be "surprisingly deficient," he composed *The Fatherhood of God, and the Brotherhood of Man* (1868), which celebrated the fact that "universal suffrage is spreading thro' the land." One verse imagined "bigots" giving way before a procession of Americans holding banners proclaiming "free suffrage." The following year he penned lyrics specifically about women's enfranchisement, which he dedicated to the Universal Suffrage and Equal Rights Association of Illinois. Appealing directly to the male voters upon whom women's suffrage depended for enactment, *Vote It*

FIG. 4.4 "The Modern Cornelia—A Veritable Rum' Un." As ratification of
the Fifteenth Amendment was before the states, this image depicted "Universal
Suffrage" as a drunken Irish American woman, sitting outside a shop window advertising gin, rum, and brandy. This modern matron proudly points to her two equally
caricatured progeny: "Female Suffrage" and "Negro Suffrage." Black suffrage and
women's suffrage were often used, as in the Kansas referenda campaigns of 1867,
to mutually indict each other. From *Frank Leslie's Illustrated Newspapers* (July 31,
1869). Courtesy of the Henry E. Huntington Library.

Right Along (1869) contemplated a heroic posterity for those men who did
the right thing. "No warrior's wreath of glory shed /A brighter lustre o'er the
head/ Than he who battles selfish pride / And votes with woman side by side."
Another song, composed by the Chicago-based married couple T. Martin

Towne and Belle Kellogg and dedicated to Lydia Maria Child, exulted that the impending "woman's vote shall usher in, The day of Jubilee."[46]

But the idea of enfranchising women also elicited musical ridicule, as seen in the 1867 song *Female Suffrage*—written in the midst of the Kansas referendum and derisively dedicated to Lucy Stone, Susan B. Anthony, Elizabeth Cady Stanton, and George Francis Train. The lyrics upheld women's subordinate status as if it were still the 1830s, informing women that they could "seek for health and riches, and marry at [their] will / But, man must wear the BREECHES, / And rule the household still." R. A. Cohen's verses paired familiar arguments from nature and history: "For nature so designed it / And so our fathers wrote / And clearly they defined it / That man, alone, should vote."[47] The chorus of another sarcastic tune promised to "fix the terrible" (then, alternately, "awful," "dreadful," "wicked") men, but the verses mocked the claims of the middle-class white women it depicted. "Oh, how we suffer, maids and wives / Although our wants very slight," the song began, before deriding women who lived in "queenly style" and spent their husbands' hard-earned money on fine carriages and new dresses. The cover art presented a mixed message (figure 4.5). It depicted a separate "ladies'" voting booth, where a white woman registrar accepts the votes from a queue of middle-class white women. The accompanying children are not neglected and, though the white middle-class men voting at their own window look on with mild surprise, everything appears orderly. And yet the voting booth is plastered with posters that both ridicule and suggest corruption. Signs urging the election of prominent activists for high office share wall space with placards proclaiming "Down with Male Rule" and exhorting women to "vote early and often."

Amidst these debates, various commentators and opinion-makers urged caution. Editorials insisted that while wars thrived on agitation and zeal, the resulting peace required reflection and reason. Not even six months after the Confederate rebellion had been vanquished, the *Christian Examiner* was already wearily (and warily) hoping that by the time "these pages are in print, the popular mind will have returned to reason" on the matter of who should be entrusted with the ballot. A commencement speaker that year urged that no harm, and only good, could come from debating matters with "calmness, candor, and patience," as well as "intelligence, sobriety, modesty, [and] moderation."[48] That "large class of moderate and intelligent thinkers" who represented the mainstream of opinion must band together, a pamphleteer insisted in 1867, identifying himself as "A Republican (not a 'Radical')." Only concerted effort could check the onward rush of "progress" and prevent "the legislation of the country from running into foolish and fanatical extremes."[49]

FIG. 4.5 Cover image from Frank Howard, *We'll Show You When We Come to Vote* (Toledo, 1869). Though the lyrics to the song mock middle-class white women and their supposed discontents, the accompanying illustration conveys jumbled attitudes toward women's enfranchisement. It depicts three well-dressed white women waiting to cast their ballots, in an orderly manner. The signs proclaiming "Down with Male Rule" and promoting the election of various prominent women for office were surely meant to be ridiculous, while the placard urging women to "vote early and often" implied corruption. Courtesy of Library of Congress, Music Division, 2002536758.

As the New York State Constitutional Convention gathered, the political theorist Francis Lieber urged delegates not to "yield to the entreaties" to expand the electorate by enfranchising women, since these were made in "a spirit which happens to be fashionable just now in our restless period." Henrietta

Crosby Ingersoll, though she supported an expanded electorate, similarly worried change was occurring too quickly and indiscriminately. She appealed to moderates to express their dissent immediately "before the tide becomes so strong that protest is of no avail."[50]

Slowing the momentum of radical change required explaining all the fallacies of enthusiasts. A chorus of commentary insisted that the suffrage could not be considered a natural or inherent "right." For whatever the vote was, these writers observed, it was clearly not among those basic human entitlements that applied equally across the adult population. The fact that even a cursory view of the law revealed multiple restrictions on the electorate made this an obvious debate point. Minors, criminals, "lunatics," and noncitizens, as well as women, were barred from voting in nearly every state.[51] The *Christian Examiner* clarified that *civil* rights were fundamental attributes of freedom; they were what made a "man or a woman a citizen." But *political* rights must be considered differently, for these "invested the holder of them with power over the lives and fortunes of his fellow-citizens." The "Republican (not a 'Radical')" even counterposed his own "natural right to be well-governed" to any claim to a "natural right to govern."[52]

Activists and democratic enthusiasts were also chided for believing that political participation was educative. It is "not true," the *Christian Examiner* asserted, that "the ballot educates." This false generalization came from earlier, specific experience of local New England self-government that Tocqueville had described in the 1830s. Perhaps that "most perfect form of democracy," where voters were already educated to a certain degree and where "thought and discussion" preceded actual voting, had elevated and instructed. But this was not the situation in cities where masses of ignorant voters simply did as they were instructed by party leaders. It was a ludicrous fantasy to believe that in this context the mere dropping of a ballot in a box provided any sort of meaningful education for voters. Until a community was already educated, the ballot was "worse than useless"—it was "like an edged tool in a child's hand."[53]

Critics lamented how Americans moved too quickly toward political inclusivity, having already enfranchised in the name of consistency voters who degraded the body politic. Blocking the enfranchisement of women thus became a necessary measure to forestall any further such degradation. Linus P. Brockett, the author of two books on women in the 1860s, urged readers to remember how an earlier generation had succumbed to a "popular and unreasoning clamor" and in a "fit of democratic generosity" had given nearly all white men the vote. Though "prompted by the best of motives," the Fifteenth

Amendment had compounded the danger by injudiciously extending the ballot to all Black men. The line must be drawn at women's enfranchisement, he insisted, especially as no clear political imperative existed for female voters of any race, as it had for Black men. If anything, prospective women's suffrage represented a deeply unpredictable element, which the New York weekly *The Round Table* captured by borrowing a metaphor from the recent anti-reform treatise of Scottish writer Thomas Carlyle and warning against shooting "the Niagara of female suffrage."[54]

Brockett dismissed those who reasoned from consistency either on principle or by arguing that "having swallowed and digested every inch of the [universal suffrage] camel," we need not strain "at the gnat" of women voters. This was faulty reasoning, he thought, as past errors hardly sanctioned future ones. Now was the time to guard against further extension of the franchise, especially as the country faced a "vast influx" of Chinese immigrants of the "lowest class." A crude cartoon in *Punchinello* visually reinforced Brockett's concern. A Black baseball player takes his turn in the "national game," swinging a bat labeled "Fifteenth Amendment." Waiting on deck is a pantaloon-clad white woman, holding a bat marked "Sixteenth Amendment," while behind her stands a Chinese man and an indigenous man from the newly acquired territory of Alaska. Consistency, the image implies, was a foolish imperative.[55]

A protracted exchange in the *Nation* magazine revealed growing anxieties over democratic consistency in the face of what would be an unprecedented enlargement of the electorate. In three lengthy letters across the spring of 1870, James Miller McKim worked through his ambivalence about women's place in American democracy. McKim—who published as "M." from Orange, Connecticut—was a Garrisonian, a Radical, and an original founder of the *Nation*. He wanted to be on the "right" side of progress, but he contemplated the possible extension of voting rights to women with considerable trepidation. He looked to Mill, along with Tocqueville, to help him think through the consequences of so large a suffrage expansion in the United States. These two non-American intellectuals were "the very apostles of democracy" upon whom he and his like-minded cohort had relied "for justification in our bold procedures." He praised Mill as "a tower of strength to the cause of woman everywhere." And yet he recalled Mill's more restrictive comments on the suffrage in *Considerations on Representative Government*, as well as the Englishman's flirtation with measures to strengthen the weight of intelligent voters. McKim gleaned, frustratingly, no clear guidance from his reading of Mill, and he found himself wondering what the Englishman would do "were he here just now, a resident and a citizen."[56]

APRIL 23, 1870.　　　PUNCHINELLO.　　　57

THE GREAT NATIONAL GAME.

OUR COLORED BROTHER. "HI YAH! STAN' BACK DAR; IT'S DIS CHILE'S INNIN'S NOW."

FIG. 4.6 "The Great National Game." This image gave visual force to the fear that constitutional change was moving too fast and too far. In front of a flag-bearing tent labeled "Congress," a caricatured Black baseball player, his belt emblazoned "41st Congress," insists that it is his "innin's now." Next in line is a white woman brandishing a "16th Amendment" bat, followed by a Chinese man and a figure identified as "Alaska." From *Punchinello* (April 28, 1870). Courtesy of the Henry E. Huntington Library.

As McKim puzzled through his own position, Martha Coffin Wright (sister of Lucretia Mott) chided him for not having "kept pace with the history of the times" or with developments on the woman question. She quibbled with his assessment that Black suffrage had meaningfully increased levels of ignorance into the electorate and echoed Frances Harper by asserting that the supposedly "ignorant slaves" knew enough to be loyal to the Union, which many highly educated white Southerners had not. She also expressed confidence that "the schools and press and pulpits of our land" would be sufficient to ensure that the country did not fail once "the principles of republican government" were fully implemented.

But still McKim was uncertain. He believed that Black manhood suffrage in the South had been necessary, and consistency required the same in the North. But women's suffrage seemed to him an uncomfortable leap in the dark, truly a shooting of Niagara. Having "under pressure of necessity" admitted "400,000 ignorant voters at the South," he wrote, we are contemplating further debasing the electorate with the admission of "400,000 more of the same class, still more ignorant, and millions besides all over the country . . . a very larger number of whom are at least as grossly ignorant as the men of the same grade who already burden us." Certainly "a body politic like ours," with its vast educating forces and training facilities, could "take in, and digest" a good deal of "raw material," but there had to be limits. He extended the metaphor, crudely. After a "meal of freedmen and coolies" and an "extra large dessert of European foreigners," the body politic ought to be allowed to rest and breathe a bit before being force-fed anything else. "The gastric solvents of a democratic body are powerful," he concluded, "but they should not be presumed to be miraculous."[57]

A barrage of articles and essays appeared to remind readers that under "our peculiar institutions," an amendment enfranchising women would enfranchise all women, not simply the women readers knew or found virtuous. One pamphleteer urged delegates to the New York State Constitutional Convention to remember that women's suffrage would lead to maids voting alongside their mistresses. "What ignorant and vulgar women, inflamed by drink and unamenable to order and discipline in a degree that no men are," this author shuddered, "will do upon exciting election days, is beyond picturing."[58] This view was vividly captured in one of the twenty-one illustrations included in Brockett's book *Woman: Her Rights, Wrongs, Privileges, and Responsibilities* (1869). The woodcut image conveyed a nightmare vision of "universal suffrage" with working-class Irish and Black women at its very center. The middle-class white men are literally marginalized, off to the side and looking on at an assortment of unsavory voters rendered in visual stereotypes. The illustration, the publisher explained, was included in a "dissuasive spirit," with the hope that "all sensible, thoughtful women" might, upon seeing it, "be led to avoid the danger, and give their powerful influence against it."[59]

WOMEN AT THE POLLS.

FIG. 4.7 "Women at the Polls." This illustration, featuring a rare nineteenth-century depiction of a Black woman at the polls, depicted the writer's nightmare vision of a truly universal suffrage. The motley crew of voters—a shirt-sleeved and smoking Black man, a severe-looking middle-class white woman, Irish and Black working-class women, and some oddly skeletal figures to the left—completely swamps the handful of white middle-class men present and marginalized off to the side. From L. P. Brockett, *Woman: Her Rights, Wrongs, Privileges, and Responsibilities* (1869). Courtesy of the Henry E. Huntington Library.

Brockett and his unnamed illustrator may have conjured this vision from their imagination, but at that moment hundreds of women, Black and white, did in fact head to the polls. Deciding conventions, petitions, and attempts at persuasion had been ineffective, these women voted or attempted to vote in elections across nearly a dozen states between 1868 and 1873. This effort would come to be known as the "New Departure," and it represented popular constitutionalism in action. Its bold and economical argument asserted that women already possessed the right to vote, having been guaranteed citizenship by the Fourteenth Amendment and thus enjoying all the associated "privileges and immunities." New Departure activists held that the right to vote was the "paramount" right and so fell under the Fourteenth Amendment's broad protections (even if the Fifteenth Amendment had made special provision to protect only the voting rights of Black men).[60] In the presidential election of 1872, Susan B. Anthony cast her ballot in Rochester, New York and was subsequently arrested for having voted "illegally." Suffragists had a chance to publicize their claims that voting was a central aspect of democratic citizenship. "Our democratic-republican government," Anthony asserted in a speech delivered repeatedly ahead of her trial, "is based on the idea of the natural right of every individual member thereof to a voice and a vote in making and executing the laws." This interpretation was refuted by the US Attorney for the case, as well as the presiding judge, who found the case so clear-cut that he directed the jury to return the verdict of guilty.[61]

It would be the Supreme Court that would ultimately decide this crucial question about the relationship between women's citizenship and suffrage in the nineteenth century. Virginia Minor, a leading activist in St. Louis, and her husband Francis Minor, a lawyer, sued the country registrar Reese Happersett after Virginia was told in 1872 that she could not register to vote, thus testing the constitutional argumentation on which the New Departure rested. Contending that voting was a fundamental right of national citizenship, the case insisted that the state constitution of Missouri, which limited the suffrage to its male inhabitants, should be overturned. After the Missouri court decided against them, the Minors appealed their case to the United States Supreme Court, which unanimously upheld the lower court's opinion.

Minor v. Happersett (1875) reiterated Attorney General Bates's opinion from 1862 but gave it the force of constitutional law that would ramify in later decisions regarding Black men. While women were clearly citizens, entitled with men to all the "privileges and immunities of citizenship" (as the Fourteenth Amendment guaranteed), voting was *not* one of those privileges and immunities. The opinion more devastatingly concluded that "the Constitution of the United States does not confer the right of suffrage upon anyone." As it pronounced that suffrage was a state and not a national matter, this opinion joined a series of decisions by the Supreme Court that narrowed the potentially expansive meanings of the Fourteenth Amendment. With this route to full political participation foreclosed, the campaign for women's suffrage began a tedious struggle to pass legislation at the state level and continue to lobby Congress to pass the proposed women's suffrage amendment it had discussed in committee but never acted on. Were that to be accomplished, ratification of the necessary three-quarters of the states would then be necessary.[62]

For those uneasy about the major changes of the postwar years, women's suffrage provided a means of slowing the momentum of "progress." It was ultimately the language of order and stability, not that of democratic consistency, that emerged triumphant. Congressional unwillingness to act on women's suffrage and a recalcitrant Supreme Court both reflected and nurtured a decreasing appetite for democratic reform. Such tendencies would continue to grow in the remaining three decades of the century. Recalling the high ideals of the immediate postwar moment and registering how far the country had traveled from them in fewer than ten years, Susan B. Anthony issued a prophetic warning at her trial: "If we once establish the false principle, that United States citizenship does not carry with it the right to vote in every state in this Union, there is no end to the petty freaks and cunning devices that will be resorted to, to exclude one and another class of citizens from the right of suffrage." Declining enthusiasm for consistent democracy and for a robust conception of political participation would not only work against women's suffrage. It would also provide a context in which the Fifteenth Amendment would be unable to preserve even the tenuous biracial aristocracy of sex that would become all white by the dawn of the twentieth century.[63]

5

Reconstructing the Woman Question

ADJUSTMENT OF THE constitutional basis of citizenship and suffrage during US Reconstruction coincided with an international outpouring of published works on the woman question. Between 1865 and 1875, American discussion of women's role in the family, society, the workplace, and the polity was part of a broader transnational consideration that was more robust than ever before. More commentary on the topic appeared across published opinion than any other decade of the nineteenth century. If there was any matter "emphatically to be considered a 'thing of the Day,'" pronounced one magazine in 1870, surely "it is this 'Woman Question.'" Within months of Union triumph, celebrity author Harriet Beecher Stowe anticipated what was to come:

> This question of Woman and her Sphere is now, perhaps, the greatest of the age. We have put Slavery under foot, and with the downfall of Slavery the only obstacle to the success of our great democratic experiment is overthrown, and there seems no limit to the splendid possibilities which it may open before the human race.

Stowe's views about women continued to diverge from those of her sister Catharine Beecher, but the two had come to a shared conviction. American women, in peace no less than in war, would play a pivotal role in determining whether democracy would survive or crumble.[1]

Much of this broader "woman question" discussion of the late 1860s and the early 1870s focused on the white middle-class Unionists who had mobilized in defense of democracy and in opposition to slavery. The most notable of the North's Republican-leading women had taken to the political stump, spoken before Congress, recruited troops, and served as nurses and missionaries across the South. Wartime publicity showered on this politically dominant, and racially and class-specific, subset of the female population carried over into the Reconstruction period. The invisibility of Black women noted by Frances Harper and Sojourner Truth in their speeches to the American Equal Rights Association was replicated in even more pronounced ways in the most widely circulating "woman question" investigations. African American venues for published opinion proliferated during this period, as existing periodicals like the *Christian Recorder* gained new readers and shared space with innovative ventures like the *New National Era* that Frederick Douglass took over in 1870. The literal reconstruction of families was a major preoccupation of such outlets, seen in the novels they serialized and the *Recorder's* "Information Wanted" column that helped freedmen and women locate dispersed family members. And yet freedwomen and free-born women of color were often relegated by nationally circulated books and journals to an aspect of the "Negro question" or the "Southern question."[2]

The more abstract the discussion about the lingering barriers of sex, the less likely nonwhite, non-Protestant, non-middle-class women featured in it. A nativism that carried over from the distrust of immigrants in the 1840s and 1850s also limited who was included in these considerations. The loyalty of Irish newcomers affiliated with the Democratic party had been placed in doubt, and the political alignment between Irish voters and former slaveholders in the wake of the Confederacy tarnished the reputation of each. Little mention was made of immigrant or rebel women in the most circulated explorations of shifting gender norms.[3]

If this era's debates encompassed only a portion of the female population, a widened scope could be found in the regular consideration of trends beyond the United States. The women's rights campaigns of English reformers, which achieved notable success in legal change and discussion of sex-neutral suffrage in these years, recurred as a frequent topic within published opinion (including the Black press). That context helps to explain why John Stuart Mill emerged as an indispensable figure in the decade's interplay of questions about women and self-government. Unlike Tocqueville and Martineau, Mill never crossed the Atlantic to observe American political institutions and social norms first-hand. But a far more effective communications network than existed in the 1830s helped him to become a vital feature of transatlantic discussion of progressive tendencies. Having already established his stature as a thinker, Mill had become the archetypal philosophical statesman during his single term in Parliament (from 1865 to 1868). He interpreted Britain's Second Reform Act and the Fifteenth Amendment as powerful indicators of progress, the momentum of which must now extend to women. Support for women's enfranchisement, he wrote to an American correspondent, was "rapidly becoming a badge of advanced liberalism" in both their countries.[4]

The appearance of Mill's *The Subjection of Women* (1869) became a publishing event. It refocused attention on marriage and the household, even as debates over women's suffrage continued.[5] As countless writers and readers engaged and responded to this philosophical treatise, many seized the opportunity for a sober second thought about the relationship between the household and the polity. These efforts, notably, would be led by women, a group of whom began in the early 1870s to mobilize in opposition to a possible Sixteenth Amendment (prohibiting the use of sex in voting laws) and on behalf of the social order that the currently constituted family provided. Their political theory offered an updated version of Beecher's domesticated democracy—reformed households, shorn of the worst features of coverture, but preserving a measure of hierarchy and subordination deemed necessary to social order. It was a vision that recognized some measure of self-governance among women as people and citizens. But it resisted treating them as individuals who were fully separate from the social units in which they were embedded, and whose participation in collective self-government was therefore either redundant or destabilizing. Their defense of the family was aided by a new round of controversies over "free love," which once again tainted reformers of all stripes. Largely evading Mill's critique of the family as a "school of despotism" ill-suited for a democracy, opponents of women's enfranchisement instead emphasized the disorderly threat they believed women's full political participation posed to the family and, by extension, to society. As Reconstruction came to an end, the United States remained an aristocracy of sex.

Querists from War to Peace

While there was much discussion about women and their loyalty during the Civil War, the momentum established in the 1850s ensured that a broader set of reflections continued. Many of the significant contributions that appeared in the 1860s had actually begun before secession and thus pursued insights largely unrelated to Union patriotism and the toppling of slavery. Boston reformer Caroline Dall devoted the greatest effort to her ongoing compilation of social scientific data about legal, economic, and educational trends within and beyond the United States. When she decided to publish a set of her lectures in 1861, she conceded there was a "certain presumption" to a book that did "not treat of the great interests which convulse and perplex" the American reader. Yet she forged ahead because she believed her fellow Americans could not "remain continually upon the rack" and because she figured a serious book on a subject of worldwide interest was bound to find a "hearty welcome." The panoramic consideration of women's legal disabilities provided in *Woman's Rights Under the Law* (1861) devoted a mere quarter of its pages to affairs within the United States, with none of the analysis relating specifically to America's enslaved population or nonwhite women. Instead, her treatment took on a more theoretical quality, as she insisted that "woman's rights" were identical to "human rights." With wry provocation, she acknowledged that the former was "a phrase we all hate," while the latter was "a phrase we all honor."[6]

Dall grew increasingly frustrated that "twaddle on the Woman question" intensified as a bloody war became more costly. She found sentimental commentary from clergy like Rev. Samuel Osgood particularly irritating. That Unitarian minister, who in 1838 had offered the first American magazine article devoted to the general "woman question," clung to the same truisms he had expressed a quarter-century earlier. What had changed by 1862 was a sharp response from the highly educated Dall, who had broadcast self-assurance across multiple sites of published opinion. Her books engaged an international public sphere; her appearances at reform conventions catalogued women's gains and losses; and her newspaper columns featured a skillfully combative back-and-forth style. She had little patience with mawkish tributes to feminine patriotism and instead linked wartime mobilization to advancement for loyal women. "All over the land," Dall observed, "a crowd of women" was emerging who were "longing for action, capable of thought, ready for organization." In this transformed context, all "women's rights women" had to do was "stand aside" and welcome these soon-to-be converts as they put "their hands to our plow." Her advice to male readers was blunt: "Do not press [women] back to the old solitude" once the war ended, but encourage them as equal participants in self-government. Dall was ready with a detailed report on global trends and challenges when women's rights conventions resumed in 1866.[7]

Dall's public profile led her to become a stand-in for the women's movement when, three decades after his mother Frances Trollope had rattled Americans with her scathing *Domestic Manners of the Americans*, British novelist Anthony Trollope featured Dall in his own commentary on the United States. He sought to make partial amends for his mother's hostility in his travel narrative *North America* (1862), which was based on a six-month trip that twice crisscrossed the North from the East Coast to the Mississippi River. The younger Trollope signaled his grudging respect for the sort of popular government widely dismissed by his mother and many earlier travelers. Unlike those who scoffed at democracy's weakness, he noted the extraordinary engagement of ordinary Americans, through an endless array of periodicals and newspapers, with political questions of the day. He mused that political participation might make the coachman, or bricklayer, or "shoeboy" less "valuable to his employer," but it undoubtedly made him "more valuable to himself." Yet Trollope's admiration had firm limits, and he shuddered at the prospect of women's political involvement. His chapter on "The Rights of Women" acknowledged that this was a "very favorite subject in America," with able advocates and "apostles" like Dall. He conceded that the basic democratic argument—that women subject to the law should help to make it— was logically "conclusive," even unanswerable. But he vaguely suggested that "mutual good relations between men and women" on which so much happiness depended must supersede democratic consistency.[8]

More robust, even adventurous, inquiries into the connections between women and democracy came from the pens of two women—one American and one French—in 1864. Elizabeth Farnham, who back in 1843 had sparred with John Neal in the pages of *Brother Jonathan*, returned to the subject twenty years later with some hard-earned wisdom that made her a critic of women's persistent political and legal disabilities. Left in New York by a California-bound husband in the 1840s, Farnham had served as matron of the female division at Sing Sing state prison and then worked for a time with Samuel Gridley Howe at his New England Asylum for the Blind. She relocated to the California ranch owned by her now-deceased husband and remarried—briefly—before divorcing this abusive spouse in 1856. Farnham then returned to the East where she wrote books, gave lectures, and studied medicine. She presented herself as a "sympathetic, yet dissenting spectator" from any "party on the Woman Question." This stance meant she could not escape "the reproaches either of its opponents or its advocates" and informed the singularity of her approach in *Woman and Her Era* (1864). This two-volume work drew on organicism, religion, phrenology, literature, art, and history. Advance publicity billed it as the "book for the century" that promised to set aside mere "discussion" and offer an "actual solution" to "the great 'woman question.'"[9]

Woman and Her Era did not so much present an "actual solution" as make a bold forecast of a superior and feminine future. If the future was female, it would also be overtly democratic. Blending popular but vague evolutionary ideas with a Romantic theory of knowledge, Farnham understood women's intrinsic and imaginative ways of knowing as superior to men's instrumental and literal ones.[10] Women, she argued, intuited and therefore grasped "self-evident Truths" long before men accepted them as "proved." She understood democracy as the "master-Truth," an affirmation of the right of every soul "to the completest development that it is capable of attaining." But every government that "Man has founded" since the dawn of time has denied or ignored this truth, except as it applied to the few. Only in the era of "feminine ascendency," Farnham argued, could "the Idea of Democracy" be fully realized. Most of her male reviewers did not in fact grasp Farnham's ideas, but the *American Phrenological Journal* generously lauded her for writing "more ably" on the woman question than Mary Wollstonecraft, Margaret Fuller, or Lydia Maria Child.[11]

The very same year an English translation of French immigrant Jenny P. d'Hericourt's *A Woman's Philosophy of Woman; or, Woman Affranchised* (1864) appeared, confirming that women's yearning for self-governance was a mounting transnational concern. A self-described "Garibaldi among women," d'Hericourt had in 1860 gained European renown with her retort to French social theorists. She vowed to make "the nineteenth century ashamed of its culpable denial of justice to half the human species." Her work rejected gendered abstractions, carving out space (as Margaret Fuller had earlier) for the full flourishing of individuality. Hard lessons learned from her native France during the Second Empire alerted her to the potential meaninglessness of the vote absent other features of democratic life, including education, freedom of the press and assembly, and a powerful public opinion that ensured the government would be responsive to the governed. More important than universal ballots was an "agonistic" politics of democratic debate that included women as well as men. She modeled this approach in her text, which consisted of lengthy exchanges between her and several male theorists, and with an imagined "Reader."[12]

These early 1860s considerations of the woman question by Dall, Trollope, Farnham, and d'Hericourt appeared as eddies in the more powerful currents of an American culture preoccupied with war. The patriotic activities of Loyal Union women, especially when placed beside the overthrow of slavery, prompted forecasts of victory that would lead to a sweeping alteration of sex roles. In May 1863, the same month that Elizabeth Cady Stanton and Susan B. Anthony launched their emancipation petition campaigns from their National Woman's Loyal League, William Lloyd Garrison Jr. (son of the old abolitionist) looked ahead to the "many questions" that would follow

Americans' reassessment of the "capacity of the negro for freedom and self-sustenance." A "searching war" had prompted the Union to begin a process of recasting inherited assumptions about racial difference; surely prevalent "bugbears" about the female half of the population would face a similar scrutiny. The claims of "both the negro and woman" were based on the "same general principles," he insisted, and the advancement of one group augured well for the other.[13]

The prospect of any radical alteration to traditional notions of womanhood, however, produced as much anxiety as enthusiasm. Even while war was ongoing, the "mooted question of woman's rights and wrongs" caused one female reader of the *New York Observer* to express caution about reformers who "descant so largely on this favorite theme." At a time when "so much fine rhetoric is expended," an average woman like herself felt bewildered and lost in "a moral fog." "Mabtha," as the Rochester-based letter-writer called herself, observed (inaccurately) that her grandmothers' generation had no such confusion about their sphere and duty. She urged patience. With the aid of their Bibles and common sense, women could navigate these new waters—"if 'the reformers' will only let us alone." *Godey's Lady's Book* circulated to far wider audiences a similar understanding of Christian womanhood. Dismissing the incessant "clamor in these days of progress," the popular women's magazine imagined new rights and privileges for women coexisting with the retention of critical boundaries. The Creator—whose "voice cannot err"—had assigned woman to be the helpmate of man, and it was in this role alone that a woman's "true nobility" resided.[14]

An underlying caution about the shift in women's possibilities was evident in two compilations that rolled off the press soon after Confederate surrender. Frank Moore's thick volume on the "heroism and self-sacrifice" of America's "Loyal Women" was supplemented by an even more mammoth book edited by Linus P. Brockett and Mary C. Vaughan. In both volumes, dozens of capsule biographies provided a rich panorama of female accomplishments in raising funds, organizing materials, caring for the wounded on the fields and in hospitals, and shoring up public sentiment. These volumes detailed stories of white women working among the freedmen, as well as a scattered set of examples of women who had served as soldiers. Yet across the nearly 1,400 combined pages, readers encountered an all-white group—and an apolitical one. Not mentioned were the battles waged by Stanton, Anna Dickinson, and others in the 1864 presidential election campaign.[15]

Rev. Henry W. Bellows, who had been a key figure in the 1863 rhetoric of loyalty, highlighted womanly reserve as a theme in introducing the Brockett and Vaughan volume. American women had demonstrated a degree of self-control and sagacity quite unlike the "spasmodic and sentimental" service of women seen elsewhere. Loyal supporters of the Union were "the products and representatives of a new social era, and a new political development," he affirmed. He praised female patriots for presiding over public meetings of other volunteer women; for serving on committees, where they drafted constitutions and bylaws; for keeping account books; and for organizing across regional and sectarian divides. "Probably never in any war in any country," he observed, "was there so universal and so specific an acquaintance on the part of both men and women, with the principles at issue, and the interests at stake." But Bellow's publicly stated opposition to women's enfranchisement stifled any possible link between such a tribute and its potential political consequences.[16]

Whether Bellow's stance was the current or the countercurrent was yet to be determined. In this context, the view from abroad suggested a possible way to discern prevailing tendencies, which helps explain the careful press scrutiny of John Stuart Mill's stunning election to Parliament in 1865. This perceived victory for Anglo-American reform held implications for a range of topics; its potential effect on the woman question was among the most important. Knowledgeable readers were aware of the 1851 *Westminster* essay by Mill's wife and his own comments on women in *Considerations on Representative Government* (1861). Even better known to American readers (especially in the North) was Mill's staunch advocacy of the Lincoln administration, which established him as England's most valuable "friend of the Union." Frances Harper might well have had Mill—along with other antislavery, pro-Union voices—in mind when she composed her poem to "Our English Friends."[17]

A new facet of Mill's progressive persona emerged from the media coverage of his transit from political philosopher to candidate to officeholder. Repeatedly, brief sketches of his most important achievements placed a series of his books alongside an arresting, and to many (especially female) observers deeply moving, dedication of *On Liberty* (1859) to his wife. Inscribed to Harriet Taylor Mill shortly after her 1858 death, this tribute publicly celebrated "the friend and wife whose exalted sense of truth and right was my strongest incitement, and whose approbation was my chief reward."[18] Many readers (including Caroline Dall who inserted a lengthy footnote on the topic in her 1861 book) were struck by a philosopher who placed an appropriate value on a life partnership and who also dealt with grief through poignant eloquence. "The love and sorrow of Petrarch are nothing," mused an article that appeared in Frederick Douglass's *New National Era*, next to the "love and sorrow of John

Stuart Mill for a wife who is buried at Avignon."[19] Mill's success, given his longstanding advocacy of women's advancement, seemed to many a sign that transnational progress on this knotty question lay just over the horizon.

Mill's celebrity status across Reconstruction-era America varied according to how commentators perceived women's rights and democratic expansion. Enthusiasm for his example among self-consciously cultivated Northern writers was reversed in *St. Elmo* (1866), the bestselling novel written by Alabamian Augusta Jane Evans. The heroine, an intellectually precocious

JOHN STUART MILL, M.P.

FIG. 5.1 "John Stuart Mill, M.P." One of nearly a dozen illustrations of Mill that appeared in American periodicals between 1865 and 1873, this engraving accompanied an article celebrating his election to Parliament, which the weekly deemed a credit to Mill and his constituents alike. Readers learned here that Mill advocated the enfranchisement of women, the extension of the franchise to working men in Britain, and "all measures which have for their object the improvement of the social, moral, intellectual, and physical condition of the people." Like nearly all articles about Mill from this period, this one also mentioned the dedication, in *On Liberty*, to his late wife. From *Harper's Weekly* (October 28, 1865). Courtesy of Dartmouth College Library.

orphan named Edna Earl, had fully memorized Mill's dedication to his wife in *On Liberty*. She is thus taken aback to learn that the dissolute St. Elmo, outraged after reading Mill's plea for women's enfranchisement, throws *Considerations on Representative Government* into a roaring fire.

Edna's further study of Mill convinces her that his noble husbandly devotion coexisted with a dangerous philosophical bent. She speaks disparagingly about Mill at a dinner party, which startles a visiting Englishman who viewed Mill's works as "so essentially democratic" that he "expected only gratitude and eulogy from his readers on this side of the Atlantic." Edna elaborates that if Mill's "theory of Liberty and Suffrage" prevailed, society would "go to ruin." Such nonsense might have been expected in England—"where a woman nominally rules, and certainly reigns"—but Edna dreaded "the contagion of such an example upon America." As the conversation intensifies, Edna works herself up to a pitch reminiscent of Louisa McCord. "At least, sir," she tells the visitor, "our statesmen are not yet attacked by this most loathsome of political leprosies. Only a few crazy fanatics have fallen victims to it . . . a few unamiable and wretched wives, and as many embittered, disappointed old maids of New England." She assures the Englishman that "the noble and true women of this continent earnestly believe that the day which invests them with the elective franchise would be the blackest in the annals of humanity." As with McCord, Edna's specific doubts about women were accompanied by musings on the fallacies of racial equality and democracy.[20]

British novelist Anthony Trollope—whose entire prodigious corpus might be said to have addressed the woman question in one form or another—presented a lighter transatlantic repartee in his 1869 novel about right and wrong marriages. One of the major subplots of *He Knew He Was Right* centered on a husband slowing going insane by his unreasonable insistence on controlling his wife, in accordance perhaps with the letter of the law but certainly not (as all the novel's other characters agree) its spirit. In a separate subplot, a pompous American and a British aristocrat engage in conversation. Though the narrator notes that the American "himself had never read a word of Mr. Mill's writings," he showily presents himself as the philosopher's booster: "Your John S. Mill is a great man." The novel appeared in the wake of Mill's Parliamentary advocacy for women's enfranchisement and just as *The Subjection of Women* began to receive press attention, but this fictional American resorts to platitudes rather than substance. "He is a far-seeing man . . . He is one of the few Europeans who can look forward and see how the rivers of civilization are running on. He has understood that women must at last be put upon an equality with men." The Englishman then glibly asked if Mill had devised a way for men to have half the babies, an absurdity meant to end an unpleasant conversation. Outside the pages of the novel, debate over Mill's plea for a "perfect equality" between men and women was only just beginning.[21]

A School of Sympathy in Equality

The very fact that *The Subjection of Women* appeared in 1869 suggested how much had changed in a mere two decades. Mill had drafted it years earlier but waited for the right moment to launch it into the world. This calculation had less to do with personal hesitancy than with his resolve to achieve the greatest impact for a reform he deemed indispensable to human progress. That right moment had come in the late 1860s—three years after women's suffrage had been seriously discussed in Parliament as well as in the US Congress and amidst continual agitation on the issue in both Britain and the United States. It also helped that his reelection loss in late 1868 gave him the time finally to complete the "little book" he had begun nearly a decade earlier.[22]

At the heart of *The Subjection of Women* was Mill's insistence that women must be self-governing and not subject to the will of husbands, social norms, or all-male governments. Unsurprisingly, it echoed Taylor Mill's "Enfranchisement of Women," and Mill characteristically attributed all that was "most striking and profound" in the text to his wife.[23] Mill stated his central premise on the opening page: that "the principle which regulates the existing social relations between the two sexes—the legal subordination of one sex to the other—is wrong itself, and now one of the chief hindrances to human improvement." He urged that this outdated principle "be replaced by a principle of perfect equality, admitting no power or privilege on the one side, nor disability on the other." Across four chapters, Mill excavated the historical foundations for women's subjection and explained how education and socialization perpetuated it; critiqued the customary institution of marriage as tyrannical; argued for removing artificial barriers to women's economic and social advancement; and detailed the benefits—to individual women, to the family, to society, and to the polity—that would accompany the full equality of women and an equal partnership between women and men on behalf of the improvement of mankind. The book was less an intellectual departure than a discussion of how many of Mill's core philosophical commitments elaborated over decades applied specifically to women. This was how contemporaries read it.[24]

The most controversial argument of *Subjection* concerned its presentation of the marital relationship, which—in a long tradition of writers following

Mary Wollstonecraft—Mill claimed was legally not unlike slavery.[25] In both institutions, holdovers from a barbaric era, the personhood of humans was legally obliterated. Mill here emphasized the most egregious features of coverture, many of which had already been or were in the process of being eliminated in both Britain and the United States. Subordination in marriage, Mill argued, was unjust to women; it was also harmful to the polity. Like his wife nearly two decades earlier, he agreed with Martineau rather than Tocqueville and Beecher on this issue, though he took from Tocqueville an emphasis on the importance of habits and training that preceded and carried over into democratic political participation. Even more forcefully than his wife, he completely inverted the connections that earlier writers had made between the family and the polity. Domestic life as currently constituted threatened, rather than promoted, representative government.

Mill agreed that the family was a key agent of political socialization. But he asked what it meant for a purportedly egalitarian polity to structure the family in contradiction to this core value. As presently constituted, "the family is a school of despotism," a formative institution where all the vices of despotism "are nourished." Here Mill echoed white analyses of the institution of slavery, going back at least to Thomas Jefferson in *Notes on the State of Virginia* (1781). Slavery was harmful not simply to slaves, Jefferson had fretted, but to slaveholders who found themselves corrupted by the despotism and tyranny they practiced on a daily basis. Jefferson expressed particular concern for how this corrupting institution would impact future (white) citizens, who watched their parents' behavior and learned from it. "Nursed, educated, and daily exercised in tyranny," the citizen cannot but "be stamped by it." This was surely no basis for republican citizenship.[26] Similarly, Mill asked his readers to imagine a boy growing up and believing that "without any merit or any exertion of his own," by the mere fact of being born a male, he was "by right the superior of all and every one of an entire half of the human race." Even if his relations with individual women are marked by chivalry, duty, and indeed affection, can we imagine it is possible that the underlying sense of superiority "does not pervert" his entire existence? Now imagine a whole society of these grown-up boys, inculcated with habits of superiority, and of women conditioned by this as well as their own internalized assumptions of inferiority.

For Mill, the virtues that would accompany women's emancipation were manifold. The most significant was that women themselves would become fully self-governing, that the newly "liberated half of the species" might live a life of "rational freedom" instead of a "life of subjection to the will of others." Simply understanding herself as "a human being like any other," one who was "entitled to exert the share of influence on all human concerns which belongs to an individual" could not help but be transformative for the individual woman. And as women were included as full members of the body politic, they would benefit from an expansion of their faculties and an enlargement in "the range of their moral sentiments." But the rest of society would benefit as well. Newly constituted families would inculcate desirable habits in the citizenry. Rather than being a school of despotism that nurtured "all the selfish propensities" and "unjust self-preference" that exist "among mankind," the family would become a "school of sympathy in equality, of living together in love, without power on one side or obedience on the other."[27]

Emancipating women and remaking the family thus also worked in tandem to safeguard representative government. In their current state of inequality and exclusion from public life, women exacerbated one of the problems Tocqueville had identified with democracy—the tendency of atomistic individuals to retreat into private affairs and foster a generalized selfishness and apathy. Women's lack of political education (an inescapable consequence of being barred from the educative effects of political participation) left them "strangers even to the elementary ideas which are presupposed in any intelligent regard for larger interests or higher moral objects." In that state they could provide no counterweight to the destructive tendencies of popular government. Worse, they served as drags on their partners, for any companionship "which is not improving is deteriorating: and the more so, the closer and more familiar it is." Thus, ending the "subjection of women"—through law, social custom, educational and economic opportunity, and political inclusion—presented an indispensable step in the improvement of mankind.[28]

Mill's "little book" met with an immediate and extensive response when it appeared in the summer of 1869. An advertisement in *Appleton's Journal* predicted that because of "Mr. Mill's high position both as a thinker and a representative of advanced ideas," the book would be "looked for with interest, and widely read." His stature gave "influence and authority to his views, such as no other living man could exert." Reviews appeared in dozens of periodicals on both sides of the Atlantic, from highbrow organs to popular illustrated magazines. In addition to the many newspaper and magazine reviews, multiple book-length responses appeared in the United States, including Horace Bushnell, *Women's Suffrage: Reform Against Nature* (1869); L. P. Brockett, *Woman: Her Rights, Wrongs, Privileges, and Responsibilities* (1869); the anonymously published *A Reply to John Stuart Mill* (1870); and Carlos White, *Ecce Femina: An Attempt to Solve the Woman Question* (1870).[29] These volumes in turn garnered their own reviews, thus extending the discussion of the woman question across published opinion in a staggering array of periodicals from the *Atlantic Monthly* to *Zion Herald*.

Mill's *Subjection* was well-known enough that the short-lived satirical magazine *Punchinello*, modeled on the London *Punch*, made more than one joke about Mill in its pages in 1870. A digest of British news noted he was hard at work on "his next book, which is to be 'On the Subjection of Horses.'" A broadly comic novel serialized in subsequent issues mocked Mill for being the author of a work on "the Revolting Injustice of Masculine Society." What Mill had observed of the 1866–1867 debate over women's enfranchisement in the House of Commons—that it generated discussion outside the movement, "in quarters where the subject had never been thought of before"—was far more true about the impact of *Subjection's* appearance.[30]

Several authors admitted as much. The author of one of the book-length replies acknowledged that though the subject "popularly known as Woman's Rights" had been discussed for years, he would never have bothered to weigh in "were it not certain that the recently published essay of Mr. Mill will create a strong public sentiment in favor of the reform therein advocated." According to *Putnam's Magazine*, the "woman question," having long been "confined to revolutionary journals," had in 1869 "risen to the dignity of Literature, in the person of Mr. John Stuart Mill."[31]

Figures within the movement unsurprisingly praised the book. They discussed it in organs such as the *Revolution* and the *Woman's Journal*. The *Revolution* even offered a promotion to renewing subscribers, promising to send a copy of "Mr. Mill's invaluable book" if they renewed "NOW."[32] Resolutions of gratitude to Mill were passed at conventions. Several activists wrote letters to Mill, or his stepdaughter Helen Taylor, eliciting letters of support in return, which were then read at conventions or published in journals. George William Curtis, who had relied on Mill in his own efforts at the 1867 New York State Constitutional Convention, "most heartily" commended this "exhaustive but small volume" to his hundreds of thousand readers of *Harper's Weekly*, at least those among them who were "interested in human progress." *Subjection* was likely the book Frances Harper's 1872 biographer had in mind when he mentioned Harper had read Mill's work. African American journalist Gertrude Mossell would, a decade later, encourage people to read Mill's work in her women's column for the Black newspaper *New York Freeman*.[33] Harriet Beecher Stowe found the book utterly persuasive, writing to a friend "it has wholly converted me—I was only right *in spots* before now I am all clear." According to Mill, she told readers of *Hearth and Home*, a magazine she briefly coedited in 1868–1869, all "popular reforms" moved through three necessary stages—"Ridicule, Discussion, and Acceptance." Thanks to works like *Subjection of Women*, the question of "Woman's Rights" was just now passing "out of the stage of ridicule into that of fair, respectful discussion." Stowe's work, along with Mill's, would contribute to that respectful discussion outside the activism of movement figures.[34]

The *Woman's Journal* agreed that a new phase had been entered. The Boston-based weekly dismissed one of the book-length reviews of *Subjection* because its sneering "tone" revealed it to be the work of "a person who is not aware that the time for trying to dispose of the Woman Suffrage question by ridicule has long since passed away." Optimism aside, the notion that the "woman question" (or, more narrowly, the "Woman Suffrage question") no longer garnered ridicule was decidedly—laughably—untrue. A satirical play, written by the husband-and-wife team of Ariana Randolph Wormley Curtis and Daniel Sargent Curtis, became a sensation throughout the 1870s and 1880s. Though only performed on the professional stage for a few weeks in Boston, *The Spirit of Seventy-Six; or the Coming Woman* (1868) ran through more than twenty print editions in the following decades. In fact, Stowe's sister, Isabella Beecher Hooker, was distressed to learn that her own daughter Alice had agreed to act in a private staging of this "burlesque"—"a mere piece of buffoonery at best"—even as Isabella was composing and reading aloud her own essays on women's suffrage.[35]

But specifically for the reception of Mill's book, the *Woman's Journal's* point about entering a post-ridicule phase stood. While there were a few outright hostile reviews, especially from the religious press, the bulk of reviewers gave *Subjection* a civil hearing and, when disagreeing with Mill, they did so rather politely and respectfully. They acknowledged his stature, expressed admiration for his "genius and character," and in some cases offered reluctant demurrals. E. L. Godkin, editor of the *Nation*, granted that the case for women's rights "has never been so ably stated as in this little volume," before finding fault with the way Mill emphasized culture and education over nature to explain women's position.[36]

The most significant book-length "response" was actually less a reply than a preemptive strike, written before Congregational minister Horace Bushnell had read *Subjection*. In *Women's Suffrage: The Reform Against Nature*, Bushnell used the subtitle to deliver a concise four-word summary of his argument. Enfranchising women, he claimed, would be as unnatural as to make "trumpets out of flutes" or "sunflowers out of violets." Bushnell was no unthinking reactionary. He had been a major force in liberal theological debates for decades. His first book, *Christian Nurture* (1847), explored his vision of the organic unity of the family, church, and nation—a vision that led him to emphasize the family as the key site of religious conversion where fathers and mothers shared responsibility. But his understanding of a joint partnership between women and men did not extend into public life. He had already in 1840 hoped to keep the female "half of society free of the broils and bruises" of corrupting and amoral democratic politics. The renewed efforts of women's suffrage activists (including his Hartford neighbors Isabella Beecher Hooker and her husband John) alarmed Bushnell enough that he felt compelled to weigh in. Even though Mill's book had not yet appeared, Bushnell demonstrated familiarity with it ("the title of his book . . . as I think I have somewhere seen, is '*The Subject Condition of Women*'"). He quoted from Mill's and Taylor Mill's earlier works and disparaged Mill's "particular bent of philosophy," which has no "respect to categories, absolute properties, or laws of kind that are immovable" but instead sees "all things, even the distinctions of morality, developed . . . by the contingent, variable operations of experience." So much did Bushnell put himself into conversation with Mill's (unread) book that *Putnam's* thought *Women's Suffrage* could "be considered as an answer in advance."[37]

Bushnell's volume began like Mill's with an historical excavation of women's condition. But where Mill's anti-essentialism emphasized brute force, education, and socialization, Bushnell based his arguments on nature and scripture. He agreed that historically women had been oppressed but thought this oppression stemmed not from domination but rather from the natural, if misdirected, efforts of men to protect women. While he encouraged an expansion of women's educational and occupational opportunities, he drew a hard line at political participation. Women's enfranchisement presented a threat not just to women but to the home, which was the foundation of society and the polity. Here history, rather than nature or scripture, proved quite useful. For "women's suffrage is not a fact of history," Bushnell observed. The whole campaign to enfranchise women was based on faulty theorizing about abstractions like "equality" and "natural rights," which obscured more than they revealed.

The Hartford minister demurred on the question of equality. Women were not equal to men: they were simply different, "equally women as men are men" and even "equally human as men," but that was not exactly the same as "equal to men." Maybe they were superior, Bushnell mused, maybe inferior; the question was not answerable in concrete terms, and these were the only terms that mattered. A presumed "right to vote" was no less an abstraction, in

Bushnell's view. "Whence comes it," he wondered, given that access to the suffrage has historically been granted to different groups at different times for different reasons (e.g., tax-payments, property, military service)? History belied the very notion of an abstract "right" to vote inhering in individual American citizens, male or female. Instead, Bushnell echoed many commentators in these years that women's suffrage must be judged at the bar of expediency. By this standard, it failed. Voting threatened to "unsex" women and to introduce a dangerous instability into the organic (and appropriately hierarchical) family.[38]

The near-simultaneity and sharply contrasting analyses they presented ensured that Bushnell and Mill were often discussed together, providing readers a convenient shorthand for the spectrum of opinion. Mill's radical egalitarianism resembled the consistent democracy of movement activists in the 1850s, while Bushnell's views echoed Beecher's domesticated democracy. Reading them both inspired Elizabeth Cady Stanton to contemplate writing her own book, hoping to go deeper on some ideas left "untouched" by either man. Many, perhaps most, readers charted themselves somewhere between these two positions, as one woman wrote in a letter to the *Nation*. She admitted that "to a firm decision we cannot instantly come; be it from superstition, timidity, or crass stupidity, such is the fact." Others echoed this self-proclaimed neutrality.[39] A young William James published the lengthiest, and most thoughtful, joint appraisal in the pages of *North American Review*, but he too agreed fully with neither writer. He had some fun mocking Bushnell's pearl-clutching fears about the potential comingling of the sexes at the polls and on the hustings ("terrible hints are given, of the naughtinesses to which women will resort in order to procure votes"). But James stumbled over Mill's insistence that historical and social conditioning accounted for nearly all of women's specific attributes. He also expressed serious reservations about Mill's view of marriage, which seemed to James more like friendship (a not uncommon criticism). The editors of *Putnam's*, finding not just Mill's and Bushnell's opinions but their very understanding of history and nature so utterly opposed, simply threw up their editorial hands: "We are somewhat at a loss to choose between Mr. Bushnell and Mr. Mill. Our readers, however, may be more fortunate, so we commit to their judgments the case of these learned doctors."[40]

Even with their differences, the books reinforced the view that discussion of the woman question had entered a critical phase. The women's movement, *Harper's Weekly* declared, could no longer "be laughed [at] or frowned down." These two important works on the subject show "how deeply it engages the attention of the most thoughtful minds." Was it not "rather a striking coincidence," asked the anonymous author of the book *A Reply to John Stuart Mill* (1870), that the two men should each publish a treatise "almost at the same moment, in different countries, and discussing the same subject?" Another critic noted that women's rights advocates had been presenting their views to the American public for over a quarter of a century, but it was only since "the close of the war" that they seemed to be making any progress. The revolutionary upheaval of that conflict and its aftermath served as a reminder to reformers and conservatives alike just how quickly change might come. Perhaps the very rapidity of that change helped explain, one critic observed, why it was that "in go-ahead republican America, one of her ablest writers [Bushnell] should take the conservative side" of the issue, while the "more radical opinion" emerged from "aristocratic Old England." This seeming reversal of national reform positions was striking: for the United States, a nation that "came into existence in defiance of the customs and regulations which have ruled the rest of the world," liked to imagine itself always in the vanguard of progress and kept a "jealous eye" on innovations elsewhere.[41]

In fact, several readers saw Mill's book as yet another sign—and this time a disturbingly transatlantic one—that reform was moving too far, too fast. As was often the case in American political rhetoric, invocations of the French Revolution were always available and helpful in distinguishing American practicality from Gallic abstraction—a tendency that would be reinforced by the Paris Commune of 1871. The evangelical *Christian Observer* admitted that "like everything that bears the 'liberté, égalite, et fraternité' stamp, there is something at first sight somewhat fascinating in the picture which Mr. Mill has unfolded to our view." But first sight had to be supplemented by a more careful reconsideration, which would reveal the folly of Mill's positions on both the equality of the sexes and the desirability of such a vast expansion of the suffrage.[42]

Some commentators worried that reform or "progress" had become its own end, regardless of any specific issue and without regard to consequences. Carlos White, the author of the book-length reply *Ecce Femina: An Attempt to Solve the Woman Question* (1870), offered an interesting case in point. He was no traditionalist or reactionary but a self-proclaimed Radical, who "had been a Garrisonian abolitionist" and "felt a natural inclination to follow the same men in the Woman's Rights movement" after Black emancipation. He noted that these reformers (whom he labeled "the Innovators") had been arguing their case since the 1840s with "little progress." But, in the aftermath of the war, the "pendulum" of "public opinion" seemed to be swinging alarmingly in their favor. He suggested that while some people had truly been converted to the cause, many others simply went along because they did not want to appear behind the times or be ridiculed. White, however, sided with "the *majority* of the women themselves," whom he claimed did not want radical reform. White was willing to concede the logical and intellectual merit of many of the Innovators' arguments, but he could not help but feel an uneasiness, "a lurking feeling that there was a fallacy" in their reasoning.[43]

William James's review offered a revealing glimpse into how intellectual and psychological or emotional responses to the woman question commingled. *The Subjection of Women*, he wrote a friend, was a "most weighty little production," "strangely startling and suggestive." He conceded that the Englishman had "justice" on his side and was quite possibly "more farseeing than the majority" on the issue. The book may well "hereafter be quoted as a landmark signaling one distinct step in the progress of the total evolution." It was simply not a step James himself was keen to take, and he suspected the "representative American" man would agree with him. However, this representative man might "shrink from expressing it in naked words," the single, twenty-seven-year-old James candidly surmised, that "the wife his heart more or less subtly craves is at bottom a dependent being." The question soon emerged: What did the "representative American woman" want? And who was entitled to answer for her?[44]

Women Without the Ballot May Possess Every Condition of a Dignified Womanhood

Mill's *The Subjection* focused attention on the woman question across published opinion, providing an opportunity for extensive discussion on a range of matters. Were women unduly "subjected" in marriage? Should the family be restructured along egalitarian lines? Ought women to be fully self-governing as individuals and partners with men in the collective endeavor of self-government? That much of this discussion sidestepped the specifics of Mill's analysis in an effort to resist further reform was not entirely surprising, given the lack of nuance that tended to accompany widespread debate. But a full understanding of Mill's precise critique of the family as currently constituted was also a casualty of a renewed wave of "free love" charges that animated traditionalist defenses of the family. These "scandals" took shape amidst a waning national appetite for further "revolutionary" reform. The enthusiasm that had been so evident across politics and published opinion only a decade earlier cooled.

As a sign of the times, in 1869 Catharine Beecher updated her bestselling work. Aware that this would be one of the last ventures of a long and productive career, Beecher collaborated with her more famous sister to redistribute material from the 1841 *Treatise on Domestic Economy* into an altered sequence of chapters of *The American Woman's Home*. Much of the homemaking advice reappeared without revision, and the multiple American editions across the 1870s featured the same techniques of fitness, medicine, and domestic management she had composed three decades earlier. What was new was the introduction, which swapped out the long passages from Tocqueville (asserting women's centrality to American democracy's success) for a set of explicitly Christian themes. This new framework anticipated the book's two overarching ideological objectives. First, Beecher pronounced her conviction, which bolstered the stance of Bushnell and others, that Americans insufficiently appreciated "the honor and duties of the family state." Her signature response to this problem was to lecture Americans on their duty to train young women for the complexities awaiting them in adulthood. Second, Beecher registered her concern that an "increasing agitation of the public mind" had given rise to "many theories" and "crude speculations as to woman's rights and duties." These theories, she warned, were leading "intelligent, reflecting, and benevolent women" astray from true Christian principles.[45]

Democracy and Christianity had been aligned in the 1841 *Treatise*, but now Beecher was decidedly more ambivalent. In essays and speeches, she repeatedly emphasized deference to divinely sanctioned authority, comparing woman's proper "subordination" in the "family state" to the subordination of her "father, husband, brother, and sons" in the "civil state." Her understanding of "the doctrine of woman's subjugation" thus explicitly repudiated "the doctrine of Stuart Mills [*sic*] and his followers," which she believed to be an affront to "common sense and Christianity" alike. As she reemerged on the national scene, she amplified the dangers of women's quest for the vote and gave increasingly short shrift to possibilities beyond women's teaching and child-rearing. Her widely quoted warnings against women's enfranchisement played a distinct role in establishing the ballot as a defining boundary between Christian manhood and Christian womanhood. Her widely quoted and reprinted essay "Something for Women Better than the Ballot" earned Beecher invitations to make a series of additional appearances that characterized voting as the "wrong means for a right end." The right end she had in mind centered on enhancing women's dignity through the important realm of household governance.[46]

Though suffrage organizations had saturated published opinion with "tracts and newspapers by hundreds of thousands," Beecher asserted that a "large majority" of women ("probably nine tenths of the most intelligent and conscientious women of our country") did not want the ballot.[47] A small chorus of voices soon emerged that claimed to speak for the "silent masses" that Beecher had invoked. Charlotte McKay, a Baltimore widow, had served as a wartime nurse and a missionary to the freedmen, two experiences that led her to date an "upheaval in the feminine forces of the country" to 1861. But she worried that this salutary shift had been commandeered by a small and unrepresentative group of women who sought "to turn these newly awakened forces into channels of political ambition." Beecher, McKay, and others found a worthy target for their coordinated efforts in the prospect of a women's suffrage amendment. They organized an "Anti-Sixteenth Amendment Society" that drew on the talent and efforts of not just Beecher and McKay but a group of other prominent women, including Madeleine Vinton Dahlgren (the widow of Civil War admiral John Dahlgren), Almira Lincoln Phelps (the sister of the notable educator Emma Willard), Susan Fenimore Cooper (daughter of the writer James), and the wives of several political figures, such as Mrs. William Tecumseh Sherman.[48]

This organized resistance—a great "counter-influence," as Beecher deemed it—sought to awaken the "multitudes of quiet and silent" women across the nation. Borrowing the tactics of the women's rights movement, they formed an organization, petitioned Congress, and founded their own journal. This last effort was particularly important, as McKay and Dahlgren agreed with Beecher that women's rights advocates had so far enjoyed the advantage in published opinion. They were determined to catch up. Their new journal, the *True Woman*, launched in April 1871. Edited by McKay in Baltimore, the new monthly combined political commentary with light literary sketches. The editors carefully monitored the larger discussion. When Susan Fenimore Cooper published a two-part essay on "Female Suffrage" in *Harper's Monthly*, the *True Woman* commended not just the author for writing it but the "Messrs. Harper" for printing it. Surely, the journal insisted, it was well past time for "the press to come out boldly against the perversion of the Rights of the True Woman." Throughout its short-lived existence, the *True Woman* paid close attention and responded directly to articles published in other newspapers and magazines.[49]

The *True Woman* and the Anti-Sixteenth Amendment Society also petitioned Congress, "begging" that "no law extending suffrage to women may be passed." They claimed to represent the "sober convictions of the majority of the women of the country." Even as women's suffrage took hold in places like Wyoming, where the territorial legislature had recently established it, they determined to thwart any national effort. *Godey's Lady's Book* printed the petition, urging readers to cut it out and collect signatures from their own communities. Only by this show of strength, the magazine contended, could women demonstrate to Congress that for every one woman who desired suffrage, there were fifty who disapproved it. Madeleine Vinton Dahlgren presented this petition with the signatures of some five thousand women who protested "against the oppression of having suffrage forced upon them."[50] To be enfranchised against their will was oppressive, they explained, because they would not disregard the duty to perform a right or privilege once granted them. Therefore, even though technically voting would not be compulsory, they would find it, in effect, to be so. When the language of "rights" surfaced across their essays and articles, it was the "right" not to be enfranchised and the "right" to remain in their own appointed sphere. "[51]

This first wave of anti-suffragists struggled against charges that they were mere reactionaries on the woman question. In fact, the *True Woman* supported educational and employment opportunities for all women, higher wages for working women, and legal redress for lingering remnants of coverture.[52] Gail Hamilton, who had issued the "Call to My Countrywomen" in 1863, dedicated a large portion of her energy and talent to the woman question, producing three books on the subject between 1867 and 1872. After presenting a searing critique of marriage in *A New Atmosphere* (1865), she turned to a blistering dismissal of what she considered weakly reasoned and mawkish arguments for women's "true sphere" in *Woman's Wrongs: A Counter-Irritant* (1868). She identified with the "woman's rights women." She shunned marriage, believing that unmarried women had "immense" advantages "over the married woman," and she held her own in a contract dispute with the publisher James T. Fields. But Hamilton agreed with the *True Woman* circle that women's advancement did not require and should not involve political participation as voters. While she initially felt only "indifference" toward suffrage, she grew more apprehensive by the time she published her third book on the subject, *Woman's Worth and Worthlessness* (1872). On closer scrutiny, she believed women's enfranchisement represented an unwarranted "revolution."[53]

The insistence that suffrage was inconsistent with true womanhood relied on a dual concern that intertwined doubts about continued democratic expansion with warnings about the American family's vulnerability. Arguments about too many voters, and the wrong kind of voters, appeared frequently in anti-suffrage writings. Henrietta Crosby Ingersoll (another avowed "woman's rights woman") balked at any possible constitutional amendment that would enfranchise all women. She approved a measure that might enfranchise women who met specific property, educational, and morality requirements, but she would prefer "no suffrage" rather than "the universal suffrage of women." Gail Hamilton made a similar point, finding in the demand for women's suffrage "no measure intended to keep the ignorant man away from the polls; only a proposition to enable him to bring his ignorant wife with him." Comments like these echoed larger anxieties about the indiscriminate enlargement of the electorate (elaborated in chapter 4) that had become increasingly vocal in the wake of Black suffrage.[54]

Anxieties about the family were equally pervasive, if somewhat less precise. A range of dangerous potential consequences seemed likely to follow from women's political participation. Wives and mothers would neglect household duties; political equality would challenge husbandly authority; electoral conflict would introduce acrimony into family life. Anti-suffragists, male and female, instead embraced the view, rooted in common law, that representative government properly represented families (embodied in the male head of household) rather than individuals. Women's enfranchisement would thus be redundant, as women were already represented by their male relatives. The fact that this view of family representation relied on an imagined congruence of interests between husbands and wives that contradicted fears of potential political conflict should women become voters did not prevent figures from making both arguments. "The *family*, and not the *individual*," Linus P. Brockett explained, "is the unit of all organized society and government"; there was, in fact, "no such thing as an *individual right of suffrage*." To enfranchise women would thus present a dangerous departure from precedent, "incompatible with the organization of society, and subversive of its best interests." President of Oberlin College James H. Fairchild affirmed this view in a series of essays on *Woman's Right to the Ballot* (1870). The family was "the great element in the structure of society," and nature and God alike decreed that it was the father who must speak for the family, vote for the family, and pay taxes for the family.[55]

Other voices chimed in to counterpose family suffrage to individual suffrage. Union College professor Tayler Lewis called it "household suffrage," likely borrowing the phrase from Britain, where it was a crucial part of electoral reform debates. This was the only legitimate basis of any form of government, he informed readers of the *Independent*. Former Wisconsin senator James R. Doolittle even proposed a household suffrage bill that would grant male heads of households of dependents two votes—one to "represent their manhood" in common with other men and a second to represent a "household, including women and children." This would have the advantage of not disfranchising anyone, but of lessening the impact of the "floating vote of homeless, houseless, unmarried men, crowded in great cities and towns." Advocates of family or household suffrage also hoped a better recognition of the family's political significance would help combat the "extreme individualism" of the era. Tayler Lewis criticized the incessant calls for this or that groups' specific rights. Men's rights, women's rights, even married women's rights: these demands were shifting the very meaning of the word: A "selfish noun" ("rights") was eclipsing the "holier adjective" ("right"). Household suffrage instead emphasized not rights but "what is right." Lewis's article prompted one reader from Iowa to write the *Independent* and bemoan that while British women had John Stuart Mill, American women were stuck with men like Lewis, who sadly "think to so little purpose on this subject."[56]

What is perhaps most striking is how much anti-suffragists evaded Mill's specific critique of the family as a school of inequality incongruous in a democratic society. They were more overt in rejecting the analogy between marriage and slavery that grounded his legal and historical analysis. Drawing on their own felt experience, these women depicted families as models of devoted, if hierarchical, interdependence. How could women feel "unrepresented," let alone "enslaved," the *True Woman* asked, when they stood at the affectionate center of this social unit and had indeed lovingly "molded" the very men who represented them?[57] If, in Mill's view, women's inequality in the family imperiled democracy, anti-suffragists in the 1870s argued that women's equality in the political sphere endangered the family—and thereby the social order, one household at a time.

The perceived threat to the family, and to gender relations more generally, was a favorite subject of illustrators and cartoonists. Americans thumbing through the pages of illustrated weeklies and monthlies or of woodcut-laden subscription books received a graphic warning about women becoming less womanly and men becoming less manly. A series of woodcuts in Brockett's *Woman: Her Rights and Wrongs* conjured up ominous visions of how politicized women would neglect their paramount duty to the family and the "sacred home" (figure 5.2). Here the woman's "sharp" visage and the "angular," "abrupt," and "self-asserting boldness" with which she throws herself into campaigning visually reinforced the author's warnings that "public life" would become "attractive" to some women and "home duties become tame."[58]

In a visual world that had made the republic's struggle for existence pal-pable, newfound attention was given to the "preservation of pure and peaceful family life," a value that emerged as relating more closely to the "well-being of the nation than any mere political question." *Godey's Lady's Book* printed a

FIG. 5.2 "The Wife and Mother at a Primary" and "The Father Stays at Home Attending to the Children." This sort of gender-reversal imagery was perhaps the most common critical visual response to the campaign for women's po-litical rights. A sharp-faced woman harangues a fellow citizen, while the harried father ushers his recalcitrant chil-dren up to bed. From L. P. Brockett, *Woman: Her Rights, Wrongs, Privileges, and Responsibilities* (1869). Courtesy of the Henry E. Huntington Library.

"Sixteenth Amendment" image that lampooned the likely consequences for traditional gender roles and the family should women become enfranchised (figure 5.3). It was not the chaos of the polling place that was depicted, but the mess that was left behind. The image depicts a man attempting to cook while soothing a distraught toddler as his wife is seen, through the window, leisurely reading a book under a tree. The accompanying article explained that "the idea" behind the image came "from the arguments of those who contend that when woman is given the political rights that at present belong solely to man, her household duties will be neglected, and her husband be compelled to take her place or starve."[59]

The Reconstruction phase of the American woman question retained many familiar features, including ridicule, even if it offered unprecedented attention and depth. But a new note of impatience and fatigue set in. This was evident when the *Christian Advocate* greeted a book-length response to Mill's *Subjection* with a yawning sigh about another work "upon the interminable 'Woman question.'" The following year a Chicago newspaper expressed its readers' weariness with the "everlasting speeches in committee" and woman suffragists who talked and talked and talked to Congressional committees "until the crack of doom." Another editor, either sensing his readers' impatience or projecting his own onto them, offered this editorial note above a multi-installment discussion in 1870: "We must ask to be spared discussion on the woman question, in order to give proper attention to other topics of immediate and perhaps not less importance."[60]

If weariness had become a feature of published opinion by the early 1870s, so too did wariness—especially in the wake of a new round of "free love" controversy. As in the 1840s, such "scandals" revealed the limits of the permissible, especially at a moment when prominent figures were already busy defending the family. No one embodied the "free love" threat more vividly than the controversial Victoria Woodhull, who had risen as a major figure in the Stanton and Anthony-led NWSA. Equal parts reformer, celebrity, and grifter, Woodhull was, in the words of historian Ellen Carol DuBois, "the most scandalous, disruptive, and transformative figure to enter into the suffrage ranks" in these years. Woodhull, née Claflin, survived an exploitative upbringing at the hands of her hustler parents, divorced her first husband, and then lived in one household with him and her new husband before emerging onto the suffrage stage in 1870. She testified before the House Judiciary Committee in 1871, sat for photographs in men's clothing, and attacked the sexual "double standard" by demanding, provocatively, not equal restraint of men but equal sexual freedom for women. While charges of

THE SIXTEENTH AMENDMENT.

FIG. 5.3 "The Sixteenth Amendment." This image also imagines the role-reversal threat of women's enfranchisement should
a fourth Reconstruction constitutional amendment be ratified.
A husband cooks and tends to the toddler while his wife sits
outside leisurely reading a book (perhaps Mill's *The Subjection
of Women*, which had been published the year before). From
Godey's Lady's Book (September 1870). Courtesy of Special
Collections, University of Vermont.

"free love" were among the oldest and most frequent way to discredit women's
rights reformers, Woodhull actually embraced the label. She took the notion
of women's "emancipation" further than nearly anyone else in the movement
was willing to go, declaring an "*inalienable, constitutional,* and *natural* right
to love whom I may."[61]

Woodhull's divisiveness, along with the general volatility of these years, can be tracked by considering the Beecher family. Catharine, Harriet, and Isabella found themselves divided not just over Mill's critique of traditional marriage but over the direction (and personnel) of the women's movement. Isabella Beecher Hooker had become a close associate of Stanton and Anthony and was captivated by Woodhull. She hoped her sisters might come to understand Woodhull's charms, but their sense of propriety (and snobbery) ruled out that possibility. Attuned to the middle-class respectability that association with the Beecher family might bring, Anthony had courted Harriet, hoping to land her as editor of the *Revolution* and urging her to write a novel that might do for the women's movement what *Uncle Tom's Cabin* had done for antislavery. That Stowe even contemplated the prospect attests to the revolutionary possibilities of the immediate postwar moment. She ultimately rejected the invitation—having unsuccessfully requested the publication's name be changed to the far less incendiary *True Republic*—and took a sharp turn toward moderation.[62]

That Harriet had parted ways with her sister Isabella as well as Anthony and Stanton became unmistakable when she began to write a novel on the "woman question" the following year. *My Wife and I* (1870) appeared serially in the *Christian Union* (a family-oriented magazine newly edited by her brother Henry) and deviated sharply from the novel Anthony had envisioned. Its attitude toward the women's rights movement became decidedly cooler as it progressed through installments, ridiculing various figures (including both her sister Isabella and Victoria Woodhull, in a character evocatively named "Miss Audacia Dangyereyes") and giving voice to a notably tepid view of women's rights. An already volatile situation became fully explosive once Woodhull, furious over hypocritical charges of sexual license, went public with accusations of Henry Ward Beecher's own illicit love affair with his female parishioner Elizabeth Tilton. The sordid public scandal hurt the campaign as a whole, and the Beecher clan more personally. Catharine and Harriet rose to Henry's defense, while Isabella stuck with Woodhull. Nobody won, least of all the women's movement.[63]

By the mid-1870s many aspects of the woman question remained unresolved. The subject had garnered attention in all corners of American culture, drawing more and more activists, querists, and critics into discussion. But the momentum so evident just a decade earlier, when the end of an emancipatory war seemed to promise transformation, had slowed. Divisions—among activists, among lawmakers, and among women in general—stalled further progress. The emergence of an organized, visible, and vocal group of anti-suffrage women represented a new and lasting force that would hamper movement figures' claims to speak on behalf of "women." The women involved in the *True Woman* and the Anti-Sixteenth Amendment Society united around a vision of what might be dubbed "benevolent coverture." The worst features of coverture, the legal obliteration of married women's personhood, had been removed, and *Minor v. Happersett* had clarified women's citizenship status. But in eschewing full political participation and embracing a vision of family representation and household suffrage, the anti-suffrage women retained a kind of political coverture. The United States remained politically, as much as it had been in the 1830s, an "aristocracy of sex."

A trip Isabella Beecher Hooker took in the spring of 1874 takes on added poignancy in this context. Traveling through Europe, she made a detour to Avignon to pay homage at the graves of Harriet Taylor Mill and her loving husband, who had died the previous year. Hooker had encountered Taylor Mill's 1851 "Enfranchisement of Women" more than a decade after it appeared, but she made up for the delay with her zeal for its message. She had published her own Taylor Mill-inspired articles, sent them to Mill, and begun a correspondence with him amidst the heady optimism of the late-1860s. In Avignon, she entreated the groundskeeper to allow her to pluck some "blossoms for pressing" from the French cemetery. Those "dear dead saints," she wrote a British acquaintance, were "the only two in all Europe at whose shrine I reverently worship." The episode felt like an elegy not just for the departed couple but for the moment of possibility that had burned so brightly before it expired.[64]

6

Unresolved Questions

IF ISABELLA BEECHER HOOKER'S graveside visit in Avignon had a touch of the elegiac, the atmosphere only became more funereal at home in subsequent decades. Enthusiastic advocacy of democracy—consistent or otherwise— began to recede from published opinion over the last decades of the nineteenth century. Uncertainty about popular government existed throughout the century, but that uncertainty grew both more acute and more conspicuous in these years. Modes of self-government that a half-century earlier had been viewed as transformational—anxiously pondered over by some but more generally hailed as America's distinct contribution to the modern world—became something narrower, less celebrated, and altogether more perplexing.

Many Americans seemed newly willing to subject "universal suffrage" and democracy itself to reappraisal, while others moved on from the topic altogether. The reasons for this were multiple. Many middle-class white, Protestant Northerners had their own anxieties over the increase in immigrant voters, which made them little inclined to quarrel with the disfranchising efforts of their white counterparts in the South. Fears of a "crisis" of urban governance and the emergence of labor unrest, especially in the wake of the Paris Commune of 1871, only exacerbated these anxieties. A further uncertainty centered on the disaffection that many Americans, from multiple perspectives and backgrounds, felt from a partisan politics that had taken organization to a new level and seemed primarily focused on the spoils of victory. Though it faced vigorous challenges from the Greenback Party, Prohibition Party, the Liberal Republican and Mugwump "bolters," and the People's (or Populist) Party, the two-party system, which had become one-party rule in the solid South, demonstrated remarkable stability. More prominently, an emboldened opposition to the "experiment" of Black suffrage in the South supplemented violence and fraud with new legislative and constitutional methods of disfranchising African American men. These efforts met little resistance from white Northerners, or from a Supreme Court that ruled poll taxes and literary tests were permissible under the Fifteenth Amendment. Finally, the late-century occupation of territories in the Caribbean and Pacific elicited new debates over self-government and the capacities it might require.

In this climate, the question of women's political participation faced a new set of hurdles. As Thomas Wentworth Higginson noted in 1881, "the commonest argument against woman suffrage" today had less to do with the hoary matters of intrinsic sex difference than with the shortcomings of democracy itself. A kind of sex equality had finally been achieved, he observed with rueful irony, in this "spasm of re-action" against "universal suffrage," as ordinary women took their place beside ordinary men in being deemed unfit for self-government.[1] Other ironies abounded. As some observers noted, after the tiny territorial legislature in Wyoming granted women the right to vote there in 1869, it was large male majorities that seemed the surest check on any democratic expansion to include women elsewhere. Individual lawmakers— in territorial and state legislatures, congressional committees, and even British Parliament—might be persuaded by movement activists, but when male electorates were asked to weigh in, they seemed generally content to uphold their "aristocratic" privilege.

Further ironies could be seen in the modification of tactics and strategies for those working against the male monopoly of voting. The largest mobilization on behalf of women's enfranchisement emerged in the 1880s, via the Women's Christian Temperance Union (WCTU), but it did so without invoking core principles of self-government. The newly united National American Woman Suffrage Association (NAWSA) dropped the "consistent democracy" theme when it rebooted the endorsement strategy first ventured in the late antebellum years. By 1893 that emphasis had given way to a simple framing of "eminent opinions" that often failed to address the larger principles of self-government and democratic participation.[2]

"Eminent opinions," however, were just as easily marshaled against women's enfranchisement, as the odd celebrity that Francis Parkman achieved in the last decades of the century revealed. Perhaps the most accomplished American historian of his generation, Parkman lent his considerable prestige to the skewering of democratic principles and what he considered their most foolhardy, if logical, consequence—the push to provide women with the ballot. His work justified the country's pivot from the idealism of the immediate post–Civil War years, and his efforts became a key reference point thereafter. Organized opponents of women's enfranchisement highlighted his fiery words in multiple editions of a pamphlet they titled *Some of the Reasons against Woman Suffrage*. Even after the author's death, his assault remained the stand-out contribution across the voluminous testimony circulated in opposition to a women's suffrage amendment. Looking back from 1915, one of the most prominent anti-suffragists dated her group's public campaign to Parkman's 1879 *North American Review* treatment of "The Woman Question."[3]

Democratic disaffection could further be seen in the rhetorical formulation that had emerged to counter the activists' decades-long criticism that "half of the population" was disfranchised. Skeptics and opponents warned instead of the dangers of "doubling the electorate," especially one that in their opinion, already rested on too wide a basis. This formulation drew its power from the way it alluded to a series of unresolved questions that had been posed for years but found expression in high-profile venues. Was Black suffrage a mistake? Did the majority of women even want to be "self-governing"? Could all citizens, including the male and female streams of immigrants in the 1870s–1890s, be assimilated and educated through political participation? Would the enfranchisement of women improve or aggravate the ills of democracy? In short, how democratic should the nation be?

One-time German revolutionary turned liberal Republican Carl Schurz captured the mood in a widely circulated piece in 1894. The American people once "flattered themselves" that they had solved "the problem of democratic government," he wrote. But that "state of self-congratulation" no longer existed. As a constitutional convention in New York state debated a women's suffrage amendment that summer, Schurz cautioned that "in the democratization of our institutions by enlargements of the suffrage we have gone fully as far as the safety of the republic will warrant."[4]

A Wide-Spread and Growing Distrust of Our Democratic Institutions

Parkman's emergence as the embodiment of Gilded Age disquiet about popular government began as a scattershot effort, dashed off with none of the care evident in his meticulous historical work. Just a few months into the centennial year of the Declaration of Independence, he took to the pages of the Boston *Advertiser* to scoff at the right to vote. His fellow Bostonian Thomas Wentworth Higginson chided him for his argument and claimed that his words might just as well have come from Jefferson Davis, Louis Napoleon, the Pope, or New England's own Federalist establishment, defunct for over a half-century. What connected that reactionary group was the belief that political participation could be curtailed if it proved to be "dangerous and harmful to the community." And in Parkman's view, women's full inclusion in the body politic would be distinctly harmful. Parkman's 1876 *Advertiser* article echoed Thomas Jefferson and Horace Bushnell on the dangers of "promiscuous" or mixed assemblies to warn that "sensualist" women invested with power would use their "charms" to seduce officeholders. The lack of "deliberate reserve" among assertive women and the weakness of men would lead to vulgar indiscretions, which along with a prurient press would further debase public deliberation. His warning implicitly invoked the recent sex scandals of Victoria Woodhull and Henry Ward Beecher. Prolific illustrator Joseph Keppler gave visual force to the hint of sexualized politics in a two-page set of images for *Puck* magazine. Keppler played on the Oliver Goldsmith poem about a "fallen" woman (one who "stooped to folly") in a series of vignettes that showed men and women behaving badly, titled "When Lovely Women Stoops to Lobby."[5]

Parkman's opposition to women's suffrage extended directly from his broader hostility to universal suffrage, and he enthusiastically elaborated both these positions in multiple essays and letters. The notion that "the ignorant, incompetent and vicious of any color or either sex should vote," he wrote Higginson privately, "I regard as a peril to civilization, and an injury to the entire community, themselves included."[6] This notion had developed over the course of his lifetime. He looked back with nostalgia to the New England of his youth, which represented (he agreed with Tocqueville) "the most successful democracy on earth." But that was before the "hordes" of Irish immigrants began flooding in, providing the labor that fed the rapidly expanding textile mills and built the railroads that transformed the United States. The Civil War seemed to him a moment of possibility—a chance for Northerners to put their selfish pursuits aside and, not incidentally, for elite Bostonians to play their rightful role as leaders in shaping national destiny. Writing amidst another wave of immigration, labor unrest, and new pockets of extreme wealth and immiserated poverty, Parkman honed his grudge against the nineteenth century's seeming fixation on mass political participation. What particularly irritated him was his sense that people who likely agreed with him felt coerced by a politically correct published opinion. Parkman himself felt no such "squeamishness." Indeed, he relished the controversy that would accompany an "attack on the sovereign Demos."[7]

What elevated Parkman from disaffected skeptic to national spokesman for reaction was a new mode of querying. Boston-born, Oxford-educated Allen Thorndike Rice had purchased the *North American Review* in 1876 and

"No Kiss till you Sign my Bill."

FIG. 6.1 Detail from J. Keppler, "When Lovely Women Stoops to Lobby—A Capital Picture." This detail from Keppler's larger series of images hints at the salacious political activity that might result from women's enfranchisement. Keppler mocked the weakness of men and the unscrupulous women who preyed on them. Along with the sexual bartering portrayed here, Keppler included images of Eve as the "original lobbyist," adulterous politicians bestowing gifts on female lobbyists, and "ugly" women being shut out of the political "game" altogether. From *Puck Magazine* (April 2, 1879). Courtesy of Dartmouth College Library.

quickly transformed the old, "dignified" New England quarterly into a "scintillating and lively" monthly that now published out of New York. Rice's key innovation, and the formula by which the *North American Review* gained expanded influence as a trend-setter, consisted of organized exchanges about the leading "questions" of the day, a mode he self-consciously borrowed from the innovative British monthly the *Nineteenth Century*. An inclination to sponsor a series of in-depth symposia coincided with Rice's push to include celebrity figures, whose standing would draw attention to full-throttled discussion of a variety of pressing matters, whether or not the authors had expertise on the topic. "Controversy," as magazine historian Frank Luther Mott observed, became "the settled policy of the magazine." And controversy paid: the *North American Review's* circulation soared under Rice's editorship.[8]

America's apparent political failings dominated Rice's early efforts to remake the *North American Review*. The first five issues under his direction featured lead stories on the 1876–1877 electoral college crisis, each from a different perspective. That "point/counterpoint" rhythm continued, with Parkman's screed on "The Failure of Universal Suffrage" in the July 1878 issue followed by Wendell Phillips's defense of broad-based voting as a "sheet-anchor" of the nation the following month. The next year, the magazine addressed the attack on Black voting by Southern "Redeemer" Democrats, with an eight-person forum responding to two questions: "Ought the Negro to Be Disfranchised? Ought He to Have Been Enfranchised?" The symposium balanced partisan and sectional (though not racial) perspectives, placing the idealism of Wendell Phillips and James Garfield (who would shortly hail Black men's voting but not women's in his inauguration as the twentieth American president) into conversation with the notably circumspect contributions of Southern whites. If no contributor responded that Black men "ought to be disfranchised," several demurred on the question of whether they should have been granted the vote in the first place. By merely posing the questions and entertaining the possibility of Black disfranchisement, the ground was laid for more strident positions that democracy worked best when limited to racially superior whites. Two years after the Black suffrage forum, a Mississippi judge offered his own withering assessment to *North American Review* readers, as he blamed voting by the freedmen for "debasing the value of the franchise in popular estimation."[9]

Such fora in a high-profile, respectable northern periodical both shaped the terms of debate, by creating what today might be called a "permission structure" for the expression of ever more extreme opinions, and helped force others into various concessions. Just as a forum on Black suffrage was followed by cruder charges, Parkman's attack on the corruption of city politics was amplified and extended both in the *North American Review* and other corners of the national discourse. A Tennessee lawyer and diplomat in 1884 lashed out against what he called "unqualified or 'tramp' suffrage" and placed the blame not on the Reconstruction amendments but on the state governments that had decades earlier "sowed the dragon's teeth" of unrestricted suffrage that he alleged created havoc in America's cities. Absent from the original state constitutions, the idea of "universal suffrage," like so many dangerous ideas, was a modern one, not "indigenous to the soil of the United States" at all but really an import from the "slums of European cities."[10] Parkman reiterated the peril of empowering women from the lower social strata in the North's rapidly urbanizing core. Middle-class women would soon be "outvoted in their own kitchens" by a more numerous servant class, he warned. Even some of his most pointed critics felt compelled to agree with parts of this analysis. Higginson, for example, conceded that women's enfranchisement might well bring with it "some of the same obstacles from ignorant and unscrupulous voting" that we already "experience on the part of men." But he countered Parkman's pessimism by insisting this was "simply the price we pay for self-government."[11]

The woman question moved from the periphery to the center of the broader debate over universal suffrage when Rice and his assistants structured an exchange of views between Parkman and "five chiefs of the woman-suffrage movement." Elizabeth Cady Stanton, Lucy Stone, Julia Ward Howe, Wendell Phillips, and Higginson provided, in a series of short responses, "The Other Side of the Woman Question." Parkman then responded to their collective rebuttal. In contrast to the respectful give-and-take of many *North American Review* fora, Parkman displayed withering condescension toward his antagonists, whom he privately dubbed "the wrathful five." They were representative of a broader group of reformers who had "spent their time for several decades in ceaseless demands for suffrage," only to see their arguments fail in "years of empty agitation." Welcoming their criticism that his comments were out of date and "unoriginal," Parkman replied that a lack of originality was hardly a knock against the convictions "of the great majority of sensible and thoughtful persons of both sexes."[12]

The collective argument made by the "Other Side" formed a cohesive whole, which stretched foundational movement convictions into the post-Reconstruction context: the educative nature of the ballot and the need to make democracy consistent by including that half of the population that had been barred from political participation. Higginson summed up the first of these after acknowledging that many women might not fully understand some public questions. If true, this fact actually constituted an argument in favor of their enfranchisement, since "all experience shows" that there was "no educational discipline like the ballot." The second point was stated most forcefully by Stone, who observed that the "principle of limited suffrage" might be "blameless" in an "aristocracy" but was simply impossible in a democracy. "Men who deny political rights to women can show no title to their own," she declared. Phillips, recalling his recent wrangling with Parkman over universal male voting, noted that "if such be his feeling toward manhood suffrage, no wonder our friend dreads extending it to women." Such a framing was meant not to sway Parkman but to discredit his position in the court of public opinion. Former congressman George Julian echoed these convictions in a string of articles he used to yoke together themes of democracy and women's rights and to warn against the "wide-spread and growing distrust of our democratic institutions." These kinds of exchanges would appear with some regularity in periodicals over the next couple of decades.[13]

Three of Parkman's "wrathful five" were affiliated with the Boston-based *Woman's Journal*, a weekly that would continue to mold a national print constituency for women's enfranchisement well into the twentieth century. The state legislature on Beacon Hill regularly heard gubernatorial pleas to extend the ballot to women beginning in 1871, and female clerks served in that body's lower House as early as the Civil War years. Harriet Robinson, who along with her daughter was among the women employed by the House of Representatives, popularized the notion of a "Woman's Hour" from the end of the Grant presidency through the mid-1880s. When the upstart Boston *Globe* used the same phrase to rebrand its weekly "Ladies Bazaar" column in 1882, it noted that the phrase had become "such a condensation of the spirit of the times" as to have "passed into a proverb." Caroline Dall invoked this Boston groundswell to explain why the monkish Parkman had been forced to lift "his head from the old French chronicles he has so profitably perused" and address the question. He could hardly avoid it: "The discussion has entered his study, and turned him out!"[14]

As had been true in the struggles over slavery, Boston's politics was neither monolithic nor trending all in one direction. Dall proved overly optimistic in her insistence that it "seems certain that this experiment [of women voting] is to be tried." In the limited case of school elections, Massachusetts women did begin to cast ballots the very same year (1879) as Parkman's first "The Woman Question" piece. For some observers, school elections were safe from the alarm about lower-class and ignorant voters that Parkman had sounded. Andrew Preston Peabody, the Plummer Professor of Christian morals at

Harvard, drew a distinction between school suffrage and what he called "political suffrage," which would draw out "ignorant and vicious" women and ex-
acerbate all the evils that currently existed among male voters. "Every woman
who ought not to vote would vote" in these contests, while "educated and
trustworthy" women steered clear of the polls. By contrast, schoolboard
elections posed little threat, especially if they were held at a separate time and
place from general political elections, and if, as in Massachusetts, the "privilege" of voting in them was based on a tax-paying requirement. These narrow
and specialized elections to guide schools would hold out no inducements to
unsavory voters or corrupt parties and would thus only attract those women
who, as mothers, were already invested in the education of the young. A series
of illustrations from voting day that appeared in *Frank Leslie's Illustrated News*
seemed to establish that warnings of impending disaster had been hyperbolic
(figure 6.2). The sky did not fall in Boston, any more than it had when women
(at least unmarried, property-holding women) began casting ballots in municipal elections in England a decade earlier or in all elections held in the territories of Wyoming (1869), Utah (1870), and Washington (1883).[15]

Neither the *North American Review* debate nor school elections fully
answered what remained a key unresolved question: whether the bulk of
women valued self-government or whether they were largely content to remain governed by the men in their lives. Parkman included no explicit reference to the "willing yoke" that Tocqueville had imagined in the pact between
the American wife and her husband. But his own sense of what most women
truly wanted aligned well with that portrait of voluntary subordination. The
anti-suffrage case rested on the conceit, articulated by the Anti-Sixteenth
Amendment Society and captured powerfully in Parkman's "The Woman
Question" essay, that "a small number of women" were attempting to "im-
pose on all the rest political duties which there is no call for their assuming,
which they do not want to assume, and which, if duly discharged, would be
a cruel and intolerable burden." Women's rights activists considered such a
sweeping charge to be too absurd to merit a reasoned response and instead
devoted energy to more and more petitions to demonstrate women's desire
for the vote. But the notion that some disempowered groups were ill-served
by "intermeddling" efforts to enfranchise them was gaining in strength as a
tenet of reactionary politics. Skeptics also pointed to low turnout in school
elections as a sign of most women's indifference.[16]

Novelist Henry James appreciated how the rift among Bostonians
could be a uniquely rich setting to explore whether enfranchisement might
hold less appeal for individual women than zealous reformers assumed. As

WOMEN CANVASSERS BESIEGING BEACON HILL VOTERS, BOSTON.

FIG. 6.2 This individual scene from the two-page spread "Massachusetts—Woman Suffrage in the Bay State," shows (tax-paying) women voting in school board elections. Women and men alike canvass voters but with no apparent damaging impact. The only element of the polling place that seems to have changed with the introduction of women is a ban on smoking, which Thomas Wentworth Higginson called "a great step toward decency and order." From *Frank Leslie's Illustrated Newspaper* (December 20, 1879). Courtesy of the Henry E. Huntington Library.

he cast about for a topic for a new novel, he sought "a very American tale, a tale very characteristic of our social conditions." He decided to revisit one of his father's chief antebellum preoccupations by composing a story that would address "the situation of women" and "the agitation on their behalf." The result was *The Bostonians*, serialized in the mass-circulation

Century Magazine beginning in 1885, which dramatized the struggle for the affection and possession of the young, beautiful Verena Tarrant, a character who, not unlike Victoria Woodhull, survived grifter parents to emerge as a charismatic performer, first of spiritualist rappings and then of speeches on women's rights. Two adversaries square off in a contest to win her over—Bostonian reformer Olive Chancellor (a "roaring radical," "a female Jacobin," someone who "would reform the solar system if she could get a hold of it") and her cousin, a Confederate veteran from Mississippi named Basil Ransom.[17]

The Bostonians can be read as an extended debate over women and self-government. Unsurprisingly, it found an eager audience in the Parkman household, each chapter read aloud when it arrived (in monthly installments) in the *Century*, a periodical that also featured ongoing discussions of the citizenship of African Americans and women.[18] Reading the novel in the context of those larger debates, what emerges is a depiction of a young woman who shows no capacity for self-governance but, more disturbingly, no desire for it either. Verena is repeatedly depicted as a cipher, thoroughly dominated by others—learning her "rule from without," to use Margaret Fuller's phrase, never unfolding it from within. She is bullied by both Olive and Basil, performing without believing the speeches Olive crams into her head and then falling at the end for the reactionary misogynist Basil. Olive complains earlier in the novel that the young working women she tries to convert to the cause always end up falling in love instead, caring more about boyfriends than the ballot. Verena not only confirms this complaint, she then chooses as a partner someone who promises to do nothing but dominate her as an unequal, who responds to her lecturing career by promising to "strike her dumb" were he to become her husband.[19]

James memorably specified Basil Ransom's politics. Ransom is a "reactionary," the narrator explains, a man who is "very suspicious of the encroachments of modern democracy." Though he enjoys "reading a volume of De Tocqueville" and thinking about "forms of government and the happiness of peoples," he recognizes that his own convictions were such that he "scarcely could think of the country where they would be a particular advantage to him." He has ambitions of being a published author and drafts "half a dozen articles," but no publisher wants them. Rejecting one paper "on the rights of minorities," a magazine editor informs Ransom that "his doctrines were about three hundred years behind the age." A magazine of the sixteenth century might have been "very happy to print them," but they would not do for the nineteenth century.

Ransom's views on women are no less antiquated. He prefers women "not to think too much, not to feel any responsibility for the government of the world." When Verena tells him she feels useful speaking so success-fully for the cause of women, Ransom informs her that "the use of a truly amiable woman is to make some honest man happy." As he contemplates marrying her, he knows he will put an end to her lecturing career. James made Ransom an increasingly less sympathetic character as the chapters proceeded, and yet he has Verena choose Ransom nonetheless. The story ends darkly, with Ransom wrenching her away, "by muscular force," just as she is about to give a women's rights lecture to a huge crowd. She claims to be happy as she leaves with him, but she is in tears. The narrator ominously informs the reader that given the marital choice she has made these tears were likely "not the last she was destined to shed." Verena's choice thus mir-rored the argument critics had been making for nearly two decades: that women did not want to vote, did not want political equality with men, and did not value self-governance.

Groups of white women, in Boston and elsewhere, would provide new ev-idence to support this claim as they mobilized against women's suffrage in the coming years. Building on the initial efforts of Madeleine Dahlgren, Charlotte McKay, and Susan Fenimore Cooper in the 1870s, new anti-suffrage organ-izations surfaced at century's end. The fact that at least some women were already voting in at least some elections forced these women to adopt the awk-ward name (and even more awkward abbreviation) that made clear they were against the "further extension" of the suffrage. The Massachusetts Association Opposed to the Further Extension of Suffrage to Women (MAOFESW) and its New York counterpart (the NYSAOWS) sprang into action in response to specific threats, such as a constitutional convention in New York in 1894 and a referendum the following year in Massachusetts. Their organizational presence, and the literature they produced and circulated, would continue to offer opponents of women's enfranchisement an easy rationale for inaction.[20]

Self-Government in a Scientific Age

Perhaps it is no wonder that democratic uncertainty increased as white middle-class Americans expressed bewilderment at a world of alarming—and alarmingly visible—inequality, labor strikes, and mass immigration. National discussions of self-government became increasingly awkward, even embar-rassing in the 1890s, as Black American men were effectively disfranchised in several southern states and the United States occupied Caribbean and Pacific islands and imposed colonial governments on their inhabitants. Other languages that better fit these times gained traction. The most dominant idiom borrowed from science, which increased in cultural authority every decade of the late nineteenth century. While evolutionary theory in general was not novel, it had found new prestige and popularity in the decades after the appearance of Charles Darwin's *On the Origins of Species* (1859). In the late nineteenth century, all manner of questions received the evolutionary treatment, and to speak in scientific, evolutionary terms was to establish cultural legitimacy.[21]

Two consequential books published in these decades reveal the larger trend: Edward Bellamy's *Looking Backward* (1888) and Charlotte Perkins Gilman's *Women and Economics: A Study of the Economic Relation Between Men and Women as a Factor in Social Evolution* (1898). Bellamy's utopian novel tapped into anxieties over economic inequality and class conflict by imagining a peaceful evolution into an egalitarian and cooperative future. The book was a veritable phenomenon, selling enough copies, in the words of one critic, to "make a ring around the world, if they were placed edge to edge." Further, and in a development that would have stunned the 1840s Fourierists, the book inspired Americans across the country to form "Nationalist" clubs devoted to turning the novelist's utopia into a reality. Bellamy's novel envisioned a harmonious world free of class conflict where all lived in an egalitarian, frictionless, and consumer-friendly welfare state. Not incidentally, it was also a world free of democratic government altogether, where the good life was "managed" not by "the people" but by a cadre of wise retired citizens. The absence of African Americans and immigrants, as well as the vagueness with which the novel treats the place of women, reveals the limits of late-nineteenth-century utopian thinking.[22]

Gilman's *Women and Economics* (1898), by contrast, represented the most significant book on the woman question to appear at century's end. Gilman had likely imbibed discussions about women's status and contributions to society in a childhood surrounded by her three great-aunts: Catharine Beecher, Harriet Beecher Stowe, and Isabella Beecher Hooker. She rejected Catharine and Harriet's emphasis on domesticity and instead critiqued women's constrained opportunities outside of marriage, reinterpreting them through an economic and evolutionary lens. Modern civilization, she argued, had created an artificial environment for women, which, in making them dependent on men through marriage, had removed them from the "struggle for existence." This harmed women, to be sure, but also held back "the race" as a whole. Gilman's analysis represented a vital and provocative new field of knowledge and interpretation, but one that largely ignored democratic governance.[23]

Self-government similarly receded from the works of a professionalizing political science, certainly compared to what it had been in the early social scientific works of Tocqueville and Martineau in the 1830s. The process of professionalization took off in the postbellum years, amidst a transformation and expansion in higher education.[24] An initial organizational effort was made by the American Social Science Association (ASSA) in 1865, which had brought together reformers and scientists from a range of backgrounds. New discipline-specific professional associations (e.g., the American Historical Association [1884], American Economic Association [1885], and the American Political Science Association [1903]) became models for narrowing specialization. Whereas Caroline Dall could play a leading role in founding the ASSA, by the end of the century "advanced" social scientific thinking, especially political science, had largely become the preserve of professional men such as Herbert Baxter Adams at Johns Hopkins, A. Lawrence Lowell at Harvard, Woodrow Wilson at Princeton, Frank Goodnow at Columbia, and Charles Merriam at Chicago (Goodnow, Lowell, and Wilson would serve as three early presidents of APSA). The focus of their works tended to emphasize the law, institutions, and statecraft more than citizens' participation. They stressed the distinction between the "scientific tendency" of their scholarship and the ideas and doctrines that continued to make up a "popular creed" among the public.[25]

The contrast between Tocqueville's *Democracy in America* and English jurist James Bryce's *American Commonwealth* (1888), written a half-century later, provides an inexact but instructive indication of the shift. Where Tocqueville had imagined democracy as a providential force, infusing an egalitarian spirit into nearly every aspect of American life, Bryce presented a more empirical and institutional approach to American statecraft. Lay people often use "the word Democracy" to mean an ethos or a tendency, Bryce acknowledged, something like the "spirit of equality." For his purposes, the term meant merely "a form of government" in which the "numerical majority rules." A disciple of Mill in the 1860s and a future president of the American Political Science Association, Bryce routinely hailed Tocqueville's *Democracy* as a masterful and penetrating work, but he urged his fellow political scientists to remember that "it is really a work of art rather than a work of science." Many others—including Johns Hopkins University president Daniel Coit Gilman, when he introduced a new edition of Tocqueville's work in 1898—would repeat versions of this distinction in the following decades, even as they praised the philosophical genius of Tocqueville.[26]

Self-government further faded from public discussion as the United States occupied new territories in the Caribbean and Pacific. Colonial possessions complicated discussions of this idea and even contributed to what University of Chicago political scientist Charles Merriam admitted might be considered "a decline of democratic faith." But as he carefully explained in his *History of American Political Theories* (1903), the phrase "consent of the governed" had never been intended in a "literal" sense through all American history. Instead, Americans had long taken the view that "liberty and natural rights" were "conditioned upon political capacity," and that "consent of the governed" was more of an aspirational principle that "in the present state of affairs, cannot be perfectly realized." A cursory examination of history would show that Native Americans, African Americans, and women of all races had routinely been subjected to the governance of others. This was the only "tenable" position for a "modern democracy" to take, as "democracy does not demand that barbarians be admitted to equal political rights with peoples long trained in the art of self-government." Judged by this standard of "political capacity" rather than "equality," Merriam could discern no democratic backsliding.[27]

If democracy narrowed and became more technical in these works, the "woman question" was widely ignored. Bryce was somewhat of an outlier in this regard. He included two full chapters on women in the *American Commonwealth* (1888), noting the progress they had made in dismantling almost the entire legal scaffolding of coverture. Like Tocqueville and Martineau, he discussed the institution of marriage, which he saw as more egalitarian than its European or English counterparts (a difference he ascribed to the "democratic feeling" of the Americans). But he observed that American men seemed to draw the line at political equality. He devoted a chapter to women's suffrage, which he did not think could be "called one of the foremost issues of to-day." The topic interested him primarily for how it illustrated the general manner in which "political proposals spring up, and are agitated and handled" in the United States. His survey of school suffrage, municipal suffrage (in Kansas), and suffrage in three territories basically elicited a shrug: "Why not?" If women's enfranchisement would likely not bring about the improvement in government some claimed for it, neither would it lead to the collapse of civilization others feared from it. As a folksy informant from Wyoming told him about its impact there: things would likely be very much what they were before, only more so.[28]

Bryce's dismissal of the "sentimentalism" involved in the question was more typical of political scientists. Though opponents of extending the right to vote had for decades insisted that the franchise was a privilege and not a right, political scientists elaborated this view and enveloped it in the authority of objectivity and expertise. For example, Russian political scientist and jurist Moisei Ostrogorski, in the prize-winning study he wrote as a political science student in Paris, presented himself as a social scientific version of the querist. Given what his English publisher noted as the "increased importance attaching to the Woman's Rights question throughout the civilized world," the book soon appeared in London and New York editions. Even-handed and dispassionate, Ostrogorski considered the law an "umpire" that might provide, amidst the partisan "din" of a thousand voices, an objective answer to the woman question. Surveying the experience and law in multiple countries, he discerned a clear trend toward women's intellectual and economic emancipation but an equally strong one against their "political equality with men"— a twofold attitude he thought the "great American democracy of the United States" perfectly encapsulated. Concerned that reviews of the earlier French edition of his book had taken him to be a partisan on the issue, he took pains to demonstrate his neutrality. He "should have exceeded" his powers had he "taken part either for or against [woman] suffrage." He sought merely to offer a methodical legal history, which demonstrated that participation in the government is simply a matter of politics, with no larger principle (such as "natural right") at stake.[29]

Movement activists reflected and participated in these scientific cultural currents. The National American Woman Suffrage Association (NAWSA) launched a "Political Science Study Series" in the 1890s, intended "to provide a systematic course of self-instruction in the principles and facts which underlie the great political questions of our day." Intriguingly, several entries in the series simply bundled together old speeches and essays by Harriet Taylor Mill, Wendell Phillips, and George William Curtis, only sometimes with introductions that contextualized and explained the enduring relevance of these midcentury efforts. Set alongside the multivolume *History of Woman Suffrage* (1882) and the collection and presentation of nearly a thousand volumes on the history of women (called the Galatea Collection) to the Boston Public Library in 1896, the "political science study series" might be seen as a context-specific adaptation of the 1848 Declaration of Sentiment's original call to "circulate tracts," "enlist" the press, and generally saturate published opinion.[30]

But inadvertently the "classic" essays by Taylor Mill, Phillips, and others called attention to how much arguments about consistent democracy and women's full self-government had disappeared as core movement convictions. The decades-long tension between the rival visions of democratic political participation as educative or as requiring prior education tilted decisively in favor of the latter by century's end. In multiple venues in the 1890s, Elizabeth Cady Stanton urged "educated suffrage" as the solution to democracy's ills. Returning to a topic she had discussed for decades, she advised Congress to "enact a law for 'educated suffrage'" that would apply to "our native-born as well as foreign rulers." Her main goal was to remove the "popular objection" to women's enfranchisement, which seemed to be the fear of "doubling the ignorant vote." If this were so, all legislators had to do, she explained, was "abolish the ignorant vote." At a minimum, Stanton argued such a measure would assuage disfranchised women who, if they were to be ruled by a "male aristocracy," would prefer at least that their rulers be "able to read and write" and "understand the principles of republican government."[31]

Lucy Stone, testifying before the House Judiciary Committee in 1892, urged Congress to pass and send to the states a Sixteenth Amendment containing an "educational qualification." Everyone should have "the right to vote who cares to vote," but anyone who did care, she reasoned (conflating education with literacy), "can learn to read." Brains, not sex, appeared to many as a safer criterion for enfranchisement, an argument illustrated in an odd book by an Ohio-based Presbyterian minister titled *Female Filosofy* (1894), which gave a crude visual statement of the contrast (figure 6.3). Stone's old collaborator on the 1858 *Consistent Democracy* pamphlet, Thomas Wentworth Higginson, bemoaned this tendency. He felt certain there were winnable allies on the question of democratic principle who were being driven into opposition by the movement itself. It "has at times seemed to me," he wrote privately to one of the organizers of the campaign for the 1895 Massachusetts referendum, "that if our whole policy was to make it as hard as possible for every Democrat, every Catholic, and every foreign-born citizen to vote on our side we could not have managed it better."[32]

Movement activists understandably had cause to doubt the wisdom of democratic electorates, given how often all-male majorities voted against extending the franchise to women. The editors of the multivolume *History of Woman Suffrage* described the hurdles that constitutional law had erected in their path. Changes to organic law required the support of the all-male electorate in various states—a far higher burden than merely a vote by a few

FIG. 6.3 "Sex the Basis for the Ballot" and "Brains the Basis for the Ballot." This crude two-panel illustration appeared in one of the more bizarre books published on the woman question. The contrasting visions of the polling place make the argument that an unrestricted male suffrage results in a rowdy electorate, prone to fighting, drinking, and pickpocketing. A sex-neutral suffrage based on "brains" however yields an orderly—and white and middle-class—electorate. From Felix Feeler, *Female Filosofy, Fished Out and Fried* (1894). Courtesy of the Henry E. Huntington Library.

dozen statesmen in a state legislature or a decision by a handful of people on a board of trustees. Had other matters been put to a mass vote, the editors darkly surmised, women would likely not have been allowed to vote in territories, to own property, or even to attend college. Structurally, women were dependent on a "prejudiced, conservative, and in a degree vicious and igno-rant electorate possessed absolutely" with plenary power to withhold or to grant women the ballot. And by the turn of the century the editors felt they were swimming upstream, campaigning for women's enfranchisement amidst a "modern skepticism as to the supreme merit of a democratic government."[33]

The paradoxical way democracy (defined as majority rule) seemed to pro-vide a check on the further extension of democracy (defined as equal political rights) became a widely noted phenomenon. Writing in 1888, Bryce observed that women had received full voting rights largely when it had been granted by tiny numbers of legislators in territorial governments; amendments submitted to the electorate had routinely failed, often by wide margins, and no majority of male voters had extended the suffrage to women. In the decade after Bryce published his book, however, male voters approved measures enfranchising women in four states—Wyoming (1889), Colorado (1893), Utah (1895), and Idaho (1896). But eminent Anglo-American historian Goldwin Smith could make the broader point in 1890, amidst debates over Wyoming statehood. Smith had been a one-time supporter of women's enfranchisement—he had even signed the petition to Parliament presented by John Stuart Mill before the end of his term in 1868—but he had changed his mind and begun to write occasional articles explaining his opposition. With his eye on the recent Third Reform Act (1884) in England, he looked with some envy on the con-stitutional means Americans had for checking the extension of the franchise. He feared MPs were too easily bullied by every "clamorous demand" for re-form, whereas women's suffrage in the United States had to go through large electorates made up of individual male voters who "are not trembling for their re-election" or "afraid of making an enemy" among nonvoting women. After all, he observed, "the American [male] citizen was satisfied of his right" and generally saw no reason to cede his privilege. Smith was part of a larger trend of British conservatives who began, at the end of the century, to study what they considered the admirable checks on the popular will that the American system provided.[34]

Democracy, historically considered, had never embraced women as polit-ical actors, according to prominent New York anti-suffragist Helen Kendrick Johnson—and that was a good thing. She devoted a full chapter to the ques-tion "Is Woman Suffrage Democratic?" in her book *Woman and the Republic* (1897). Her answer: no. Surveying multiple democracies and republics across time and space, this densely argued tome found that none of them included women as equal political participants. Yet history showed that women had played significant political roles in monarchies, despotisms, and aristocracies

of various kinds. So, judging by the historical record, women's political participation was not part of the democratic inheritance. Further, Johnson
made much of the fact that Utah was among the first places to introduce
women's suffrage in the United States—a territory, and subsequently a state,
rife with Mormonism, which she considered a combination of communism
and polygamy. The "introduction of woman suffrage within our borders," she
concluded, was thus "not only undemocratic, it was anti-democratic." Women
had made tremendous progress across the centuries, but none of that progress
depended on them participating in the polity. In fact, the "dogma of Woman
Suffrage" was "fundamentally at war with true democratic principles."[35]

That the language of democracy—and even more a robust understanding
of self-government—was in eclipse became evident when adherents actually
spoke in these terms in the 1890s. Stanton, even with her fixation on educated suffrage, ended her career as she began it: as one of the most powerful
proponents of self-government. Her "Solitude of Self" (1892) has been well
recognized by historians and political theorists as a profound statement of
liberal feminism, an argument about the fundamental isolation of the individual self and the need for the resources to navigate the turbulent waters of
existence. But another essay she wrote the following year, to be read at the
World's Congress of Representative Women in Chicago, captured the more
broadly democratic aspects of her thinking. In "The Ethics of Suffrage" (1893),
Stanton considered the "right of self-government" as the foundational idea of
the American republic. It was the right to "govern one's self," to participate
meaningfully in the work of government, and to exercise one's freedom.[36]

Stanton considered the longing for self-government to be a universal
human impulse. Men liked to think that women preferred "masculine domination to self-government" and that on this point women are peculiar, differing
from all other groups of people in preferring to be "governed by others." But
to claim so, Stanton argued, was to "falsify every page of history." Stanton
wanted homes, schools, and the polity to reflect this fact of human nature. Full
self-government, she maintained, extended well beyond voting. Women must
be equally represented in legislatures but also on juries and even police forces
(so that, she warned, "young girls when arrested during the night, intoxicated
and otherwise helpless, may be under the watchful eye of a judicious woman,
and not left wholly to the mercy of a male police"). But self-government also
entailed "equal authority in the home" and in professions and trades. As the
vote was the political mechanism of self-government, women's suffrage posed
"the greatest question ever before any nation"—every other question sinks
"into utter insignificance when compared with the emancipation of one-half

the human race." She thus urged all women to make their enfranchisement "the primal question in their own estimation." For all its rhetorical power and intellectual force, Stanton's effort met with a resounding silence. The piece generated little discussion and left barely a trace in published opinion.[37]

American Households Protected and Betrayed

Even when women mobilized politically in ever greater numbers, they did not necessarily do so under the banner of democracy. The 1880s witnessed the largest infusion of women into the women's suffrage movement thanks to the WCTU. But the self-governance of women never registered as a central concern of that mass organization. Only with a reluctant sense that their anti-saloon, anti-liquor goals could not be achieved without the ballot did the WCTU formally endorse women's suffrage in 1881. Frances E. Willard, who became the WCTU's forceful president in 1879, had generally eschewed conversations about women's equality, finding them unhelpfully controversial for her narrower purposes. Temperance women, she wrote in 1879, cared about the "human question" rather than the "woman question." She preferred to approach the enfranchisement of women obliquely, rather than head-on, by emphasizing women's selfless work on behalf of children and humanity rather than themselves. Outfitted in this "rhetorical suit of armor," as historian Charles Postel has recently argued, Willard and the massive organization she led were able to engage in political activities—public speaking, lobbying, canvassing—yet also "fend off the blows" from any critics that their behavior was unwomanly. And yet the ballot became an indispensable, if still controversial, instrument in the WCTU struggle, a crucial part of Willard's larger "Do Everything" strategy, along with work on kindergartens, prison reform, labor activism, and international peace.[38]

Willard crafted a "Home Protection Ballot" campaign that rhetorically narrowed the meaning and purpose of the vote. It also intriguingly reversed the relationship between home and polity that earlier domestic writers had envisioned. If they had understood the home as an educative site that would protect America from the disorders of democracy, Willard and the WCTU now understood that the household's need for protection required a new role for women. Whereas Catharine Beecher had once instructed women that their role in the household would safeguard the polity, temperance women were being told they must participate in the polity to safeguard the household.

But even on these narrowed terms, the question of voting remained controversial in the WCTU, at the national level as well as in local and state

auxiliaries. Many temperance women understood women's political participation as a threat to their familial roles. As anti-suffragist (and temperance
advocate) Helen Kendrick Johnson put it: "Woman suffrage and the home
are incompatible." Some of this controversy played out in the pages of the
WCTU's organ *The Union Signal*, where, for example, editor Mary Willard
(sister-in-law of Frances) insisted that women's suffrage should be qualified
and not "increase the number of vicious votes."[39] In deference to divided
opinion, the WCTU left the question of suffrage up to local unions to support or not. Such deference was particularly important in the southern states,
where the question of Black voters loomed over any discussion of women's
suffrage. National leadership also deferred to local unions on the matter of
interracial work.

Frances Ellen Watkins Harper's experience with the WCTU revealed the
enduring challenges she faced as a Black woman navigating public life in the
last decades of the century. That the WCTU would appeal to Harper is no
surprise. It combined several tenets of her democratic vision: the uplift of
family life, the remediation of male immortality, and the enfranchisement of
all women. Women's vulnerability to the threat of male drunkenness, an important theme in her writing since the 1850s, drove the plot of her novella
Sowing and Reaping (1876). In a story primarily concerned with temperance,
Harper staged a conversation among moderate women to demonstrate the
necessity of the suffrage. When one character confesses that she is content "to
let my father and brothers do all the voting for me," her mother chides her.
Not only did "millions of women" lack supportive fathers or brothers, but
even those lucky ones who had them still suffered the "painful inequalities"
that stemmed from laws written exclusively by men. Harper joined the local
WCTU branch in Philadelphia and quickly rose through the leadership
ranks, ultimately serving for seven years as the national superintendent for
"Work Among the Colored People of the North."[40]

The notion of "Home Protection" had more visceral connotations for
Black Americans living in the South, as Harper routinely emphasized. The
most pressing of unresolved questions at century's end remained, she urged,
whether or not democratic America could "deal justly with our millions of
people" who had only recently relocated from "the old oligarchy of slavery
to the new commonwealth of freedom." In no other "civilized country," she
observed in 1875, were so many people "brutally and shamefully murdered
with or without impunity as in this republic within the last ten years." This
question was one she would be forced to return to again and again for the
next twenty-five years, as Reconstruction gave way to Redemption and then

to an era of unprecedented lynching and the systematic disfranchisement of Black men. "Protection to human life," she insisted in 1894, was the most immediate claim citizens could make on their government.[41]

Harper's elevation within the WCTU stemmed from the prominence she had achieved through her writing and activism—a prominence recognized when she shared the stage, and a speaking program, with the likes of Frederick Douglass and Henry Wilson, the vice president of the United States. That prominence did not mean her views reached as wide a circulation as they might have, since the most influential periodicals treated America's "woman question" and its "race problem" as distinct from one another. If the intertwined burdens of sex and color prejudice generally remained an unexamined topic in the major circuits of national published opinion, they found an audience among women's activists in Britain. Harper's "The Coloured Women of America" (1878), an effort to address the distinctive challenges borne by millions of nonwhite women, appeared in the London-based *Victoria*

VISIT OF THE KU-KLUX.—Drawn by Frank Bellew.—[See Page 157.]

FIG. 6.4 Frank Bellew, "Visit of the Ku-Klux." While "Home Protection" became a major theme for the WCTU in the 1880s, this engraving depicts the persistent vulnerability of Black homes and the bodies within them. Frances Harper addressed this issue repeatedly in the postwar decades. From *Harper's Weekly* (February 24, 1872), 160. Courtesy of Dartmouth College Library.

Magazine in its entirety and then in excerpted form in *The Englishwoman's Review*. For Black womanhood to attract comparatively more attention in the non-US Anglosphere continued a pattern begun with the antislavery editorial work of Mary Shadd Cary in Canada and the occasional essays of Sarah Parker Remond for the British press and extending through the anti-lynching writings of Ida B. Wells.[42]

Harper's powerful and distinctive response to the late-nineteenth century reckoning with popular government was registered in such appearances, which were intermittently recorded and usually transmitted only to discrete sections of the reading public. A steady output of didactic poetry and fiction was most eagerly consumed by a mass African American readership. The composite nature of her writing in the last quarter of the nineteenth century has attracted considerable scholarly attention, but the centrality of self-government as a unifying theme has not been fully appreciated. Seeing her multifaceted work as a whole reveals Harper's poignant sense of closing opportunities. If the waning of earlier idealism drew her attention, of greater concern were the increasingly dire social conditions she witnessed first-hand in her travels. Her post-Reconstruction efforts extended a key feature of her reform work in the 1850s and 1860s, blending forward-looking, religiously inflected optimism with brutal frankness about escalating racist violence.[43]

"The Coloured Women of America" (1878) was Harper's broadest nonfictional account of the disappointment that followed the exhilarating period of emancipation and Black male enfranchisement. Presented as an address to the 1877 Woman's Congress gathering in Cleveland, Ohio, it began by acknowledging a basic division among the freed people of the South. Formerly enslaved women reaped the benefits of "personal freedom" and the collective gain that represented, but they continued to suffer from being "retained in political thraldom" because they were still barred from the polls. Being "left behind to serve" the men of their families, the female half of the freed population was abandoned and had only themselves to rely on to overcome "sad inheritances" and to seize the "opportunity for social advancement and individual development." The only way forward, Harper urged, lay in the "self-redemption" of the "coloured woman" so that she might "take her place in the great ranks of American womanhood." Speaking to an audience of predominantly white women, Harper pointed to crucial differences among women as well. Formerly enslaved women had been "weighted down with a hundred pounds' weight." It would hardly be "just" to expect them to run as swiftly as those with "unfettered limbs and unretarding garments." Black women had made considerable progress, to be sure, but much work remained to repair the damage inflicted by slavery on their "self-respect" and their regard for "the marriage relation."[44]

As with her earlier efforts, Harper was also candid about Black men's shortcomings. Her remarks were tempered by an acknowledgment of slavery's brutal impact on Black men, who had themselves just "emerged from a wretched school" of "despotism," in which the "sacred claims and rights of women" had been constantly diminished. An explicit reference to John Stuart Mill noted how "very fine ideas about the 'subjection of women'" did not come automatically to a people only recently released from tyranny, and that Black male heads of household sometimes resorted to "subjection by force." Freedmen's desire to protect newly won family prerogatives was accompanied by an unwillingness to enfranchise women. Reference to men's narrow self-interest expanded upon her critique, delivered via popular poetry, of Black votes being sold to the highest bidder. Whether such corruption yielded "just three sticks of candy" or was used to procure the "flour and meat" needed for family sustenance, Harper portrayed Black women who chided their men for electoral chicanery. Her folksy character of "Aunt Chloe" in the early 1870s modeled the path of political virtue with her couplet: "Though I think a heap of voting/ I go for voting clean." How formerly enslaved men might ultimately come around as advocates of women's suffrage did not figure into her poetry for another decade and a half. Then her 1885 "Dialogue on Woman's Rights," published in a New York newspaper, depicted in verse how one fair-minded Black man convinced a skeptical friend to support his wife's enfranchisement because "wrong is wrong, and right is right."[45]

Significantly, Harper's concern for clean or "honest voting" never led her to scapegoat Black voters. If it was "shabby for an ignorant colored man" to sell his vote, one of her fictional characters asked, "wasn't it shabbier for an intelligent man to buy it?" Ignorance was a temporary and improvable condition, not a permanent deficiency, and required education, not disfranchisement. Her early efforts in the WCTU seemed to take a similar view of racial prejudice, the cure for which she believed was also education. If she had imagined the ballot as a "normal school" for women back in 1866, she hoped the organizational work of the WCTU might be similarly educative for northern white women. She urged them to overcome their prejudices and recognize that while they brought decades of rich cultural resources to the effort, Black women had to overcome an inheritance of "slavery, ignorance and poverty."[46]

The WCTU's commitment to securing the ballot for Black women remained another unresolved question. As the organization appealed to white women in the Deep South, by allowing the local unions to set the color line, Harper was put on the defensive. She justified the launching of separate "colored" groups within the WCTU as a way for a community with distinct needs and challenges to act autonomously, free of the condescending supervision of white women. In 1890, amidst these tensions and a general lack of support for her work, Harper's position was eliminated in an organizational restructuring. This development occurred the same year that a new Mississippi constitution unleashed a wave of measures to disfranchise Southern Black men through constitutional (as well as violent) means. Having already expressed some concern lest women's enfranchisement "increase the number of vicious votes," it was hardly surprising that the WCTU did little to condemn the stripping of the ballot from Black men, who were often presented as foes of temperance. Harper followed her departure from the WCTU with a stinging assault on the white supremacist resurgence of lynching and other injustices, as well as the government's bitter betrayal of Black Americans who had shown staunch loyalty during the Civil War.[47]

All Harper's major concerns came together in *Iola Leroy* (1892), her last and most commercially successful novel. She once again used fiction to imagine solutions to current problems and present answers to unresolved questions. Discussion of racial equality, women's rights, Black political power, and a reformed understanding of marriage was set in a hopeful moment—the Civil War and early Reconstruction years—as a way to condemn trends in evidence in the early 1890s. A chapter on "Open Questions"—a nod to the journalistic querying format of the late 1870s—gathered a group of Black and white, northern and southern professionals in the North (all of them men), to debate the question of Black political participation. A white doctor (and suitor of Iola) echoes the white moderates in the 1879 *North American Review* forum about the wisdom of Black suffrage, observing that "wisely, or unwisely the Government has put the ballot" into the hands of the freedman and it would be vastly "better to teach him to use that ballot aright than to intimidate him by violence or vitiate his vote by fraud." A Black doctor (and Iola's eventual choice as husband) makes the case for Black loyalty and civic virtue, but in terms more resonant of the 1890s than the novel's supposed 1860s setting. It is not "the negro" who is "plotting in beer-saloons against the peace and order of society," he points out, nor are his fingers "dripping with dynamite" or "flaunting the red banner of anarchy in your face." Both men agree that what in published opinion was generally framed as a "negro problem" should be reframed as the "problem of the nation." The real question centered not on what Americans "will do with the negro" but what they "will do with the reckless, lawless white men who murder, lynch, and burn their fellow-citizens."[48]

Such reasonable conversation is no match for the two most worrisome elements Harper portrays in the novel: the violent intransigence of the white South and the hypocritical racism and general indifference of the white North. The chapter's most volatile character, the white Southern doctor, declares that the white South will never submit to Black rule and then advocates a push to "eliminate" Black men "from the politics of the country" by "suppressing the negro vote." America, he insists in an echo of 1850s Democrats, was "a white man's government and a white man's country." Northern white people hold out little more hope in the novel. They say the right things but balk at full racial equality, revealing an "aristocracy of color" to be a national, not regional, condition. "In dealing with Southern prejudice against the negro," Iola's kindly white employer acknowledges, "we Northerners could do it with better grace if we divested ourselves of our own." Iola ultimately marries the "successful doctor," a Black man who understand the "depths in her nature" and the "aspirations of her soul." While she teaches Sunday School, her brother and his wife are "at the head of a large and flourishing school." Mutually supportive marriages, nurturing households, and education—in the absence of federal and northern resolve—appear the way forward.

The year after her novel appeared, Harper seemed to perceive the limits of merely seeking the "uplift" of nonwhite Americans, and particularly of women. The ominous turn of American politics in the 1890s made her eager to sound the alarm about the country's spiral into racist violence reminiscent of slavery days. Doubts predominated both about reform and about the problem of democracy itself, and her pronouncements began to absorb some of the narrowing impulses of the times and to dispense with earlier, more expansive ones. "What we need today is not simply more voters, but better voters," she insisted at the 1893 Woman's Congress, voters who would uphold democratic principles not impugn them by interfering with others' right to vote. She called upon American women to "create a healthy public sentiment" that would, in a turn of phrase she repurposed from her novel, "brand with everlasting infamy that lawless and brutal cowardice that lynches, tortures, and burns your own countrymen."

In the face of such violent betrayal, Harper grew exasperated with the limitations of democratic governance. Like so many of her contemporaries, she expressed doubt about "unrestricted and universal suffrage for either men or women." She supported "moral and educational tests," though her idea of such tests undoubtedly differed radically from that of white Southern Democrats.

She never wavered in her insistence that women be full partners in the project of self-government, believing American democracy, like that of any nation, could not succeed if "one-half of it is free" while the "other half is fettered." Still, she conveyed she was agnostic about what women's enfranchisement might achieve. "The ballot in the hands of woman means power added to influence. How well she will use that power I cannot foretell."[49]

At the close of an extraordinary century, uncertainty about democracy was widely evident, even among some reformers who had imbued it with such elevating promise a half-century earlier. Across published opinion, the very concept of self-government had been drained of its robust meanings and had come to be routinely qualified in terms of "fitness," or "capacity," or "preparedness." This involved a tendency to lump recent immigrants, African American men, and new subjects of colonial occupation, as well as all women, into a suspect category whose right to have a say in the government was contingent. The new president of the NAWSA, Carrie Chapman Catt, who replaced octogenarian Susan B. Anthony when she finally stepped down in 1900, bluntly assessed the state of play at the dawn of the twentieth century. The women's movement faced a new context, one characterized by "inertia in the growth of Democracy." An unease had followed the inclusion into the "body politic of vast numbers of irresponsible citizens" and had made "the nation" anxious and timid. "Democracy has been the boast of our country for a hundred years," Catt announced matter-of-factly before an annual convention of predominantly white middle-class women, but enthusiasm for it had waned. "Men believe in the theory, but do not like its apparent results." Women's inclusion at partners in self-government, dependent as ever on the votes of men, would be the work of a new century.[50]

Epilogue

NEW WOMEN, NEW QUESTIONS IN 1893

A WOMAN LIKE Helen Watterson might have been the target audience of the celebrated World's Congress of Representative Women held in 1893. A college-educated journalist in her early thirties, Watterson had already established her reputation as one of the nation's first female newspaper columnists and was becoming a regular presence in the high-toned monthlies that set the direction of published opinion. Her good will toward the events she wrote about mattered. Yet when Watterson trained her sights on a Chicago gathering billed as a milestone event, she did not cheer. She sighed. All the talk offered by the hundreds of speakers—which stretched across seventy-six sessions and six full days—was well and good. Yet Watterson wanted readers of the *Forum* to appreciate that windy discussion by itself only "serve[d] charmingly to keep alive that intangible something called the 'Woman Question,' of which men are already very tired, and of which women ought to be."[1]

Watterson's impatience was one indication of how the woman question discourse was losing cultural traction in the waning years of the nineteenth century. A query that had attracted such intense commentary in the 1860s and 1870s had become both overly familiar and the source of frustration in never really yielding meaningful answers. Its tendency to abstraction, in interrogating the condition and prospects of a singular "Woman," seemed increasingly to smack of a bygone era. Those who did not fit the norm chafed at its generality, as did those who preferred individual action to ponderous analysis.

Looking back a quarter-century after the appearance of *The Subjection of Women*, Watterson dismissed the "earnest followers of Mr. Mill and his question-begging book" as irrelevant to a generation that would soon be

dubbed "New Women." The gumption and worldliness of this generation
would allow them to chart the future in novel ways. To ride a bicycle (or, in
Watterson's view, wield a typewriter) seemed a surer path to modern female
liberation than working to preserve democratic self-government writ large.
As the twentieth century drew near, novelist and college professor Jennette
Barbour Perry conveyed a playful disdain for collective female self-scrutiny
in a short story she titled "The Woman Question." Discussing Charlotte
Perkins Gilman's *Women and Economics* (1898), one of characters confesses
she "had to shake [her]self after reading" it to confirm she was still "an intelligent person of the nineteenth century" and not an "antediluvian" drudge.
Suffering page-by-page as she read the treatise, the fictional college woman
reported that "I felt like Woman, with a capital W, all the way through."[2]

Resistance to being classed as "Woman with a capital W" fit the self-image
of the burgeoning college-educated professionals of the 1890s. Watterson (a
graduate of the College of Wooster) and others in this cohort were acutely
conscious of being pioneers, which led some of them to disregard the efforts
of earlier innovators.[3] At Wellesley College, efforts to establish a sense of tradition among highly educated women came in 1886, when a marble statue of
Harriet Martineau ended up in College Hall. Students there were unlikely
to be familiar with the 1837 *Society in America* as, having enjoyed none of
the enduring renown of Tocqueville's more famous work from the 1830s, it
had long been out of print. Martineau's likeness thus inspired campus mirth
rather than modeled social scientific inquiry. First-year students who were
pushed and pulled—"wriggling painfully, with gasps and giggles"—through
the rungs of the chair on which Martineau sat could thereafter claim to have
experienced a rite of passage known as "going through Harriet."[4]

But for all Watterson's impatience with the phrase, the "woman question"
did not completely disappear. Instead, it multiplied and segmented across a
media landscape that grew ever more varied. Though its organizers continued
to speak in the oracular singular, the Congress of Representative Women actually demonstrated how plural woman questions had become. The six-day
convention promised to showcase "the progress of women, in all lands and
in all departments of human progress." It delivered. Old stalwarts from the
early days of activism were there: Lucy Stone, who reviewed "The Progress
of Woman"; Frances Harper, who gave her address on "Woman's Political
Future"; Elizabeth Cady Stanton, who sent her eloquent argument for self-
government "The Ethics of Suffrage" to be read aloud for her in absentia;
and Susan B. Anthony, who as the most famous attendee, appeared in several
separate presentations. But the Chicago event also gave a platform to more

ONE OF THE FIRST STEPS IN OUR EDUCATION.

FIG. E.I "One of the First Steps in Our Education." This drawing illustrates a first-year ritual at Wellesley College, centered on the Harriet Martineau sculpture that Maria Weston Chapman had commissioned shortly after the Englishwoman's death in 1876. Called "Going Through Harriet," the rite of passage involved gently forcing first-year students through the pedestaled chair upon which Harriet Martineau sat. The statue, and College Hall in which it was exhibited, were destroyed in a fire in 1914. From *Legenda* (Wellesley, 1913). Courtesy of Wellesley College Archives.

than eight hundred women whose speeches ranged across political, literary, scientific, aesthetic, industrial, economic, social, and religious concerns.[5]

Two of those speakers would emerge as important theorists of democracy for the twentieth century: Anna Julia Cooper and Jane Addams. They used their allotted time to explore subsets of the female population they had already considered in print. Cooper's address on "The Intellectual Progress of the Colored Women of the United States" and Addams's "Domestic Service and the Family Claim" made the concerns of Black women and working class-immigrant women central to the questions they asked.[6] Both speeches highlighted the persistent family obligations that defined lives of unheralded "new women" generally ignored in the press. The struggles of the enslaved mother to protect daughters from sale or sexual violation was, for Cooper, a dark prelude to the maternal self-sacrifice that after 1865 fought to give a free-born generation bracing new opportunities. Addams explained immigrant working women's strong family attachments; like women in general they sought "to live with their parents, their brothers and sisters, and kinsfolk, and will sacrifice a good deal to accomplish this."[7]

These paired observations underscored the resilience of gendered roles within households and kin structures that persisted, some in the Chicago audience might have reflected, even as the rigid legal structures of common-law coverture had been dismantled. Notably, on this occasion at least, neither the widowed Cooper nor the unmarried Addams offered any analysis on the relation of husband and wife that had been at the heart of the woman question in earlier decades.[8] To the extent that women's advancement depended on remodeling familial obligations and duties, the pursuit of legal change became less important than a shift of cultural conventions that lacked any obvious government sanction. The distinction between law-based and culture-based barriers was never clear-cut, and nineteenth-century reformers had of course pursued both. But twentieth-century feminism pursued agendas and deployed language that risked obscuring the inherently democratic basis of their project to remodel the household as well as the polity. That shift in emphasis has allowed critics to reduce feminism to rights-based individualism and misleadingly to cast it as antagonistic to the common good.[9]

Other key questions that animated Cooper and Addams's democratic thought appeared in the significant works they had published within months of each other on the eve of their appearances before the World's Congress. Unsurprisingly, Addams had the easier time in gaining a national audience for her first venture into published opinion. She enjoyed immediate success when she pitched two lectures about her settlement house project to the same *Forum* editor who opened that monthly's pages to Helen Watterson.[10] Cooper's inaugural work appeared in a small North Carolina religious journal she herself helped to edit. She supplemented this first brief article with seven other pieces she compiled in a breathtakingly ambitious book that introduced the author as an archetypal "Black Woman of the South." Issued by an obscure press near Ohio's Wilberforce University, *A Voice from the South* echoed Frances Harper and Sojourner Truth in centering the voice of an individual whose perspective was neglected in the culture's focus on a "woman question" and a "race problem."[11]

From their different vantages, in distinct ways, and to two separate audiences, Cooper and Addams updated elements of consistent democracy and a robust understanding of self-government and applied these to a new era. Addams's power as a thinker lay not in rejecting outmoded questions but in recasting them. She saw the nineteenth century's fixation on political democracy as limited and "partial," beholden to an eighteenth-century understanding that would not suffice for the twentieth.[12] A more consistent democratic ethos would not stop at the ballot, she insisted, as it had with Black men who had never overcome the intensely racialized and deeply rooted "practical social ostracism" of the post–Civil War years. She imagined Hull House, the social settlement she established in Chicago in 1889, as a living, breathing democracy in microcosm, where fundamental human respect toward newly arrived immigrants was a core principle. The settlement resembled nothing so much as a multicultural, female-centered embodiment of a Tocquevillean association, complete with literal "citizenship schools" that sought to help first- and second-generation immigrants acquire the habits of self-government. Never a one-way transfer of knowledge and experience, Hull House, like democracy, was always, insistently, a conversation conducted in a distinctly educative mode. Since in a democracy all progress must come from the people, Addams argued that people must share a desire for progress. The "blessings which we associate with a life of refinement and cultivation" thus must be made universal and "incorporated into our common life."[13]

Educative self-government also grounded Cooper's democratic theory. A basic test of the soundness of the country's "political institutions" and the very "possibilities of a liberal and progressive democracy" lay precisely in their tendency to "cultivate the faculties of all individuals." What good was America's "vaunted 'rule of the people'" if it did not "breed nobler men and women than monarchies have done?" she asked. Democratic consistency for Cooper also meant recognizing the pluralism and diversity at the very heart of America's democratic endeavor. In the provocative essay "Has America a Race Problem? If So, How Can It Best Be Solved?," Cooper theorized the origins of democracy by setting aside a white/nonwhite binary and addressing the settlement of peoples from all different lands, religions, and ideologies. The radical pluralism of "a hundred free forces" all "lustily clamoring for recognition" and power, where "all interests must be consulted" and "all claims conciliated," determined that America would have to become a "democratic" republic. Consistency also meant calling out a women's movement that had narrowed its struggle over the decades. In her forceful essay titled "Woman and the Indian," she took white suffrage leaders to task for counterposing their own claims to the claims of others. Why did these women feel the need to pit "the intelligent woman versus the ignorant woman" or "white woman versus the black, the brown, and the red" or even "cause of woman versus man"? Instead, she insisted that the "cause of freedom" was "not the cause of a race or a sect, a party or a class"; it was the cause of all humankind, "the very birthright of humanity."[14]

Differences that separated Cooper and Addams were certainly meaningful, but they should not obscure their shared heritage of the nineteenth-century demand that a consistent democracy must include women as full partners. The debt they owed to over a half-century's discussion of female self-governance was obvious and self-conscious. They learned early—and clung to the conviction—that while consistency required extending the franchise to all adult citizens, that achievement hardly settled the question. Both democracy and consistency had to be interrogated and thought through. Accordingly, though both Cooper and Addams hailed the passage of the Nineteenth Amendment, neither considered it an end in itself. Nor was the only democratic challenge left in its aftermath the need to secure suffrage rights to women who, because of race, ethnicity, or class, faced lingering barriers to the ballot after the 1920 breakthrough.

The educative mode of democracy, rooted in an emphasis on self-government broadly considered, lost its power in the twentieth century. In some ways, its nineteenth-century theorists were themselves to blame as they allowed their anxieties about popular rule to muddle their aspirations for democracy's emancipatory potential. Uncertainty about whether participation was educative or required prior education reflected a larger wariness about mass democratic electorates composed of voters whose trustworthiness was suspect, whether these were white slaveholders, newly arrived immigrants, workers, nonwhite citizens, or women in these and other categories.

Democracy's meaning was also hollowed out by broader forces and by prevailing usages that diminished the idealism of nineteenth-century theorists. A set of associations between popular government and the projection of American power abroad gained currency when an American president justified entry into the Great War as a way to "make the world safe for democracy." Wilsonian talk of democratic self-governance differed from Lincolnian formulations in many critical respects. Chief among these was its tendency to ratify, rather than disrupt, the color-consciousness that operated both within the United States and across the globe as a dominant feature of modern world affairs. Wilson's sanctimonious cant was rejected by Adams in a 1922 book that extended her reputation and ultimately helped her earn a Nobel Peace

Prize in 1931. Cooper's pursuit of a doctorate from the Sorbonne in 1925 allowed her to reflect on, and reject, the arguments of those who used democratic idioms of the interwar period to justify white racial dominance.[15]

Looking back at the intersecting discussions of democracy and the woman question, before later associations took hold, might dampen the understandable tendency to cynicism about American democracy. Nineteenth-century perspectives might also help twenty-first-century Americans cease to take popular government for granted, which can become a formula for not reinvigorating it as times demand.

Central to the earlier era's enthusiasm for self-government was a devotion to dignifying and elevating ordinary men and women. Many saw in it as well a promise to remake the family and the polity simultaneously. None of the visions for change went uncontested in a larger culture that often resisted reform. But the debate itself constitutes the history of American democracy. and clashing visions are a vital embodiment of how a democratic people understands itself and its government.

Posing challenging questions about women and democracy was the work of the nineteenth century. Answering them remains the work of our own.

Notes

INTRODUCTION

1. [John Stuart Mill], "De Tocqueville on Democracy in America," *The London Review* (October 1835): 92.
2. The precise timing of a democracy that included all adult white males is a matter of some scholarly debate; see Donald Ratcliffe, "The Right to Vote and the Rise of Democracy, 1787–1828," *Journal of the Early Republic* 33, no. 2 (2013): 219–254; Alexander Keyssar, *The Right to Vote: The Contested History of Democracy in the United States* (New York: Basic Books, 2000); and Sean Wilentz, *The Rise of American Democracy: Jefferson to Lincoln* (New York: Norton, 2005). Ancient democracies were minoritarian, excluding foreigners, slaves, and women from citizenship. Deborah Kamen, *Status in Classical Athens* (Princeton, NJ: Princeton University Press, 2013).
3. The salience of "adulthood" to American political citizenship is developed in Corinne T. Field, *The Struggle for Equal Adulthood: Gender, Race, Age, and the Fight for Citizenship in Antebellum America* (Chapel Hill: University of North Carolina, 2014).
4. [John Stuart Mill], "De la Démocratie en Amérique," *The Edinburgh Review* 145 (October 1840), 5. Mill here summarized Tocqueville's view in the second volume of *Democracy in America* (1840).
5. The phrase comes from Madison's *Federalist #39*. The changing meaning of self-government is more fully discussed in chapter 2.
6. Languages of liberalism and democracy, along with languages of republicanism and Christianity, were intertwined and overlapping throughout the nineteenth century, as James T. Kloppenberg has argued for decades. See his "The Virtues of Liberalism: Christianity, Republicanism, and Ethics in Early American Political Discourse," reprinted in *The Virtues of Liberalism* (New York: Oxford University Press, 1998) and "From Hartz to Tocqueville: Shifting the Focus from Liberalism

to Democracy in America," in *The Democratic Experiment*, edited by Meg Jacobs, William J. Novak, and Julian E. Zelizer (Princeton, NJ: Princeton University Press, 2009), 150–180. My emphasis on the democratic connotations of individual self-governance is just that: an emphasis. It is not meant to replace more conventional liberal understandings of selfhood in the nineteenth century (more clearly evoked by a term such as "self-possession"), with which it coexisted. On liberal ideas of the self as applied to women, see especially Amy Dru Stanley, *From Bondage to Contract: Wage Labor, Marriage, and the Market in the Age of Slave Emancipation* (New York: Cambridge University Press, 1998).

7. The problematic category of "woman" in the singular has been interrogated in classic works by Denise Riley, *"Am I That Name?": Feminism and the Category of "Women" in History* (Minneapolis: University of Minnesota Press, 1988) and Joan W. Scott, "Gender: A Useful Category of Historical Analysis," *American Historical Review* 91, no. 5 (December 1986): 1053–1075, while a foundational Black feminist critique of the "grammar" of gender can be found in Hortense Spillers, "'Mama's Baby, Papa's Maybe': An American Grammar Book," in *Black, White, and In Color: Essays on American Literature and Culture* (Chicago: University of Chicago Press, 2003), 203–229.

8. A large literature addresses how enslavement stripped African-descended women of personhood and self-sovereignty, a topic handled with particular sophistication by Imani Perry, *Vexy Thing: On Gender and Liberation* (Durham, NC: Duke University Press, 2018) and, for an earlier time period, Jennifer L. Morgan, *Reckoning with Slavery: Gender, Kinship, and Capitalism in the Early Black Atlantic* (Durham, NC: Duke University Press, 2021).

9. The disabilities imposed by racial caste (whether legal or social) on women of color are delineated in Rosalyn Terborg-Penn, *African-American Women in the Struggle for the Vote, 1850–1920* (Bloomington: Indiana University Press, 1998) and in two works by Martha S. Jones, who has most fully resurrected woman question debates within what she terms Black "public culture" (of which print was one component). See her *All Bound Up Together: The Woman Question in African American Public Culture, 1830–1900* (Chapel Hill: University of North Carolina Press, 2007) and *Vanguard: How Black Women Broke Barriers, Won the Vote, and Insisted on Equality for All* (New York: Basic Books, 2020).

10. The Anglo-American legal tradition, in giving husbands property rights in their wives (and other dependents), empowered them to govern those dependents in the household and represent them in the polity. See Nancy F. Cott, *Public Vows: A History of Marriage and the Nation* (Cambridge, MA: Harvard University Press, 2000), 11–12, 62. Thus, the effort to make women self-governing would require restructuring the family as well as voting rights. As Reva B. Siegel has argued, though the Nineteenth Amendment is often remembered as merely "adding voters," what was actually at stake was the "democratization of the family," "The Nineteenth Amendment and the Democratization of the Family," *Yale Law Journal Forum*

(January 20, 2020): 450–494. See also Reva B. Siegel, "'She the People': The Nineteenth Amendment, Sex Equality, Federalism, and the Family," *Harvard Law Review* 1115 (February 2002): 948–1045.

11. Harriet Martineau, *Society in America* (New York, 1837), vol. 1, chapter 3, section vii. On coverture in practice (which was often less absolute than in theory), see Kirsten Sword, *Wives Not Slaves: Patriarchy and Modernity in the Age of Revolutions* (Chicago: University of Chicago Press, 2021). A broad-based handling of how this legal edifice was dismantled can be found in Carole Shammas, *A History of Household Governance in America* (Charlottesville: University of Virginia Press, 2002).

12. Joan Kelly, "Early Feminist Theory and the *Querelle des Femmes*, 1400–1789," in *Women, History, and Theory: The Essays of Joan Kelly* (Chicago: University of Chicago Press, 1986), 65–109; Lucy Delap, "The 'Woman Question' and the Origins of Feminism," in *The Cambridge History of Nineteenth-Century Political Thought*, edited by Gareth Stedman Jones and Gregory Claeys (Cambridge: Cambridge University Press, 2011), chapter 10.

13. Holly Case, *The Age of Questions* (Princeton, NJ: Princeton University Press, 2018); Leslie Butler, "The 'Woman Question' in the Age of Democracy: From Movement History to Problem History," in *The Worlds of American Intellectual History*, edited by Joel Isaac, James T. Kloppenberg, Michael O'Brien, and Jennifer Ratner-Rosenhagen (New York: Oxford University Press, 2017), 37–56.

14. Thomas C. Holt, "Marking: Race, Race-making, and the Writing of History," *American Historical Review* 100, no. 1 (1995): 1–20; Barbara J. Fields and Karen E. Fields, *Racecraft: The Soul of Inequality in American Life* (New York: Verso Books, 2014).

15. Elizabeth K. Helsinger, Robin Lauterbach Sheets, and William Veeder noted this dialogic framework years ago in their edited volume. "Almost any public statement bearing on the Woman Question . . . was likely to generate a chain of responses, and to be read as a response to prior statements in an ongoing public discussion. To view any of these statements out of context, which as modern readers we often do when we study a novel or a painting, may properly emphasize the integrity of imaginative creation but can only distort our perception of Victorian thinking about women," *The Woman Question: Society and Literature in Britain and America, 1837–1883* (Manchester: Manchester University Press, 1983), vol. 1, xi.

16. Though she was referring to the postbellum years, historian Lisa Tetrault's recent observation applies to the century as a whole: that scholars have yet to grapple with just how "regularly—and seriously—citizens as well as politicians" discussed aspects of the woman question. "Women's Rights and Reconstruction," part of an online scholarly forum at *Journal of the Civil War Era*, https://www.journalofthe civilwarera.org/forum-the-future-of-reconstruction-studies/ (accessed February 20, 2023).

17. Scholarly appreciation for the opinion-shaping work of America's rapidly expanding visual culture include, for example, Gary L. Bunker, "Antebellum Caricature and Woman's Sphere," *Journal of Women's History* 3 (Winter 1992): 6–43; Caroline Winterer, "Venus on the Sofa: Women, Neoclassicism, and the Early American Republic," *Modern Intellectual History* 2, no. 1 (2005): 29–60; Joshua Brown, *Beyond the Lines: Pictorial Reporting, Everyday Life, and the Crisis of Gilded Age America* (Berkeley: University of California Press, 2002); Jasmine Nichole Cobb, *Picture Freedom: Remaking Black Visuality in the Early Nineteenth Century* (New York: New York University Press, 2015); Teresa A. Goddu, *Selling Antislavery: Abolition and Mass Media in Antebellum America* (Philadelphia: University of Pennsylvania Press, 2020); Aston Gonzalez, *Visualizing Equality: African American Rights and Visual Culture in the Nineteenth Century* (Chapel Hill: University of North Carolina Press, 2020); and Allison K. Lange, *Picturing Political Power: Images in the Women's Suffrage Movement* (Chicago: University of Chicago Press, 2020).

18. Leslie Butler, "From the History of Ideas to Ideas in History," *Modern Intellectual History* 9, no. 1 (2012): 157–169. Digitized source databases especially important for this work include Making of America; American Periodical Series Online; American Antiquarian Society Periodicals; Hathi Trust; Accessible Archives (one of the rare databases that focuses on the Black press); Gerittsen Collection; Nineteenth-Century Collections Online; Library of Congress's Chronicling America: Historic American Newspapers; and GoogleBooks.

19. Carl F. Kaestle, "The History of Literacy and the History of Readers," *Review of Research in Education* 12 (1985): 11–53; Lee Soltow and Edward Stevens, *The Rise of Literacy and the Common School in the United States: A Socioeconomic Analysis to 1870* (Chicago: University of Chicago Press, 1981); Johann N. Neem, *Democracy's Schools: The Rise of Public Education in America* (Baltimore: Johns Hopkins University Press, 2017). On the communications revolution, see Daniel Walker Howe, *What Hath God Wrought: The Transformation of America, 1815–1848* (New York: Oxford University Press, 2007); and Richard R. John, *Spreading the News: The American Postal System from Franklin to Morse* (Cambridge, MA: Harvard University Press, 1995) and *Network Nation: Inventing American Telecommunications* (Cambridge, MA: Harvard University Press, 2010).

20. The Black press has drawn increasing attention, as evident in Teresa Zackodnik, *Press, Platform, Pulpit: Black Feminist Publics in the Era of Reform* (Knoxville: University of Tennessee Press, 2007); Ivy G. Wilson, "The Brief, Wondrous Life of the *Anglo-African Magazine*; Or, Antebellum African American Editorial Practice and Its Afterlives," in *Publishing Blackness: Textual Constructions of Race Since 1850*, edited by George Hutchinson and John K. Young (Ann Arbor: University of Michigan Press, 2013), 18–38; Eric Gardner, *Black Print Unbound: The Christian Recorder, African American Literature and Periodical Culture* (New York: Oxford University Press, 2015); Benjamin Fagan, *The Black Newspaper and the Chosen*

Nation (Athens: University of Georgia Press, 2016); Derrick R. Spires, *The Practice of Citizenship: Black Politics and Print Culture in the Early United States* (Philadelphia: University of Pennsylvania Press, 2019). Scholarship on Black women intellectuals has also flourished and with it a lessening of the tendency to treat its protagonists as "activists" rather than "thinkers," the "objects" of intellectual activity rather than "the producers of knowledge." See Mia E. Bay, Farah J. Griffin, Martha S. Jones, and Barbara D. Savage, *Toward an Intellectual History of Black Women* (Chapel Hill: University of North Carolina Press, 2015), quotation at p. 2.

21. On reprinting, see Meredith L. McGill, *American Literature and the Culture of Reprinting, 1834–1853* (Philadelphia: University of Pennsylvania Press, 2003). On print networks in the Anglosphere, see Leslie Butler, "The Liberal North Atlantic," in *The Cambridge History of America and the World: Volume 2, 1820–1900*, edited by Kristin Hoganson and Jay Sexton (New York: Cambridge University Press, 2021), 617–641.

22. The nineteenth-century association of democracy with modernity was powerful, though a specialized scholarly literature has recently emphasized how practices of broad consultation and collective rule have existed across all of human history. A helpful summation of this deeper perspective appears across Benjamin Isakhan and Stephen Stockwell, eds., *The Edinburgh Companion to the History of Democracy* (Edinburgh: University of Edinburgh Press, 2012) and David Stasavage, *The Decline and Rise of Democracy: A Global History from Antiquity to Today* (Princeton, NJ: Princeton University Press, 2020) and is applied to the case of Native Americans in the Southwest by Maurice Crandall, *These People Have Always Been a Republic: Indigenous Electorates in the U.S.–Mexico Borderlands, 1598–1912* (Chapel Hill: University of North Carolina Press, 2019).

23. Jürgen Osterhammel, *The Transformation of the World: A Global History of the Nineteenth Century* (Princeton, NJ: Princeton University Press, 2015), 594. Making a similar point, Oliver Hidaldgo argues that after 1850, the question was no longer "if democracy was within the historic horizon, but simply what kind of democracy" lay ahead, "Conceptual History and Politics: Is the Concept of Democracy Essentially Contested?" *Contributions to the History of Concepts* 4, no. 2 (October 2008): 176–201, quotation at 184.

24. James T. Kloppenberg, *Toward Democracy: The Struggle for Self-Rule in European and American Thought* (New York: Oxford University Press, 2016), 5. A crisp distillation of the "woolliness of democracy," along with a forgotten version of it, can be found in Steven W. Sawyer, "The Forgotten Democratic Tradition of Revolutionary France," *Modern Intellectual History* 18, no. 3 (September 2021), 1–29.

25. Multiplicity is the theme of Reeve Huston, "Rethinking 1828: The Emergence of Competing Democracies in the United States," in *Democracy, Participation and Contestation*, edited by Emmanuelle Avril and Johann N. Neem (New York: Routledge, 2014), chapter 1 and Adam I. P. Smith, "The 'Fortunate

Banner': Languages of Democracy in the United States, c. 1848," in *Re-Imagining Democracy in the Age of Revolutions: America, France, Britain, and Ireland, 1750–1850*, edited by Joanna Innes and Mark Philp (New York: Oxford University Press, 2013), chapter 2, as well as several of the essays in *Practicing Democracy: Popular Politics in the United States from the Constitution to the Civil War*, edited by Daniel Peart and Adam I. P. Smith (Charlottesville: University of Virginia Press, 2015) and the collected essays in *Democracies in America: Keywords for the Nineteenth Century and Today*, edited by D. Berton Emerson and Gregory Laski (New York: Oxford University Press, 2023). An explosion of work on American democracy has occurred over the last decade and a half. In addition to the works cited above, see also Johann N. Neem, *Creating a Nation of Joiners: Democracy and Civil Society in Early National Massachusetts* (Cambridge, MA: Harvard University Press, 2008); W. Caleb McDaniel, *The Problem of Democracy in the Age of Slavery: Garrisonian Abolitionists and Transatlantic Reform* (Baton Rouge: Louisiana State University Press, 2013); Kyle G. Volk, *Moral Minorities and the Making of American Democracy* (New York: Oxford University Press, 2014); Christopher James Bonner, *Remaking the Republic: Black Politics and the Creation of American Citizenship* (Philadelphia: University of Pennsylvania Press, 2020); Jon Grinspan, *The Virgin Vote: How Young Americans Made Democracy Social, Politics Personal, and Voting Popular in the Nineteenth Century* (Chapel Hill: University of North Carolina Press, 2016); John L. Brooke, *"There is a North": Fugitive Slaves, Political Crisis, and Cultural Transformation in the Coming of the Civil War* (Amherst: University of Massachusetts Press, 2019). Recent work in nineteenth-century American literature has also made democracy a central theme. See, for example, Sandra M. Gustafson, *Imagining Deliberative Democracy in the Early American Republic* (Chicago: University of Chicago Press, 2011); Stacey Margolis, *Fictions of Mass Democracy in Nineteenth-Century America* (New York: Cambridge University Press, 2015); Gregory Laski, *Untimely Democracy: The Politics of Progress After Slavery* (New York: Oxford University Press, 2017).

26. Besides Kloppenberg (who relates developments in France and Great Britain), see Pierre Rosanvallon, *Democracy Past and Future*, edited by Samuel Moyn (New York: Columbia University Press, 2006), especially chapter 4; John Dunn, *Setting the People Free: The Story of Democracy* (London: Atlantic Books, 2005); Hilda Sabato, *Republics of the New World: The Revolutionary Experiment in Nineteenth-Century Latin America* (Princeton, NJ: Princeton University Press, 2018); James E. Sanders, *The Vanguard of the Atlantic World: Creating Modernity, Nation, and Democracy in Nineteenth-Century Latin America* (Durham, NC: Duke University Press, 2014); and Marilyn Lake and Henry Reynolds, *Drawing the Global Colour Line: White Men's Countries and the Question of Racial Equality* (Melbourne: Melbourne University Press, 2008). A mapping of women's acquisition of democratic rights (pertinent mainly to the end of the period this

book covers) is offered by John Markoff, "Margins, Centers, and Democracy: The Paradigmatic History of Women's Suffrage," *Signs* 29, no. 1 (2003): 85–116.

27. John Stuart Mill's writings clarified some of what was at stake in the broader view, and his influence is evident on the rendering of democracy as ethos in Kloppenberg, *Toward Democracy*. More typical is the minimal definition of self-government, which involves broad-based elections and rights of speech and association, as laid out, for instance, in Robert Wiebe, *Self-Rule: A Cultural History of American Democracy* (Chicago: University of Chicago Press, 1995).

28. But see the essays in Ellen Carol Dubois and Richard Candida Smith, *Elizabeth Cady Stanton, Feminist as Thinker: A Reader in Documents and Essays* (New York: New York University Press, 2007) for rich treatments of Stanton's democratic thought.

PRELUDE

1. Samuel Osgood, "The Woman Question," *The Western Messenger: Devoted to Religion, Life, and Literature* 6 (November 1838): 3 and "Three Views of Democracy; Sismondi-Heeren-De Tocqueville," *Western Messenger* 6 (December 1838); Robert D. Habich, "An Annotated List of Contributions to the *Western Messenger*," *Studies in the American Renaissance* (1984): 93–179. Basic biographical material on Osgood appears in Perry Miller, *The Transcendentalists: An Anthology* (Cambridge, MA: Harvard University Press, 1950), 163–165 and Judith Kent Green, "A Tentative Transcendentalist in the Ohio Valley: Samuel Osgood and the *Western Messenger*," in *Studies in the American Renaissance*, edited by Joel A. Myerson (Charlottesville: University Press of Virginia, 1984), 79–92. This Unitarian should not be confused with the Congregationalist clergyman bearing the same name from Springfield, Massachusetts, who was a correspondent of William Lloyd Garrison.

2. Holly Case, *The Age of Questions* (Princeton, NJ: Princeton University Press, 2018).

3. Habich, "An Annotated List of Contributions to the *Western Messenger*," 9.

4. Southern white querists were evident across the antebellum period, though they were more attuned to politics than reform. Representative of a large group of essays is George Tucker, "The Missouri Question," *Niles Register*, February 26, 1820: 453–458 and Alexander Hamilton Sands, "A Calm Discussion of the Know-Nothing Question" *Southern Literary Messenger* 20 (September 1854): 540–543.

5. Marilyn Richardson, *Maria W. Stewart: America's First Black Woman Political Writer* (Bloomington: Indiana University Press, 1988); Manisha Sinha, *The Slave's Cause: A History of Abolition* (New Haven, CT: Yale University Press, 2016), 266–298; Kathryn Kish Sklar, *Women's Rights Emerges within the Antislavery Movement, 1830–1870: A Brief History with Documents* (New York: Bedford St. Martin's, 2000); Martha S. Jones, *All Bound Up Together: The Woman Question in African American Public Culture, 1830–1900* (Chapel Hill: University of North Carolina

Press, 2007); Martha S. Jones, *Vanguard: How Black Women Broke Barriers, Won the Vote, and Insisted on Equality for All* (New York: Basic Books, 2020).

6. Whittier to Angelina and Sarah Grimké, April 14, 1837, in Sklar, *Women's Rights Emerges within the Antislavery Movement*, 129; "Communications," *Pennsylvania Freeman*, July 12, 1838, which published Whittier's comment to a reader's response to his earlier "Letter from the Editor," *Pennsylvania Freeman*, June 14, 1828; "The Woman Question," *Advocate of Freedom*, August 2, 1838.

7. The distinctiveness of Garrisonians' engagement with nineteenth-century democracy informs the work of W. Caleb McDaniel, *The Problem of Democracy in the Age of Slavery: Garrisonian Abolitionists and Transatlantic Reform* (Baton Rouge: Louisiana State University Press, 2013) and Enrico Dal Lago, *William Lloyd Garrison and Giuseppe Mazzini: Abolition, Democracy, and Radical Reform* (Baton Rouge: Louisiana State University Press, 2013).

8. Whittier quoted in William Sloane Kennedy, *John G. Whittier: The Poet of Freedom* (New York: Funk & Wagnalls, 1892), 158. On nonresistance, see Lewis Perry, *Radical Abolitionism: Anarchy and the Government of God in Antislavery* (Ithaca, NY: Cornell University Press, 1973).

9. *History of the Book in America Volume 3: The Industrial Book, 1840–1880*, edited by Scott E. Casper, Jeffrey D. Groves, Stephen W. Nissenbaum, and Michael Winship (Chapel Hill: University of North Carolina Press, 2007); Aileen Fyfe, *Steam Powered Knowledge: William Chambers and the Business of Publishing, 1820–1860* (Chicago: University of Chicago Press, 2012); Daniel Walker Howe, *What Hath God Wrought: The Transformation of America, 1815–1848* (New York: Oxford University Press, 2007).

10. *Freedom for Women: Speech of Wendell Phillips, Esq. at the Convention Held at Worcester, October 15 and 16, 1851* (Syracuse, 1851).

11. Joan Kelly, "Early Feminist Theory and the *Querelle des Femmes*, 1400–1789," in *Women, History, and Theory: The Essays of Joan Kelly* (Chicago: University of Chicago Press, 1986), 65–109. On the stadial theory of history, as it related to women, see Sylvana Tomaselli, "The Enlightenment Debate on Women," *History Workshop Journal* 20 (Autumn 1985): 101–124; Rosemarie Zagarri, "Morals, Manners, and the Republican Mother," *American Quarterly* 44, no 2 (June 1992): 192–215; Barbara Taylor, *Mary Wollstonecraft and the Feminist Imagination* (Cambridge: Cambridge University Press, 2003); Sylvana Tomaselli, "Civilisation, Gender and Enlightened Histories of Woman," in *Women, Gender, and Enlightenment*, edited by Sarah Knott and Barbara Taylor (New York: Palgrave Macmillan, 2005), 117–135; and Jane Rendall, "Women and the Enlightenment, c. 1690–1800," in *Women's History: Britain, 1700–1850*, edited by Hannah Barker and Elaine Chalus (New York: Routledge, 2005), 9–32.

12. Wollstonecraft, *A Vindication of the Rights of Women* (London, 1792); Condorcet, "On the Emancipation of Women," [1790], in *Condorcet: Political Writings*, edited by Steven Lukes and Nadia Urbinati (Cambridge: Cambridge University

Press, 2012), 156, 161; Judith Sargent Murray, "On the Equality of Sexes," reprinted in *Selected Writings of Judith Sargent Murray*, edited by Sharon M. Harris (New York: Oxford University Press, 1995), 3–14.

13. Linda Kerber, "The Republican Mother: Women and the Enlightenment—an American Perspective," *American Quarterly* 28, no. 2 (Summer 1976): 187–205; Jan Lewis, "The Republican Wife: Virtue and Seduction in the Early Republic," *William and Mary Quarterly* 44, no. 4 (October 1987): 689–721; Zagarri, "Morals, Manners, and the Republican Mother." On female politicians and women voters in New Jersey, see Rosemarie Zagarri, *Revolutionary Backlash: Women and Politics in the Early American Republic* (Philadelphia: University of Pennsylvania Press, 2007), 30–37; Jan Lewis, "Rethinking Woman Suffrage in New Jersey, 1776–1807," *Rutgers Law Review* 63, no. 3 (August, 2011): 1017–1035. On women's participation in the public sphere of the early American republic, see Susan Branson, *These Fiery Frenchified Dames: Women and Political Culture in Early National Philadelphia* (Philadelphia: University of Pennsylvania Press, 2001); Cynthia A. Kierner, *Beyond the Household: Women's Place in the Early South, 1700–1835* (Ithaca, NY: Cornell University Press, 1998); and Catherine Allgor, *Parlor Politics: In Which the Ladies of Washington Help Build a City and a Government* (Charlottesville: University of Virginia Press, 2000). On women's education and participation in civil society, see Mary Kelley, *Learning to Stand and Speak: Women, Education, and Public Life in America's Republic* (Chapel Hill: University of North Carolina Press, 2006).

14. Zagarri, *Revolutionary Backlash*, 155–164. On voting expansion and contraction, see Alexander Keyssar, *The Right to Vote: The Contested History of Democracy in the United States* (New York: Basic Books, 2000).

15. Elisabeth Gibbels, "The Wollstonecraft Meme: Translations, Appropriations, and Receptions of Mary Wollstonecraft's Feminism," in *The Routledge Handbook of Translation, Feminism and Gender*, edited by Luise von Flotow and Hala Kamal (New York: Routledge, 2020) 173–183. William Thompson and Anna Wheeler, *Appeal of One Half the Human Race, Women, Against the Pretensions of the Other Half, Men, to Retain Them in Political, and Thence in Civil and Domestic, Slavery: In Reply to a Paragraph of Mr. Mill's Celebrated "Article on Government"* (London, 1825). Not only did an American edition never appear, the *Appeal* seems to have generated no conversation in American periodicals.

16. Aimé-Martin, *De L'Éducation des Mères de Famille* (1834); translated into English in 1842 (in a London edition) and then printed in the United States in 1843. On Aimé Martin, see Jennifer Popiel, *Rousseau's Daughters: Domesticity, Education, and Autonomy in Modern France* (Durham: University of New Hampshire Press, 2008).

17. Elizabeth Cady Stanton, "Address to the American Antislavery Society" *Liberator*, May 18, 1860; Julie Roy Jeffrey, *The Great Silent Army of Abolitionism* (Chapel Hill: University of North Carolina Press, 1998); Sinha, *The Slave's Cause*, especially chapter 9; Lois A. Brown, "William Lloyd Garrison and Emancipatory Feminism in Nineteenth-Century America," in *William Lloyd Garrison at Two Hundred,*

edited by James Brewer Stewart (New Haven, CT: Yale University Press, 2008), 41–76; Dorothy C. Bass, " 'The Best Hope of the Sexes': The Woman Question in Garrisonian Abolitionism" (PhD diss., Brown University, 1981).

18. E. P. Hurlbut, *Essays on Human Rights and their Political Guarantees* (New York, 1845); Lori D. Ginzberg, *Untidy Origins: A Story of Woman's Rights in Antebellum New York* (Chapel Hill: University of North Carolina Press, 2006).

19. Samuel Osgood, "The Ideal of Womanhood," *The Hearth-Stone: Thoughts Upon Home-life in Our Cities* (New York, 1854): 38.

CHAPTER 1

1. The intellectual novelty of these observing visitors is a theme of Aurelian Craiutu, "What Kind of Social Scientist Was Tocqueville?" in *Conversations with Tocqueville: The Democratic Revolution in the Twenty-First Century*, edited by Aurelian Craiutu and Sheldon Gellar (Lanham, MD: Lexington Books, 2009), 55–81 and Valerie Sanders and Gaby Weiner, eds., *Harriet Martineau and the Birth of Disciplines: Contribution to Fields of Knowledge* (New York: Routledge, 2017); Beaumont's tilt to social science, evident in the appendices to his novel, has yet to be fully appreciated.

2. Joe Eaton, *The Anglo-American Paper War: Debates about the New Republic, 1800–1825* (New York: Palgrave-Macmillan, 2012); Sam W. Haynes, *Unfinished Revolution: The Early American Republic in a British World* (Charlottesville: University of Virginia Press, 2010), chapter 2; Elizabeth J. Deis and Lowell T. Frye, "British Travelers and the 'Condition-of-America' Question': Defining American in the 1830s," in *Nineteenth-Century British Travelers in the New World*, edited by Christine DeVine (Farnham: Ashgate, 2013), 121–150. Bridging the period of the paper war and the bestselling travelogue was Frances Wright, *Views of Society and Manners in America* (London, 1822), whose impact on published opinion never approached the work of the 1830s.

3. "Tours in America, by Latrobe, Abdy, &c," *London Quarterly Review* (September 1835): 205; Robert Wiebe, *Self-Rule: A Cultural History of American Democracy* (Chicago: University of Chicago Press, 1995), chapter 2; Dona Brown, "Travel Books," in *A History of the Book in America, Volume 2: An Extensive Republic: Print, Culture, and Society in the New Nation, 1790–1840*, edited by Robert A. Gross and Mary Kelley (Chapel Hill: University of North Carolina Pres, 2010), 449–458.

4. [Charles Sumner], "Grund's *Americans*," *North American Review* (January 1838): 106; Frances Trollope, *Domestic Manners of the Americans* (New York, 1832), vol. 1, 198; Thomas Moore's poem "To Lord Viscount Forbes: From the City of Washington," in *The Works of Thomas Moore* (Paris, 1823), vol. 2, 147–157; Christopher Leslie Brown, *Moral Capital: Foundations of British Abolitionism* (Chapel Hill: University of North Carolina Press, 2006), 134–154. Slavery and racial prejudice were especially prevalent in E. S. Abdy, *Journal of a Residence and Tour in the United States of North*

America, From April, 1833, to October 1834, 3 volumes (London, 1835), vol. 1, 133, 117;
J. S. Buckingham, *America: Historical, Statistic, and Descriptive* (London, 1841), 78;
and Buckingham's sequel, *The Slave States in America* (London, 1842). Slavery's prevalence as a theme for foreign travelers is evident across the essays featured in DeVine,
Nineteenth-Century British Travelers in the New World, while treatments of the
intertwined nature of slavery and popular government in Jacksonian America can be
found in Andrew Robertson, "Democracy: America's Other 'Peculiar Institution,'"
in *Democracy, Participation, and Contestation: Civil Society, Governance, and the
Future of Liberal Democracy*, edited by Emmanuelle Avril and Johann N. Neem
(New York: Routledge, 2015), chapter 5; and W. Caleb McDaniel, *The Problem of
Democracy in the Age of Slavery: Garrisonian Abolitionists and Transatlantic Reform*
(Baton Rouge: Louisiana State University Press, 2013).

5. "Prince Pickler Muscat and Mrs. Trollope," *North American Review* 78 (January
   1833): 42. Frederika Bremer, *The Homes of the New World* (New York, 1853); Francis
   Lieber, *The Stranger in America* (Philadelphia, 1835), 224; Amanda Claybaugh, *The
   Novel of Purpose: Literature and Social Reform in the Anglo-American World* (Ithaca,
   NY: Cornell University Press, 2007); Quarles Quickens, Esq., *English Notes;
   Intended for Very Extensive Circulation* (Boston, 1842). "Quickens" described the
   wretchedness of the poor in London, exclaiming that "having come to the country
   as much to observe the habits and condition of its people as to add to my present
   popularity among them I propose to give here, as I have a whole chapter which
   I cannot well fill in any other way, the history of this family," 59–60.

6. [John Stuart Mill] "State of Society in America," *London Review* II (January
   1836): 93; Harriet Martineau, *How to Observe Moral and Manners* (London, 1838).

7. Sandra M. Gustafson, "Histories of Democracy and Empire," *American Quarterly*
   59 (March 2007): 107–133, which offers an excellent exploration of the vagueness
   of the term, among scholars and early/antebellum Americans alike. On democratic
   developments of the era, see Sean Wilentz, *The Rise of American Democracy: Jefferson
   to Lincoln* (New York: Norton, 2005); Daniel Walker Howe, *What Hath
   God Wrought: The Transformation of America, 1815–1848* (New York: Oxford
   University Press, 2007); James T. Kloppenberg, *Toward Democracy: The Struggle
   for Self-Rule in European and American Thought* (New York: Oxford University
   Press, 2016), 592–594; Daniel Peart, *Era of Experimentation: American Political
   Practices in the Early Republic* (Charlottesville: University of Virginia Press, 2014);
   and the essays in *Practicing Democracy: Popular Politics in the United States from
   the Constitution to the Civil War*, edited by Daniel Peart and Adam I. P. Smith
   (Charlottesville: University of Virginia Press, 2015).

8. Trollope, *Domestic Manners*, vol. 1, iii. The French painter Auguste Hervieu traveled
   with the Trollope family, working as tutor to the Trollope children, and provided
   the twenty-four illustrations for the book. On Hervieu, see Sara R. Danger, "The
   Bonnet's Brim: The Politics of Vision in Frances Trollope's *Domestic Manners of the
   Americans*," *Philological Quarterly* 88, no. 3 (2009): 239–258. On the likely writing

of the preface by the publisher, see Ada B. Nisbet, "Mrs. Trollope's 'Domestic Manners,'" *Nineteenth-Century Fiction* (March 1950): 319–324.

9. Alexis de Tocqueville to M. Stoffels, February 21, 1835, in *Memoir, Letters, and Remains of Alexis de Tocqueville* (London, 1861), vol. 2, 397. On Tocqueville and Beaumont's travels, see George Wilson Pierson, *Tocqueville in America* (1938; Baltimore: Johns Hopkins University Press, 1996) and Olivier Zunz, ed., *Alexis de Tocqueville and Gustave de Beaumont in America: Their Friendship and Their Travels* (Charlottesville: University of Virginia Press, 2010). Five editions of *Marie* appeared in Paris between 1835 and 1842.

10. [Calvin Colton], *A Voice from America* (London, 1839), 3. Adam I. P. Smith has argued, based on tracking usage of the word in newspaper titles, that "democracy" became vastly more prevalent after 1830 than before; see Adam I. P. Smith, "The 'Fortunate Banner': Languages of Democracy in the United States, c. 1848," in *Re-imagining Democracy in the Age of Revolutions: America, France, Britain, and Ireland 1750–1850*, edited by Joanna Innes and Mark Philp (Oxford: Oxford University Press, 2013), 28–39. Even so, "democracy," as both word and concept, was never absent from late eighteenth- and early nineteenth-century discussion, as James Kloppenberg demonstrates in *Toward Democracy*, chapter 14. Joanna Innes and Mark Philp have recently argued that Tocqueville was the "most influential promoter" of the view that democracy represented a modern, nineteenth-century tendency in Europe, in " 'Democracy' from Book to Life: The Emergence of the Term in Active Political Debate, to 1848," in *Democracy in Modern Europe: A Conceptual History*, edited by Jussi Kurunmäki, Jeppe Nevers, and Hank te Velde (New York: Berghahn Books, 2018), chapter 1.

11. On Tocqueville's long-term reception, see James T. Kloppenberg, "Life Everlasting: Tocqueville in America," La Revue Tocqueville/Tocqueville Review 17 (1996): 19–36; Matthew J. Mancini, *Alexis de Tocqueville and American Intellectuals: From His Time to Ours* (Lanham, MD: Rowman & Littlefield, 2006).

12. Tocqueville, *Democracy in America*, translated by Henry Reeve, esq. (1835; New York, 1838), ii, xxiii, xvi. Hereafter, all references to the first volume of *Democracy in America* will be cited as *Democracy in America* 1 and the 1840 volume as *Democracy in America* 2. I have chosen to quote from the original English translation by Henry Reeve, as this was the translation the non-French speaking readers in the 1830s and 1840s would have read and discussed. For a more elegant recent translation, see Arthur Goldhammer, trans., *Democracy in America* (New York, 2004). On the politics and poetics of translating this work, see the forum "Translating Tocqueville" in *French Politics, Culture, and Society* 21 (Spring 2003).

13. Tocqueville, *Democracy in America* 1, xxviii. On the imprecision of his use of the word "democracy," see James T. Schlefer, *The Making of Tocqueville's Democracy in America* (Charlottesville: University of Virginia Press, 1980), chapter 19.

14. *Quarterly Review* of Basil Hall quoted in Deis and Frye, "British Travelers and the 'Condition-of-America' Question': Defining American in the 1830s," 121–150,

which offers a nice discussion of the conventional wisdom that Tocqueville would help to overturn.

15. Tocqueville, *Democracy in America* 1, 408. Johann N. Neem provides a smart analysis of the development of voluntary associations as a complex, new civic "technology," complete with new modes of circulating information through print, in *Creating a Nation of Joiners: Democracy and Civil Society in Early National Massachusetts* (Cambridge, MA: Harvard University Press, 2008), chapter 4, while Kevin Butterfield examines the "legal culture" that enabled the vibrant associational life Tocqueville witnessed in *The Making of Tocqueville's America: Law and Association in the Early United States* (Chicago: University of Chicago Press, 2015).

16. Tocqueville, *Democracy in America* 1, 280, 233, 232. The question of political participation in Tocqueville's era has been a lively subject of debate among historians for decades. See, for example, the discussion in the *Journal of American History* responding to the skeptical work of Glenn C. Altschuler and Stuart M. Blumin, with responses by Harry L. Watson, Jean Harvey Baker, and Norma Basch, "Political Engagement and Disengagement in Antebellum America: A Round Table," *Journal of American History* 84 (December 1997): 855–909.

17. Americans were not more virtuous than other people, Tocqueville argued, but they had figured out that their own self-interest was linked with the fate of others in a variety of ways. He called this instinct *"l'intérêt bien-entendu,"* which translators have rendered as self-interest "properly" or "rightly" understood.

18. Tocqueville, *Democracy in America* (New York, 1840), 112 (hereafter cited as *Democracy in America* 2). Goldhammer puts this more elegantly: "American democracy prospers not because of its elected officials but because its officials are elected," *Democracy in America*, 593. With this insight, Olivier Zunz has recently observed, Tocqueville "taught Americans how to understand themselves anew," see *The Man Who Understood Democracy: The Life of Alexis de Tocqueville* (Princeton, NJ: Princeton University Press, 2022), 126.

19. [Mill], "De Tocqueville on Democracy in America," *London Review* (October 1835); [Mill], "De la Démocratie en Amérique," *The Edinburgh Review* 145 (October 1840). Responding to Mill's review of the 1840 volume, Tocqueville told Mill that he planned to have the review bound with his own copy of the book, so thoroughly did Mill understand him, in Richard Swedberg, *Tocqueville's Political Economy* (Princeton, NJ: Princeton University Press, 2009), 95.

20. Mill, "State of Society in America," 93. While Tocqueville and Beaumont both used the language of aristocracy and nobility when discussing race, the analogy between European feudalism and American racial hierarchy has only recently drawn sustained scholarly attention. See, for example, Jennie C. Ikuta and Trevor Latimer, "Aristocracy in America: Tocqueville on White Supremacy," *Journal of Politics* 83 (March 2021): 547–559.

21. [Mill], "De Tocqueville on Democracy in America," Mill's review of the first volume, appeared as a stand-alone pamphlet: *A Review of M. De Tocqueville's Work on "Democracy in America"* (New York, 1836).

22. Tocqueville, *Democracy in America* 1, 426. See, for example, W., "De Tocqueville's *Democracy in America*: A Review of Those Sections of Chapter XVII Which Relate to the Colored People in the United States," which appeared in three issues of the *Colored American*, January 23, February 6, May 15, 1841; and Justitia, "Reviewer of De Tocqueville," *Colored American*, May 1, 1840. On the Black response to Tocqueville, see Alvin B. Tillery Jr., "Reading Tocqueville Behind the Veil: African American Receptions of Democracy in America, 1835–1900," *American Political Thought* 7, no. 1 (2018): 1–25 and "Tocqueville as Critical Race Theorist: Whiteness as Property, Interest Convergence, and the Limits of Jacksonian Democracy," *Political Research Quarterly* 62, no. 4 (2009): 639–652.

23. Gustave de Beaumont, *Marie or, Slavery in the United States: A Novel of Jacksonian America* (Baltimore: Johns Hopkins University Press, 1999). Nell Irvin Painter, "Was Marie White? The Trajectory of a Question in the United States," *Journal of Southern History* (February 2008): 3–30. Sara M. Benson has urged scholars to treat the three American works by Tocqueville and Beaumont (the novel plus the works on prisons and on democracy) as a trilogy that centers "unfreedom" as much as free institutions. "Democracy and Unfreedom: Revisiting Tocqueville and Beaumont in America," *Political Theory* 45, no. 4 (2017): 466–494.

24. "Introduction," *The Collected Works of John Stuart Mill: Later Letters*, edited by Francis E. Mineka and Dwight N. Lindley (Toronto: University of Toronto Press, 1972), vol. XIV, xxv. Kathryn Gleadle, *The Early Feminists: Radical Unitarians and the Emergence of the Women's Rights Movement, 1831–51* (New York: St. Martin's Press, 1995); R. K. Webb, *Harriet Martineau: Radical Victorian* (London: Heinemann, 1960), 118–119. Mill in fact harbored an enduring dislike of Martineau, whom he believed had made disparaging comments about his unconventional relationship with the married Harriet Taylor. Martineau (not unlike several of her male contemporaries) was an often strident, prudish, and difficult character. Her reputation has undergone a shift in the past generation or so, though that work has been mostly done by literary scholars, sociologists, and political theorists rather than historians. See Deborah Anna Logan, *The Hour and the Woman: Harriet Martineau's 'Somewhat Remarkable' Life* (DeKalb: Northern Illinois University Press, 2002) and Deirdre David, *Intellectual Women and Victorian Patriarchy: Harriet Martineau, Elizabeth Barrett Browning, George Eliot* (Ithaca, NY: Cornell University Press, 1987).

25. The full title made the critique of James Mill explicit: *Appeal of One Half the Human Race, Women, Against the Pretensions of the Other Half, Men, to Retain Them in Political, and thence in Civil and Domestic Slavery; In Reply to a Paragraph of Mr. Mill's Celebrated "Article on Government"* (London, 1825). This book was curiously not reprinted in the United States. On Thompson-Wheeler tract, see Abbie L.

Cory, "Wheeler and Thompson's 'Appeal': The Rhetorical Revisioning of Gender," *New Hiberian Review/Iris Éireannach Nua* (Summer 2004): 106–120 and James Jose, "Feminist Political Theory without Apology: Anna Doyle Wheeler, William Thompson, and the Appeal of One Half of the Human Race, Women," *Hypatia* 34, no. 4 (2019): 827–851.

26. "Lines. On Miss Martineau," *Southern Literary Messenger* (February 1835): 319 (brackets in original). The poem also mentioned the ear trumpet: "So I waited upon her, and venturing near, // I whispered some words in her ivory ear." Above the poem was a brief article on Martineau's stay in Richmond, pronouncing her "a woman of fine understanding; a ready talker; easy, affable, and unaffected in her manners; and altogether more feminine and pleasing than we had expected of her." The author looked forward to her book, which would surely be "something rather better than the scandal of Mrs. Trollope, or the blunders of Basil Hall." This writer was undoubtedly disappointed when *Society in America* appeared two years later.

27. Harriet Martineau, *Society in America* (New York, 1837), vol. 1, xiv. Shortly after Tocqueville's death, Martineau dismissively observed that *Democracy in America* "might have been written in his own library, without the trouble of the voyage." Perhaps confusing him with Charles Dickens, whose travel narrative *American Notes* appeared in 1843, she claimed Tocqueville "did not go southwards beyond Washington," when the Frenchman had in fact traveled fairly extensively through the slave states. Martineau, "Representative Men: Political Philosophers: Machiavelli, Montesquieu, De Tocqueville," *Once a Week*, September 7, 1861, 293. Lisa Pace Vetter has explicated Martineau's dialogic approach to the study of democracy—which combined the "imaginative sympathy" of Adam Smith with an insistence on conversation—in *The Political Thought of America's Founding Feminism* (New York: New York University Press, 2017), chapter 2. Martineau elaborated her methodology in *How to Observe Morals and Manners*. See also the essays in Michael R. Hill and Susan Hoecker-Drysdale, *Harriet Martineau: Theoretical and Methodical Perspectives* (New York: Routledge, 2001).

28. Martineau, *Society in America*, vol. 1, 2. Whether or not Martineau was aware, this Madisonian phrase was set out in *Federalist #39* nearly a half-century earlier. By contrast, Tocqueville rooted self-government in the colonial past rather than in the anti-monarchical revolutionary founding of 1776.

29. Martineau, *Society in America*, vol. 1, iv, vi; vol. 2, 368. Martineau wrote about her "conversion" to Garrisonianism, in the context of violent threats to her personally, in *Harriet Martineau's Autobiography* (Boston, 1877). See Webb, *Harriet Martineau*, 151–156 and Logan, *The Hour and the Woman*, chapter 3.

30. Martineau, *Society in America*, vol. 2, 226–227; vol. 1, 149.

31. Martineau, *Society in America*, vol. 1, 149, 153, 154.

32. Martineau, *Society in America*, vol. 2, 259. The analogy between slavery and marriage was a constant theme of early feminist thinkers, starting at least with Mary Wollstonecraft. This did not involve a claim that the institutions were equivalent

or that being a wife was somehow comparable experientially to being a slave. Rather it conveyed, as Nancy F. Cott has aptly put it, that "structurally, conceptually, and legally" the relations of husband to wife and master to slave "were parallel," though the former was entered into voluntarily and at least theoretically sustained by affection, while the latter was imposed by violence or heredity and sustained by coercion. Nancy F. Cott, *Public Vows: A History of Marriage and the Nation* (Cambridge, MA: Harvard University Press, 2000), 62. On family law, see Michael Grossberg, *Governing the Hearth: Law and the Family in Nineteenth-Century America* (Chapel Hill: University of North Carolina Press, 1998). For a history of the slave/marriage analogy, see Ana Stevenson, *The Woman as Slave in Nineteenth-Century American Social Movements* (London: Palgrave Macmillan, 2020).

33. Martineau, *Society in America*, vol. 1, 226, 224; vol. 2, 121; Martineau, *Retrospect of Western Travel* (New York, 1838), vol. 1, 263. Martineau observed that "a walk through a lunatic asylum" was far less painful than a visit to the slave quarter of any plantation, where "the natural good taste, so remarkable in free negroes," was entirely extinguished, *Society in America*, vol. 1, 224. She acknowledged that the story of Madame Lalaurie, while infamous in New Orleans, was not known in England. She decided to publish it, over her informant's express request not to, because it revealed "what may happen in a slaveholding country, and can happen nowhere else," *Retrospect of Western Travel*, vol. 1, 263.

34. Martineau, *Society in America*, vol. 2, 123. Martineau may well have gotten the story from Lydia Maria Child, who included it in her *Brief History of the Condition of Women, In Various Ages and Nations* (New York, 1835), vol. 2, 215. Martineau attributed the story to "a southern lady" who told it "in the hearing of a company, among whom were some friends of mine."

35. Martineau, *Retrospect of Western Travel*, vol. 2, 163; She admiringly recounted hearing the famed "Father [Edward Thompson] Taylor" preach in Boston but censured the "unchristian distinction of races" within the chapel, 215.

36. Martineau, *Retrospect of Western Travel*, vol. 1, 180. Martineau heard about Freeman from a lyceum lecture (by Henry Sedgwick in 1831, printed in the *Anti-Slavery Record* in 1836) and from conversations with Catharine Maria Sedgwick, with whom she had become friends. Nearly all that is known about Freeman comes from Sedgwick-mediated documents, much of which made Theodore Sedgwick (and his family) the hero of the story. Martineau's version certainly flattered the Sedgwicks—and dwelt on Freeman's grateful devotion to them—but it centered Freeman as the principal actor in her story. On the way the "Mumbet" story has been used, see Sari Edelstein, "'Good Mother, Farewell': Elizabeth Freeman's Silence and the Stories of Mumbet," *New England Quarterly* (December 2019): 584–614.

37. Martineau, *How to Observe Morals and Manners*, 145.

38. Martineau, *Society in America*, vol. 2, 236. Gleadle, *The Early Feminists*.

39. Jan Lewis, "The Republican Wife: Virtue and Seduction in the Early Republic," in *William and Mary Quarterly* (1987): 689–721; Cott, *Public Vows*; Kirsten

Sword, *Wives Not Slaves: Patriarchy and Modernity in the Age of Revolutions* (Chicago: University of Chicago Press, 2021); Grossberg, *Governing the Hearth*. Caleb Cushing anticipated Martineau's "liberal-minded" lawyer in his "The Legal Condition of Women," *North American Review* 26 (April 1828): 316–319.

40. Martineau, *Society in America*, vol. 2, 222; vol. 1, 384; vol. 2, 116. Martineau might have added to this list of burdens by addressing the "mixed status" marriages forged between free Black and enslaved spouses, as set out in Tera W. Hunter, *Bound in Wedlock: Slave and Free Black Marriage in the Nineteenth Century* (Cambridge, MA: Harvard University Press, 2017), 91–101.

41. Martineau, *Society in America*, vol. 2, 163.

42. Martineau, *Society in America*, vol. 1, 102–103; see also Sarah M. Grimké's September 6, 1837 entry in *Letters on the Equality of the Sexes, and the Condition of Women* (Boston, 1838), 81–82, where she also observed that American women have "no political existence." See Woody Holton, "Equality as Unintended Consequence: The Contracts Clause and the Married Women's Property Acts," *Journal of Southern History* 81, no. 2 (2015): 313–340. The importance of achieving the entire American population's "consent" (however attenuated that was for the enslaved or for married women) is laid out in François Furstenberg, *In the Name of the Father: Washington's Legacy, Slavery and the Making of a Nation* (New York: Penguin, 2006) and John L. Brooke, "Consent, Civil Society, and the Public Sphere in the Age of Revolution and the Early American Republic," in *Beyond the Founders: New Approaches to the Political History of the Early American Republic*, edited by Jeffrey L. Pasley, Andrew W. Robertson, and David Waldstreicher (Chapel Hill: University of North Carolina Press, 2004), 209–250.

43. Beaumont, *Marie*, 58; Tocqueville, *Democracy in America* 1, 363–364.

44. Tocqueville, *Democracy in America* 1, 364; Beaumont, "The Test: Episode of Onéda," *Marie*, chapter 11.

45. Tocqueville, *Democracy in America* 2, 194, 196, 195, 198, 199–200. Eileen Hunt Botting, "A Family Resemblance: Tocqueville and Wollstoncraftian Protofeminism," in *Feminist Interpretations of Alexis de Tocqueville*, edited by Jill Locke and Eileen Hunt Botting (University Park, PA: Penn State University Press, 2009), 99–124. On Tocqueville's own marriage, see Ross Carroll, "The Hidden Labors of Mary Mottley, Madame de Tocqueville," *Hypatia* 33, no. 4 (2018): 643–662. Tocqueville's initial letters home sounded more like Beaumont. He gave marriage a more positive slant only when he wrote the second volume of *Democracy*. See Jean Elisabeth Pedersen, "Outrageous Flirtation, Repressed Flirtation, and the Gallic Singularity: Alexis de Tocqueville's Comparative Views on Women and Marriage in France and the United States," *French Politics, Culture, and Society* 38, no. 1 (March 2020): 67–90.

46. Tocqueville, *Democracy in America* 2, 198–201. Two generations of women's historians have demonstrated the inaccuracy of Tocqueville's observations even for white middle-class women. See, for example, Nancy F. Cott, *Bonds of*

Womanhood: "Woman's Sphere" in New England, 1780–1835 (New Haven, CT: Yale University Press, 1977); Mary P. Ryan, *Cradle of the Middle Class: The Family in Oneida County, New York, 1790–1865* (New York: Cambridge University Press, 1981); Linda K. Kerber, "Separate Spheres, Female Worlds, Woman's Place: The Rhetoric of Women's History," *Journal of American History* 75, no. 1 (1988): 9–39.

47. Tocqueville, *Democracy in America* 2, 201.

48. Tocqueville, *Democracy in America* 2, 212, 225. Tocqueville did, however, think that the precarious volatility that accompanied economic mobility—where "the same man" might rise and sink again through all "the grades which lead from opulence to poverty"—took a toll on American women, who seemed prematurely aged and careworn (213).

49. Tocqueville, *Democracy in America* 2, 602, 601. Sheldon Wolin argues that marriage in Tocqueville's schema was not a model for but a "check" on democracy and an institution directed to restricting "the extension of democracy into the structure of the family," Wolin, *Tocqueville Between Two Worlds* (Princeton, NJ: Princeton University Press, 2003), 333–334.

50. Lydia Maria Child, *The Mother's Book* (Boston, 1831), 163–164.

51. Martineau, *Society in America*, vol. 2, 236–237, 235, 244. On Wollstonecraft and marriage, see Barbara Taylor, *Mary Wollstonecraft and the Feminist Imagination* (Cambridge: Cambridge University Press, 2003); Eileen Hunt Botting, *Family Feuds: Wollstonecraft, Burke, and Rousseau on the Transformation of the Family* (Albany: State University of New York Press, 2006).

52. Tocqueville, *Democracy in America* 2, 600, 603. On developments in America between the first and second volumes of Tocqueville's work, see Leslie Friedman Goldstein, "Europe Looks at American Women, 1820–1840" *Social Research* 54, no. 3 (Autumn 1987): 519–542. Early nineteenth-century sex radicalism is addressed in Claire Goldberg Moses, *French Feminism in the Nineteenth Century* (Albany: State University of New York Press, 1984); Margaret McFadden, *Golden Cables of Sympathy: The Transatlantic Sources of Nineteenth-Century Feminism* (Lexington: University Press of Kentucky, 1999); Bonnie S. Anderson, *Joyous Greetings: The First International Women's Movement, 1830–1860* (New York: Oxford University Press, 2000); and Karen M. Offen, *The Woman Question in France, 1400–1870* (Cambridge: Cambridge University Press, 2017).

53. "Democracy in America. Part II. The Social Influence of Democracy," *Methodist Quarterly Review* (July 1841); [Colton], *A Voice from America*, 266. Olivier Zunz, "Tocqueville and the Americans: *Democracy in America* as Read in Nineteenth Century America," in *The Cambridge Companion to Tocqueville*, edited by Cheryl B. Welch (Cambridge: Cambridge University Press, 2006).

54. Justitia, "Reviewer of De Tocqueville," *Colored American*, May 1, 1841, a piece contextualized in Tillery Jr., "Reading Tocqueville Behind the Veil"; [Robert Walsh], "Review of *Democracy in America*," *American Quarterly Review* 19 (March 1836); "European Views of Democracy—No. II," *The United States Magazine and*

Democratic Review (July 1838): 337–358; Martineau, *Society in America*; [John Greenleaf Whittier], *Views of Slavery and Emancipation from "Society in America"* (New York, 1837).

55. Mill, "State of Society in America," 365–366. The two Chapman-translated chapters appeared in the London-based monthly *The British Friend of India* (December 1845): 180–193; another chapter, one that was wholly unrelated to racial boundaries, was translated in *Western Monthly Magazine, and Literary Journal* 5 (August 1836), 471–482; and some other excerpts in "Caste in the United States: A Review," in *Quarterly Anti-Slavery Magazine* (January 1837): 175–199. See also "American Republication of Foreign Quarterlies," *Southern Literary Messenger* (July 1835): 651; "Republicanism and It Commentators," *The Knickerbocker* (July 1835): 81–82; and the reprint of the *London Quarterly* review in *Museum of Foreign Literature, Science, and Art* (1835): 33. For publication background on Beaumont's novel, see the helpful introduction by Gerard Fergerson in *Marie, Or Slavery in the United States: A Novel of Jacksonian America*, trans. by Barbara Chapman (Baltimore: Johns Hopkins University, 1999), ix–xi and Zunz, *Alexis de Tocqueville and Gustave de Beaumont*, xxxiii–xxxvi.

56. [Whittier], *Views of Slavery and Emancipation from "Society in America"*; [Daniel K. Whitaker], "Society in America," *The Southern Literary Journal and Monthly Review* (August 1837): 568–570; [William Gilmore Simms], *Slavery in America, Being A Brief Review of Miss Martineau on that Subject. By a South Carolinian* (Richmond, 1838); *The Proslavery Argument* (Charleston, 1852).

57. [James T. Boyle], *A Review of Miss Martineau's Work on 'Society in America'* (Boston, 1837). Such a stance was productive for readers as well as reviewers, and one balanced review concluded by simply encouraging "the reader to *study* the work." "Review of New Books," *Journal of Belles-Lettres*, June 27, 1837.

58. George Sidney Camp, *Democracy* (New York, 1841), 142. Camp's book intriguingly found its way to South America where it was translated and serialized in 1852. There it apparently helped form the basis of the Radical program in the Republic of New Granada in the 1850s. See Robert Louis Gilmore, "Nueva Granada's Socialist Mirage," *Hispanic American Historical Review* 36 (May 1956): 190–210.

59. Camp, *Democracy*, 45, 85; "The Book Trade," *Hunt's Merchants' Magazine*, December 1841, 554. On the habitual lumping of women with infants and children, see Corinne T. Field, *The Struggle for Equal Adulthood: Gender, Race, Age, and the Fight for Citizenship in Antebellum America* (Chapel Hill: University of North Carolina Press, 2014).

60. Boyle, *A Review of Miss Martineau's Work*, 33–34, 51; "Notes on Miss Martineau," *New Yorker*, July 1, 1837.

61. Hubbard Winslow, *Woman as She Should Be* (Boston, 1843), 32; "An American Physician," introduction and appendix to Alexander Walker, *Woman Physiologically Considered as to Mind, Morals, Marriage, Matrimonial Slavery, Infidelity, and Divorce* (New York, 1842), xii, 373–382. Scottish physiologist Walker's book

appeared in multiple editions in Britain and America. Robyn Cooper, "Definition and Control: Alexander Walker's Trilogy on Woman," *Journal of the History of Sexuality* 2, no. 3 (1992): 341–364. The "American physician" who edited and introduced the volume for American readers included an extended discussion of Martineau in the appendix, blaming her for having "first infected American women . . . with this absurd notion in relation to the equality of the sexes." Ellen Wallace, *The Clandestine Marriage: And the Sisters* (London, 1840), 259–262, an English novel, distilled Martineau in ways that made sense on both sides of the Atlantic. The chapter on "political non-existence" prompts a character to exclaim: "Ah tyrants! Where are our parliaments and votes! Our hustings where are our liberties! Our representatives!" 260.

62. "Miss Martineau's Works," *The American Biblical Repository* (October 1838); [John L. O'Sullivan], "American Women," *The United States Magazine and Democratic Review* (August 1839): 139–142; [William Leggett], (New York) *Plaindealer*, June 17, 1837. Brownson declared himself "non-committal" in opening his journal to a pro-Martineau essay, "Rights of Women" *Boston Quarterly Review* (July 1839): 350. Only after his conversion to Catholicism would he explore "The Woman Question" in sharply anti-reform articles from 1869 and 1873, included in *The Works of Orestes A. Brownson* (1885).

63. Margaret McFadden, "Boston Teenagers Debate the Woman Question, 1837–1838," *Signs* 15, no. 4 (1990): 832–847; George W. Julian, *Political Recollections 1840 to 1872* (Chicago, 1884), 324–325.

CHAPTER 2

1. Catharine Beecher, *A Treatise on Domestic Economy* (Boston, 1841).

2. Kathryn Kish Sklar, *Catharine Beecher: A Study in American Domesticity* (New Haven, CT: Yale University Press, 1973); Sarah A. Leavitt, *From Catharine Beecher to Martha Stewart: A Cultural History of Domestic Advice* (Chapel Hill: University of North Carolina Press, 2002).

3. See especially Nancy F. Cott, *Bonds of Womanhood: 'Woman's Sphere' in New England, 1780–1835* (New Haven, CT: Yale University Press, 1977); Mary P. Ryan, *Cradle of the Middle Class: The Family in Oneida County, New York, 1790–1865* (New York: Cambridge University Press, 1981).

4. Classic treatments of domesticity, which historians of the 1960s developed in dialogue with feminism's "second-wave," begin with Barbara Welter, "The Cult of True Womanhood," *American Quarterly* 18, no. 2 (1966): 151–174; Aileen S. Kraditor, *Up from the Pedestal, Selected Writings in the History of American Feminism* (Chicago: Quadrangle, 1970); Cott, *Bonds of Womanhood*; Linda K. Kerber, "Separate Spheres, Female Worlds, Woman's Place: The Rhetoric of Women's History," *Journal of American History* 75, no. 1 (1988): 9–39; Glenna Matthews, *Just a Housewife: The Rise and Fall of Domesticity* (New York: Oxford University

Press, 1989). On Black women's relation to domesticity, see Shirley J. Yee, "Black Women and the Cult of True Womanhood," in *Black Women Abolitionists: A Study in Activism, 1828–1860* (Knoxville: University of Tennessee Press, 1992), 40–59.

5. Alexis de Tocqueville, *Democracy in America* (New York, 1840), chapter 13 (hereafter cited as *Democracy in America* 2). On the mobility and volatility of these decades, see Charles Sellers, *The Market Revolution: Jacksonian America, 1815–1846* (New York: Oxford University Press, 1991); Robert Wiebe, *Self-Rule: A Cultural History of American Democracy* (Chicago: University of Chicago Press, 1995); Edward Balleisen, *Navigating Failure: Bankruptcy and Commercial Society in Antebellum America* (Chapel Hill: University of North Carolina Press, 2001); Jonathan Levy, *Freaks of Fortune: The Emerging World of Capitalism and Risk in America* (Cambridge, MA: Harvard University Press, 2014). On the many ways women were not walled off from the market but immersed within it, see Christine Stansell, *City of Women: Sex and Class in New York, 1789–1860* (Urbana: University of Illinois, 1986); Jeanne Boydston, *Home and Work: Housework, Wages, and the Ideology of Labor in the Early Republic* (New York: Oxford University Press, 1990).

6. William A. Alcott, *The Young Housekeeper* (Boston, 1838), 18.

7. "From Facts from the People," *Colored American*, July 8, 1837. James Madison wrote in *Federalist #39* of "that honorable determination which animates every votary of freedom, to rest all our political experiments on the capacity of mankind for self-government." Harriet Martineau had quoted Madison (the man, not *Federalist #39*) in the opening pages of *Society in America*, as discussed in chapter 1.

8. Alexis Tocqueville, *Democracy in America* (New York, 1835), 384 (hereafter cited as *Democracy in America* 1). In a more recent translation, Arthur Goldhammer renders the phrase as "that every person is born with the faculty to govern himself"; *Democracy in America* (New York, 2004). [M. A. Richter], *On Self-Government; Together with General Plans of a State Constitution, and a Constitution for a Confederation of States, founded on the Principle of Self-Government . . .* (Boston, 1847), 1. Francis Lieber, who traced the etymology of the compound word in 1853, was unsure if it originated in England or the United States, but he was certain it was an Anglo-American concept, used in English even by French and German speakers. See *On Civil Liberty and Self-Government* (Philadelphia, 1853), vol. 1, 268.

9. George Sidney Camp, *Democracy* (New York, 1841), 55–56; "Notices of New Books," *United States Democratic Review* (December 1847); "Principles at Issue in the Continental Struggle," *Littel's Living Age*, September 22, 1849. President Polk's widely reprinted message to Congress (December 1847) insisted that the United States had proven that "man is capable of self-government," reprinted in "Massachusetts Quarterly Review—Literature and Politics," *National Era*, December 30, 1847. Edward Everett, "Colonizing Africa," *Christian Register*, October 13, 1849, on importance to the cause of emancipation of a demonstration of Africans' "capacity for self-government."

10. On the era of reform, see Alice Felt Tyler, *Freedom's Ferment: Phases of American Social History to 1860* (Minneapolis: University of Minnesota Press, 1944); Ronald G. Walters, *American Reformers, 1815–1860* (New York: Hill and Wang, 1978); Steven Mintz, *Moralists and Modernizers: America's Pre–Civil War Reformers* (Baltimore: Johns Hopkins University Press, 1995); Michael P. Young, *Bearing Witness against Sin: The Evangelical Birth of the American Social Movement* (Chicago: University of Chicago Press, 2006). On reform as response to the expansion of democracy, see Kyle G. Volk, *Moral Minorities and the Making of American Democracy* (New York: Oxford University Press, 2014), chapter 1.

11. "The Graham System. What Is It?," *The Graham Journal of Health and Longevity*, April 18, 1837. On Graham and other varieties of bodily regulation (including sex reform), see Stephen Nissenbaum, *Sex, Diet, and Debility in Jacksonian America* (Westport, CT: Greenwood Press, 1980); Helen Lefkowitz Horowitz, *Rereading Sex: Battles over Sexual Knowledge and Suppression in Nineteenth-Century America* (New York: Knopf, 2002) and Carol Faulkner, *Unfaithful: Love, Adultery, and Marriage Reform in Nineteenth-Century America* (Philadelphia: University of Pennsylvania Press, 2019). On sex reform more generally, also William Leach, *True Love and Perfect Union: The Feminist Reform of Sex and Society* (New York: Basic Books, 1980); Wendy Hayden, *Evolutionary Rhetoric: Sex, Science, and Free Love in Nineteenth-Century Feminism* (Carbondale: Southern Illinois University Press, 2013). And on phrenology see Carla Bittel, *A Most Useful and Peculiar Science: Phrenology in Practice in the Nineteenth Century* (Cambridge University Press, forthcoming). William Ellery Channing put a Unitarian spin on this broader phenomenon in *Self-Culture* (Boston, 1838), a celebrated work that also aligns with some of the leading "self-making" features of New England Transcendentalism.

12. Heman Humphrey, *Domestic Education* (Amherst, MA, 1840), 24. Lydia Maria Child's *The Frugal American Housewife* (Boston, 1829) addressed itself specifically to poor and middling women, a gambit that resulted in over six thousand copies being sold in its first year and thirty reprintings of the work between 1829 and 1845.

13. "Publisher's Preface" to John Mather Austin's *A Voice to the Married: Being a Compendium of Social, Moral, and Religious Duties, Addressed to Husbands and Wives* (Boston, 1847); Patricia Okker, *Our Sister Editors: Sarah J. Hale and the Tradition of Nineteenth Century American Women Editors* (Athens: University of Georgia Press, 1995). On changing ideas about child-rearing in the 1830s, see Bernard Wishy, *The Child and the Republic* (Philadelphia: University of Pennsylvania Press, 1968).

14. William A. Alcott, *The Young Man's Guide* (Boston, 1833), 22–23. On Alcott, the cousin of Bronson Alcott (father of Louisa May Alcott), see Louis B. Salomon, "The Least-Remembered Alcott," *New England Quarterly* 34 (March 1961): 87–93. Catharine Maria Sedgwick, *Means and Ends, or Self-Training* (Boston, 1839), 13–15. The ubiquity of domestic published opinion is evident in Mary Ryan, *Empire of the Mother: American Writings about Domesticity, 1830–1860* (New York: Haworth

Press, 1982); John F. Kasson, *Rudeness & Civility: Manners in Nineteenth-Century Urban America* (New York: Macmillan, 1990); Jane E. Rose, "Conduct Books for Women, 1830–1860: A Rationale for Women's Conduct and Domestic Role in America," *Nineteenth-Century Women Learn to Write* (Charlottesville: University of Virginia Press, 1995), 37–58; while complementary development within an English context is addressed in Kay Boardman, "The Ideology of Domesticity: The Regulation of the Household Economy in Victorian Women's Magazines," *Victorian Periodicals Review* 33, no. 2 (2000): 150–164.

15. Alcott, *The Young Man's Guide.* On the centrality of self-making to American culture, see Daniel Walker Howe, *Making the American Self: Jonathan Edwards to Abraham Lincoln* (Cambridge, MA: Harvard University Press, 1997).

16. Carole Shammas, *A History of Household Government in America* (Charlottesville: University of Virginia Press, 2002). On marriage reform, see also Norma Basch, *In the Eyes of the Law: Women, Marriage, and Property in Nineteenth-Century New York* (Ithaca, NY: Cornell University Press, 1982); Michael Grossberg, *Governing the Hearth: Law and the Family in Nineteenth-Century America* (Chapel Hill: University of North Carolina Press, 1988); Nancy F. Cott, *Public Vows: A History of Marriage and the Nation* (Cambridge, MA: Harvard University Press, 2000); Hendrick Hartog, *Man and Wife in America* (Cambridge, MA: Harvard University Press, 2000).

17. Matthew Carey, *Philosophy of Common Sense: Practical Rules for the Promotion of Domestic Happiness. Containing Rules of Marriage* (Philadelphia, 1838); George W. Burnap, *The Spheres and Duties of Woman* (Baltimore, 1841), 206–208. Alcott was no less insistent in his guidance to young husbands. He chastised would-be domestic tyrants who, succumbing to "this fell disease of our sex," treated their wives and children as mere drudges, in *The Young Husband, or Duties of Man in the Marriage Relation* (Boston, 1839). Horace Bushnell offered a specifically theological defense of family care in his *Views of Christian Nurture* (1847). For a thoughtful discussion of Bushnell's coherent social theory, see Daniel Walker Howe, "The Social Science of Horace Bushnell," *Journal of American History* (September 1983): 305–322.

18. Lydia Maria Child, *The Mother's Book* (Boston, 1831), 167. In the wake of the 1832 foundation of the Boston Phrenological Society, Orson Squire Fowler, an Amherst College graduate and notable phrenologist, circulated these often-reprinted titles: *Matrimony, or Phrenology and Physiology Applied to the Selection of Suitable Companions for Life* (Philadelphia, 1841); *Love and Parentage* (New York, 1846); and, with his brother Lorenzo, *Marriage: Its History and Ceremonies with a Phrenological and Physiological Exposition of the Functions and Qualifications for Happy Marriages* (New York, 1848), a volume that went into at least 22 editions. Attention to the reception and use of this literature is provided in Carla Bittel, "Woman, Know Thyself: Producing and Using Phrenological Knowledge in 19th-Century America," *Centaurus* 55, no. 2 (2013): 104–130; and Bittel, *A Most Useful and Peculiar Science.*

19. Alcott, *The Young Man's Guide*, 48; Howard P. Chudacoff, *The Age of the Bachelor: Creating an American Subculture* (Princeton, NJ: Princeton University Press, 2000); Lee Virginia Chambers-Schiller, *Liberty, A Better Husband: Single Women in America: The Generations of 1780–1840* (New Haven, CT: Yale University Press, 1984). Domestic advice literature was also unrelentingly heteronormative. On alternative pairings in practice, see Rachel Hope Cleves, *Charity and Sylvia: A Same-Sex Marriage in Early America* (New York: Oxford University Press, 2014) and Jen Manion, *Female Husbands: A Trans History* (New York: Cambridge University Press, 2020).

20. [Samuel Griswold Goodrich], *Fireside Education* (New York, 1838); Harriet Martineau, *Household Education* (Philadelphia, 1849), 1.

21. William A. Alcott, *Familiar Letters to Young Men on Various Subjects* (Boston, 1849), 263 and *The Young Wife* (Boston, 1838), 285.

22. On 1840, see Elizabeth R. Varon, "Tippecanoe and the Ladies, Too: White Women and Party Politics in Antebellum Virginia," *Journal of American History* 82 (September 1995): 494–521 and *We Mean to Be Counted: White Women and Politics in Antebellum Virginia* (Chapel Hill: University of North Carolina Press, 1998); Ronald Zboray and Mary Saracino Zboray, "Whig Women, Politics, and Culture in the Campaign of 1840: Three Perspectives from Massachusetts," *Journal of the Early Republic* 17 (Summer 1997): 277–315 and *Voices Without Votes: Women and Politics in New England* (Durham: University of New Hampshire Press, 2010).

23. Lydia H. Sigourney, *Letters to Mothers* (Hartford, 1838), 13–15.

24. This relationship continues to be framed in the terms set and questions posed in two classic works: Nancy Hewitt, *Women's Activism and Social Change: Rochester, New York, 1822–1872* (Ithaca, NY: Cornell University Press, 1984) and Lori D. Ginzberg, *Women and the Work of Benevolence: Morality, Politics, and Class in the Nineteenth-Century United States* (New Haven, CT: Yale University Press, 1990). On the education that enabled this entry into civic life, see Mary Kelley, *Learning to Stand and Speak: Women, Education, and Public Life in America's Republic* (Chapel Hill: University of North Carolina Press, 2006).

25. [Goodrich], *Fireside Education*, iii–vi. This manual went into multiple editions and reprintings between 1838 and 1846. Goodrich was best-known for his Peter Parley series of books for children. On whiteness and citizenship in this era, see James Brewer Stewart, "The Emergence of Racial Modernity and the Rise of the White North, 1790–1840," *Journal of the Early Republic* (Summer 1998): 181–217.

26. Shammas, *A History of Household Government in America*. On African American marriage and family, see Tera W. Hunter, *Bound in Wedlock: Slave and Free Black Marriage in the Nineteenth Century* (Cambridge, MA: Harvard University Press, 2017); Amy Dru Stanley, *From Bondage to Contract: Wage Labor, Marriage, and the Market in the Age of Slave Emancipation* (New York: Cambridge University Press, 1998); Cott, *Public Vows*. On Southern households see Stephanie McCurry, *Masters of Small Worlds: Yeoman Households, Gender Relations, and the Political*

Culture of the Antebellum South Carolina Low Country (New York: Oxford University Press, 1995). On slave catechisms, see Janet Duitsman Cornelius, *"When I Can Read My Title Clear": Literacy, Slavery, and Religion in the Antebellum South* (Columbia: University of South Carolina Press, 1991); Tammy K. Byron, " 'A Catechism for their Special Use': Slave Catechisms in the Antebellum South" (PhD diss., University of Arkansas, 2008).

27. Lydia Maria Child, *Brief History of the Condition of Women, In Various Ages and Nations* (New York, 1835), vol. 2, 212; Virginia Cary, *Letters on Female Character: Addressed to a Young Lady on the Death of her Mother* (Richmond, 1828), 202–207. On the significance of the family and gender to abolitionist rhetoric, see Kristin Hoganson, "Garrisonian Abolitionist and the Rhetoric of Gender, 1850–1860," *American Quarterly* 45, no. 4 (1993): 558–595; Cott, *Public Vows*; Amy Dru Stanley, "Home Life and the Morality of the Market," in *The Market Revolution in America: Social, Political, and Religious Expressions, 1800–1880*, edited by Melvyn Stokes and Stephen Conway (Charlottesville: University of Virginia Press, 1996), 74–96. Slavery's "outrage upon the family" would become a central theme of Harriet Beecher Stowe's wildly successful *Uncle Tom's Cabin* (1852).

28. "A Good Wife," *Colored American*, January 23, 1841, and "Family Sympathies," *Colored American*, July 7, 1838. Further examples of domesticity in *Colored American* can be seen in "How to Reduce Your Household Expenses," August 17, 1839, "Moral Influence of the Wife on the Husband," November 17, 1838, "Hints to Young Ladies," November 14, 1840. Erica L. Ball offers a sensitive reading of this material and demonstrates how it linked up to the politics of freedom in *To Live an Antislavery Life: Personal Politics and the Antebellum Black Middle Class* (Athens: University of Georgia Press, 2012). On *Freedom's Journal*, see Jacqueline Bacon, Freedom's Journal: *The First African American Newspaper* (Lanham, MD: Lexington Books, 2007); Benjamin Fagan, *The Black Newspaper and the Chosen Nation* (Athens: University of Georgia Press, 2016), chapter 1.

29. Hélène Quanquin makes this astute point about Douglass's marriage certificate in *Men in the American Women's Rights Movement, 1830–1890* (New York: Routledge, 2020), 72, n. 80. On the marriage of Douglass and Murray, see Leigh Fought, *Women in the World of Frederick Douglass* (New York: Oxford University Press, 2017) and David Blight, *Frederick Douglass: Prophet of Freedom* (New York: Simon & Schuster, 2018). And on the complicated ways that freedom and the prerogatives of patriarchal authority over wives were entangled, see Amy Dru Stanley, "Home Life and the Morality of the Market" and Maurice O. Wallace, " 'I Rose a Freeman': Power, Property, and the Performance of Manhood in the Slave Narratives," in *Oxford Handbook of the African American Slave Narrative*, edited by John Ernest (New York: Oxford University Press, 2014), 260–276.

30. Catharine Beecher to Edward Beecher, August 23, 1828, in Jeanne Boydston, Mary Kelly, and Anne Margois, *The Limits of Sisterhood: The Beecher Sisters on Women's Rights and Woman's Sphere* (Chapel Hill: University of North Carolina Press,

1988), 41; "best boy" quoted on 17. For a contemporaneous sketch of the Beecher family history, see Harriet Beecher Stowe, *Uncle Sam's Emancipation: Earthly Care, A Heavenly Discipline, and Other Sketches* (Philadelphia, 1853).

31. Sklar, *Catharine Beecher*, 99.

32. Beecher, *Treatise*, 56, 247; "Monthly Literary Record: Notices of New Books," *The United States Magazine, and Democratic Review* (December 1841): 42. The word "calisthenics" had just begun to appear in print as a specifically female version of gymnastics. See, for example, Gustavus Hamilton, *The Elements of Gymnastics, for Boys; and of Calisthenics, for Young Ladies* (London, 1827), which was reviewed fairly widely in American periodicals, and "Calisthenics," *Lady's Book* (May 1836), which explained "this hard name is given to a gentler sort of gymnastics, suited to girls." Beecher eventually published a book devoted specifically to just this subject: *Physiology and Calisthenics: For Schools and Families* (New York, 1856). Dolores Hayden, *The Grand Domestic Revolution: A History of Feminist Designs for American Homes, Neighborhoods, and Cities* (Cambridge, MA: MIT Press, 1982). On Lyman Beecher's reform efforts, see Johann N. Neem, *Creating a Nation of Joiners: Democracy and Civil Society in Early National Massachusetts* (Cambridge. MA: Harvard University Press, 2008), chapter 4 and Volk, *Moral Minorities and the Making of American Democracy*, chapter 4.

33. Beecher, *Treatise*, 207, 39; Catharine Beecher, *Letters to Persons Who Are Engaged in Domestic Service* (New York, 1842). Mrs. A. J. Graves quoted Tocqueville extensively in her own advice manual but she stuck mainly to his comments on the "superiority" of American women, rather than the democratic aspects of domesticity. See *Woman in America; Being an Examination into the Moral and Intellectual Condition of American Female Society* (New York, 1841).

34. Lydia Maria Child and Eliza Farrar targeted the "newly married" audience with greatest success. A few others crossed generational boundaries such as Miss Eliza Leslie, *The House Book; or a Manual of Domestic Economy* (Philadelphia, 1840), which Beecher herself invoked as a competitor in the preface to the first (1841) edition of the *Treatise*, ix–x.

35. Catharine Beecher, *Suggestions Respecting Improvements in Education* (Hartford, 1829), 7.

36. This relocation allowed her to boast of having resided in eight American states, while making extended stays in five others, a matter that lent credibility to her claims to possess a truly American perspective. She invoked the scope of her experiences, beginning in the second edition of the *Treatise*, to combat the most biting commentary about American women that appeared in Harriet Martineau's *Society in America*.

37. Catharine Beecher, *Essay on Slavery and Abolitionism: With Reference to the Duty of American Females* (Philadelphia, 1837); Alisse Portnoy, *Their Right to Speak: Women's Activism in the Indian and Slave Debates* (Cambridge, MA: Harvard University Press, 2005). Beecher's general argument that women's calming and

purportedly apolitical ministrations would tame the passions of partisan politics echoes the distaste for women's politicization addressed in Rosemarie Zagarri, *Revolutionary Backlash* (Philadelphia: University of Pennsylvania Press, 2007).

38. Beecher, *Treatise*, 27.

39. Beecher, *Treatise*, 36–37. In sentiments like this one, stripped of any specific democratic language, Beecher's domesticity most clearly resembled earlier formulations of republican womanhood.

40. Horace Bushnell, "American Politics," *American National Preacher* 14 (December 1840): 198–199. Mark Edwards offers a compelling analysis of Bushnell's gendered worldview in " 'My God and My Good Mother': The Irony of Horace Bushnell's Gendered Republic," *Religion and American Culture: A Journal of Interpretation* 13 (Winter 2003): 111–137. See also Michiyo Morita, *Horace Bushnell on Women in Nineteenth-Century America* (New York: New York University Press, 2004).

41. Beecher, *Essay on Slavery and Abolitionism*; Beecher, *Letters to Persons who are Engaged in Domestic Service*. On the Stowe-Jackson encounter, see Susanna Ashton, " 'The Genuine Article': John Andrew Jackson and Harriet Beecher Stowe," *Commonplace* 13 (Summer 2013), https://commonplace.online/article/genuine-article/ (accessed February 24, 2023). Jackson became a writer himself, publishing a memoir while living in England, *The Experience of a Slave in South Carolina* (London, 1862). On Catharine's aid to Harriet while she wrote *Uncle Tom's Cabin*, see Sklar, *Catharine Beecher*, 233 and Joan D. Hedrick, *Harriet Beecher Stowe: A Life* (New York: Oxford University Press, 1995), 220–221. On the novel's importance to political culture, see especially John L. Brooke, *"There is a North": Fugitive Slaves, Political Crisis, and Cultural Transformation in the Coming of the Civil War* (Amherst: University of Massachusetts Press, 2019).

42. *New York Weekly Tribune*, March 26, 1842. On Fourier, see Jonathan Beecher, *Charles Fourier: The Visionary and His World* (Berkeley: University of California Press, 1990); on Fourierism in the United States, see Carl J. Guarneri, *The Utopian Alternative: Fourierism in Nineteenth-Century America* (Ithaca, NY: Cornell University Press 1991).

43. "Prospectus of the *New York Weekly Tribune*," *The New World: A Weekly Family Journal of Popular Literature, Science, Art and News*, August 28, 1841. Brisbane's column in the *Tribune* came after a series of earlier collaborations in published opinion. On Greeley, see Adam Tuchinsky, *Horace Greeley's New-York Tribune: Civil-War Era Socialism and the Crisis of Free Labor* (Ithaca, NY: Cornell University Press, 2009); James M. Lundberg, *Horace Greeley: Print, Politics, and the Failure of American Nationhood* (Baltimore: Johns Hopkins University Press, 2019); and Mitchell Snay, *Horace Greeley and the Politics of Reform in Nineteenth-Century America* (Lanham, MD: Rowman & Littlefield, 2011). Greeley began the European edition in 1850. See Richard Allen Schwarzlose, *The Nation's Newsbrokers: The Formative Years, From Pretelegraphy to 1865* (Evanston, IL: Northwestern University Press, 1988), 53.

44. Parke Godwin, *Democracy: Constructive and Pacific* (New York, 1844), 3. This volume was a reworking of the Fourier-disciple Victor Considerant's "Manifeste" of his journal *La Démocratie Pacifique* (1843). Greeley himself mixed hoopla campaigning with broad-gauged reform. He was a key innovator of sensational electioneering through his organ *The Log Cabin*, which in 1840 drew 60,000 Whig subscribers.

45. Philip F. Gura, *Man's Better Angels: Romantic Reformers and the Coming of the Civil War* (Cambridge, MA: Harvard University Press, 2017) emphasizes the links between reformism and the 1837 economic downturn, while the utopian impulse is explored in Christopher Clark, *The Communitarian Moment: The Radical Challenge of the Northampton Association* (Amherst: University of Massachusetts Press, 1995) and Richard Francis, *Transcendental Utopias: Individual and Community at Brook Farm, Fruitlands, and Walden* (Ithaca, NY: Cornell University Press, 1997). Alcott and his partner, Englishman Charles Lane, wrote a manifesto of sorts that was published in the *Liberator* (among other newspapers): "The Consociate Family Life," *Liberator*, September 22, 1843, 152. On the "sisterhood of reforms" (a phrase of Thomas Wentworth Higginson's), see Ronald G. Walters, *American Reformers, 1815–1860* (1978; rev. ed., New York: Hill and Wang, 1997), xiii.

46. "Othello—Jealousy," *Harbinger*, September 25, 1847; Albert Brisbane, *The Social Destiny of Man* (Philadelphia, 1840), 6; George Ripley, "Influence of Association upon Woman," *Harbinger*, September 27, 1846; William Henry Channing, "Woman," *The Present* (December 1843). Guarneri discusses the outreach toward women in *The Utopian Alternative*. On debates over the woman question in French socialist thought, see Leslie F. Goldstein, "Early Feminist Themes in French Utopian Socialism: The St-Simonians and Fourier," *Journal of the History of Ideas* (January–March 1982): 91–108.

47. Henry Jarvis Raymond and Horace Greeley, *Association Discussed: Or, The Socialism of the Tribune Examined; Being a Controversy Between The New York Tribune and the Courier and Enquirer* (New York, 1847). See the discussion of Fourier's ideas about sex in Beecher, *Charles Fourier*, chapter 15. On the Raymond-Greeley controversy, see Tuchinsky, *Horace Greeley's New-York Tribune*, 112–117.

48. *Love, Marriage, Divorce and the Sovereignty of the Individual. A Discussion by Henry James, Horace Greeley, and Stephen Pearl Andrew* (New York, 1853) concluded a conversation that began in the pages of the *Harbinger* in the fall of 1848. For more on the controversy, see Alfred Habegger, *Henry James and the "Woman Business"* (New York: Cambridge University Press, 1989), chapter 2 and *The Father: The Life of Henry James, Sr.* (New York: Farrar, Straus and Giroux, 1994), chapter 18; Tuchinsky, *Horace Greeley's New-York Tribune*, chapter 4. On the broader context of sex reform, see especially Leach, *True Love and Perfect Union*; Horowitz, *Rereading Sex*; and Faulkner, *Unfaithful*.

49. S. Margaret Fuller, *Woman in the Nineteenth Century* (New York, 1845). Another indispensable text in this one-hundred-and-fifty-year span is John Stuart Mill's *The Subjection of Women* (1869), discussed in chapter 5.

50. Greeley's reflections on his relationship to Fuller appears in *Memoirs of Margaret Fuller Ossoli* (Boston, 1852) 2: 152–163 and is effectively handled in Lundberg, *Horace Greeley*, 46–50. On Fuller and Fourierites, see Charles Capper, *Margaret Fuller: An American Romantic Life. Volume 2. The Public Years* (New York: Oxford University Press, 2007), 111–112, 179.

51. [Margaret Fuller], "The Great Lawsuit. Man *versus* Men. Woman *versus* Women," *The Dial* (July, 1843): 11; Fuller, *Woman in the Nineteenth Century*, 159. The complexity of Fuller's engagement with the Transcendental female self is laid out in Howe, *Making the American Self*, chapter 8; Phyllis Cole, "Woman Questions: Emerson, Fuller, and New England Reform," in *Transient and Permanent: The Transcendentalist Movement and its Contexts*, edited by Charles Capper and Conrad Wright (Boston: Massachusetts Historical Society, 1999), 408–446; Capper, *Margaret Fuller*; Corinne T. Field, *The Struggle for Equal Adulthood: Gender, Race, Age, and the Fight for Citizenship in Antebellum America* (Chapel Hill: University of North Carolina, 2014), 66–71; Megan Marshall, *Margaret Fuller: A New American Life* (New York: Houghton Mifflin Harcourt, 2013); and Tiffany K. Wayne, *Woman Thinking: Feminist and Transcendentalism in Nineteenth-Century America* (Lanham, MD: Lexington Books, 2005).

52. Fuller, "The Great Lawsuit."

53. Fuller, "The Great Lawsuit," 7; *Woman in the Nineteenth Century*, 13, 26. Fuller looked to Martineau as a potential mentor during her 1834–1836 American tour, but the two had a falling out after Fuller criticized *Society in America*. Though the book nearly tripled in length, it did not fundamentally alter the thesis of the article. On both texts, see especially Capper, *Margaret Fuller*, 111–112, 176–118; Howe, *Making the American Self*, chapter 8; and Field, *The Struggle for Equal Adulthood*, 66–71.

54. Fuller, *Woman in the Nineteenth Century*, 16. Though "self-dependence," not unlike Emerson's "self-reliance," can call to mind a constrained sort of liberal individualism, such an understanding fails to capture its more robust meanings associated with human flourishing. "Democratic individuality" is thus a better phrase. See, for example, Alex Zakaras, *Individuality and Mass Democracy: Mill, Emerson, and the Burdens of Citizenship* (New York: Oxford University Press, 2009).

55. Capper, *Margaret Fuller*, 166; [Fuller], "What Fits a Man to be a Voter? Is it to be White Within, or White Without?" *New-York Daily Tribune*, March 31, 1846; "1st January, 1846," *New-York Daily Tribune*, January 1, 1846. The 1846 New York state constitution imposed a property tax on Black men alone. Capper dates Fuller's political awakening to debates over the annexation of Texas in 1844. Charles Capper, "Getting from Here to There: Margaret Fuller's American Transnational Odyssey," in *Margaret Fuller Transatlantic Crossings in a Revolutionary Age*, edited by Charles Capper and Cristina Giorcelli (Madison: University of Wisconsin Press, 2007), 3–26

56. The complicated, state-by-state, process of married women's property laws is traced in Basch, *In the Eyes of the Law* and Cott, *Public Vows*.

57. Capper, *Margaret Fuller*, 188.
58. Elizabeth Oakes Smith, *Woman and Her Needs* (New York, 1851).

CHAPTER 3

1. Elizabeth Oakes Smith in *Proceedings of the Woman's Rights Convention, Held at Syracuse* (Syracuse, 1852), 16; Harriet Martineau, *Society in America* (New York, 1837), vol. 1, 102.
2. Lori D. Ginzberg, *Elizabeth Cady Stanton: An American Life* (New York: Hill and Wang, 2009), 58.
3. Frederick Douglass, "Some Thoughts on Woman's Rights," *Frederick Douglass' Paper*, June 10, 1853, reprinted in Philip S. Foner, *Frederick Douglass on Women's Rights* (Westport, CT: Greenwood Press, 1976), 58–60.
4. John Neal, "Men and Women: A Brief Hypothesis Concerning the Difference in their Genius," *Blackwood's Magazine* 16 (October 1824): 387; W. P. Daggett, *A Down-East Yankee from the District of Maine* (Portland: A. J. Huston, 1920), 35; and Boyd Guest, "John Neal and 'Women's Rights and Women's Wrongs,'" *New England Quarterly* 18 (December 1945): 508–511. Daggett puts the number in attendance at "between two and three thousand." Neal's recollections of his conversations with Mill can be found in John Neal, *Wandering Recollections of a Somewhat Busy Life* (Boston, 1869), 50, 59 and were recounted in *History of Woman Suffrage, Volume 3, 1876–1885*, edited by Elizabeth Cady Stanton, Susan B. Anthony, and Matilda Josyln Gage (Rochester, NY, 1886), 354. Joining the London Debating Society, he proposed a debate on the proposition that "the intellectual powers of the sexes may be equal." A subsequent article for *Blackwood's Magazine* revealed his indebtedness to Mary Wollstonecraft as it offered a simple declaration: "I am for treating women like rational beings." Neal, "Men and Women," 387.
5. *The Radical* [Bowling Green, MO], April 22, 1843; Daggett, *A Down-East Yankee*, 36–37. Park Benjamin reworked his thoughts and committed them to print as "The True Rights of Woman," *Godey's Magazine and Lady's Book* 29 (June 1844): 271–274. For recollections of the Broadway Tabernacle lecture, see Paulina W. Davis, *A History of the National Woman's Rights Movement, for Twenty Years . . .* (New York, 1870), 12, which was then reprinted in *A History of Woman Suffrage, Volume 2, 1861–1876*, edited by Elizabeth Cady Stanton, Susan B. Anthony, and Matilda Josyln Gage (New York, 1882), 435–436. Neal recalled the debate decades later in "The Subjection of Women," *Revolution*, October 14, 1869.
6. John Neal, "Rights of Women," *Brother Jonathan*, June 17, 1843, 183–185. Neal chided his friend Margaret Fuller, when her *Woman in the Nineteenth Century* (1845) appeared, for failing to go all the way and insist that women's full autonomy required them to be politically self-determining selves. "All you and others are doing to elevate woman," he told her, "is only fitted to make her feel more sensibly the long abuse of her understanding, when she comes to her senses." "You

go for thought—I for action." He maintained that women must not only become voters but be entitled to serve on juries, hold elective office, and work in government agencies and bureaus. Neal to Fuller, March 4, 1845, in Bell Gale Chevigny, *The Woman and the Myth: Margaret Fuller's Life and Writings* (1976; rev. ed. Boston: Northeastern University Press, 1994), 234.

7. The Farnham-Neal debate ran through these issues of *Brother Jonathan*: "From the N.Y. Correspondence of the *National Intelligencer*," February 18, 1843, 191; "What We Have to Say," April 29, 1843, 494; Mrs. T. J. Farnham, "Rights of Women. Reply to Mr. Neal's Lecture," June 21, 1843, 236; Mrs. T. J. Farnham, "Rights of Women. Reply to Mr. Neal's Lecture," July 1, 1843, 266, Neal, "Woman!: Letter to Mrs. T. J. Farnham, on the Rights of Women," July 15, 1843, 306; "The Rights of Women! Mrs. Farnham's Reply to John Neal, Esq.," July 29, 1843. Re-encountering the print debate decades later, Neal mused that they should have been printed as a small volume. On Farnham at Sing Sing, see Janet Floyd, "Dislocations of the Self: Eliza Farnham at Sing Sing Prison," *Journal of American Studies* 40, no. 2 (2006): 311–325. Farnham would return to the theme of women's spiritual superiority in her two-volume work *Woman and Her Era* (1864), discussed in chapter 5.

8. Timothy Walker, *Introduction to American Law: Designed as a First Book for Students* (Philadelphia, 1837); Elisha P. Hurlbut, *Essays on Human Rights and Their Political Guaranties* (New York, 1845). An 1834 antislavery address by Harvard's Charles Follen had noted that the Americans' treatment of wives lagged behind even "the law of continental Europe," in "The Cause of Freedom in Our Country," *Quarterly Anti-Slavery Magazine* 2 (October 1836): 61–72. On the usage of slavery when discussing married women's legal disabilities, see Ana Stevenson, *The Woman as Slave in Nineteenth-Century American Social Movements* (London: Palgrave Macmillan, 2020).

9. Hurlbut, *Essays on Human Rights*, 3; Timothy Walker, "The Legal Condition of Women," *Western Law Journal* (January 1849): 145–146; Walker, *The Reform Spirit of the Day: An Oration Before the Phi Beta Kappa Society of Harvard University* (Boston, 1850), 17. Despite Hurlbut and Walker's political differences, Lucretia Mott paired them in her *Discourse on Woman* (Philadelphia, 1850), 15–17 and in *Proceedings of the National Women's Rights Convention Held at Cleveland*, 57. On the rowdiness of antebellum elections, see David Grimsted, *American Mobbing, 1828–1861: Toward Civil War* (New York: Oxford University Press, 1998); Richard Franklin Bensel, *The American Ballot Box in the Mid-Nineteenth Century* (New York: Cambridge University Press, 2004); Jon Grinspan, *The Virgin Vote: How Young Americans Made Democracy Social, Politics Personal, and Voting Popular in the Nineteenth Century* (Chapel Hill: University of North Carolina Press, 2016); and Andrew Wender Cohen and Carol Faulkner, "Enforcing Gender at the Polls: Transing Voters and Women's Suffrage Before the American Civil War," *Journal of Social History* 56, no. 2 (2022): 386–420.

10. Samuel J. May, *Some Recollections of Our Antislavery Conflict* (Boston, 1869), 236, 233–235; Samuel J. May, *The Rights and Condition of Women* [1846] (reprinted: Boston, 1854), 4; May, *Memoir of Samuel J. May* (1873), 190. On May, see Donald Yacovone, *Samuel Joseph May and the Dilemmas of the Liberal Persuasion, 1797–1871* (Philadelphia: Temple University Press, 1991).

11. Knight copied sentences from May and circulated them among British women in the late 1840s. The lack of attribution, or any other indication that the lines were taken from May's Syracuse sermon, ultimately led to the weaving of his phrasing into the history of the British suffrage movement, where it has been regarded as a foundational text authored by Anne Knight and an equivalent to America's Declaration of Sentiments. That interpretation (which remains a feature of popular lore) seems to have first been ventured in Helen Blackburn, *Women's Suffrage A Record of the Women's Suffrage Movement in the British Isles* (London: Williams & Norgate, 1902), 19.

12. R., "An Inquiry into the Meaning of 1 Corinthians xi. 10," *Evangelical Repository* (February 1843): 409–412; Elizabeth Wilson, *A Scriptural View of Woman's Rights and Duties, in All the Important Relations of Life* (Philadelphia, 1849), v–vi, 222; "A Scriptural View of Woman's Rights and Duties," *Evangelical Repository* (April 1850): 541–545. A report that women's rights had been "a favorite topic of discussion with [Wilson] for years," appeared in the *Cadiz Sentinel*, June 19, 1850, while Lucretia Mott informed Elizabeth Cady Stanton that Wilson's work represented "the labor of 10 years," suggesting she began even earlier than 1843. See Mott to Stanton, October 25, 1849, in *Selected Letters of Lucretia Coffin Mott*, edited by Beverly Wilson Palmer (Urbana: University of Illinois Press, 2002), 191. Existing scholarship on Wilson is scanty, with the notable exceptions of Nancy Isenberg, *Sex and Citizenship in Antebellum America* (Chapel Hill: University of North Carolina Press, 1998), esp. 29–32 and, on her anti-Catholicism, John T. McGreevy, *Catholicism and American Freedom* (New York: Norton, 2003), chapter 4.

13. Wilson, *A Scriptural View of Woman's Rights and Duties*, 80–86 and throughout.

14. Wilson, *A Scriptural View of Woman's Rights and Duties*, 376, 223, 252. Martha S. Jones, *All Bound Up Together: The Woman Question in African American Public Culture, 1830–1900* (Chapel Hill: University of North Carolina Press, 2007), 59–85 and *Vanguard: How Black Women Broke Barriers, Won the Vote, and Insisted on Equality for All* (New York: Basic Books, 2020), 59–62 shows that Black women took a similar tack within the African Methodist Episcopal church.

15. "Declaration of Sentiments," in *Report of the Woman's Rights Convention, Held at Seneca Falls, N.Y., July 19th and 20th, 1848* (Rochester, NY, 1848), 5–7. On the Colored National Convention at Cleveland, see *Report of the Proceedings of the Colored National Convention Held at Cleveland, Ohio, on Wednesday, September 6, 1848...* (Rochester, NY, 1848), https://omeka.coloredconventions.org/items/show/280 and, on its exclusion of Black women's voices, Jones, *Vanguard*, 64–65. On the origins of Seneca Falls, see Judith Wellman, *The Road to Seneca Falls: Elizabeth*

Cady Stanton and the First Woman's Rights Convention (Urbana: University of Illinois Press, 2004); Sally G. McMillen, *Seneca Falls and the Origins of the Women's Rights Movement* (New York: Oxford University Press, 2008) and on contestation over its memory Lisa Tetrault, *The Myth of Seneca Falls: Memory and the Women's Suffrage Movement, 1848–1898* (Chapel Hill: University of North Carolina Press, 2014).

16. "Declaration of Sentiments," 7; review in *Mechanic's Advocate* [Albany, NY], quoted in *History of Woman Suffrage, Volume 1, 1848–1861*, edited by Elizabeth Cady Stanton, Susan B. Anthony, and Matilda Joslyn Gage, 802–803.

17. *The Proceedings of the Woman's Rights Convention, Held at Worcester, October 23rd & 24th* (Boston, 1851), 4. A notice in the *Boston Post* for May 31, 1850, mentions that a convention "in favor of securing to women the exercise of political rights" had been planned for October. The official call circulated fairly widely in August and September. See, for example, the *Anti-Slavery Bugle*, August 24, 1850; *Liberator*, September 6, 1850; and the *National Era*, September 19, 1850.

18. *New-York Daily Tribune*, October 25 and 26, 1859; "Remarks," *New York Daily Tribune*, November 2, 1850.

19. John Stuart Mill to Harriet Taylor, [after October 29, 1850], in *The Collected Works of John Stuart Mill: Later Letters*, edited by Francis E. Mineka and Dwight N. Lindley (Toronto: University of Toronto Press, 1972), vol. XIV, 49.

20. On the history of the essay's composition, see Alice Rossi, "Sentiment and Intellect: The Story of John Stuart Mill and Harriet Taylor Mill," *Essays on Sex Equality*, edited by Alice Rossi (Chicago: University of Chicago Press, 1970), 3–63; Evelyn L. Pugh, "John Stuart Mill, Harriet Taylor, and Women's Rights in America, 1850–1873," *Canadian Journal of History* 13, no. 3 (1978): 423–442. Even though Mill insisted that the essay was Taylor Mill's work, a long-running debate among scholars has taken up issues of influence and authorship, a dialogue continued in such recent feminist accounts as Michèle Le Doeuff, *Sex of Knowing* (New York: Routledge, 2003) and Emmalon Davis, "On Epistemic Appropriation," *Ethics* 128, no. 4 (2018): 702–727.

21. [Harriet Taylor Mill], "The Enfranchisement of Women," *Westminster Review* (July 1851): 300.

22. [Harriet Taylor Mill], "The Enfranchisement of Women," 292. Mill exempted himself and Harriet from the charge of frightened servility. John Stuart Mill to Harriet Taylor, [after October 29, 1850], in *The Collected Works of John Stuart Mill: Later Letters*, vol. XIV, 49.

23. [Harriet Taylor Mill], "The Enfranchisement of Women."

24. The essay appeared in the *New York Tribune* on July 18, 1851. Lucretia Mott to William Lloyd Garrison, September 11, 1851, in Palmer, *Selected Letters of Lucretia Coffin Mott*, 208–209. Mott wrote the Scottish phrenologist George Combe that "it is one of the best essays on Woman's Rights that I have seen." She also commented on the authorship question that would befuddle so many in the coming months

(and scholars for generations). It was written, Mott wrote, by "Mrs. Taylor a widow who has recently married J. S. Mill" but "part of it is from his pen. Indeed, she says, *he* wrote it—he says, *she* wrote it." Mill certainly did not minimize the confusion in his dealings with the editor of the *Westminster*, William Hickson, where he clearly led him to believe the essay was by him. See the multiple letters from Mill to Hickson in *The Collected Works of John Stuart Mill: Later Letters*, vol. XIV, 55–69. "Enfranchisement of Women" would be the first work, but far from the last, to stir up this confusion about authorship with the Mills.

25. As Martineau's letter conveys, confusion around authorship continued at the 1851 convention. One speaker claimed it had been written by "the mother of J. Stewart [*sic*] Mill," *Proceedings of the Woman's Rights Convention, Held at Worcester, October 15th and 16th, 1851* (New York, 1852). Phillips's speech, with additional paragraph, in *History of Woman Suffrage*, vol. 1, 227. Pugh, "John Stuart Mill, Harriet Taylor and Women's Rights in America, 1850–1873."

26. On those other circuits, for example involving French radicals like Jean Deroin, see Margaret McFadden, *Golden Cables of Sympathy: The Transatlantic Sources of Nineteenth-Century Feminism* (Lexington: University Press of Kentucky, 1999); Bonnie S. Anderson, *Joyous Greetings: The First International Women's Movement, 1830–1860* (New York: Oxford University Press, 2000).

27. [Louisa S. McCord], L.S.M., "Enfranchisement of Woman," *Southern Quarterly Review* (April 1852): 322–341. Michael O'Brien argued that McCord was "among the earliest Americans habitually to use the word 'conservative' to describe her ideology," in *Conjectures of Order* (Chapel Hill: University of North Carolina Press, 2004), vol. 1, 274–284. On the opposite ways that abolitionists and proslavery ideologues paired their cause with women's rights, see Kristin Hoganson, "Garrisonian Abolitionists and the Rhetoric of Gender, 1850–1860," *American Quarterly* 45, no. 4 (1993): 558–595; Amy Dru Stanley, "Home Life and the Morality of the Market," in *The Market Revolution in America: Social, Political, and Religious Express, 1800–1880*, edited by Melvyn Stokes and Stephen Conway (Charlottesville: University of Virginia Press, 1996), 74–96; Nancy F. Cott, *Public Vows: A History of Marriage and the Nation* (Cambridge, MA: Harvard University Press, 2000).

28. [McCord], "Enfranchisement of Woman," 329, 327; [Louisa S. McCord] L.S.M., "Diversity of Races," *Southern Quarterly Review* (April 1851): 403. The proslavery Christian republicanism in which McCord was situated socially and ideologically is thoroughly excavated in Stephanie McCurry, *Masters of Small Worlds: Yeoman Households, Gender Relations, and the Political Culture of the Antebellum South Carolina Low Country* (New York: Oxford University Press, 1995).

29. [McCord], "Enfranchisement of Woman," 339–340.

30. [McCord], "Enfranchisement of Woman," 325–326. Had she known about it, the appearance, also in 1851, of a chapter on "The Rights of Women" by the English polymath Herbert Spencer would have only increased McCord's outrage that the

poison had spread (though Spencer would recant these early views by the 1880s). Carlyle's essay inspired a furious response from John Stuart Mill the following year. On this exchange, see David Theo Goldberg, "Liberalism's Limits: Carlyle and Mill on 'the Negro Question,'" *Nineteenth-Century Contexts* 22, no. 2 (2008): 203–216.

31. McCord followed up this review with another that fall, an essay on Elizabeth Oakes Smith's *Woman and Her Needs* for *Debow's Review* (September 1852). For discussions of the McCord marriage, see the brief but insightful discussion in O'Brien, *Conjectures of Order*, vol. 1, 274–284; and Leigh Fought, *Southern Womanhood and Slavery: A Biography of Louisa S. McCord, 1810–1879* (Columbia: University of Missouri Press, 2003), 83–100.

32. Senex, "Chivalry vs. Women's Enfranchisement," *The Lily*, February 1, 1855, with subsequent installments in the April 1 and July 1 issues. He is identified as Bingham in the *History of Woman Suffrage*, vol. 1, 688.

33. Catharine Beecher, *The True Remedy for the Wrongs of Woman* (Boston, 1851), 23. Norma Basch, *In the Eyes of the Law: Women, Marriage, and Property in Nineteenth-Century New York* (Ithaca, NY: Cornell University Press, 1982); Cott, *Public Vows*. On women in churches, see Isenberg, *Sex and Citizenship* and Jones, *All Bound Up Together*.

34. On the theatrical quality of conventions, see Isenberg, *Sex and Citizenship*, chapter 2; and on constitutional conventions as a genre, Rowland Berthoff, "Conventional Mentality: Free Blacks, Women, and Business Corporations as Unequal Persons, 1820–1870," *Journal of American History* 76, no. 3 (December 1989): 753–784. Derrick R. Spires offers a powerful analysis of Colored Conventions as both practice and published text in *The Practice of Citizenship: Black Politics and Print Culture in the Early United States* (Philadelphia: University of Pennsylvania Press, 2019), chapter 2. On Oakes Smith, see Adam Tuchinksy, "'Woman and Her Needs': Elizabeth Oakes Smith and the Divorce Question," *Journal of Woman's History* 28 (Spring 2016): 38–59.

35. "Woman's Rights," *New York Evangelist*, December 11, 1856. Paulina Wright Davis wanted to establish a "National Organ of the Woman's Rights Movement" in New York City, a proposal that was debated—but ultimately rejected—at the Syracuse (1852) and Cleveland (1852) conventions. See the record of debate in *History of Woman Suffrage*, vol. 1, 377–379. For similar debates within the Colored Conventions movement, see Benjamin Fagan, "The Organ of the Whole: Colored Conventions, the Black Press, and the Question of National Authority," in *The Colored Conventions Movement: Black Organizing in the Nineteenth Century*, edited by P. Gabrielle Foreman, Jim Casey, and Sarah Lynn Patterson (Chapel Hill: University of North Carolina Press, 2021), 195–210.

36. On Truth, see Nell Irvin Painter, *Sojourner Truth: A Life, A Symbol* (New York: Norton, 1997), 111–132, 258–286; Susan Ware, *Why They Marched: Untold Stories of the Women Who Fought for the Right to Vote* (Cambridge, MA: Harvard University Press, 2019), 29–39; and Jones, *Vanguard*, 77–83. Truth's autobiography was

Narrative of Sojourner Truth: A Northern Slave (Boston, 1850). Harriet Beecher Stowe wrote the introduction to the 1855 edition. On Lucy Stone, see Andrea Moore Kerr, *Lucy Stone: Speaking Out for Equality* (New Brunswick, NJ: Rutgers University Press, 1992); Sally G. McMillen: *Lucy Stone: An Unapologetic Life* (New York: Oxford University Press, 2015). On how both women used images of themselves to promote their celebrity and amplify their message, see Allison K. Lange, *Picturing Political Power: Images in the Woman Suffrage Movement* (Chicago: University of Chicago Press, 2020).

37. Jones, *Vanguard*, especially chapter 3; Rosalyn Terborg-Penn, *African American Women in the Struggle for the Vote, 1850–1920* (Bloomington: Indiana University Press, 1998), 16–17 and "African-American Women and the Woman Suffrage Movement," in *One Woman, One Vote*, edited by Marjorie Spruill Wheeler (Troutdale, OR: New Sage Press, 1995), 135–156. Close reading of the *Proceedings* reveals occasional moments of biracial awareness, such as when in Cincinnati in 1855, a woman identified as "Mrs. Swift, of Elyria, Ohio" urged all "friends of Freedom to manifest, by prompt and earnest action, their sympathy with the oppressed" and explicitly linked the causes of "[all] women and colored men." I thank Sharla Fett for calling my attention to this lithograph.

38. On sales of *Woman in the Nineteenth Century*, see Charles Capper, *Margaret Fuller: An American Romantic Life, Volume 2. The Public Years* (New York: Oxford University Press, 2007), 192; Theodore Parker, *Of the Public Function of Woman* (Boston, 1853); Paul E. Teed, *A Revolutionary Conscience: Theodore Parker and Antebellum America* (Lanham, MD: University Press of America, 2012), 91–92. Parker had opened his pulpit to Elizabeth Oakes Smith and Rev. Antoinette Brown Blackwell earlier. Emerson, "Woman" (1855), in *Miscellanies* (Boston, 1878), 281–296. As with abolition, Emerson's attitude toward the women's movement has been a subject of lively debate among scholars. See Len Gougeon, "Emerson and the Woman Question: The Evolution of his Thought," *New England Quarterly* 71 (December 1998): 570–592; and Phyllis Cole, "Emerson and Women's Rights: Pain and Protest in the Emerson Family" and Armida Gilbert, " 'Pierced by the Thorns of Reform': Emerson on Womanhood," both in *The Emerson Dilemma: Essays on Emerson and Social Reform*, edited by T. Gregory Garvey (Athens: University Press of Georgia, 2001), 67–92, 93–114.

39. Frederick Grimke, *Considerations upon the Nature and Tendency of Free Institutions* (Cincinnati, 1848). Grimke had dropped the accent from his last name.

40. Frederick Grimke, "The Rights of Women in a Democratic Republic," in *The Works of Frederick Grimke* (Columbus, OH, 1871). David Brion Davis made a similar point when he wrote that "the revolution of all revolutions has been the relatively recent, peaceful, and still continuing equalization of men and women," "The Other Revolution," reprinted in *In the Image of God: Religion, Moral Values, and Our Heritage of Slavery* (New Haven, CT: Yale University Press, 2001), 360.

41. Grimke directed that his works be published and distributed to "certain libraries and colleges in each of the States." The executor of his will decided (against Grimke's wishes) to include the essay on women's rights in the two-volume collection of his works he published in 1871, deeming it too valuable "a contribution to a subject now so largely agitating the public mind." The intriguing history of this essay's composition and eventual publication has recently been excavated, along with a modern printing of the essay, by Donald F. Melhorn Jr. in Frederick Grimke, *The Rights of Women in a Democratic Republic.* (Bloomington: Indiana University Press, 2016). According to Melhorn, Sarah Grimké had tried unsuccessfully to get the essay published in the late 1850s, after which Frederick came to doubt its conclusions. On Grimke's larger political thought, embodied in his *Considerations upon the Nature and Tendency of Free Institutions*, see also Arthur A. Ekirch Jr., "Frederick Grimke: Advocate of Free Institutions," *Journal of the History of Ideas* 11 (January 1850): 75–92.

42. See William John Mahar, *Behind the Burn Cork Mask: Early Blackface Minstrelsy* (Urbana: University of Illinois Press, 1999). On sheet music, see Dale Cockrell, "Nineteenth-Century Popular Music," in *The Cambridge History of American Music*, edited by David Nicholls (New York: Cambridge University Press, 2004), 158–185.

43. "Lecture LXVI: Woman's Rights" in Julius Caesar Hannibal, *Black Diamonds; or Humor, Satire, and Sentiment, Treated Scientifically* (New York, 1857), 219–221; Louisa May Alcott's journal from 1855, in *Louisa May Alcott: Her Life, Letters, and Journals*, edited by Ednah D. Cheney (Boston, 1890), 81.

44. Katie Horn, *Woman's Rights: A Right Good Ballad Rightly Illustrating Woman's Rights* (Boston, 1853). The song was "dedicated without permission" to "Mrs. Oakwood Smith and Mrs. Amelia Bloomer." Oakes Smith's mistaken name may well have come from parodies of her on the minstrel stage, where a cross-dressing performer was identified as "Mrs. E. Oakwood Smith." See Mahar, *Behind the Burnt Cork Mask*, 94.

45. Fred Folio, *Lucy Boston, or Woman's Rights and Spiritualism, Illustrating the Follies and Delusions of the Nineteenth Century* (Boston, 1855). David S. Reynolds includes an interesting discussion of this novel in *Beneath the American Renaissance: The Subversive Imagination in the Age of Emerson and Melville* (New York: Knopf, 1988), 478–479.

46. Michael D. Pierson, *Free Hearts and Free Homes: Gender and American Antislavery Politics* (Chapel Hill: University of North Carolina Press, 2003), chapters 4 and 5; Stephen Douglas in Rodney O. Davis and Douglas L. Wilson, *The Lincoln-Douglas Debates* (Urbana: University of Illinois Press, 2008), 163. In addition to Pierson, other scholars have recently explored the importance of gender to party politics in the 1850s. See especially Joshua A. Lynn, *Preserving the White Man's Republic: Jacksonian Democracy, Race, and the Transformation of American Conservatism* (Charlottesville: University of Virginia Press, 2019) and Lauren

N. Haumesser, *The Democratic Collapse: How Gender Politics Broke a Party and Nation* (Chapel Hill: University of North Carolina Press, 2022). On the centrality of culture to politics, see John L. Brooke, *"There is a North": Fugitive Slaves, Political Crisis, and Cultural Transformation in the Coming of the Civil War* (Amherst: University of Massachusetts Press, 2019).

47. Republicans followed earlier Whig party overtures to women that are investigated in Elizabeth R. Varon, *We Mean to be Counted: White Women and Politics in Antebellum Virginia* (Chapel Hill: University of North Carolina Press, 1998). Republicans' efforts are explored in Rebecca Edwards, *Angels in the Machinery: Gender in American Party Politics from the Civil War to the Progressive Era* (New York: Oxford University Press, 1997), chapter 1; Pierson, *Free Hearts, Free Homes,* chapters 4 and 5; Lynn, *Preserving the White Man's Republic* and Haumesser, *The Democratic Collapse.*

48. This was the domestic corollary to free soil and free labor. Pierson, *Free Hearts, Free Homes,* chapters 4 and 5. On Buchanan's bachelordom and rumors about his sexuality, see Thomas J. Balcerski, *Bosom Friends: The Intimate World of James Buchanan and William Rufus King* (New York: Oxford University Press, 2019).

49. "The Fine Old Fossil Bachelor" and "The Bachelor Candidate," both in *The Campaign of 1856: Fremont Songs for the People* (Boston, 1856). Republicans' insistence that all men "take a wife" meant just one wife—thus the polygamy of Mormonism posed an even greater danger than bachelordom to their cultural/political vision.

50. On the Democrats' fear of fanatical degradation, see Lynn, *Preserving the White Man's Republic,* especially chapter 2 and Haumesser, *The Democratic Collapse,* throughout. On the reform agenda of the Republican Party during the 1856 election, see Matthew Karp, "The People's Revolution of 1856: Antislavery Populism, National Politics, and the Emergence of the Republican Party," *Journal of the Civil War Era* 9 (December 2019): 524–545.

51. *Proceedings of the Seventh National Woman's Rights Convention, Held in New York City* (New York, 1856), 632.

52. *Consistent Democracy: The Elective Franchise for Women. Twenty-Five Testimonies of Prominent Men* (Worcester, 1858). Higginson, possibly with Stone, also published a *Woman's Rights Almanac for 1858* (Worcester, 1858), containing "facts, statistics, arguments, records of progress, and proofs of the need of it."

53. *Consistent Democracy.* The leaflet silently abridged the full passage from the Ohio senate report excerpt, which was unmistakably taken from Taylor Mill's "Enfranchisement of Women" and reads: "To declare that a voice in the government is the right of all, and demand it only for a part,—the part, namely, to which the claimant himself belongs,—is to renounce even the appearance of principle." See "Enfranchisement of Women," 292; *Report of the Select Committee of the Ohio Senate on Giving Suffrage to Females* ([Columbus, OH], 1857), 4.

54. "I, too, wish to save the dinner," he admitted, "Yet it seems more important, after all, to save the soul," Thomas Wentworth Higginson, *Woman and Her Wishes: An Essay Inscribed to the Massachusetts Constitutional Convention* (Boston, 1853); "Ought Women to Learn the Alphabet?" *Atlantic Monthly* (February 1859), 120.

55. Higginson, *Woman and Her Wishes*, 6, 12, 13. Another foreign visitor in these years echoed this view. Englishwoman Barbara Leigh Smith Bodichon, an important women's rights activist at home, toured the United States on her honeymoon. She wrote in her diary how proudly the German and French immigrants she talked to insisted on their American-ness. "This comes of their right to vote," she thought. "It makes them feel at home, gives them an importance which they probably never had before, makes them respect themselves, gives them a standing which creates a new motive for self-improvement." She drew the parallel with women and concluded "American women will not be worth much until they get this right." Bodichon, *An American Diary* (London: Routledge & Kegan Paul, 1972), 73.

56. Stefan Collini, *Public Moralists: Political Thought and Intellectual Life in Britain, 1850–1930* (Oxford: Clarendon Press, 1991).

57. See Jane Rendall, *Equal or Different: Women's Politics, 1800–1914* (New York: Basil Blackwell, 1987); Barbara Caine, *Victorian Feminists* (Oxford: Oxford University Press, 1992); Christine Bolt, *The Women's Movements in the United States and Britain from the 1790s to the 1920s* (Amherst: University of Massachusetts, 1993), 84–125.

58. Mill discussed the significance of his reading of Tocqueville in his autobiography published after his death in 1873, see *Autobiography* (London, 1873), 191. For a useful discussion of *On Liberty* and *Considerations on Representative Government* in the context of Mill's biography, see Richard Reeves, *John Stuart Mill: Victorian Firebrand* (London: Atlantic Books, 2007), chapters 11–12.

59. For an introduction to the debate over Mill's commitment to democracy (which is vast and lively), see Georgios Varouxakis, "Mill on Democracy Revisited," in *A Companion to Mill*, edited by Christopher Macleod and Dale E. Miller (Oxford: Wiley Blackwell, 2017), 454–471. There are far too many works to list here, but books that emphasize his democratic theory include Dennis F. Thompson, *John Stuart Mill and Representative Government* (Princeton, NJ: Princeton University Press, 1976); Nadia Urbinati, *Mill on Democracy: From the Athenian Polis to Representative Government* (Chicago: University of Chicago Press, 2002); Collini, *Public Moralists*; and Alex Zakaras, *Individuality and Mass Democracy: Mill, Emerson, and the Burdens of Citizenship* (New York: Oxford University Press, 2009). A recent account makes a compelling case for reassessing Mill as a (non-Marxist) socialist, Helen McCabe, *John Stuart Mill: Socialist* (Montreal: McGill-Queens University Press, 2021).

60. *On Liberty* and *Considerations on Representative Government* both "proclaimed self-rule as the highest form of government," as Dipesh Chakrabarty has put it, "and yet argued against giving Indians or Africans self-government on grounds" that they

were "*not yet* civilized enough to rule themselves," *Provincializing Europe: Postcolonial Thought and Historical Difference* (Princeton, NJ: Princeton University Press, 2000), 8. Thorough treatments of the way foreign policy and empire shaped and limited Mill's political thought can be found in Uday Mehta, *Liberalism and Empire: A Study in Nineteenth-Century British Liberal Thought* (Chicago: University of Chicago Press, 1999); Jennifer Pitts, *A Turn to Empire: The Rise of Imperial Liberalism in Britain and France* (Princeton, NJ: Princeton University Press, 2005); Gregory Claeys, *Mill and Paternalism* (Cambridge: Cambridge University Press, 2013); and Georgios Varouxakis, *Liberty Abroad: J. S. Mill on International Relations* (Cambridge: Cambridge University Press, 2014).

61. John Stuart Mill, *Considerations on Representative Government* (London, 1861) 66–69; *On Liberty* (London, 1859), 197. Dale E. Miller explicates Mill's emphasis on participation in "John Stuart Mill's Civic Liberalism," *History of Political Thought* 21, no. 1 (Spring 2000): 88–113. *On Liberty* was more skeptical about the virtues of political engagement. On this tension, and the way Mill's view of "democratic individuality" sought to circumvent it, see Alex Zakaras "John Stuart Mill, Individuality, and Participatory Democracy," in *J. S. Mill's Political Thought: A Bicentennial Reassessment*, edited by Nadia Urbinati and Alex Zakaras (New York: Cambridge University Press, 2007), 200–220. As Wendy Donner shows, education (and the "improvement" it implied) was the unifying key of Mill's political thought. Donner, "John Stuart Mill on Democracy and Education," *J. S. Mill's Political Thought*, 250–274.

62. *Considerations on Representative Government*, 156–159; 175–180. Mill argued that voting should be contingent on the ability to read, write, and perform basic arithmetic, though he did not think these requirements violated the larger principle since he insisted that "the means of attaining these elementary" skills must be made available to every person "either gratuitously" or at a minimal expense. While in the United States such requirements would be restrictive, this was not the case in Britain where before the Second Reform Act (1867) fewer than a third of adult males possessed the franchise.

63. *Considerations on Representative Government*, 180.

64. George William Curtis, *An Address, Vindicating the Rights of Woman* (New York, 1858), 6–7. "The Contest in America," *Fraser's* (February 1862). For Mill's views on the Civil War, see John O. Waller, "John Stuart Mill and the American Civil War," *Bulletin of the New York Public Library* 51, no. 66 (October 1962): 505–518; T. Peter Park, "John Stuart Mill, Thomas Carlyle, and the U.S. Civil War," *Historian* 54, no. 1 (Autumn 1991): 93–106; John W. Compton, "The Emancipation of the American Mind: J. S. Mill on the Civil War," *The Review of Politics* 70, no 2 (Spring 2008): 221–244; Brent E. Kinser, *The American Civil War in the Shaping of British Democracy* (Burlington, VT: Ashgate, 2011); and Georgios Varouxakis, "'Negrophilist' Crusader': John Stuart Mill on the American Civil War and Reconstruction," *History of European Ideas* 39, no. 5 (September 2013): 729–754.

INTERLUDE

1. Charles Nordhoff, "A Tilt at the Woman Question," *Harper's New Monthly Magazine* (February 1863): 350–356.

2. Gail Hamilton, *A Call to My Countrywomen, Reprinted from the Atlantic Monthly* (New York, 1863), 23; also in Hamilton, *Gala Days* (Boston, 1863), 249–264; Lyde Cullen Sizer, *The Political Work of Northern Women Writers* (Chapel Hill: University of North Carolina Press, 2000), 121–133.

3. William A. Blair, *With Malice toward Some: Treason and Loyalty in the Civil War Era* (Chapel Hill: University of North Carolina Press, 2014); Matthew J. Gallman, *Defining Duty in the Civil War: Personal Choice, Popular Culture, and the Union Home Front* (Chapel Hill: University of North Carolina Press, 2015).

4. Henry Bellows, *Unconditional Loyalty* (New York, 1863); Henry Bellows, *To the Loyal Women of America* (October 1861 broadside); Hamilton, *A Call to My Countrywomen*, 5; Nina Silber, *Gender and the Sectional Conflict* (Chapel Hill: University of North Carolina Press, 2008).

5. Gail Hamilton, "A Countercharm," in *Skirmishes and Sketches* (Boston, 1865), 321–324; letter dated April 21, 1863 in *Gail Hamilton's Life in Letters*, edited by H. Augusta Dodge (Boston: Lee and Shepard, 1901), vol. 1, 347. Lincoln's implicit understanding of citizenship as a male category, both in the dedication remarks in Pennsylvania and across his presidency, are handled in Jean Baker, "Engendering the Gettysburg Address: Its Meaning for Women," in *The Gettysburg Address: Perspectives on Lincoln's Greatest Speech*, edited by Sean Conant (New York: Oxford University Press, 2015), 233–251 and Elizabeth Brown Pryor, *Six Encounters with Lincoln: A President Confronts Democracy and Its Demons* (New York: Viking, 2017), 213–268.

6. LeeAnn Whites, *Gender Matters: Civil War, Reconstruction, and the Making of the New South* (New York: Palgrave Macmillan, 2005), 25–44; Nina Silber, *Daughters of the Union: Northern Women Fight the Civil War* (Cambridge, MA: Harvard University Press, 2011), 12–13; Wendy Hamand Venet, *Neither Ballots nor Bullets: Women Abolitionists and the Civil War* (Charlottesville: University of Virginia Press, 1991); Faye E. Dudden, *Fighting Chance: The Struggle over Woman Suffrage and Black Suffrage in Reconstruction America* (New York: Oxford University Press, 2011). Critical material on the emergence of the May 1863 meeting appears in *The Selected Papers of Elizabeth Cady Stanton and Susan B. Anthony. Vol. II: Against an Aristocracy of Sex*, edited by Ann D. Gordon (New Brunswick, NJ: Rutgers University Press, 2000), 480–500.

7. Mrs. O. S. Baker, "Ladies Loyal League," *Continental Monthly* (July 1863): 51–56; E. O. Sampson Hoyt and Anthony interchange recorded in *Proceedings of the Meeting of the Loyal Women of the Republic, Held in New York, May 14, 1863* (New York, 1863): 20–23.

8. "Address of Mrs. Elizabeth Cady Stanton to the Women of the Republic," *New York Tribune*, April 24, 1863; "Call for a Meeting of the Loyal Women of the Nation," *Liberator*, April 24 and May 8, 1863; *Manchester (U.K.) Guardian*, May 8, 1863;

"Speech of Mrs. E. Cady Stanton," in *Proceedings of the Meeting of the Loyal Women of the Republic*, 4–10.

9. "Address of Mrs. Blackwell," *Proceedings of the Meeting of the Loyal Women*, 35–42.

10. "Annual Message to Congress, December 1, 1862," in Roy P. Basler, *Collected Works of Abraham Lincoln* (New Brunswick, NJ: Rutgers University Press, 1953), vol. 5, 537.

11. Adrian J. Ebell, "The Indian Massacres and the War of 1862," *Harper's New Monthly Magazine* (July 1863), which featured Native or settler women in nine of its seventeen woodcut illustrations of the episode. See also Linda M. Clemmons, *Dakota in Exile: The Untold Stories of Captives in the Aftermath of the US-Dakota War* (Iowa City: Iowa University Press, 2019).

12. The plight of native peoples, the phenomenon of Confederate oaths, and the cautious optimism of Black Americans have been expertly handled, respectively, in Steven Hahn, "Slave Emancipation, Indian Peoples, and the Projects of a New American Nation-State," *Journal of the Civil War Era* 3, no. 3 (2013): 307–330; LeeAnn Whites and Alecia P. Long, eds. *Occupied Women: Gender, Military Occupation, and the American Civil War* (Baton Rouge: Louisiana University Press, 2009); Elizabeth R. Varon, *Armies of Deliverance: A New History of the Civil War* (New York: Oxford University Press, 2019); and Thavolia Glymph, *The Women's Fight: The Civil War's Battles for Home, Freedom, and Nation* (Chapel Hill: University of North Carolina Press, 2019).

13. "Mrs. Frances E. Watkins Harper on the War and the President's Colonization Scheme," *Christian Recorder,* September 27, 1862; Manisha Sinha, "The Other Frances Ellen Watkins Harper," *Commonplace* 16, no. 2 (Winter 2016), http://common-place.org/book/the-other-frances-ellen-watkins-harper/ (accessed February 10, 2023); Harper to William Still, [January 1863] in William Still, *The Underground Railroad* (Philadelphia, 1872), 766; Eric Gardner, "Frances Ellen Watkins Harper's 'National Salvation': A Rediscovered Lecture on Reconstruction," *Commonplace* 17 (Summer 2017), http://commonplace.online/article/vol-17-no-4-gardner/ (accessed February 10, 2023); Bettye Collier-Thomas, "Frances Ellen Watkins Harper: Abolitionist and Feminist Reformer, 1825–1911," in *African-American Women and the Vote, 1837–1965*, edited by Ann D. Gordon and Bettye Collier-Thomas (Amherst: University of Massachusetts Press, 1997), 41–65; Eric Gardner, "The Return of Frances Ellen Watkins Harper," *ESQ: A Journal of Nineteenth-Century American Literature and Culture* 66, no. 4 (2020): 591–643.

14. "The New Liberty Bell," *National Antislavery Standard*, February 28, 1863, (selected lyrics from this verse later published as "The Freedom Bell"). Harper also intertwined values of country and family in "The Massachusetts Fifty-Fourth," *The Anglo-African*, October 10, 1863 and "The Sin of Achan," *The Anglo-African*, December 12, 1863; both discussed in R. J. Weir and Elizabeth Lorang, " 'Will Not These Days Be by Thy Poets Sung': Poems of the *Anglo-African* and *National*

Anti-Slavery Standard, 1863–1864," *Scholarly Editing* 34 (2013), https://scholarly editing.org/2013/editions/intro.cwnewspaperpoetry.html (accessed June 9, 2023).

15. Jane Rhodes, *Mary Ann Shadd Cary: The Black Press and Protest in the Nineteenth Century* (Bloomington: Indiana University Press, 1999); Nell Irvin Painter, *Sojourner Truth: A Life, A Symbol* (New York: Norton, 1997); Sirpa Salenius, *An Abolitionist Abroad: Sarah Parker Remond in Cosmopolitan Europe* (Amherst: University of Massachusetts Press 2016); Still, *Underground Railroad*, 749, a book that included portraits of four additional Black women.

16. Sarah Hopkins Bradford, *Scenes from the Life of Harriet Tubman* (Auburn, 1869), ii; Milton C. Sernett, *Harriet Tubman, Myth, Memory, and History* (Durham, NC: Duke University Press, 2007), 74–75.

CHAPTER 4

1. Eric Gardner, "Frances Ellen Watkins Harper's 'National Salvation': A Rediscovered Lecture on Reconstruction," *Commonplace* 17 (Summer 2017), http://common place.online/article/vol-17-no-4-gardner/ (accessed February 10, 2023). This speech was reprinted in full in the *Philadelphia Evening Telegraph* and then an excerpt appeared under the title "The Power of an Idea" (but misidentifying Harper as "Mrs. F. S. W. Harper") in a popular reader: Erastus F. Beadle, *Beadle's Dime Standard Speaker: A Collection of Choice Extracts and Passages from the Best American Orators and Authors in Prose and Verse* (New York, 1867), 35–36.

2. Harper, *Minnie's Sacrifice [1869]*, in *Minnie's Sacrifice; Sowing and Reaping; Trial and Triumph: Three Rediscovered Novels*, edited by Frances Smith Foster (Boston: Beacon Press, 1994), 74, 75–76, 78, 79; William Still, *The Underground Railroad* (Philadelphia, 1872); *Proceedings of the Eleventh Woman's Rights Convention* (New York, 1866). Harper repeated a version of this sentiment (about the institution of slavery being "overthrown" but the spirit still living on), in her (newly rediscovered) 1867 speech on "National Salvation" and in her 1892 novel (set in the 1860s) *Iola Leroy*.

3. Elizabeth Cady Stanton, *Eighty Years and More, 1815–1897* (New York, 1898), 241. The phrase "popular constitutionalism" is associated with Larry Kramer's *The People Themselves: Popular Constitutionalism and Judicial Review* (New York: Oxford University Press, 2004), but it has been employed and defined in different ways by legal theorists and historians in the last couple decades. A recent interpretation can be found in Elizabeth Beaumont, *The Civic Constitution: Civic Visions and Struggles in the Path Toward Constitutional Democracy* (New York: Oxford University Press, 2014), which includes a chapter on "gender justice constitutionalism." Eric Foner reveals the significance of Reconstruction-era popular constitutionalism in *Second Founding: How the Civil War and Reconstruction Remade the Constitution* (New York: Norton, 2019). Alison M. Parker excavates the political thought of six activist women in *Articulating Rights: Nineteenth-Century Women*

on Race, Reform, and the State (DeKalb: Northern Illinois University Press, 2010); and Christopher James Bonner demonstrates the crucial role African American activists played in redefining citizenship in *Remaking the Republic: Black Politics and the Creation of American Citizenship* (Philadelphia: University of Pennsylvania Press, 2020).

4. Lea VanderVelde, *Mrs. Dred Scott: a Life on Slavery's Frontier* (New York: Oxford University Press, 2010); Ellen Carol DuBois, "Outgrowing the Compact of the Fathers: Equal Rights, Woman Suffrage, and the United States Constitution, 1820–1878," *Journal of American History* 74, no. 3 (1987): 836–862; Liette Gidlow, "The Sequel: The Fifteenth Amendment, the Nineteenth Amendment, and Southern Black Women's Struggle to Vote," *Journal of the Gilded Age and Progressive Era* (July 2018): 433–449.

5. Martha S. Jones, *Birthright Citizens: A History of Race and Rights in Antebellum America* (New York: Cambridge University Press, 2018).

6. *Opinion of Attorney General Bates on Citizenship* (Washington, DC, 1862), 4–5; James P. McClure, Leigh Johnsen, Kathleen Norman, and Michael Vanderlan, "Circumventing the Dred Scott Decision: Edward Bates, Salmon P. Chase, and the Citizenship of African Americans," *Civil War History* 43, no. 4 (1997): 279–309; Bonner, *Remaking the Republic*, chapter 5.

7. Frederick Douglass, "The Mission of the War," in *Frederick Douglass Papers*, edited by John W. Blassingame (New Haven, CT: Yale University Press, 1979), vol. 4, 11; "Speech of Frederick Douglass," [December 4, 1863], in *Proceedings of the American Anti-Slavery Society at Its Third Decade* (New York, 1864), 118.

8. "The Right of Franchise" and "Universal Suffrage," *Christian Recorder*, June 10 and June 24, 1865; Louis P. Masur, *Lincoln's Last Speech: Wartime Reconstruction and the Crisis of Reunion* (New York: Oxford University Press, 2015). Johnson's consistent hostility received its most thorough expression in his veto message opposing the "untimely extension of the elective franchise" to residents of Washington, as reprinted in *Baltimore Sun*, January 7, 1867, and then excerpted in his 1867 State of the Union address. On Black soldiers, see Brian Taylor, *Fighting for Citizenship: Black Northerners and the Debate Over Military Service in the Civil War* (Chapel Hill: University of North Carolina Press, 2020).

9. Frederick Douglass, "What the Black Man Wants: Speech of Frederick Douglass," in *The Equality of All Men Before the Law: Claimed and Defended* (Boston, 1865), 37. Douglass affirmed here that his "heart and voice go with the movement to extend suffrage to woman."

10. Henry Ward Beecher, *Woman's Duty to Vote* (New York, [1866] 1867), 9; "Universal Suffrage a Universal Tendency," *Christian Recorder*, April 7, 1866; George William Curtis, *Equal Rights for Women* (New York, 1867), 15. The *Christian Recorder* would publish a variety of opinion on women's enfranchisement in the coming years but a new editor in 1868 (Benjamin Tanner) seemed generally in favor of it. See for example Schuyler, "A Glance at Three of the Minor Objections to Female Suffrage,"

August 29, 1868, which easily debunked each objection; E. B. S., "Female Suffrage,"
October 24, 1868, which expressed a Christian woman's preference for praying
rather than voting; and R. G. M, "Women's Rights," January 15, 1870, which urged
the AME (and its paper) to take a stand for "women's right to the ballot," else the
world "the world will justly regard us as behind the times." Women's suffrage, this
author argued, was in harmony with scripture, justice, and "the genius of our free
institutions."

11. "Constitution of the American Equal Rights Association," printed in *Proceedings
     of the First Anniversary of the American Equal Rights Association* (New York, 1867),
     70; also printed in *History of Woman Suffrage. Volume 2*, edited by Elizabeth Cady
     Stanton, Susan B. Anthony, and Matilda Joslyn Gage (Rochester, 1881), 173.

12. *Petition Asking for an Amendment of the Constitution that Shall Prohibit the Several
     States from Disfranchising Any of Their Citizens on the Ground of Sex*; 1/29/1866;
     (HR 39A-H14.9); *Petitions and Memorials, 1813–1968*; *Records of the U.S. House of
     Representatives, Record Group* 233; National Archives Building, Washington, DC
     (available at https://www.docsteach.org/documents/document/petition-prohi
     bit-disfranchisement, July 15, 2021). As Laura Free observes, these petitions likely
     had the unintended consequence of ensuring that Republicans would not rely on
     gender-neutral language, which might be misconstrued by woman suffragists, but
     would instead make their assumptions about the connection between manhood
     and suffrage explicit. Free, *Suffrage Reconstructed: Gender, Race, and Voting Rights
     in the Civil War Era* (Ithaca, NY: Cornell University Press, 2015), 104–106. On
     petitioning more generally, see Susan Zaeske, *Signatures of Citizenship: Petitioning,
     Antislavery, and Women's Political Identity* (Chapel Hill: University of North
     Carolina Press, 2003) and Daniel Carpenter, *Democracy by Petition* (Cambridge,
     MA: Harvard University Press, 2021), which includes a rich discussion of state-
     level suffrage petitions in the 1850s.

13. Foner, *Second Founding*.

14. Eric Foner, *Reconstruction: America's Unfinished Revolution, 1863–1877*
     (New York: Harper & Row, 1988); Steven Hahn, *A Nation Under Our Feet: Black
     Political Struggles in the Rural South from Slavery to the Great Migration* (Cambridge,
     MA: Harvard University Press, 2003).

15. Stanton (letter to Gerrit Smith, January 1, 1866), quoted in Ellen Carol Dubois,
     *Feminism and Suffrage: The Emergence of an Independent Woman's Movement in
     America, 1848–1869* (Ithaca, NY: Cornell University Press, 1978), 161; Caroline
     Dall to Charles Sumner, January 14, 1866, quoted in *Selected Journals of Caroline
     Healey Dall* (Boston: Massachusetts Historical Society, 2013), edited by Helen
     Deese, vol. 2, 622; On the movement's response, see also Faye E. Dudden, *Fighting
     Chance: The Struggle over Woman Suffrage and Black Suffrage in Reconstruction
     America* (New York: Oxford University Press, 2011) and Free, *Suffrage Reconstructed*.

16. The fracturing of the movement has long been a well-established feature of the schol-
     arship. See Eleanor Flexner, *Century of Struggle: The Woman's Rights Movement*

in the United States (Cambridge, MA: Harvard University Press, 1996); 137–139; DuBois, *Feminism and Suffrage*; and especially Dudden, *Fighting Chance*, which provides a detailed account of the political calculations involved on all sides. Kathi Kern and Linda Levstik point out that the rupture, complete by 1869, occupies more space in textbooks than nearly any other woman-centered issue in these years. See "Teaching the New Departure: *The United States v. Susan B. Anthony*," *Journal of the Civil War Era* 2, no. 1 (2012): 127–141.

17. Ann D. Gordon, "Stanton and the Right to Vote: On Account of Race or Sex," 111–127, and Michele Mitchell, "'Lower Orders,' Racial Hierarchies, and Rights Rhetoric: Evolutionary Echoes in Elizabeth Cady Stanton's Thought during the Late 1860s," both in *Elizabeth Cady Stanton, Feminist as Thinker: A Reader in Documents and Essays*, edited by Ellen Carol DuBois and Richard Cándida Smith (New York: New York University Press, 2007), 128–151.

18. See, for example, "The British," *Douglass' Monthly* (March 1863), which reprinted a letter hailing Mill as "one of the greatest in England."

19. John Stuart Mill to Parker Pillsbury, July 4 [1867], in *The Collected Works of John Stuart Mill: The Later Letters*, edited by Francis E. Mineka and Dwight N. Lindley (Toronto: University of Toronto Press, 1972), vol. XVI, 1289. On Mill and the women's movement in the UK, see Evelyn L. Pugh, "John Stuart Mill and the Women's Question in Parliament, 1865–1868," *The Historian* 42 (May 1980): 399–418; Ann Robson, "No Laughing Matter: John Stuart Mill's Establishment of Women's Suffrage as a Parliamentary Question," *Utilitas* 2, no 1 (1999): 88–101; Jane Rendall, *The Origins of Modern Feminism: Women in Britain, France, and the United States, 1780–1860* (London: Macmillan, 1984); Barbara Caine, *Victorian Feminists* (Oxford: Oxford University Press, 1992). On the Second Reform Bill more generally, see Catherine Hall, Keith McClellan, and Jane Rendall, *Defining the Victorian Nation: Class, Race, Gender, and the British Reform Act of 1867* (New York: Cambridge University Press, 2000).

20. Julian in *Congressional Globe*, December 8, 1868. On suffrage debates in Congress, see Xi Wang, *The Trial of Democracy: Black Suffrage and Northern Republicans, 1860–1910* (Athens: University of Georgia Press, 2012) and, for Washington, DC, Kate Masur, *An Example for all the Land: Emancipation and the Struggle for Equality in Washington, DC* (Chapel Hill: University of North Carolina Press, 2010).

21. Stanton, "Stand by your Guns, Mr. Julian," *Revolution*, May 20, 1869 (emphasis added); Foster in *History of Woman Suffrage*, vol. 2, 381.

22. The earlier history of debates over an "informed" citizenry is the theme of Richard D. Brown, *The Strength of a People: The Idea of an Informed Citizenry in America, 1650–1870* (Chapel Hill: University of North Carolina Press, 1996) and Michael Schudson, "The Informed Citizenry in Historical Context," *Research in the Teaching of English* 30 (October 1996): 361–369.

23. James Russell Lowell, "Reconstruction," *North American Review* (April 1865): 554.

24. Wendell Phillips, *Proceedings of the Ninth National Woman's Rights Convention . . . with a Phonographic Report of the Speech of Wendell Phillips, by J.M.W. Yerrinton* (Rochester, 1859), Beecher, *Woman's Duty to Vote*, 5–6.

25. Julian in *Congressional Globe*, January 16, 1866. On the invocation of Mill during Reconstruction, see Evelyn L. Pugh, "John Stuart Mill in America" (PhD diss., American University, 1966).

26. Stanton, "Sound Argument," *Revolution*, February 4, 1869; discussed in DuBois, *Feminism and Suffrage*; Dudden, *Fighting Chance*, 169–170; Tetrault, *The Myth of Seneca Falls*. Stanton used the "aristocracy of sex" phrasing in resolutions at conventions in 1869, where she powerfully observed that a "man's government is worse than a white man's government, because in proportion as you increase the rulers you make the conditions of the ostracized more hopeless and degraded," *History of Woman Suffrage, Volume 3*, edited by Elizabeth Cady Stanton, Susan B. Anthony, and Matilda Joslyn Gage (Rochester, NY, 1886), 641. The editors of Stanton and Anthony's papers made this the title to the second volume of the collected work: Ann D. Gordon, ed., *The Selected Papers of Elizabeth Cady Stanton and Susan B. Anthony. Vol. II: Against an Aristocracy of Sex* (New Brunswick, NJ: Rutgers University Press, 2000).

27. John Stuart Mill to Stanton, printed in *Revolution*, May 13, 1869. Mill recommended both periodicals to a Danish correspondent who asked for the best works on the woman question (or "la situation sociale des femmes," as he called it); John Stuart Mill to Georg Brandes, February 24, 1870, *The Collected Works of John Stuart Mill: Later Letters*, vol. XVII, 1700; Julia Ward Howe, "Women as Voters," *The Galaxy* 7 (March 1869): 364–371. Isabella Beecher Hooker made her intellectual debt to Harriet Taylor Mill clear in her "Two Letters on Woman Suffrage," *Putnam's Monthly* (November and December 1868), which caught the attention of Mill.

28. *Proceedings of the Eleventh Woman's Rights Convention* (New York, 1866), 90–93. On Harper, see Bettye Collier-Thomas, "Frances Ellen Watkins Harper: Abolitionist and Feminist Reformer, 1825–1911," in *African-American Women and the Vote, 1837–1965*, edited by Ann D. Gordon and Bettye Collier-Thomas (Bloomington: Indiana University Press, 1998), 41–65.

29. On Harper as a reader of Tocqueville and Mill, Still, *Underground Railroad*, 778; On this 1866 speech, see C. C. O'Brien, "'The White Women All Go for Sex': Frances Harper on Suffrage, Citizenship, and the Reconstruction South," *African American Review* 43, no. 4 (2009): 605–620 and Jen McDaneld, "Harper, Historiography, and the Race/Gender Opposition in Feminism," *Signs* 40, no. 2 (2015): 393–415.

30. Harper, "All Bound Up Together," in *A Brighter Coming Day: A Frances Ellen Watkins Harper Reader*, edited by Francis Smith Foster (New York: Feminist Press, 1990), 219.

31. *Proceedings of the First Anniversary of the American Equal Rights Association* (New York, 1867); Stephanie McCurry, "The Story of the Black Soldier's Wife," in *The Women's War: Fighting and Surviving the American Civil War* (Cambridge, MA: Harvard University Press, 2019), 63–123 and Amy Dru Stanley, "Instead of Waiting for the Thirteenth Amendment: The War Power, Slave Marriage, and Inviolate Human Rights," *American Historical Review* 115, no. 3 (2010): 732–765. On Truth and Harper, see Nell Irvin Painter, "Voices of Suffrage: Sojourner Truth, Frances Watkins Harper, and the Struggle for Woman Suffrage," in *Votes for Women*, edited by Jean H. Baker (New York: Oxford University Press, 2002), 42–55.

32. Jones, *Birthright Citizens*. On divisions among women during the Civil War era more generally, see Thavolia Glymph, *The Women's Fight: The Civil War's Battles for Home, Freedom, and Nation* (Chapel Hill: University of North Carolina Press, 2019).

33. In addition to the poetry, Child also included a short narrative passage of Harper's "The Air of Freedom" (written at Niagara Falls). Lydia Maria Child, *The Freedmen's Book* (Boston, 1865). Harper's views aligned with other free Black women writers. See, for example, Carla L. Peterson, "Frances Harper, Charlotte Forten, and African American Literary Reconstruction," in *Challenging Boundaries: Gender and Periodization*, edited by Joyce E. Warren and Margaret Dickie (Athens: University of Georgia Press, 2000), 39–61; P. Gabrielle Foreman, "The *Christian Recorder*, Broken Families, and Educated Nations in Julia C. Collins's Civil War Novel *The Curse of Caste*," *African American Review* (Winter 2017): 1063–1074.

34. On Harper's Southern lecture tour, visiting all states but Texas and Arkansas, see Still, *Underground Railroad*, 767–773, which includes a report from the white *Mobile Register* expressing grudging support for Harper's talents as a lecture. The editor could not discern "a single grammatical inaccuracy of speech, or the slightest violation of good taste in manner or matter" and found her not simply "intelligent and educated" but, what is rarer and more valuable, "enlightened," 775.

35. Eliza Frances Andrews, "Georgia—The Elections," *New York World*, November 6, 1867.

36. Harper in Still, *Underground Railroad*, 770, 773.

37. "The Two Offers," originally published in the *Anglo African* in 1859, reprinted in Foster, *A Brighter Coming Day*, 109, 114. Marriage as site of contested autonomy and self-governance was also a theme in Julia C. Collins incomplete novel, *The Curse of Caste* (1865), possibly the "first" novel by an African American woman. It was serialized in the *Christian Recorder*, but Collins died suddenly before she was able to finish it. *The Curse of Caste; or The Slave Bride: A Rediscovered African American Novel by Julia C. Collins*, edited by William L. Andrews and Mitch Kachun (New York: Oxford University Press, 2006).

38. Harper, *Minnie's Sacrifice*, 74, 75–76, 78, 79. As Corinne T. Field has astutely observed, the way Harper wove the "same phrases through political speeches to predominantly white activists and in fiction written for the black press" worked to

advance her nationalist stance in *The Struggle for Equal Adulthood: Gender, Race, Age, and the Fight for Citizenship in Antebellum America* (Chapel Hill: University of North Carolina Press, 2014), 154.

39. Harper, *Minnie's Sacrifice*, 74, 75–76, 78, 79.

40. See *The Fifteenth Amendment* (Savannah, GA, 1870), which features a central panel of Black and white men, including President Lincoln, Frederick Douglass, Hiram Revels, and General Sherman; and *The Result of the Fifteenth Amendment, And the Rise and Progress of the African Race in America and its Final Accomplishment, and Celebration on May 19th, A.D. 1870* (Baltimore, 1870), which features the efforts of Black men. Even the vignette on education concerns men: "Education will be our pride," the caption reads, and it shows a male teacher instructing male students.

41. James C. Beard, *The Fifteenth Amendment* (New York, 1870). On this more expansive understanding of African American political community, see especially Elsa Barkley Brown, "Negotiating and Transforming the Public Sphere: Afro-American Political Life in the Transition from Slavery to Freedom," in *Public Culture* 7, no. 1 (1994): 107–146; Laura F. Edwards, *Gendered Strife and Confusion: The Political Culture of Reconstruction* (Urbana: University of Illinois Press, 1997); Tera Hunter, *Bound in Wedlock: Slave and Free Marriage in the Nineteenth Century* (Cambridge, MA: Harvard University Press, 2017); and Martha S. Jones, *Vanguard: How Black Women Broke Barriers, Won the Vote, and Insisted on Equality for All* (New York: Basic Books, 2020).

42. Stanton, *Eighty Years and More*, 241; George W. Julian, "The Slavery Yet to Be Abolished," *Later Speeches on Political Questions, With Select Controversial Papers*, edited by Grace Julian Clarke (Indianapolis, 1889), 58.

43. "Suffrage," *The Youth's Companion*, March 11, 1869, 77; "Female Suffrage," *Youth's Companion*, June 9, 1870. The magazine explained that while there was "no uniformity of voting" in the United States, "recent events" suggested the time was approaching when "Congress will dictate a uniform mode of voting," at least for all "national offices." It further mistakenly informed its young readers that the constitutional amendment recently passed by Congress would, if ratified, make "all citizens of the United States voters in all the states," "Voting in America," *The Youth's Companion*, March 18, 1869.

44. Nast would go on to draw far less benign images of these types in the coming years, especially African Americans and Irish Americans. For an excellent discussion of the use of racial typologies and the visual rendering of Black citizens, see Vanessa Meikle Schulman, "Visualizing Race at the Polling Place: Thomas Waterman Wood's American Citizens," *American Art* 33 (Spring 2019): 24–51.

45. The story of Cornelia, originated with the first-century Roman Valerius Maximus, but was repeated ad nauseam across periodicals and books in the nineteenth century. Clearly *Frank Leslie's,* a popular illustrated weekly, assumed its readers would be familiar with the story. See for example Rev. J. Few Smith, "Our Nation's Jewels," *Evangelical Review* (July 1853): 79 and "Haec Ornamenta Mea Sunt" *Ladies*

Repository 26 (April 1858): 386–387. Sorosis, organized in 1868, was incorporated in New York in 1869. Along with the Boston-based New England Woman's Club, it spurred the woman's club movement over the next few decades. Mrs. J. C. Croly, *A History of the Woman's Club Movement in America* (New York, 1898).

46. John Wallace Hutchinson, *The Story of the Hutchinsons* (Boston, 1896), 436–437, 439. John W. Hutchinson, *The Fatherhood of God and Brotherhood of Man* (Chicago, 1868) and Hutchinson, *Vote it Right Along: Song and Chorus* (Chicago, 1869); T. Martin Towne, *Let Woman Vote: Song and Chorus* (Chicago, 1869). Though he was a staunch supporter of women's rights, Hutchinson developed a reputation as a philanderer in later years, according to Scott Gac, *Singing for Freedom: The Hutchinson Family Singers and the Nineteenth-Century Culture of Reform* (New Haven, CT: Yale University Press, 2008).

47. *Female Suffrage: Song and Chorus.* Words by R. A. Cohen, With Symphonies, Accompaniments, &c by George H. Briggs (St. Joseph, MO, 1867).

48. "South Carolina, One of the States," *Christian Examiner* (September 1865); Orville Dewey, "Radicalism and Conservatism: An Address to the Graduating Class at the Cambridge Divinity School, April 17, 1865," reprinted in *Christian Examiner* (September 1865), 219. David Roediger captures the revolutionary sense contemporaries had of the moment they were living through in *Seizing Freedom: Slave Emancipation and Liberty for All* (New York: Verso Books, 2014).

49. A Republican (not a "Radical"), *Universal Suffrage. Female Suffrage* (Philadelphia, 1867), 3. The pamphlet was published anonymously, but the author was Thomas W. Hartley. See *Catalogue of the Galatea Collection of Books Relating to the History of Woman in the Public Library of the City of Boston* (Boston, 1898), 19. Mrs. H. C. Ingersoll, *A Woman's Plea for Partial Suffrage* (Washington, DC, 1869).

50. Francis Lieber, "Reflections on the Changes Which May Seem Necessary in the Present Constitution of the State of New York," [1867], in Lieber, *Contributions to Political Science* (Philadelphia, 1880), 204; Ingersoll, *A Woman's Plea for Partial Suffrage.*

51. *Universal Suffrage. Female Suffrage*, 12. Anglo-Irish reformer Frances Power Cobbe objected to this categorical lumping in her *Fraser's* article titled "Criminals, Idiots, Minors, and Women" (December 1868), which became a widely circulated tract both in the United States and Great Britain.

52. "South Carolina, One of the States," 239; Alexander Keyssar, *The Right to Vote: The Contested History of Democracy in the United States* (New York: Basic Books, 2000), 56. On the larger European "discourse of capacity" among liberal critics of mass democracy, see Alan S. Kahan, *Liberalism in Nineteenth-Century Europe: The Political Culture of Limited Suffrage* (Basingstoke: Palgrave Macmillan, 2003).

53. "South Carolina, One of the States," 233.

54. L. P. Brockett, *Woman: Her Rights, Wrongs, Privileges, and Responsibilities* (Cincinnati, 1869), 265, 267, 278; "A New Phase of the Woman Question," *The Round Table*, June 5, 1869. Carlyle's *Shooting Niagara: And After?* had appeared

in 1867, first in *Macmillans* (April 1867) and then separately as a pamphlet later that year. It was reprinted and discussed in American periodicals. See, for example, *Littel's Living Age*, September 14, 1867, which introduced it with the disclaimer that as the work of "the leading prophet of Toryism,—Absolutism,—Slavery," they felt they could not ignore it. The postwar period represented another chapter in the long history of disagreement between Mill and Carlyle over American slavery and democracy. On that see T. Peter Park, "John Stuart Mill, Thomas Carlyle, and the U.S. Civil War," *The Historian* 54, no. 1 (Autumn 1991): 93–106; and Leslie Butler, *Critical Americans: Victorian Intellectuals and Transatlantic Liberal Reform* (Chapel Hill: University of North Carolina Press, 2007), 105–108, 126–127.

55. William Gillette, *Retreat from Reconstruction, 1869–1879* (Baton Rouge: Louisiana State University Press, 1981); David Montgomery, *Beyond Equality: Labor and the Radical Republicans, 1862–1872* (Urbana: University of Illinois Press, 1981).

56. M., "The Vexed Question" (Parts I, II, and III) *Nation*, March 24, 30, and April 14, 1870, 189–190, 205–206, 237–238; quotation at 189–190.

57. M., "The Vexed Question," 189–190, 205–206, 237–238; and M. C. W., "Opposition of Women to Female Suffrage," *The Nation*, April 7, 1870, 222–223.

58. *An Appeal Against Anarchy of Sex. To the Constitutional Convention and the People of the State of New-York. By a Member of the Press* (New York, 1867), 12.

59. Brockett, *Woman*, 3.

60. Kathi Kern and Linda Levstik place the number of women involved at seven hundred, in "Teaching the New Departure." On the efforts of Black women in the New Departure endeavor, see Rosalyn Terborg-Penn, *African-American Women in the Struggle for the Vote, 1850–1920* (Bloomington: Indiana University Press, 1998), 36–42 and Jones, *Vanguard*, 117–120. On the "New Departure" more generally, see Ellen Carol DuBois, "Taking the Law into Our Own Hands: Bradwell, Minor, and Suffrage Militance in the 1870s" and "Outgrowing the Compact of our Fathers: Equal Rights, Woman Suffrage, and the United States Constitution, 1820–1878," both in Dubois, *Woman Suffrage and Women's Rights* (New York: New York University Press, 1998), 81–113 and 114–138. As Andrew Wender Cohen and Carol Faulkner have recently argued, some Americans challenged gender limitations on voting in "nearly every election cycle" between 1830 and 1860, but without the backing of an organized movement; "Enforcing Gender at the Polls: Transing Voters and Women's Suffrage Before the American Civil War," *Journal of Social History* 56, no. 2 (2022): 386–420.

61. *An Account of the Proceedings on the Trial of Susan B. Anthony, on the Charge of Illegal Voting . . .* (Rochester, 1874), 151; *Gerrit Smith to Susan B. Anthony, Peterboro, February 5th, 1873.* https://www.loc.gov/item/rbpe.23701400/. The US Attorney rejected this view, citing the prior practice of all states excluding women (and many others) from the right to vote throughout their history. He also drew attention to the use of the word "male" in section 2 of the Fourteenth Amendment, which he

argued precluded "the theory or supposition that the right to vote, was, by that amendment, conferred upon females."

62. This case followed two earlier decisions that sought to narrow the scope of the Fourteenth Amendment—the *Slaughterhouse Cases* (1873) and *Bradwell v. Illinois* (1873)—and was in turn followed by two cases that weakened the power of the Fifteenth Amendment: *United States v. Reese* (1875) and *United States v. Cruikshank* (1875). Ellen Carol Dubois argued that the link between the judicial dismissal of women's rights and the repudiation of the Reconstruction amendments has been underappreciated in "Taking the Law into Our Own Hands: *Bradwell, Minor,* and Suffrage Militancy in the 1870s." See also Norma Basch, "Reconstructing Female Citizenship: *Minor v. Happersett,*" in *The Constitution, Law, and American Life: Critical Aspects of the Nineteenth-Century Experience,* edited by Donald G. Nieman (Athens: University of Georgia Press, 1992), 52–66; Gretchen Ritter, *Constitution as Social Design: Gender and Civic Membership in the American Constitutional Order* (Stanford, CA: Stanford University Press, 2006), 18–27; Foner, *Second Founding,* chapter 4.

63. Anthony, "Is it a Crime," [January 16, 1873], in *Selected Papers of Elizabeth Cady Stanton and Susan B. Anthony,* Vol. 2, 569.

CHAPTER 5

1. "Things of the Day. The Woman Question," *Galaxy* (June 1870): 841; Harriet Beecher Stowe, "The Chimney Corner—The Woman Question; or, What Will You Do with Her," *Atlantic Monthly* 16 (December 1865).

2. See Heather Andrea Williams, *Help Me Find My People: The African American Search for Family Lost in Slavery* (Chapel Hill: University of North Carolina Press, 2012); Jean Lee Cole, "Information Wanted: *The Curse of Caste, Minnie's Sacrifice,* and the *Christian Recorder,*" *African American Review* 40 (Winter 2006): 731–742; P. Gabrielle Foreman, "The *Christian Recorder,* Broken Families, and Educated Nations in Julia C. Collins's Civil War Novel *The Curse of Caste,*" *African American Review* 50 (Winter 2017): 1063–1074; Eric Gardner, *Black Print Unbound: The* Christian Recorder, *African American Literature and Periodical Culture* (New York: Oxford University Press, 2015).

3. Recent historical work obviously ventures more widely than contemporary commentary did, a theme developed in Catherine A. Jones, "Women, Gender, and the Boundaries of Reconstruction," *Journal of the Civil War Era* 8, no. 1 (2018): 111–131.

4. John Stuart Mill to Parker Pillsbury, July 4, [1867], in *The Collected Works of John Stuart Mill: Later Letters,* edited by Francis E. Mineka and Dwight N. Lindley (Toronto: University of Toronto Press, 1972), vol. XVI, 1289. He compared British and American electoral expansion in a letter to Ralph Waldo Emerson (August 12, 1867), where he predicted that "all the fundamental problems of politics and

society, so long smothered by general indolence and apathy, will surge up and demand better solutions than they have ever yet obtained," 1306–1307.

5. Mill's *An Examination of Sir William Hamilton's Philosophy* (London, 1865), a follow-up to his own earlier *System of Logic* (London, 1843), also caused a stir in the 1860s, at least in more rarefied theological and philosophical circles. The soon-to-be president of Princeton, James McCosh, weighed in to defend Hamilton in *An Examination of J. S. Mill's Philosophy* (London, 1866).

6. Caroline H. Dall, *Woman's Rights Under the Law. In Three Lectures, Delivered in Boston, January, 1861* (Boston, 1861), v; xviii–xix; 143.

7. Osgood's remarks about "twaddle," the Osgood-Dall exchange, and Dall's *Christian Inquirer* piece, from October 11, 1862, appear in *Selected Journals of Caroline Healey Dall*, edited by Helen Deese (Boston: Massachusetts Historical Society, 2013), vol. 2, 402, 665–668.

8. Anthony Trollope, *North America* (New York, 1862), 4, 272; 253, 261–262. Brent E. Kinser, *The American Civil War in the Shaping of British Democracy* (Burlington, VT: Ashgate, 2011), chapter 2. The family pattern caused one reviewer to wonder "whether future generations of Americans are to be discussed by future Trollopes." The English public may or may not be "heartily sick" of "books about this country" as well as of the Trollopes, but that the American public was sick of both "could not be doubted." "Trollope's *North America*," *Philobiblion* 9 (August 1862): 204.

9. Elizabeth W. Farnham, *Woman and Her Era* (New York, 1864), iii; *Literary Gazette and Publishers' Circle*, March 1, 1864 and April 1, 1864. John Neal also reemerged in the 1860s to resume his insistence on women's claim to full self-governance (individual and collective) in "Masquerading," *The Northern Monthly* (March 1864): 1–5 and his two-part series "Woman's Rights—and Woman's Wrongs," *American Phrenological Journal* (March and April 1867). For Farnham's California years, see Ellen Carol DuBois, "Seneca Falls in Santa Cruz: Eliza W. Farnham and the Varieties of Women's Emancipation in Nineteenth-Century California," *Commonplace* 9 (2009), http://commonplace.online/article/seneca-falls-santa-cruz/ (accessed June 10, 2023).

10. Farnham, *Woman and Her Era*, iii. Farnham's philosophy echoed Auguste Comte's positivism and Herbert Spencer's evolutionary theories, though rather than discuss either man she relied on the English historian Henry Thomas Buckle, a popularizer of Comte. Buckle's lecture "The Influence of Women on Progress of Knowledge" (1858) and his *History of Civilization in England* (1864) appeared repeatedly in ways that form an American counterpart to the story laid out in Fiona McIntosh-Varjabédian, "Henry Thomas Buckle's The History of Civilization in England in France (1865–1918): A Transnational Reception Case," *Reception: Texts, Readers, Audiences, History* 11, no. 1 (2019): 40–57.

11. Farnham, *Woman and Her Era*, iii; "Mrs. Eliza W. Farnham: Biography," *American Phrenological Journal* (February 1865): 57. Reviews ran the gamut, with some

praising her "masculine vigor of style" and others deriding her central argument as "the veriest trash of feminine sentimentalism," *American Literary Gazette and Publishers' Circular*, March 1, 1864, April 1, 1864, May 16, 1864; "Woman and Her Era," *Harper's New Monthly Magazine* 29 (June 1864): 130. Knowing its audience, the *American Phrenological Journal* also informed readers that the "larger and better developed brain" Farnham possessed was housed in a head "nearly twenty-three inches in circumference."

12. *A Woman's Philosophy of Woman; or, Woman Affranchised* (New York, 1864) excluded some European details seen in *La Femme Affranchie Réponse à MM. Michelet, Proudhon, É. de Girardin, A. Comte et aux autres novateurs modernes par Jenny P. d'Héricourt* (Paris, 1860). Stephen Sawyer labels d'Hericourt's theory "agonistic democracy" in *Demos Assembled: Democracy and the International Origins of the Modern State, 1840–1880* (Chicago: University of Chicago Press, 2018), chapter 5. See also Karen Offen, "A Nineteenth-Century French Feminist Rediscovered: Jenny P. D'Hericourt, 1809–1875," *Signs* 13 (Autumn 1987): 144–158; Claire G. Moses, *French Feminism in the Nineteenth Century* (Albany: State University of New York Press, 1984); and Karen Offen, *The Woman Question in France, 1400–1870* (New York: Cambridge University Press, 2017). On the hollowness of democracy in the Second Empire, see James T. Kloppenberg, *Toward Democracy: The Struggle for Self-Rule in European and American Thought* (New York: Oxford University Press, 2016), 657–658.

13. William Lloyd Garrison Jr., "Woman and the War," *Liberator*, May 8, 1863, 74.

14. "Mabtha," "The Woman Question," *The New York Observer and Chronicle*, February 25, 1864, 61. "The Rights of Women," *Godey's Lady's Book and Magazine* (September 1863): 229.

15. Frank Moore, *Women of the War: Their Heroism and Self-Sacrifice* (Hartford, CT, 1866); L. P. Brockett, M.D., and Mrs. Mary C. Vaughan, *Woman's Work in the Civil War: A Record of Heroism, Patriotism and Patience* (Philadelphia, 1867); Frances M. Clarke, "Forgetting the Women: Debates over Female Patriotism in the Aftermath of America's Civil War," *Journal of Women's History* 23, no. 2 (2011): 64–86; Alice Fahs, "The Feminized Civil War: Gender, Northern Popular Literature, and the Memory of the War, 1861–1900," *Journal of American History* 85, no. 4 (1999): 1461–1494. On Dickinson's political efforts during the election, see Matthew Gallman, *America's Joan of Arc: The Life of Anna Elizabeth Dickinson* (New York Oxford University Press, 2006).

16. Bellows in Brockett and Vaughan, *Woman's Work in the Civil War*, 40.

17. Harper praised "the regal men/whose brows ne'er wore a diadem" but whose true nobility was revealed as they "grandly made our cause their own, / Till Slavery tottered on her throne." "Our English Friends" appeared in the *Woman's Journal*, September 21, 1872, reprinted in *A Brighter Coming Day: A Frances Ellen Watkins Harper Reader*, edited by Frances Smith Foster (New York: Feminist Press, 1990), 196.

18. Obsession with the Taylor-Mill marriage may have begun with Mill's contemporaries, but it continued in twentieth-century scholarship. Friedrich Hayek devoted a whole volume to the topic in 1951: *John Stuart Mill and Harriet Taylor: Their Friendship and Subsequent Marriage* (Chicago: University of Chicago Press, 1951). And the question of Harriet's influence sparked Gertrude Himmelfarb's "two Mills" thesis in *On Liberty and Liberalism: The Case of John Stuart Mill* (New York: Knopf, 1975). A more recent discussion can be found in Alan Ryan, "The Passionate Hero, Then and Now," *New York Review of Books*, December 8, 2011.

19. Justin M'Carthy [*sic*], "John Stuart Mill," *New National Era*, December 8, 1870; Dall, *Woman's Rights Under the Law*, 94–96. Richard T. Greener, a fellow editor at the *New National Era*, referred to Mill and his women's rights activism with some regularity. A lengthy discussion, and rejection, of Mill's argument for a sex-neutral suffrage came in [Andrew Peabody], "Mill on Representative Government," *North American Review*, 95 (July 1862), 228. Among the more notable discussions of this candidacy, unprecedented in US coverage of English politics, were "Stuart Mill," *New York Tribune*, July 26, 1865; Moncure Conway, "The Great Westminster Canvass," *Harper's New Monthly Magazine*, 31 (November 1865): 732; "John Stuart Mill, M.P.," *Harper's Weekly*, October 28, 1865.

20. Augusta Jane Evans, *St. Elmo; Or, Saved at Last* (New York, 1866), 262–263; 394; 393.

21. Anthony Trollope, *He Knew He Was Right* (London, 1869), vol. 2, 46–47.

22. On the composition of *Subjection* and delay in publication see *Sexual Equality: Writings by John Stuart Mill, Harriet Taylor Mill, and Helen Taylor*, edited by Ann P. Robson and John M. Robson (Toronto: University of Toronto Press, 1994), xxix–xxx; Alice S. Rossi, "Sentiment and Intellect: The Story of John Stuart Mill and Harriet Taylor Mill," in *Essays on Sex Equality*, edited by Alice S. Rossi (Chicago: University of Chicago Press, 1970), 3–5; 56–57. Mill's delay in publishing *Subjection* offers an intriguing parallel to Frederick Grimke's similar hesitation at publishing his essay on "The Rights of Women in a Democratic Republic," which would ultimately appear (to little attention) two years after *Subjection*.

23. John Stuart Mill, *Autobiography* (London, 1873), 265–266. He also credited his stepdaughter Helen Taylor for having "enriched" the work. On the differences between "Enfranchisement" and *Subjection*, see Rossi, "Sentiment and Intellect."

24. Given the importance of this text to the origins and development of liberal feminism, philosophers and political theorists have generated an enormous body of scholarship. The classic works include: Julia M. Annas, "Mill and the Subjection of Women," *Philosophy* 52, no. 200 (1977): 179–194; Susan Moller Okin, "John Stuart Mill, Liberal Feminist," in *Women in Western Political Thought* (Princeton: Princeton University Press, 1979), 197–232; Susan Hekman, "John Stuart Mill's *The Subjection of Women*: The Foundations of Liberal Feminism," *History of European Ideas* 15, no. 4-6 (1992): 681–686. More recent work has argued that Mill's concern with questions of patriarchal domination far exceeds

the limits of "liberal" feminism. See here, for example, Wendy Donner, "John Stuart Mill's Liberal Feminism," *Philosophical Studies* 69 (March 1993): 155–166; Maria H. Morales, *Perfect Equality, John Stuart Mill on Well-Constituted Communities* (Lanham, MD: Rowman & Littlefield, 1996); Maria H. Morales, "Rational Freedom in John Stuart Mill's Feminism," in *J. S. Mill's Political Thought: A Bicentennial Reassessment*, edited by Nadia Urbinati and Alex Zakaras (New York: Cambridge University Press, 2007), 43–65; Helen McCabe, "John Stuart Mill, Utility and the Family: Attacking 'the Citadel of the Enemy,'" *Revue Internationale de Philosophie* 2, no. 272 (2015): 225–235.

25. In the wake of the abolition of slavery, Mill wrote, "marriage is the only actual bondage known to our law. There remain no legal slaves, except the mistress of every house"; John Stuart Mill, *The Subjection of Women* (New York, 1869), 147. Ana Stevenson examines the woman/slave analogy over time in *The Woman as Slave in Nineteenth-Century American Social Movements* (London: Palgrave Macmillan, 2020).

26. Mill, *The Subjection of Women*, 81; Thomas Jefferson, *Notes on the State of Virginia* (Philadelphia, 1781), Query XVIII (on "Manners").

27. Mill, *The Subjection of Women*, 148–150.

28. Mill, *The Subjection of Women*, 178.

29. "Critical Notices," *Fortnightly Review* (July 1869): 119. Horace Bushnell, *Women's Suffrage: The Reform Against Nature* (New York, 1869); L. P. Brockett, *Woman: Her Rights, Wrong, Privileges, Responsibilities* (Cincinnati, 1869); [Donald McCaig] *A Reply to John Stuart Mill on the Subjection of Women* (Philadelphia, 1870); and Carlos White, *Ecce Femina: An Examination of Arguments in Favor of Female Suffrage by John Stuart Mill and Others, and a Presentation of Arguments Against the Proposed Change in the Constitution of Society* (Hanover, NH, 1870).

30. "Great Britain," *Punchinello*, May 7, 1870, 86; Orpheus C. Kerr, "The Mystery of Mr. E. Drood," *Punchinello*, July 9, 1870, 228 (a spoof of Charles Dickens's current novel); Review of White, *Ecce Femina* in "Book Notices," *Christian Advocate*, April 7, 1870, 106. McCaig kept a scrapbook of the notices of his book, which includes favorable quotations from newspapers in Philadelphia, Cincinnati, Charleston, and Chicago. *Copies of Certificates, Testimonials, &c. Obtained During a Course of Fourteen Years' teaching: also, Literary Notices on a Work Written in Reply to John Stuart Mill on the Subjection of Women* (Microfilm, from copy held at University of Guelph).

31. [McCaig], *A Reply to John Stuart Mill*, 1; "Literature—at Home," *Putnam's Magazine* (October 1869): 503.

32. *Revolution*, December 23, 1869.

33. George William Curtis, "Men and Women in Convention," *Harper's Weekly*, July 31, 1869, 483; William Still, *The Underground Railroad* (Philadelphia, 1872), 778; on Mossell, see Rosalyn Terborg-Penn, *African American Women in the Struggle for the Vote, 1850–1920* (Bloomington: Indiana University Press, 1998), 51.

34. Stowe to Fanny Fern in Joan Hedrick, *Harriet Beecher Stowe: A Life* (New York: Oxford University Press, 1995), 360.

35. T. P. Eliot, "A Reply to John Stuart Mill," *Woman's Journal*, July 16, 1870, 219. Hooker quoted in Susan Campbell, *Tempest-Tossed: The Spirit of Isabella Beecher Hooker* (Middletown, CT: Wesleyan University Press, 2016), 91. Ariana Wormeley Curtis and Daniel Sargent Curtis, *The Spirit of Seventy-Six; or the Coming Woman: A Prophetic Drama* (Boston, 1868). Several suffragists commented on the success of the play in these years.

36. [E. L. Godkin], "Mr. Mill's Plea for Women," *Nation*, July 22, 1869. Sharper responses came from those who faulted Mill for ignoring the "Scripture laws on the subject," as in, for example, "J. Stuart Mill on the Subjection of Women," *New York Observer and Chronicle*, July 29, 1869.

37. Bushnell, *Women's Suffrage*, 164–165; Bushnell, "American Politics," *American National Preacher* 14 (December 1840): 198–199; "Literature—at Home," 503.

38. Bushnell, *Women's Suffrage*, 110; 35–36, 40.

39. Elizabeth Cady Stanton to Paulina Wright Davis, [August 12, 1869], in *Selected Papers of Elizabeth Cady Stanton and Susan B. Anthony. Volume Two: Against an Aristocracy of Sex, 1866–1873*, edited by Ann D. Gordon (New Brunswick, NJ: Rutgers University Press, 2000), 94; Lulu Gray Noble, "An Explanation from the 'Looker-On,'" *Nation*, March 10, 1870, 156. Stanton contemplated retiring from the movement and spending the next five years of her life alone, "with my own thoughts." That did not happen, and she never did write a single-volume book on the woman question (though her speeches and writings have filled multiples volumes). For a compelling reading of Stanton's engagement with Mill, see Barbara Caine, "Elizabeth Cady Stanton, John Stuart Mill, and the Nature of Feminist Thought," in *Elizabeth Cady Stanton, Feminist as Thinker: A Reader in Documents and Essays*, edited by Ellen Carol DuBois and Richard Cándida Smith (New York: New York University Press, 2007), 50–65.

40. [William James], "Bushnell's Women's Suffrage, and Mill's Subjection of Women," *North American Review* 109 (October 1869): 556–565. Henry James Sr. also reviewed both books, returning to a subject in which he had been interested for decades. "The Woman Thou Gavest With Me," *Atlantic Monthly* (January 1870): 66–72; "Literature—at Home," 503. As Cady Stanton remarked in the pages of the *Revolution*, "we find a general dissatisfaction among the ladies with Horace Bushnell's book, and all are waiting impatiently for the philosophical and logical presentation of the question by John Stuart Mill," *Revolution* (July 1, 1869).

41. "Men and Women in Convention," *Harper's Weekly*, July 31, 1869, 483; [McCaig], *A Reply to John Stuart Mill*, 7; White, *Ecce Femina*, 7. Alexander Keyssar, *The Right to Vote: The Contested History of Democracy in the United States* (New York: Basic Books, 2000); Faye E. Dudden, *Fighting Chance: The Struggle over Woman Suffrage and Black Suffrage in Reconstruction America* (New York: Oxford University Press, 2011); and David Roediger, *Seizing Freedom: Slave Emancipation and Liberty for*

All (New York: Verso Books, 2014) all contextualize suffragists newly raised hopes in the 1860s–1870s, precisely in this lived experience of witnessing so revolutionary a change in their lifetimes.

42. "Mr. Mill on the Condition of Women," *Christian Observer* (August 1869), in *The Subjection of Women: Contemporary Responses to John Stuart Mill*, edited by Andrew Pyle (Bristol: Thoemmes Press, 1995), 80.

43. White, *Ecce Femina*, 7, 10, 8.

44. [James], "Bushnell's Women's Suffrage, and Mill's Subjection of Women," 565; Letter to Henry Bowditch, in *The Correspondence of William James*, edited by Ignas K. Skrupskelis and Elizabeth M. Berkeley (Charlottesville: University of Virginia Press, 1992–2004), vol. 4, 382–383. For a fuller discussion of James's response to Bushnell and Mill, see Leslie Butler, "Encountering the Smashing Projectile: William James on John Stuart Mill and the Woman Question," in *William James and the Transatlantic Conversation: Pragmatism, Pluralism, and the Philosophy of Religion*, edited by Martin Halliwell and Joel Rasmussen (Oxford: Oxford University Press, 2014), 115–130.

45. Catharine E. Beecher and Harriet Beecher Stowe, *The American Woman's Home; or, Principles of Domestic Science* (New York, 1869), 16; a brief quotation from Tocqueville on the superiority of democratic over aristocratic manners was retained at pp. 209–210. The text appeared under two different titles: as an 1870 textbook, *Principles of Domestic Science: As Applied to the Duties and Pleasures of Home* and, with the addition of 500 recipes, as the 1873 *The New Housekeeper's Manual, Embracing a New Revised Edition of the American Woman's Home, Or, Principles of Domestic Science*. A final edition, stripped of commentary about women's rights, came in 1874.

46. Catharine Beecher, *Woman Suffrage and Woman's Profession* (Hartford, CT, 1871), 181; Beecher, "Something for Women Better than the Ballot," *Appleton's Journal* 2 (September 1869): 81–84, this essay was reprinted in its entirety as an appendix in Brockett, *Woman*, 393–412 and in *Scott's Monthly Magazine* (October 1869).

47. Catharine Beecher, *Woman's Profession as Mother and Educator, With Views in Opposition to Woman Suffrage* (Philadelphia, 1872), 181.

48. *Memorial of C. E. McKay, Remonstrating Against the Right of Suffrage Being Granted to Women.* (February 10, 1870). Capsule biographies of McKay appeared in both Moore, *Women of the War* and Brockett and Vaughan, *Woman's Work in the Civil War*.

49. "Literary Notices," *True Woman*, April 1871. See, for example, Mrs. Dahlgren, "Journalism and Woman Suffrage," *True Woman*, October 1871, 60–61; "What the Washington Papers Say," *True Woman*, January 1872, 85. Fenimore Cooper's articles appeared as "Female Suffrage: A Letter to the Christian Women of America," in *Harper's New Monthly Magazine* 41 (August and September 1870).

50. *Memorial of C. E. McKay, Remonstrating Against the Right of Suffrage Being Granted to Women*, February 10, 1870. The *True Woman* put that number at 7,000

signatures by July of 1871 in "A History of Protests Against Woman Suffrage," *True Woman*, July 1871, 29. A full text of this petition can be found in Madeleine Vinton Dahlgren, *Thoughts on Female Suffrage and in Vindication of Women's True Rights* (Washington, DC, 1871), 4 and was included in "Notes and Notices," *Godey's Lady's Book* (May 1871): 476. The same issue also noted that four hundred women from the Illinois Normal School had sent an anti-suffrage remonstrance to Congress and predicted that the people of Wyoming Territory were about to "abandon woman suffrage as both mischievous and impracticable." The *New York Times* printed the petition, along with a lengthy letter of explanation by Almira Lincoln Phelps, on May 27, 1871.

51. Dahlgren even underscored the basic human rights of children neglected by their mothers too focused on political rights. Dahlgren, "Children's Rights," in *Thoughts on Female Suffrage and in Vindication of Woman's True Rights*, 10–11.

52. See for example "What to Do with Single Women," February 1, 1873; "Help Those Women," April 1, 1873; "Women as Teachers," June 1, 1873. The *True Women* circle also took umbrage at being described by suffrage advocates as "wealthy, sentimental, and ignorant," even though most did come from comfortable backgrounds, "Woman Without the Ballot," *True Woman*, April 1870. Nineteenth-century anti-suffrage activism is still understudied. But see the first chapters in Thomas J. Jablonsky, *The Home, Heaven, and Mother Party: Female Anti-Suffragists in the United States, 1868–1920* (Brooklyn: Carlson Pub., 1994); Susan E. Marshall, *Splintered Sisterhood: Gender and Class in the Campaign against Woman Suffrage* (Madison: University of Wisconsin Press, 1997); and Susan Goodier, *No Votes for Women: The New York State Anti-Suffrage Movement* (Urbana: University of Illinois Press, 2013).

53. M. A. Dodge to [Mr. James], March 20, 1865, in *Gail Hamilton's Life and Letters*, edited by H. Augusta Dodge (Boston: Lee and Shepard, 1901), vol. 1, 488; Gail Hamilton, *Woman's Worth and Worthlessness* (New York, 1872), v–vi. Writing for the *Woman's Journal* (where Hamilton and her work were frequently discussed), Thomas Wentworth Higginson found her essays on the woman question wrong-headed but genuinely worth reading (she was a "generous partisan"—often "unreasonable, but never willfully unfair"), T. W. H. "Gail Hamilton's Warnings," *Woman's Journal*, April 1, 1871.

54. Mrs. H. C. Ingersoll, *A Woman's Plea of Partial Suffrage* (Washington, DC, 1869); Gail Hamilton, *Woman's Wrongs: A Counter-Irritant* (Boston, 1868), 104.

55. Brockett, *Woman*, 271–272; James Harris Fairchild, *Woman's Right to the Ballot* (Oberlin, OH, 1870), 60. Centuries of republican political theory and common law alike considered independent male heads of household as the proper governors of their own dependent family members and as their representatives in the polity. For a probing constitutional history of sex equality and a discussion of how women's suffrage contributed to the "democratization of the family," see the two excellent articles by Reva B. Siegel, "'She the People': The Nineteenth Amendment,

Sex Equality, Federalism, and the Family," *Harvard Law Review* 1115 (February 2002): 948–1045 and "The Nineteenth Amendment and the Democratization of the Family," *Yale Law Journal Forum* (January 20, 2020): 450–494.

56. Tayler Lewis, "Household Suffrage," *The Independent*, December 20, 1866; James R. Doolittle's proposal was summarized, approvingly, in the *New York Evangelist*, September 30, 1869 and excerpted in the *Baptist Quarterly Review* (October 1869); M. E. S., "Appeal of a Western Woman," *The Independent*, January 24, 1867. Lewis repeated his argument in "Female Politicians," *The Guardian* (March 1867).

57. "For the True Woman," *True Woman*, June 1872, 28–29; Mrs. Dahlgren, "Are the Women of America Slaves?," *True Woman*, February 1872, 90. In fact it was suffrage itself that would entail a kind of slavery. Many anti-suffrage women emphasized the coercive, involuntary elements of women's enfranchisement, arguing instead that women should have the "right not to vote." "Compulsory Character of the Woman Suffrage Movement," *True Woman*, March 1872, 7–8.

58. Quotations from Bushnell, *Women's Suffrage*, 135; Fairchild, *Woman's Right to the Ballot*, 62.

59. A. B. C., "Why Women Should Not Vote," *True Woman*, July 1871, 39; *Godey's Lady's Book* (September 1870).

60. Review of Carlos White, *Ecce Femina* in "Book Notices," *Christian Advocate*, April 7, 1870, 106; *Chicago Tribune*, January 3, 1871; *Nation*, April 7, 1870, 223 (the editorial note was in response to McKim Miller's multiple letters, discussed in chapter 4).

61. Victoria C. Woodhull, *"And the Truth Shall Make You Free:" A Speech on the Principles of Social Freedom* (New York, 1872), 23 (emphasis in original). There is no shortage of work on Woodhull, a character who has fascinated historians as much as her contemporaries. Good, balanced accounts of her impact on the movement can be found in Ellen Carol DuBois, *Suffrage: Women's Long Battle for the Vote* (New York: Simon & Schuster, 2021), 83–95 and Lisa Tetrault, *The Myth of Seneca Falls: Memory and the Women's Suffrage Movement, 1848–1898* (Chapel Hill: University of North Carolina Press, 2014), 56–59, 63–66. See also, Amanda Frisken, *Victoria Woodhull's Sexual Revolution: Political Theater and the Popular Press in Nineteenth-Century America* (Philadelphia: University of Pennsylvania Press, 2004).

62. Hedrick, *Harriet Beecher Stowe*, 357–358; Amy Easton-Flake, "Harriet Beecher Stowe's Multifaceted Response to the Nineteenth-Century Woman Question," *New England Quarterly* 86 (March 2013): 29–59.

63. Stowe, *My Wife and I; Or Harry Henderson's History* (New York, 1870); Easton-Flake, "Harriet Beecher Stowe's Multifaceted Response to the Nineteenth-Century Woman Question," 29–59 and Barbara A. White, *The Beecher Sisters* (New Haven, CT: Yale University Press, 2003) offers a detailed discussion of these events from the perspective of all three women. See also, Hedrick, *Harriet Beecher Stowe*. On the Beecher-Tilton trial, see Richard Wightman Fox, *Trials of Intimacy: Love and Loss in the Beecher-Tilton Scandal* (Chicago: University of Chicago Press, 1999);

Debby Applegate, *The Most Famous Man in America: The Biography of Henry Ward Beecher* (New York: Doubleday, 2007); and on the larger impact of sex and marriage reform, Carol Faulkner, *Unfaithful: Love, Adultery, and Marriage Reform in Nineteenth Century America* (Philadelphia: University of Pennsylvania Press, 2019).

64. Hooker to Mill, August 9, 1869, reprinted in Hooker, *Womanhood: Its Sanctities and Fidelities* (Boston, 1874), 33–34; Isabella Beecher Hooker to Josephine Butler, May 27, 1874, in Mill-Taylor Collection, London School of Economics (LSE).

CHAPTER 6

1. Thomas Wentworth Higginson, "Too Many Voters Already," in *Common Sense About Women* (Boston, 1882), 299–302.

2. *Consistent Democracy: The Elective Franchise for Women. Twenty-Five Testimonies of Prominent Men* (Worcester, 1858); "Should Women Vote? Important Affirmative Authority," *The Emporia News*, June 14, 1867; *Eminent Opinions on Woman Suffrage* (Boston, 1893). Versions of this list were reproduced in multiple volumes, see for example the bizarre [Rev. L. E. Keith] Felix Feeler, *Female Filosofy, Fished Out and Fried* (Cleona, PA, 1894), 218–228 and the amusing Mrs. Hattie A. Burr, *The Woman Suffrage Cookbook* (Boston, 1886), 144–148.

3. Both Parkman's *Some of the Reasons against Woman's Suffrage Views* (a composite sampling of his two "Woman Question" articles from the 1879 and 1880 *North American Review*) and the much shorter *An Open Letter to a Temperance Friend* appeared in multiple, undated versions, which records suggest proliferated as tracts of various anti-suffrage societies between 1887 and 1918. Mrs. Charles E. Guild's 1916 recollection of how anti-suffrage women gained their "first achievement" by inducing Parkman to contribute to the *North American Review* is noted in Susan E. Marshall, *Splintered Sisterhood: Gender and Class in the Campaign against Woman Suffrage* (Madison: University of Wisconsin Press, 1997), 80–82. The anti-suffragists' search for origins echoed the similar "movement history" considered in Lisa Tetrault, *The Myth of Seneca Falls: Memory and the Women's Suffrage Movement, 1848–1898* (Chapel Hill: University of North Carolina Press, 2014).

4. Carl Schurz, "Woman Suffrage," *Harper's Weekly*, June 16, 1894, 554.

5. [Francis Parkman], "Some of the Reasons against Woman Suffrage," *Boston Daily Advertiser*, March 24, 1876; J. Keppler, "When Lovely Women Stoops to Lobby—A Capital Picture," *Puck Magazine* (April 2, 1879). Parkman's article elicited two quick responses. [Henry Browne Blackwell] "Some of the Reasons for Woman Suffrage," *Boston Daily Advertiser*, March 27, 1876; [Thomas Wentworth Higginson], "Modern Feudalism," *The Woman's Journal*, April 8, 1876.

6. Francis Parkman to Higginson, June 5, 1876, cited in Charles Haight Farnham, *A Life of Francis Parkman* (Boston, 1901), 272. Compelling discussions of Parkman can be found in Kim Townsend, "Francis Parkman and the Male Tradition," *American Quarterly* 38, no. 1 (1986): 97–113; Nicholas Carr, "'I Have Not

Abandoned Any Plan: The Rage in Francis Parkman," *Massachusetts Historical Review* 17 (2015): 1–34; and Jon Grinspan, *Age of Acrimony: How Americans Fought to Fix their Democracy* (New York: Bloomsbury, 2021).

7. Francis Parkman, "The Failure of Universal Suffrage," *North American Review* (July–August 1878): 3, 2; Parkman, "The Tale of the 'Ripe Scholar,'" *Nation*, December 23, 1869; Parkman to Abbé Henri-Raymond Casgrain, November 2, 1878, in *The Letters of Francis Parkman*, edited by Wilbur R. Jacobs (Norman: University of Oklahoma Press, 1960), vol. 2, 119.

8. F. L. Mott, "One Hundred and Twenty Years," *North American Review* (June 1935), 144–175. According to Mott, the circulation climbed from 1200, when Rice bought the magazine in 1876, to 7,500 by 1880 and 17,000 by the time of Rice's death in 1889. Frank Luther Mott, *A History of American Magazines. Vol. III: 1865–1885* (Cambridge, MA: Harvard University Press, 1938).

9. Wendell Phillips, "The Outlook," *North American Review* (July–August 1878): 97–116; James G. Blaine, James A. Garfield, Montgomery Blair, L. Q. C. Lamar, Alexander H. Stephens, Thomas A. Hendricks, Wade Hampton and Wendell Phillips, "Ought the Negro to Be Disfranchised? Ought He to Have Been Enfranchised?," *North American Review* (March 1879); H. H. Chalmers, "The Effects of Negro Suffrage," *North American Review* (March 1881), 239–248. On the crucial role that Blaine played in the forum and in calling out the intransigence of Southern Democrats more generally, see Stephen A. West, "Remembering Reconstruction in its Twilight," *Journal of the Civil War Era* 10, no. 4 (December 2020): 495–523.

10. Parkman, "Review of Current Literature," *The Unitarian Review and Religious Magazine* (April 1877): 450; William Lindsay Scruggs, "Restriction of the Suffrage," *North American Review* (November 1884).

11. Parkman, *Some of the Reasons against Woman Suffrage*, 5; Thomas Wentworth Higginson, "Unsolved Problems in Woman Suffrage," *Forum* (January 1887): 445. George W. Julian made similar concessions, though also without backtracking from a universal, sex-neutral suffrage. See Julian, "Pending Ordeals of Democracy," *The International Review* 5 (November 1878); George W. Julian, "Suffrage a Birthright," *The International Review* (January 1879), 2–20; George W. Julian, "The Abuse of the Ballot and Its Remedy" *The International Review* (May 1880), 534.

12. Julia Ward Howe, Lucy Stone, Thomas Wentworth Higginson, Elizabeth Cady Stanton, and Wendell Phillips, "The Other Side of the Woman Question," *North American Review* (November 1879). The correspondence between Parkman and Higginson, and the remark made to *North American Review* associate editor John S. Barron about the "wrathful five," appear in *Letters of Francis Parkman*, vol. 2, 134.

13. "The Other Side of the Woman Question"; George W. Julian, "Is the Reformer Any Longer Needed?" *North American Review* (September–October 1878): 237–260; and "Suffrage a Birthright." On similar exchanges see, for example, Ouida, "Female Suffrage," *North American Review* (September 1886) with a response by Mary Livermore, "Woman Suffrage," *North American Review* (October 1886).

14. Harriet H. Robinson, *Massachusetts in the Woman Suffrage Movement* (Boston, 1881); Robinson, "Massachusetts" in *History of Woman Suffrage. Volume 3*, edited by Susan B. Anthony, Matilda Joslyn Gage, and Elizabeth Cady Stanton (Rochester, 1881), 265–315; "The Woman Question," in *"Warrington" Pen-Portraits*, edited by W. S. Robinson (Boston, 1877), 547; Boston *Weekly Globe*, August 1, 1882; Caroline H. Dall, "Mr. Parkman on Woman Suffrage in the 'North American Review,'" *The Unitarian Review and Religious Magazine* (March 1880): 223.

15. Prof. A. P. Peabody, "The Voting of Women in School Elections," *Journal of Social Science* (October 1879). "Massachusetts—Woman Suffrage in the Bay State," *Frank Leslie's Illustrated*, December 20, 1879. The Russian political scientist Moisei Ostrogorski conducted a transnational study of women's involvement in local self-government (as opposed to national politics) and concluded that these narrow modes of participation stemmed mostly form "concrete economic interests" and were thus largely independent of modern "democratic principles." Ostrogorski, "Woman Suffrage in Local Self-Government," *Political Science Quarterly* 6 (December 1891): 711. On *Frank Leslie's* and women voters, see Joshua Brown, *Beyond the Lines: Pictorial Reporting, Everyday Life, and the Crisis of Gilded Age America* (Berkeley: University of California Press, 2002), 226–232. On Western suffrage, see Rebecca J. Mead, *How the Vote Was Won: Woman Suffrage in the Western United States, 1869–1914* (New York: New York University Press, 2004).

16. Parkman, "Woman Question"; Edmund B. Thomas Jr., "School Suffrage and the Campaign for Women's Suffrage in Massachusetts, 1879–1920," *Historical Journal of Massachusetts* 25 (Winter 1997): 1–17. James Parton blamed hostility to the freedmen on the fact the vote had been "hurled" upon them "unprepared" in "Antipathy to the Negro," *North American Review* (November–December 1878), 476–491. Matilda Gage made a similar argument about Native Americans, detailed in Allison L. Sneider, *Suffragists in an Imperial Age* (New York: Oxford University Press, 2008).

17. Henry James to Macmillan, January 25, [1886], in *The Correspondence of Henry James and the House of Macmillan, 1877–1914*, edited by R. S. Moore (London: Palgrave Macmillan, 1993), 120. Not only had Henry James Sr. been caught up in the controversy surrounding Fourierism and free love when the future novelist was a boy, the father had continued to weigh in on the woman question right up to the decade before his death in 1882. He and Henry's brother William had both reviewed Mill's *The Subjection of Women*, which the brothers discussed in their correspondence. See Leslie Butler, "Encountering the Smashing Projectile: William James on John Stuart Mill and the Woman Question," in *William James and the Transatlantic Conversation: Pragmatism, Pluralism, and the Philosophy of Religion*, edited by Martin Halliwell and Joel Rasmussen (Oxford: University of Oxford Press, 2014), 115–130.

18. The book's publisher made sure to share an author's copy of the novel with Parkman when it appeared as a single volume the following year. Parkman wrote to

congratulate James on his "masterly" novel. He remarked that while he had never known such a woman as Olive Chancellor, he "had the ill-luck to know her component parts." Believing as he did that the "great majority of sensible and thoughtful persons of both sexes" shared his own views, he could only imagine the novel would do some good. Francis Parkman to Henry James, September 15, 1885, in *Letters of Francis Parkman*, vol. 2, 178.

19. Margaret Fuller, *Woman in the Nineteenth Century* (New York, 1845), 29. On the publication context of the novel, see especially Emily Coit's excellent discussion of the novel in *American Snobs: Transatlantic Novelists, Liberal Culture, and the Genteel Tradition* (Edinburgh: University of Edinburgh Press, 2021). An immense literature on the politics of *The Bostonians* includes Alfred Habegger's identification of it as James's "most reactionary book," *Henry James and the "Woman Business"* (New York: Cambridge University Press, 1989); Judith Fetterly's possibility for a resistant feminist reading in *The Resisting Reader: A Feminist Approach to American Fiction* (Bloomington: Indiana University Press, 1978); and Leslie Petty, *Romancing the Vote: Feminist Activism in American Fiction, 1870–1920* (Athens: University of Georgia Press, 2006).

20. James J. Kenneally, "Woman Suffrage and the Massachusetts 'Referendum' of 1895," *The Historian* 30, no. 4 (1968): 617–633; and more generally, Manuela Thurner, "'Better Citizens Without the Ballot': American Antisuffrage Women and their Rationale During the Progressive Era," *Journal of Women's History* 5, no. 1 (Spring 1993): 33–60; Marshall, *Splintered Sisterhood*.

21. On science, evolution, and cultural authority, see Cynthia Eagle Russett, *Darwin in America: The Intellectual Response, 1865–1912* (San Francisco: Freeman, 1976); Gail Bederman, *Manliness and Civilization: A Cultural History of Gender and Race and in American History, 1880–1917* (Chicago: University of Chicago Press, 1995).

22. Katharine Pearson Woods, "Mr. Bellamy Replies," *The Bookman: A Review of Books and Life* (August 1897); Edward Bellamy, *Looking Backward* (Boston, 1888). In subsequent writing, including the novel *Equality* (1897), Bellamy offered a clearer sense of how transformative his Nationalism would be for women, who, freed by technology and cooperation from most domestic labor, would serve in the industrial army and earn an equal state-guaranteed income with men. The new order would thus free women from their current economic dependence on marriage—which Bellamy called "the most ancient form of bondage." Bellamy, "Woman in the Year 2000," *The Ladies Home Journal* (February 1891).

23. Charlotte Perkins Gilman, *Women and Economics: A Study of the Economic Relation Between Men and Women as a Factor in Social Evolution* (1898). On evolutionary science and women, see Cynthia Eagle Russett, *Sexual Science: The Victorian Construction of Womanhood* (Cambridge, MA: Harvard University Press, 1991); Lois S. Magner, "Darwinism and the Woman Question: The Evolving Views of Charlotte Perkins Gilman," in *Critical Essays on Charlotte Perkins Gilman*, edited by Joanne B. Karpinsky (New York: G. K. Hall & N. Co., 1992); and Kimberly A.

Hamlin, *From Eve to Evolution: Darwin, Science, and Women's Rights in Gilded Age America* (Chicago: University of Chicago Press, 2014), which examines Gilman within a group she calls "Darwinian feminists" who used Darwin's theory of sexual selection—developed most fully in *Descent of Man* (1871)—to advance the cause of women. Gilman blended together evolutionary, eugenicist, and white supremacist ideas. On this, see especially Bederman, *Manliness and Civilization*, chapter 4 and Louise Michelle Newman, *White Women's Rights: The Racial Origins of Feminism in the United States* (New York: Oxford University Press, 1999), chapter 6.

24. Hugh Hawkins, *Between Harvard and America: The Educational Leadership of Charles W. Eliot* (New York: Oxford University Press, 1972); Julie A. Reuben, *The Making of the Modern Research University: Intellectual Transformation and the Marginalization of Morality* (Chicago: University of Chicago Press, 1996); Caroline Winterer, *The Culture of Classicism: Ancient Greece and Rome in American Intellectual Life, 1780–1910* (Baltimore: Johns Hopkins University Press, 2002).

25. Charles Edward Merriam, *A History of American Political Theories* (New York: Macmillan, 1903), 333. On the ASSA and early social science, see the classic works by Thomas L. Haskell, *The Emergence of Professional Social Science: The American Social Science Association and the Crisis of Nineteenth-Century Authority* (Urbana: University of Illinois 1977); Dorothy Ross, *The Origins of American Social Science* (New York: Cambridge University Press, 1991); Daniel T. Rodgers, *Contested Truths: Keywords in American Politics Since Independence* (Cambridge, MA: Harvard University Press, 1998); Robert Adcock, *Liberalism and the Emergence of American Political Science: A Transatlantic Tale* (New York: Oxford University Press, 2014). Nonprofessional male journalists also contributed works that received serious attention, for example, E. L. Godkin, *Problems of Modern Democracy* (New York, 1896) and Gamaliel Bradford, *Lessons of Popular Government* (New York, 1899).

26. James Bryce, "Predictions of Hamilton and De Tocqueville," *John Hopkins University Studies in Historical and Political Science* (September 1887): 28. The word "democracy," he elaborated in his final work, had "become encrusted with all sorts of associations attractive or repulsive, ethical or poetical, even religious," *Modern Democracies* (New York, 1920), ix. Daniel Coit Gilman explained that Bryce "gathers facts, arranges them under appropriate heads, takes care to verify, by repeated visits to this country," in "Alexis de Tocqueville and His Book on America," *Century* (September 1898), 706–709. Bryce worked through his methodological difference with Tocqueville's deductive method in a seminar he taught at John Hopkins. Herbert B. Adams, "Jared Sparks and Alexis de Tocqueville," *John Hopkins University Studies in Historical and Political Science* (December 1898): 16–17. An extended discussion of Bryce's view of Tocqueville can be found in Edmund Ions, *James Bryce and American Democracy* (New York: Humanities Press, 1970) and Hugh Tulloch, *James Bryce's* American Commonwealth: *The Anglo-American Background* (London: Royal Historical Society, 1988), 62–70.

27. Merriam, *A History of American Political Theories*, 345–347. Some Americans did argue for self-government in Cuba, Hawaii, Puerto Rico, and the Philippines. See, for example, the insistence on this bedrock "principle," which belongs to all, that people must make and execute the laws under which they live. If a "principle is right," the article concluded, "its application is safe" universally, "The Bottom Principle of Self-Government," *The Independent* (October 20, 1898). But a contrary view, which worried about women voters in Cuba and ignorant voters in "Porto Rico," can be found in "What is Self-Government," *Outlook* (July 21, 1900). On how debates over American colonies intersected with women's suffrage debates, see Sneider, *Suffragists in an Imperial Age*.

28. Bryce, *American Commonwealth* (New York, 1888), 521–522. Accustomed to applying this principle of democratic equality "to all sorts and conditions of men," the Americans were "naturally the first to apply to it women," at least in social and legal matters. Bryce concluded this chapter with an echo of Tocqueville's comment on the superiority of American women: no country owes "more to its women than America does" (522). Bryce sensed that "questions" were now dependent on parties, rather than a less organized published opinion. As he wrote Moisei Ostrogorski in 1905, mass-based parties "seem to be a necessary machinery for formulating public questions . . . formerly the issue made parties; now the parties make the issue," quoted in Pablo Pombeni, "Starting in Reason, Ending in Passion: Bryce, Lowell, Ostrogroski, and the Problem of Democracy," *The Historical Journal* 37, no. 2 (June 1994): 319–341.

29. M. Ostrogorski, *The Rights of Woman: A Comparative Study in History and Legislation* (New York, 1893), 190–196. According to the English publisher's preface, the earlier (1891) French version of what became this book won the top prize in an international competition, organized by the Paris Faculté du Droit, for the best essay on the woman question. On the collective hostility to women's suffrage among the first generation of political scientists, see Mary G. Dietz and James Farr, "'Politics Would Undoubtedly Unwoman Her': Gender, Suffrage, and American Political Science," in *Gender and American Social Science: The Formative Years*, edited by Helene Silverberg (Princeton, NJ: Princeton University Press, 1998), chapter 3.

30. *Prospectus No. 2* (New York, 1896). The series appears to have begun in 1895 and was presented as an effort to inculcate "the principles of good citizenship," *Woman's Tribune*, July 13, 1895. Higginson explained his collection and the gift to BPL in the 1896 letter reprinted as the preface to *Catalogue of the Galatea Collection of Books* (Boston, 1898). Kathi Kern explores the way Stanton's turn to science in the late decades of the nineteenth century likely amplified or reinforced her racial thinking, in *Mrs Stanton's Bible* (Ithaca, NY: Cornell University Press, 2001).

31. Stanton, "Educated Suffrage Justified," *Woman's Journal*, November 3, 1894; Stanton, "Educated Suffrage Our Hope," *Woman's Journal*, December 8, 1894; Stanton, "Educated Suffrage," *The Independent*, February 14, 1895. A small debate

on "educated" and "ignorant" suffrage ensued across the pages of the *Woman's Journal,* involving Stanton, William Lloyd Garrison Jr., the Nantucket activist Anna Gardner, and Stanton's daughter Harriot Stanton Blatch. Stanton's paper was also read at the annual convention. See Ann D. Gordon, "Stanton and the Right to Vote: On Account of Race or Sex," in *Elizabeth Cady Stanton: The Feminist as Thinker,* edited by Ellen Carol DuBois and Richard Cándida Smith (New York: New York University Press, 2007), chapter 7; Ellen Carol DuBois, *Harriot Stanton Blatch and the Winning of Woman Suffrage* (New Haven, CT: Yale University Press, 1997), 72–73; Lori D. Ginzberg, *Elizabeth Cady Stanton: An American Life* (New York: Hill and Wang, 2009), 162–164. The issue became something of a "hobby-craze" for Stanton in the 1890s, to the annoyance of Susan B. Anthony. See Anthony's diary entry in Ann D. Gordon, *The Selected Papers of Elizabeth Cady Stanton and Susan B. Anthony. Volume VI: An Awful Hush, 1896–1906* (New Brunswick, NJ: Rutgers University Press, 2013), 161.

32. "Address of Mrs. [*sic*] Lucy Stone," in *Hearing of the Woman Suffrage Association before the Committee on the Judiciary, Monday, January 18, 1892* (NP, 1892); Feeler, *Female Filosofy, Fished Out and Fried*; Higginson to Mary Clark Smith, November 9, 1895, Calvin W. Smith Papers, Massachusetts Historical Society, box 2 folder 11.

33. *History of Woman Suffrage, Volume 4, 1883–1900,* edited by Susan B. Anthony and Ida Husted Harper (Rochester, NY, 1902), vol. 4, xiv

34. Goldwin Smith, "Female Suffrage," *Macmillans* (June 1874); Smith, "Woman's Place in the State," *The Forum* (January 1890), 516–517. Smith's essay met with searing criticism from some quarters. Mrs. Marion Todd, a graduate of Hastings College of Law (Berkeley), who was active in the Greenback, Farmer's Alliance, and eventually Populist politics published a book-length rebuttal. She was irritated that Smith's ideas, though retrograde, were being taken seriously simply because of his status as an Anglo-American intellectual and college professor. See *Prof. Goldwin Smith and His Satellites in Congress* (Battle Creek, MI, 1890), 34. Francis Minor, the husband of Virginia Minor (plaintiff in *Minor v. Happersett*) dissected Smith's article with surgical precision as well in "Woman's Political Status," *Forum* (March 1890), 150–158. This issue also included an essay by the jurist Albion Tourgée warning of the vulnerability of Black voting rights with only the Fifteenth Amendment to protect them. See "The Right to Vote" *Forum* (March 1890), 78–92.

35. Helen Kendrick Johnson, *Woman and the Republic: A Survey of the Woman-Suffrage Movement in the United States and a Discussion of the Claims and Arguments of its Foremost Advocates* (New York, 1897), chapter 2, 321. On Mormons and women's suffrage, see Sarah Barringer Gordon, "'The Liberty of Self-Degradation': Polygamy, Woman Suffrage, and Consent in Nineteenth-Century America," *Journal of American History* (December 1996): 815–847. On suffrage in the territories, see Sneider, *Suffragists in an Imperial Age.*

36. Here Stanton joined a centuries-long intellectual tradition of understanding freedom as political participation, not the pursuit of economic gain. On this

tradition, see Annelien de Dijn, *Freedom: An Unruly History* (Cambridge, MA: Harvard University Press, 2020).

37. Stanton, "The Ethics of Suffrage," in *The World's Congress of Representative Woman*, edited by May Wright Sewall (Chicago, 1894), vol., 2, 482–488. Stanton's address garnered very little response. It was published, without commentary, in the *New York Sun*, September 17, 1893, and then reprinted (also without commentary) in a few venues, including *Providence News*, September 26, 1893; the *Helena Independent*, October 8, 1893, and *Current Literature* (December 1893).

38. Frances Willard "Home Protection," *The Independent*, June 28, 1894; Charles Postel, *Equality: An American Dilemma, 1866–1896* (New York: Farrar, Straus, and Giroux 2019), 130.

39. Johnson, *Woman and the Republic*, 316; Mary Willard quoted in Postel, *Equality*, 132. On Willard, see Ruth Bordin, *Frances Willard: A Biography* (Chapel Hill: University of North Carolina Press, 2014). See also Sara Egge, *Woman Suffrage and Citizenship in the Midwest, 1870–1920* (Iowa City: University of Iowa Press, 2018).

40. Frances Ellen Watkins Harper, "Sowing and Reaping," in *Minnie's Sacrifice, Sowing and Reaping, Trial and Triumph: Three Rediscovered Novels by Frances E. W. Harper*, edited by Frances Smith Foster (Boston: Beacon Press, 1994), chapter xvii. The novel was serialized in the *Christian Recorder* beginning in August 1876. Like other of Harper's novels, chapters of this one continue to be rediscovered. See Eric Gardner, "Sowing and Reaping: A 'New' Chapter from Frances Ellen Watkins Harper's Second Novel," *Commonplace* (October 2012), http://commonplace.onl ine/article/sowing-reapinga-new-chapter-frances-ellen-watkins-harpers-second-novel/ (accessed February 10, 2023).

41. Frances Ellen Watkins Harper, "The Great Problem to Be Solved," *Centennial Anniversary of the Pennsylvania Society, for Promoting the Abolition of Slavery* (Philadelphia, 1875), 29–32; Harper, "How to Stop Lynching," *Women's Era*, quoted in Alison M. Parker, "Frances Watkins Harper and the Search for Women's Interracial Alliance," in *Susan B. Anthony and the Struggle for Equal Rights*, edited by Christine L. Ridarsky and Mary H. Huth (Rochester: University of Rochester Press, 2012), chapter 5. Harper supported Ida B. Wells in her battle with Willard over the tentativeness of the WCTU in confronting lynching. On Harper and Wells, see Mia Bay, *To Tell the Truth Freely: The Life of Ida B. Wells* (New York: Hill and Wang, 2009).

42. On joint appearance of Harper, Douglass, and Wilson, see *Centennial Anniversary of the Pennsylvania Society, for the Promotion of the Abolition of Slavery* (Philadelphia, 1875). The "Woman question" / "race problem" rhetoric of Anna Julia Cooper, discussed in the epilogue, captured a prevailing tendency that reached back to the early antislavery movement. Harper, "The Coloured Women of America," in *Victoria Magazine* (January 1878), 229–238 and *The Englishwoman's Review of Social and Industrial Questions*, January 15, 1878, 10–15. On Wells in England, see

Bederman, *Manliness and Civilization*, chapter 2; and Bay, *To Tell the Truth Freely*, chapter 5.

43. Harper's Cleveland appearance, but not the text of her address, was reported in "The Colored Women of America," *Cincinnati Daily Gazette*, October 25, 1877. Harper's framing, reported in full by *Victoria Magazine*, was omitted in *The Englishwoman's Review*, which focused on the observational reports she made about Black female life rather than its relation to the Civil War and its implications for American democracy. That shorter version has received more attention, largely because of its inclusion in *A Brighter Coming Day: A Frances Ellen Watkins Harper Reader*, edited by Frances Smith Foster (New York: Feminist Press, 1990).

44. Harper, "The Coloured Women of America," *Victoria Magazine*, 227, 238, 228.

45. Harper, "The Coloured Women of America," 227–228; Harper, "Aunt Chloe's Politics," *Sketches of Southern Life* (Philadelphia, 1872); "John and Jacob—A Dialogue on Woman's Rights," *New York Freeman*, November 28, 1885, reprinted in Foster, *A Brighter Coming Day*, 240–242.

46. Harper, *Iola Leroy; or, Shadows Uplifted* (Philadelphia, 1893), 178; Harper, "Work Among the Colored People of the North," *The Union Signal*, May 28, 1885. She took to the pages of the WCTU's organ to remind her northern white "sisters and co-workers" that "the vote of the most ignorant and vicious counts just the same as that of the wisest and best," and that there may be well be "colored voters" who could help tip the balance toward the latter.

47. Harper, "The Woman's Christian Temperance Union and the Colored Woman," *AME Church Review* 12 (1888): 313–316, quoted in Parker, "Frances Watkins Harper and the Search for Women's Interracial Alliances," 145–171. On the WCTU and race, see especially Glenda Gilmore, *Gender and Jim Crow: Women and the Politics of White Supremacy in North Carolina, 1896–1920* (Chapel Hill: University of North Carolina Press, 1996), 45–57.

48. Harper, *Iola Leroy*, chapter 26. As she did in earlier novels, here Harper repurposed phrases and whole sentences in both speeches and novels. The main character Iola even delivers a paper on "The Education of Mothers," which closely resembled a talk Harper gave on "Enlightened Motherhood" before the Brooklyn Literary Society in 1892 (where Harper flirted with a version of eugenics), Foster, *A Brighter Coming Day*, 285.

49. Harper, "Woman's Political Future," in Sewell, *The World's Congress of Representative Women*, vol. 2, 433–447. An aging Frederick Douglass gave voice to a similar disenchantment at the semicentennial celebration of the Seneca Falls Convention. "At any rate," he concluded, "seeing that the male governments of the world have failed, it can do no harm to try the experiment of a government by man and woman united," *Life and Times of Frederick Douglass* (Boston, 1892), 576.

50. Catt's presidential address was printed in *Woman's Journal*, June 8, 1901. A debate over the "lumping" of different categories of people as unfit for self-government appeared in the *Westminster Review* in 1890–1891. Ellen B. Dietrick defended

Black men and white and Black women from such charges in "Woman and Negro Suffrage" (April 1891), which was a response to Alice Bodington's "The Importance of Race and Its Bearing on the 'Negro Question'" (October 1890).

EPILOGUE

1. Helen Watterson, "Women's Excitement Over 'Woman,'" *Forum* 16 (September 1893): 15; Helen Watterson, "The Fair Unvisited," *Harper's Bazaar*, November 11, 1893.

2. Helen Watterson, *The Unquiet Sex* (New York, 1898), 51; Jennette Barbour Perry, "The Woman Question," *The Critic* 35 (October 1899): 890–893; Martha H. Patterson, ed., *The American New Woman Revisited: A Reader, 1894–1930* (New Brunswick, NJ: Rutgers University Press, 2008) dates the term "New Woman" to the debate sparked by Sarah Grund, "The New Aspect of the Woman Question," *North American Review* (March 1894): 270–276. On generational dynamics in the women's movement, see Christine Stansell, *The Feminist Promise, 1792 to the Present* (New York: The Modern Library, 2011).

3. Barbara Miller Solomon, *In the Company of Educated Women: A History of Women and Higher Education in America* (New Haven, CT: Yale University Press, 1985); Lynn D. Gordon, *Gender and Higher Education in the Progressive Era* (New Haven, CT: Yale University Press, 1990); Helen Lefkowitz Horowitz, *Alma Mater: Design and Experience in the Women's Colleges from Their Nineteenth Century Beginnings to the 1930s* (New York: Knopf, 1984); and the essays in *Women and Higher Education in American History*, edited by John Mack Faragher and Florence Howe (New York: Norton, 1988). On Black institution of higher education, see James D. Anderson, *The Education of Blacks in the South, 1865–1930* (Chapel Hill: University of North Carolina Press, 1988); Glenda Gilmore, *Gender and Jim Crow: Women and the Politics of White Supremacy, 1896–1920* (Chapel Hill: University of North Carolina Press, 1996).

4. "One of the First Steps in Our Education," *Legenda* (Wellesley College Yearbook, 1913); "Harriet," *Youth's Companion*, June 11, 1914. Maria Weston Chapman commissioned the work shortly after Martineau's death in 1876 and chose the American sculptor Anne Whitney—a former abolitionist and women's rights activist—to execute it for Boston University, though it found its way instead to nearby Wellesley. See Lisa B. Reitzes, "The Political Voice of the Artist: Anne Whitney's 'Roma' and 'Harriet Martineau,'" *American Art* (Spring 1994): 44–65.

5. "Preface" in May Wright Sewall, *The World's Congress of Representative Women* (Chicago, 1894), xxii. Ellen Carol DuBois details the events at the World's Congress in *Suffrage: Women's Long Battle for the Vote* (New York: Simon & Schuster, 2021), 130–133. A compelling examination of the whole event can be found in Kristy Maddux, *Practicing Citizenship: Women's Rhetoric at the 1893 Chicago's World's Fair* (Philadelphia: University of Pennsylvania Press, 2019), who puts the number of speakers at over eight hundred.

6. Mrs. A. J. Cooper, "The Intellectual Progress of Colored Women of the United States" and Jane Addams, "Domestic Service and the Family Claim," in Sewall, *The World's Congress*, 711–715, 626–631.

7. Addams, "Domestic Service and the Family Claim," 628. Two helpful reviews of evolving interpretations of these women's reformist ideas are: Beverly Guy-Sheftall, "Black Feminist Studies: The Case of Anna Julia Cooper," *African American Review* 43, no. 1 (2009): 11–15 and Louise Knight, "Scholarship and Jane Adams," in *Citizen: Jane Addams and the Struggle for Democracy* (Chicago: University of Chicago Press, 2005), 405–412. While no scholarly biography of Cooper has been executed, many of her writings are available in Charles Lemert and Esme Bahn, *The Voice of Anna Julia Cooper: Including* A Voice from the South, *and Other Important Essay, Papers, and Letters* (Lanham, MD: Rowman & Littlefield, 1998) and notable interpretations of her ideas are advanced in Deborah Gray White, *Too Heavy a Load: Black Women in Defense of Themselves, 1894–1994* (New York: Norton, 1999); Vivian M. May, *Anna Julia Cooper: Visionary Black Feminist. A Critical Introduction* (New York: Routledge, 2007); Brittney C. Cooper, *Beyond Respectability: The Intellectual Thought of Race Women* (Urbana: University of Illinois Press, 2017); and essays across the special issue of *African American Review* (Spring 2009). Especially pertinent in the more developed field of scholarship on Jane Addams are Knight, *Citizen*; Jean Bethke Elshtain, *Jane Addams and The Dream of American Democracy* (New York: Basic Books, 2002), and Victoria Bissell Brown, *The Education of Jane Addams* (Philadelphia: University of Pennsylvania Press, 2004).

8. Cooper's husband died two years after she married him, at age nineteen. As she had no children, the path was cleared for her to attend Oberlin. She did, however, end up adopting the children of her brother after their mother died. Addams formed long-term partnerships and emotionally intimate relationship with Ellen Gates Starr and Mary Rozet Smith, as set out in Knight, *Citizen*, 217–218.

9. Reva B. Siegel has offered a particularly cogent plea to appreciate the democratic underpinnings of nineteenth- and twentieth-century efforts to critique family constraints. See "She the People: The Nineteenth Amendment, Sex Equality, Federalism, and the Family," *Harvard Law Review* 115 (February 2002): 948–1045 and her updated account in "The Nineteenth Amendment and the Democratization of the Family," *Yale Law Journal Forum* 129 (January 2020): 450–494.

10. Addams, "Hull-House, Chicago: An Effort Toward Social Democracy," *Forum* 14 (October 1892): 226–241; Addams, "A New Impulse to an Old Gospel," *Forum* 14 (November 1892): 342–356. While both these essays were subsequently reprinted in full in *Philanthropy and Social Progress*, edited by Henry C. Adams (New York, 1893), only the latter appeared in Addams, *Twenty Years at Hull-House with Autobiographical Notes* (New York: Macmillan, 1910) under its original title "The Subjective Necessity of Social Settlements."

11. "Mrs. A. J. Cooper," "Higher Education of Woman," *The Southland* (April 1891): 186–202; [Anna Julia Cooper], *A Voice from the South* (Xenia, OH: Aldine

Printing House, 1892). Frances Harper's poem "The Rallying Cry" was published in this same issue of *The Southland*.

12. Addams, "A New Impulse to an Old Gospel," 346. Addams was among the non-voting women who became key agents of Progressive era state-building, s story set out in Paula Baker, "The Domestication of Politics: Women and American Political Society, 1780–1920," *American Historical Review* 89 (June 1984): 620–647 and part of a the cohort of self-consciously democratic state-builders, as discussed in William J. Novak, *The New Democracy: The Creation of the Modern American State* (Cambridge, MA: Harvard University Press, 2022).

13. Addams, "A New Impulse to an Old Gospel," 348; Addams, *Democracy and Social Ethics* (New York: Macmillan, 1902) further developed how ethical relationships were constitutive of meaningful self-rule.

14. Anna Julia Cooper, "Has America a Race Problem? If So, How Can It Best Be Solved?" and "Womanhood: A Vital Element in the Regeneration and Progress of a Race," both in *A Voice from the South*, 164, 121. On Cooper's political thought, see Jane Anna Gordon, "Unmasking the Big Bluff of Legitimate Governance and So-Called Independence: Creolizing Rousseau through the Reflections of Anna Julia Cooper," *Critical Philosophy of Race* 6, no. 1 (2018): 1–25.

15. Jane Addams, *Peace and Bread in the Time of War* (New York: Macmillan, 1922), reissued, with an introductory essay by John Dewey in 1945; Cooper, "Equality of Races and the Democratic Movement" (1925), reprinted in Lemert and Bahn, *The Voice of Anna Julia Cooper*, 291–288.

Index

For the benefit of digital users, indexed terms that span two pages (e.g., 52–53) may, on occasion, appear on only one of those pages.
Page numbers followed by n. indicate endnotes. Page numbers followed by f. indicate figures.